COMPLICATED GAME

INSIDE THE SONGS OF XTC

**ANDY PARTRIDGE
AND TODD BERNHARDT**

JAW
BONE

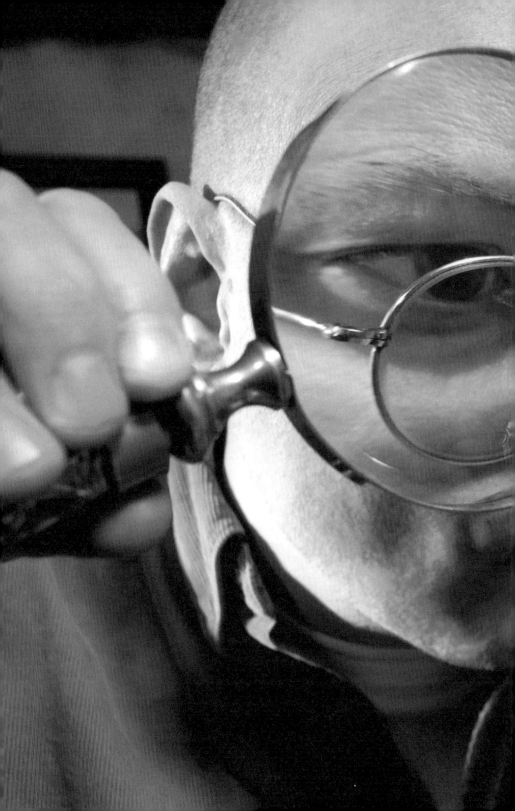

COMPLICATED GAME
INSIDE THE SONGS OF XTC
ANDY PARTRIDGE
AND TODD BERNHARDT

A JAWBONE BOOK
FIRST EDITION 2016
PUBLISHED IN THE UK AND THE USA BY
JAWBONE PRESS
OFFICE G1
141–157 ACRE LANE
LONDON SW2 5UA
ENGLAND
WWW.JAWBONEPRESS.COM

ISBN 978-1-908279-78-1

EDITOR JOHN MORRISH
JACKET DESIGN MARK CASE

PRINTED BY SHORT RUN PRESS, EXETER

3 4 5 6 28 27 26 25

CONTENTS

INTRODUCTION

BY TODD BERNHARDT

I first met Andy Partridge on a cold night in February 1998, when he attended a show in New York celebrating the release of David Yazbek's second album, *Tock* (which features a song co-written by the two friends). When I found out several days before the show that I might have the chance to finally meet Andy, I knew I had to find a way to say something more to him than, 'Wow, I really like your music'—though, of course, that's the truth.

Then it hit me: I had written articles for *Modern Drummer* magazine previously, and I knew that they had a column—called 'A Different View'— in which musicians who are not drummers talk about drumming and the drummers they've played with. An e-mail or two later, I'd found out that there were XTC fans on the editorial staff, and that the magazine would indeed be interested in an interview with Mr. P.

I pitched the idea to Andy when I met him, and he graciously agreed, asking me to call him when he got back to England. The two-hour interview yielded a transcript of about 18,000 words. I whittled that down to an article of about 4,000 words for the magazine, but I was frustrated by the fact that I had to get rid of so much humour and insight—so much *Andy*—to meet the word-count limitations of a printed publication. So, with the help of John Relph, I posted a full-figured version for the devoted XTC fan on his venerable website, Chalkhills.

Five years into the new century, a social-media site known as MySpace was beginning to catch fire, especially with musicians and their fans. My friend (and sound engineer of choice) Rob Cosentino had started a page about XTC, and—knowing that Andy and I had continued to do occasional interviews— asked if I wanted to help with it. Sure, I said. How much work could it be, after all?

A lot, after all. But I didn't mind. I wanted to help the band raise its online profile and ultimately move some product, so I started fiddling around with and fleshing out the content—writing a bio, posting pictures, and constantly changing the songs on the page's music player. The number of followers started to slowly build. Then, because I do corporate communications work for a living, I began to wonder how I could leverage some basic online-marketing principles to further build traffic and make the XTCfans MySpace site 'sweet and sticky'— sweet enough to attract new fans, sticky enough to keep them around.

After I posted an extended interview with Andy about lyric writing (in another effort to compensate for good material lost because of the word-count limitations of the book that the original was included in), we gained lots of followers, there were lots of comments, and—even more important—lots of requests for *more*. I realised I'd hit upon something.

So I talked to Andy, who already had told me about his frustration regarding the lack of space dedicated to each of the band's songs in *Song Stories*, the 1998 book covering the band's catalogue. There are no word-count limitations on the web, I told him—we can explore the story behind each song to our hearts' content. He enthusiastically agreed, and we posted the first interview, about 'Merely A Man', on October 29 2006.

By the time we wrapped things up, almost four years later, Andy and I had done interviews about eighty-three of his songs, about his record label and its projects, and about his influences and technique as a guitarist, while answering countless fan questions. I had also been lucky enough to connect with Colin, Dave, and Terry, as well as the drummers who succeeded him: Pete Phipps, Ian Gregory, Prairie Prince, Pat Mastelotto, Dave Mattacks, and Chuck Sabo. When I posted the final interview on September 12 2010, the blog counter showed it had been viewed just shy of 370,000 times.

The next year, my friend and editor extraordinaire John Morrish reached out with the idea of turning these interviews into a book. Great idea, I said, but right now I'm busy trying to push my guts back inside me as I go through a divorce—can we talk later? Yes, said John, who showed great patience until 2014, when he insisted that I put down my ex's dictionary and get to work. Stupidly happy with a new love and a new life, I agreed.

And so get to work we did. The book you're now reading includes expanded versions of thirty of the MySpace interviews; a new interview about Andy's approach to songwriting; a guide by Mr. Morrish to Mr. Partridge's Swindon; and a foreword by the supremely talented Steven Wilson—the only person I know who might be a bigger fan of Andy, and of the band, than I am.

And speaking of fellow fans: through the years I've become friends with a number of like-minded people whom I should acknowledge for their help in getting this all started and keeping it going. My thanks go to David Yazbek for making the initial introduction; to Mitch Friedman for essential info and advice; to John Relph for keeping the fire burning; to Rob Cosentino for getting all up in MySpace; to J.D. Mack for valuable and timely backup services; to Mike Versaci for empathy, good humour, and perspective; to Dom Lawson, Wes Long, Paul Myers, and Harrison Sherwood for inspiration, benchmarking, and camaraderie; to the DC Chalkfest crew for fun music and late nights; to the gentlemen at Jawbone (John, Tom Seabrook, Nigel Osborne) for skill, patience, and making this all possible; and to all of the too-numerous-to-name fellow fans with whom I've played through the years. Your engagement and encouragement has made all the difference.

Finally, I must thank Andrew John Partridge for his friendship and generosity—with his time, trust, wit, insight, advice, and gifts—and for excellent recommendations about wine, books, music, movies, and pornography. And thanks for sharing your art with all of us, Andy. We're looking forward to what comes next.

FOREWORD

BY STEVEN WILSON

I'll get this out of the way early: I *love* XTC.

And like many people who love a band who are apparently under the radar or underrated in some way, I have become an evangelist for them and their music, spreading the word ever since I became a fan back in the late 80s. These days I find myself in the privileged position of being able to remix the catalogue, deconstructing and reconstructing the music from the drums (and wires) up, and it's been fascinating to rediscover the songs and appreciate just how much depth there is in both the songwriting and production. It's also been a thrill to watch Andy go through this same process of rediscovery, re-evaluating his own songs as we've worked on the remixes. Seeing a big grin form on his face as he listened to the 5.1 mix of one of my all-time favourite songs—'Complicated Game'—was one of the most rewarding moments of my career as a producer / remix engineer, as was hearing the exhilaration in his voice at the end when he proclaimed, with typical Andy understatement, 'We weren't actually that bad, were we?' No, mate — you really weren't!

This book you're reading now—this *Complicated Game*—is a similar journey of discovery. With Todd's help, Andy looks back on the creation, context, and craft of each song, sometimes surprising even himself as one memory leads to another and brings up details about the songs that haven't been covered elsewhere. What you'll gain from this book is an insight into the creative process of one of the great songwriters of our generation. The way the world appears through the prism of Andy Partridge's songwriting can be strange, beautiful, nostalgic, funny, and heartbreaking—sometimes all at the same time.

My first memories of XTC are when they had a handful of hit singles in the UK in the late 70s and early 80s. I was maybe eleven years old when I first heard the name, and my friends and I were listening to the punk and new wave music of the day. XTC came up through that scene, so I saw them as being part of a bunch of bands I quite liked at the time, including The Stranglers, Public Image Ltd, The Clash, Japan, etc. But I was a school kid who could only afford to buy singles, so I never investigated the albums.

Fast-forward a few years, and in the mid 80s I came across a copy of *Mummer* on CD. I had bought a CD player with money earned from my first proper job, and was looking through the limited inventory at a local record store—there wasn't so much to buy on CD at the time, especially if you had an interest in music outside of the mainstream, as I did. I think it was the song titles that piqued my interest—'Love On A Farmboy's Wages', 'Human Alchemy', 'Me And The Wind', 'Frost Circus'—these didn't seem like the titles of your run-of-the-mill rock band. So, without any notions of what kind of music XTC made at the time, I bought it. And, honestly, I can't say I liked it the first time I listened to it. But as with all the music I've come to love over the years, something made me curious enough to want to go back to it. There was something special there; I just needed to decode it. Sure enough, after a few more listens it *clicked*, and I was blown away by the musical range, depth, literacy, sensitivity, melodicism, and inventive production. It just wasn't that common to hear such depth in pop or rock music in the 80s. From that moment I hungrily worked my way through the XTC back catalogue and bought each new single and album as it was released (though new XTC albums were few and infrequent from that time on).

I've asked myself (not to mention found myself trying to explain to other people over the years) what it is that I love so much about the band. In many ways, that's an intangible thing. Why does *any* music resonate with us the way it does? But one thing I *can* identify that I admire is the way that almost every XTC song inhabits its own musical world, with an approach and sonic palette that distinguishes it from almost every other XTC song. In this they have much in common with Andy's heroes, The Beatles, who on their later albums rarely used the same instrumentation or production approach on more than one song. This is a rare thing in popular music, with many bands effectively refining and recycling the same basic modus operandi and sound over a whole career.

Another thing I can say that I love about XTC songs is the many layers they have—even after countless listens there can still be an idea, musical twist, or 'punch line' that will reveal itself to me for the first time. The combination of Andy's inspired songwriting, Dave Gregory's exquisite arrangement touches, Colin Moulding's ever-inventive and never-obvious bass lines (and his own songs of course, which would often be the perfect complement to Andy's),

Terry Chambers's creative powerhouse drumming (and the drumming of those who followed him), the contributions of the different producers they worked with—all these things combined to create something beautifully unpredictable and multifaceted.

So, given this, why aren't XTC household names, and why are they referenced most frequently in the press as cult favourites, or as a 'musician's band'? It does seem that XTC have a large percentage of fans who are themselves musicians. Perhaps it's because, having more than a passing interest in the art form, we musicians tend to be a little more obsessive about discovering music that isn't in the mainstream. Of course, it didn't help that after 1982 there were no live performances, nor that they were hardly the kind of musicians who would embrace the idea of being celebrities or media personalities (despite Andy being a brilliant and funny conversationalist and raconteur, as this book will demonstrate). But for anyone who believes that the quality of the work should be enough, it still baffles and frustrates me that the band is not better known, especially as I never considered XTC's music to be 'difficult'. Yes, the songs may be considerably more sophisticated than your average pop tunes, and require a little more perseverance from the listener, but at the same time there are so many wonderfully accessible hooks and melodies. What a shame we live in world where people seem less and less inclined to engage with music in anything but the most superficial way.

Let's also consider the astounding musical arc of XTC's catalogue, and Andy's growth as a songwriter over the years. How many other bands can you think of that over the course of a career created the breadth of music covered in the journey from *White Music* to *Apple Venus*? Again, I would say that only The Beatles made a similar journey with such consistently brilliant results. I love every one of XTC's albums, and each has a valid and valuable place in their discography. That's a singular artistic achievement; one most bands can only dream of. But at the same time, that's never going to be an easy pill for the predominantly conservative music industry to swallow—which box do we put this band in? Andy is largely incapable of thinking in these terms and doing the 'right thing' for his career, and that's because he makes music primarily to please himself—which of course is why I, and I imagine most XTC fans, love it so much. It's selfish music in the sense that nearly all great art is borne of a selfish need by the creator to create, and not simply to entertain or please others.

So, what can you expect to learn from a book like this? One thing it won't do is teach you how to write songs like Andy Partridge. Explaining songwriting is like trying to catch the breeze. I'm sure Andy can't explain it either. His uniqueness and musical vocabulary come from many sources: the country and town he was born and raised in, the music he grew up listening to, the books and comic books he read, nostalgia for his own childhood, his sense of humour and love of the absurd, his obsessive attention to details and love of collecting things (which, as has been noted before, is reflected back at him in the obsessive-collector nature of many XTC fans)—you can recognise all of these things in the songs.

If you're a fan already, then this book is a way to gain new understanding of the context and inspirations behind the songs, and hopefully it will make you go back and listen again with new ears. And if you are an aspiring musician or artist yourself, I hope it will provide something to inspire you, too—not to copy what Andy does, but to understand that sometimes the longer and more difficult way is ultimately the most rewarding way. So much generic music achieves short-term success, but is quickly forgotten and becomes indistinguishable from the rest. Though it may be less celebrated than the music of The Beatles, I believe the music of XTC and the songs of Andy Partridge will live on in the same way. They are truly unique and timeless.

Steven Wilson
September 2015

Steven Wilson has been active over the past twenty-five years as a musician and producer. He is best known as the frontman of the band Porcupine Tree and more recently as a successful solo artist. In parallel with his own music, he's been busy as a producer and sound engineer specialising in remixing classic albums, with a focus on 5.1 surround sound, for which he has received four Grammy nominations. To date he has worked on remixing the back catalogues of, among others, King Crimson, Roxy Music, Jethro Tull, Tears for Fears, Yes, and—most pertinent to this book—XTC, a band he considers to be one of his all time favourites. He has worked closely with Andy Partridge to create new stereo and 5.1 surround-sound mixes of Nonsuch, Drums And Wires, *and* Oranges & Lemons, *for a highly acclaimed series of definitive XTC reissues, with plans (if all the multitrack tapes can be located) to ultimately complete the whole back catalogue.*

SWINDON: A PERAMBULATION

BY JOHN MORRISH

Before you criticise a man, they say, walk a mile in his shoes. That way, he's a mile away, and you've got his shoes.

But we are not here to criticise Andy Partridge. We're going to try to understand him, by following his footsteps around the town with which he will always be associated. Imagine that Swindon is laid out before you like a board game. In his life, Andy has travelled from north to south, but also from the lowest part of the town to the highest. We're going to follow on foot, except when we catch a bus. We're not going to drive. There are no cars in Andyland.

Penhill

We're going to start in Penhill, three miles north of the modern town centre. Andy did not start there. He was born on November 11 1953, in Malta, then a British colony in the Mediterranean Sea. His father, John Partridge, was a Royal Navy Seaman. His mother, Vera, was a seaman's wife. After three years they came to Britain, first to unlovely Portsmouth and then to Swindon.

To the south and west of Swindon are the chalk hills and downlands of Wiltshire. Old Town, formerly Old Swindon, formerly just Swindon, is on a hill south of the modern town, which is in a depression. Penhill is, as the name suggests, also on a bit of high ground. But the Valley, the part of Penhill where Andy arrived when he was three, is not.

In 1956, when the Partridges arrived, The Valley—a nickname—was still under construction. Swindon had been booming since 1952, when steps were taken to reduce its reliance on the famous railway works. New estates of council housing were being thrown up to accommodate incomers, invited in from the more overcrowded parts of London.

Penhill, a sprawling council estate for 8,000 people, was all finished by

1957. The Valley, though, was an afterthought. It came about in a hurry because of some glitch in the planning process, and was built on land earmarked for a pleasant open space. Like Penhill itself, it was thrown up fast and cheaply, and the latest technology was used: prefabrication. Many of the houses are made of concrete panels that quickly turned grey and stayed that way. In parts of Penhill, even today, you could be in a grim northern industrial town: and in a way, that's what Swindon was in the 50s, except that it was situated in a lovely southern county of rolling hills and farmland.

Affluence floats uphill; deprivation sinks. The well-off live on the hills, while the strugglers are at the bottom. (Rio de Janiero is an exception, just one of the ways in which it differs from Swindon.) Swindon's middle class was tiny, and it aspired to the heights of Old Town. Most Swindonians were skilled working class. Those who sank, though, ended up somewhere like the Valley, a steep walk downhill from the modest rise on which the rest of Penhill stands. Penhill is not a terrible place, but it has always had its problems. It was often called Swindon's worst estate: and the Valley was the worst part of Penhill. Built without amenities of any kind, a stiff uphill walk to the nearest bus stop, it was at one time said to have three times the crime rate even of the rest of Penhill.

Find your way down to Latton Close. Ask for directions, but don't be surprised if you get some hostile looks. This is where we start our perambulation. Latton Close is not Heritage Britain. Andy's house was in the middle of a small terrace; observe the decaying garden furniture out the front, the overflowing bin bags, the forlorn football on the bald lawn. It was less like that in 1957. The houses were new and the tenants were delighted to have them. They offered amenities that many Swindonians had never known. Andy's grandparents, for instance, still had an outside lavatory. Number 40 Latton Close was a good place to bring up children, especially in the free-range fashion of the day. But the Valley became notorious. Council road-menders learned to lock away their shovels when they took a break; otherwise the Valley kids would fill in the holes they had just dug. You can imagine Andy laughing.

Walk down past Andy's house and you will find a little stream, sometimes ornamented with an abandoned shopping trolley. Beyond it is a little strip of thicket, all that is left of the countryside Andy knew: the perfect place for the building of dens, the bandying of sticks, the pulling of girls' hair, the throwing of knives and all manner of glorious play activities now discouraged on account of their death rate. The farms where Andy was menaced by farmers' boys have gone. The stream now marks a very British class frontier. North and west: owner-occupied homes, German cars, fancy brickwork, visits from the Ocado van. South and east: rented housing, rusty cars, Union Jacks in the window, dogs on chains, people shouting in the street.

The Partridges, though, struck lucky, and were able to move up. Walk up the hill, left into Ramsbury Avenue, then right and uphill again along Minety Road (where an infant Colin Moulding once lived), past a playing field with trees, swings, and a climbing frame, then left into Downton Road (there is no Abbey nearby), then right into Allington Road, and right again into Southwick Avenue. Andy and his family arrived here after two years at the bottom of the hill.

It was a step up from the Valley, though still Penhill, which had, by the 60s, deteriorated badly. Today many of the houses are owner-occupied, and the owners have taken advantage of the freedom that has given them to brighten things up. Andy's family home, number 10, now has a white exterior, a pleasant change from the prevailing grey, and the former front garden is paved with little tiles. A river of geraniums runs down each side. Some residents have gone further. The house next door has become a kind of Spanish hacienda.

It was here that Andy did his growing up, much of it with his friend, Steve Warren, who lived across the way in Number 15. Andy was outside sometimes, in the aforementioned fields and the mean streets of Penhill, making a nuisance of himself, but he was also inside, watching television, drawing, making games, and, at some point, teaching himself guitar by listening to pop music. He had no known teacher—a pattern that would reoccur.

There are many theories as to why Partridge is so extraordinary, such a bubbling font of creativity and invention. The 'genius' word is used. One definition of a genius is 'someone with exceptional abilities in his or her chosen field of work'. That's Charles Darwin or Stephen Hawking or John Maynard Keynes. But that's not really Andy. Look at all the things he's good at: playing the guitar, writing music, writing lyrics, painting and drawing, making things, devising games, singing, making people laugh … it doesn't seem fair to those struggling to acquire or perfect a single talent.

So why is Andy the way he is, a fizzing bundle of imagination who, even when depressed and feeling unappreciated, keeps on creating? Someone suggested to me that he must have been given lots of creative tools when he was a child and encouraged to play with them. Another observer, close to the band, said he is the product of an unhappy home—a 'child of divorce', although no actual divorce took place—who was always seeking to impress one or other parent even in his unhappiness. He was always 'a handful'. He still is.

Long-distance psychoanalysis is bogus, but we can't leave Southwick Avenue without a glance at Andy's parents. John Partridge was at sea in Andy's first few years. Then he had unskilled jobs around Swindon. He did not present a role model, at least professionally. But he was musical, and he left a guitar hanging around for Andy to try. Creative people, though, tend to have special relationships with their mothers. Mother is the first audience in a child's life. *Look mummy! Look at me!*

We know, from the interviews in this book, that Vera Partridge was tidy to the point of obsession, and that she threw Andy's toys away if they disturbed that order. She disapproved of drinking and long hair. When Andy's musical friends came to call, she sent them away. Unaccountably, she could not find it in herself to admire Captain Beefheart. But she also indulged her only child, buying the catalogue clothes he needed for each change of image.

Maybe there is something in his schooling that will help us understand the Partridge phenomenon? Choice barely existed for working-class people in the 50s, and they didn't expect it. Andy started at Penhill Infants School. Let's find our way there. It's uphill again. Carry on south along Southwick Avenue, observing the grey concrete housing on your right: that's what the estate would have looked like when Andy lived here.

At the end, turn left and carry on until you come to Penhill Drive, the loop road that runs around the top part of the estate: true to form, it is the nicest part, especially if the sun is out. If you turn right, you will come to St Peter's Church, built along with the estate, concrete with a brick skin. The Church did its best to engender a community spirit. It started social evenings when the Valley acquired a makeshift Common Room, suggesting 'Beetle, Bedlam, Gooffey, or Whist Drives'. No one turned up, not even for Gooffey, whatever that was. But St Peter's little church hall, on its left flank, would eventually host performances by one of the earliest of the bands that Partridge saw while getting the music bug: Dave Gregory's Pink Warmth. Look inside, if you can. With its shiny dance floor and curtained stage, it was a fine place for starter gigs.

Now reverse your steps, and go round Penhill Drive in the other direction:

anti-clockwise. Pass the library and the pub. Keep going, over two mini-roundabouts—Swindon does love a roundabout—until you see a road on your right called Alton Close. This is where Penhill Infant School and Penhill Junior School were situated. The buildings are still there but the schools have been renamed and rebranded. Don't hang around outside; someone will call the police. This is Britain.

Andy attended first one, from the age of four, and then the other. We know nothing about his primary schooldays, except that he learnt to read and write. Probably there was lots of painting and cutting out and sticking and looking at pictures of smiling black people working in the cocoa plantations out there in the British Empire. There was a lot of that in primary schools in the early 60s. How much promise did he show at that stage? It doesn't really matter. The next stage of his education would do its best to stamp that out.

Let's go to Andy's secondary school. There was really no element of choice here either. He went to Penhill Secondary. You can find it by retracing your steps down Alton Close, then going right into Penhill Drive, then second left into Grafton Road, until you emerge on Cricklade Road, the main road into Swindon. The school is on the left-hand side of the road as you go down the hill into town. There's a footbridge. Climb up and you can get a glimpse. It's a big two- and three-storey building in brick and concrete with big windows and spacious playing fields behind a spiked fence. Plenty of room there to be bruised by the bullies, if you were a somewhat sensitive, somewhat solitary young man with artistic hobbies and no interest in sport. The school is now called St Luke's. It specialises in children with behavioural and educational difficulties; much worse educational and behavioural difficulties than Andy's. Don't hang round here either.

It was at Penhill School that a crucial development took place. Vera Partridge was subject to bouts of mental instability. Once she was an in-patient at Roundway Hospital in Devizes, Wiltshire. Roundway was originally the Wiltshire County Lunatic Asylum, and although it was no longer so vast and intimidating, in-patient treatment remained a scary prospect to patient and relatives alike. To this day, Andy has no idea what was wrong with her; he asked his father, and was told it was 'nerves'. It must have preyed on the mind of the sensitive boy. Poor mum. Could it happen to me?

Some time later, the twelve-year-old began displaying signs of agitation and over-excitement at school, manifested in the need to use the toilet very frequently. Vera was summoned to meet the headmaster; somehow Andy too was diagnosed with 'nerves' and put on a course of Valium, a psychiatric wonder-drug only introduced a couple of years earlier. He wouldn't come off it for thirteen years, which means for many of his most productive years he was on an addictive medication whose side effects can include depression and impaired concentration but also, paradoxically, nervousness, irritability, excitement, and, in some cases, rage and violence. Perfect fuel for the punk years. On the other hand, it made him shun recreational drugs: Andy's brilliance has never required artificial assistance.

Andy did quite well at senior school, then got bored. He could have moved to Headlands School, further down Cricklade Road, which had a sixth form designed to prepare people for university. But he had by now detached himself from the educational process, finding it boring and oppressive. He was already setting himself apart from his peers, both in his manner of dress and his interests. Christmas 1965 brought him a little tape recorder. In March 1968 he won £10 for drawing Mickey Dolenz in a *Monkees Monthly* competition and put it toward a much better tape recorder, a Grundig. He was starting to make music.

At fifteen, Andy left Penhill School. University was a remote prospect for working-class boys in those days and besides, he was sick of the classroom. He was pretty much finished with Penhill, too, and so are we. Wander further down Cricklade Road and find a bus stop. You want the number 17. They come every ten minutes, and it'll take you about twelve minutes to get into town. There's free wi-fi in the bus, but you'll be in town by the time you've connected. Better to look out the window at north Swindon's older suburbs, and think about what move Andy could have made next.

New Swindon
There was work in Swindon, especially if you were male. It was an industrial town, with several big employers: the railway works, in permanent decline but still important in the 60s; Pressed Steel Fisher, a car-body plant; the Vickers-Armstrong aerospace factory; and Plessey, a semiconductor manufacturer.

New Swindon—the Swindon that grew up after the Great Western Railway works was established in 1843—was a working-class, male town from the start. By 1851 Swindon boasted more than a dozen pubs. In the words of the local writer Richard Jefferies, the publicans 'had discovered that steel filings make men quite as thirsty as hay dust'. It was dangerous, too. In his 1975 book, *Swindon: A Town In Transition*, Michael Harloe noted that between

1840 and 1850, the average age of death in Swindon dropped from thirty-six to twenty-six. I'll repeat that: the average age of death was twenty-six.

From the 1950s, by dedicated efforts to diversify, Swindon began to attract more white-collar work, which would in time modify the gender and class imbalances in the town's labour market. But Andy's parents—he was still under sixteen, and in 1969 your parents' views counted—put him on a different track, away from both factory and desk. They had noticed that the boy had artistic talent and decided that could be harnessed. He would become what was often then called a 'commercial artist': a graphic designer.

So off he went to Swindon College, whose 1969 prospectus declared, 'The course aims to develop the student's creative personality at the same time as training him in the skills and techniques involved in the practice of advertising'. But Andy's creative personality did not require developing. Nor was he interested in being trained, like a garden plant up a trellis. After eighteen months, bored, and convinced he was a better artist than the course required, he left. It was a turning point. No-one would ever be able to teach Andy Partridge anything again. From now on he would be self-taught, an autodidact, a voracious reader, listener, and observer. He would come at the artistic world without preconceptions or prejudices, not knowing what he 'should' like. It was one source of his originality.

It was about now that Andy discovered his destiny was to be an artist, and not a commercial one either. If you look at his career in XTC, he always chose originality over popularity. Each album was different from its predecessor. More, he made each song different from the next. The point was to be true to himself as an artist.

It's sometimes illuminating to divide artists and art movements into two types: Romantic and Classical. The watchword of the Classical artist is beauty. They observe what has moved people throughout the ages, and they do everything they can to build on that tradition. Classical architecture is balanced, harmonious, and reassuring. But punk rock, in its way, was Classical music. It has no musical originality at all. The chord changes are as old as Methuselah. But it affected people. Romantic artists are more interested in truth than beauty, but their watchword is 'I'. They want to give you *their* truth, as they see it at that moment. To do that they scorn tradition and attempt to create everything anew.

Geniuses (that word again) create the taste by which they will be judged. No one knew the world wanted simple ballads about ordinary rural folk, written by professional poets, before Wordsworth and Coleridge started doing them. No one knew there was a market for rhythm & blues music played by English boys. As a Romantic artist, you can keep your audience by repeating yourself, but your very nature is to move on, to innovate. To succeed like that you have to convince your audience that it likes everything you do. You have to become more and more like yourself. That takes a psychological toll, particularly when you start working alone.

But we're not there yet. We're on a bus travelling south and need to decide where to get off. We could go to the old Swindon College, now being converted to flats. We could go to the offices of the *Swindon Evening Advertiser* (known as 'the *Adver*'). It was there that Andy secured his first job after college, thanks to the intervention of his father, who was working there as a driver. Andy was a tea-boy/messenger/dogsbody. In 1969, dads could wangle jobs for their sons, even sons as ill-disposed toward work as A. Partridge.

But the bus doesn't go that way. Ask to be dropped at Fleming Way. It's the main stop for the centre of town. Look across the dual carriageway and you will see a long grey concrete cuboid, with the word Debenhams emblazoned in one corner. This excrescence is Swindon's premier department store. In 1972, it was known as Bon Marché, and in its record department you could find Andy 'Rocky' Partridge, sporting a flowing mane and a pair of red satin loon pants which, he later recalled, made his legs look like he'd borrowed them from a passing flamingo.

It was all starting to happen in Partridge's life. Soon he would meet his first proper girlfriend, Linda Godwin, and start playing with a drum'n'bass duo known as Terry Chambers and Colin Moulding. You might want to poke your head into Debenhams to get a sense of the era. There's a dreary pedestrian underpass. Welcome to the 70s.

By 1975, Andy was in a band called XTC. The next year, the year of punk, he got a job as a poster painter and window-dresser in a fabulous Victorian emporium known as McIlroy's. In true Swindonian fashion, it no longer exists. On the site, in Regent Street, is a bland branch of H&M, the clothing chain. A clock has been placed on one corner as some sort of half-baked reminder of the old building. But we're not going there; one of the rules of this perambulation is that we only go where there's something to see.

It was while working at McIlroy's that Andy first encountered a young woman called Marianne Wyborn. Theirs was not a straightforward courtship (biographies are available), but in August 1976 they moved in together. Their flat was at 7 Gladstone Street. Head due east along Fleming Way, and at the roundabout turn left into Corporation Street.

(It's not part of this tour, but turn right if you want to find Regent Circus, where you can see the old Swindon College, the Town Hall, and a nightclub called Medina, once the Affair. It was at the Affair that XTC acquired a manager. We'll say no more about that, except that Andy thought he was climbing a ladder but was in fact treading on a snake.)

But we're going north along Corporation Street. After about 200 yards, Corporation Street goes under a railway bridge. You need to turn sharp right before that. You are in Station Road, which, as you might expect, runs parallel to the railway line. No one wanted to live by a noisy, dirty railway line, and these are cheap houses, thrown up by speculators in the Victorian era, many of them badly 'improved' and now often broken up into so-so flats and bedsits for a shifting population. Not to mention would-be rock stars and their girlfriends.

Second on the right is Gladstone Street. Number 7 is featureless. Its exterior is finished in beige pebbledash, the British exterior treatment that was so unaccountably popular in the 60s and 70s. Andy and Marianne rented, which meant Andy was not supposed to redecorate. He ignored that, first painting seven-foot palm trees and then Second World War German aircraft on the wall, as you do. Despite the surroundings, they were happy, though their landlord was not.

Let's move on. Gladstone Street is scruffy but it is respectable (without being 'Respectable Street', of which more later). You wouldn't say that about the next place the pair lived. Head north along Gladstone Street until you come to a crossroads with a busy thoroughfare, Manchester Road. (The observant will note that you have already been along it, on the number 17 bus.) Manchester Road is bustling with commercial activity by day. It is at night, too. Andy recalls it as Swindon's red-light district, and it was.

Turn right and look for 12 Manchester Road, where the pair had their flat. Until recently this was the Manchester, a guest house. A friendly note on the letterbox declared 'No Cold Callers'. It did not look the place for a romantic weekend break. But now it has been given a lick of paint and turned back into housing.

Why are we bothering with this? Because we are interested in where Andy came from. The scrappy, underprivileged circumstances of his early life explain some of his frustration when, in the punk years and after, he was patronised as a bumpkin, a yokel, a tractor-driver and someone who knew nothing about the grit of city life. It did not help that these comments came from people who had learned their spiky attitudes in the sylvan suburbs of our biggest cities.

Manchester Road is lively, chaotic, and multi-cultural, with its secondhand shops, takeaways, slot machine arcades, ethnic supermarkets, and Kuba's Polski Sklep. It's very twenty-first century. It's not quite how New Swindon, the town built for the railway, was meant to be.

Having seen a fair bit of the Swindon no one likes, it might be nice now to go and see the bit of Swindon that some people think qualifies it for World Heritage status. Keep on along Manchester Road, back to the junction with Corporation Street. You've been here before. Turn right, up to the bridge, but this time turn left into the other half of Station Road, the part that goes west past the station. Considering New Swindon was built around the Great Western Railway ('God's Wonderful Railway' to its admirers), what happened to its station in the 1960s and 70s is sad and symbolic. You pass it on your right, which gives you the chance to admire it in all its apologetic glory. It's an office block, with a low grey-clad slot in the front to insert passengers.

Keep walking alongside the Victorian rubble wall that now contains the station car park. Everything gets scruffy again, until you come to some Victorian workshops (industrial units/offices to let) on your right and, almost opposite them, as the name of the road changes from Sheppard Street to London Street, a row of solid, elegant, uniform, and externally unimproved terraced cottages. This is the railway village, built by the GWR for its workers in 1842, only two years after the railway line had reached Swindon in its rapid progress toward Bristol. There are eight little streets of cottages, perfectly preserved. They are well worth a wander.

But for now, walk a few more yards along London Street. On your left you will see hoardings and scaffolding and, hidden inside that, Swindon's most famous (and possibly most embarrassing) architectural sight. The Mechanics' Institute (or Institution) was created by the railway workers to provide a place for recreation and education, as well as wholesome food. The building was opened in 1855. It had a library, a community centre, and a covered market. Later it became the base for Swindon's very own health service. It closed in 1986, and no one has ever come up with a viable plan for a new use for it. A Victorian fantasy of pitched roofs and spires built around a central fly-tower, it has fallen into the hands of the Crown Estate, which is to say the Government. In 1978, it provided the inspiration for a song called 'Meccanik

Dancing'. In 1983, its central hall scenery store provided space for XTC to rehearse *Mummer.*

The tourist trail heads north through a tunnel, built to take the railway workers from their cottages to the gigantic engine-building sheds on the other side of the tracks. The works covered 300 acres. Some of the buildings still exist, but mostly there's a shopping mall and STEAM, the museum of the Great Western Railway. It's well worth a visit.

But we're not tourists; we're following in the footsteps of Andy Partridge. A street called Emlyn Square runs down the side of the battered Mechanics'. Walk that way, going south, then turn left into Farringdon Road. On the corner is another fine building, now the Platform, a centre for young musicians. Built in 1849 as a lodging house for the railway, it subsequently became a Wesleyan Chapel. In 1960 it was converted into the Railway Museum, and it was here that the photographs for *The Big Express* were taken. The photos show the three-man band in GWR outfits on the footplate of Lode Star, a Swindon-built locomotive. They look like they're having the time of their lives, but they weren't employed in Swindon Works. The same was about to be true of 2,375 Swindonians. In February 1985, British Rail Engineering Limited promised, in the face of rumours, that it would have a continuing presence in the town. Three months later, it decided to close completely. An inquiry into the likely consequences of the closure noted that it would add to 'an already disastrous level of unemployment at Penhill'. Poor old Penhill.

Some way up Farringdon Road, on your right, you will come to Holmes Music, which plays a small part in Partridge's story. A frieze above the door declares 'God Save Our Queen'. This ornament is not thought to be in honour of the Sex Pistols. It was known in 1976 as the John Holmes Organ Centre, which didn't sound so funny at the time. Organs were downstairs, guitars upstairs, and it was there that Partridge saw a card on the wall, from a keyboard player looking to join a band. The keyboard player, of course, was Barry Andrews. Andrews had a London accent: not so unusual in Swindon in the 70s, which had been taking in Londoners and their children since 1952. Holmes Music still has a bustling notice-board; it's downstairs.

Turn round and head west. The first turning on your left is Farnsby Street. It heads south-east, which is where we want to go. You pass Swindon's market, which is covered by a tensile structure (a tent, in English). Looking down on it is the town's most notable (indeed, unavoidable) modern building, the Brunel Tower (properly known as the David Murray John tower, after a man who served as town clerk for thirty-six years, earning himself the coveted nickname 'Mr Swindon'). Completed in 1976, it was one of the first modern buildings to escape the tyranny of the rectangle. It is a skyscraper, but with rounded corners which make it look like a radio or a toaster. It is rather good. It dominates the Swindon landscape, but then Swindon is very flat.

Farnsby Street joins Commercial Road. Keep going south-east, pass a zebra crossing, and there on your left is Kempster & Son, another important stepping stone in the Partridge story. A long narrow shop, full of guitars, amps, and accessories, Kempster's has always been a second home to Swindon's musicians. Andy would sit on the floor playing the guitar for hours until Jeff Kempster threw him out 'in the nicest possible way'. In the summer of 1977, with some Virgin money burning a hole in his pocket, Andy went into the shop intending to buy a Gibson Les Paul and came out with the unfashionable instrument that has always been his pride and joy: an Ibanez Artist 2619. 'It was love at first twang,' he said later. He thought it was Spanish, on account of its name, then learned it was Japanese, but he didn't care. He certainly didn't care what anyone else thought about it. He has always been his own man, in this as everything else.

Time to take stock. Andy has his band. He has his instrument. He has his (first) wife-to-be. Time to start climbing the hill. Do you have your oxygen gear? Almost directly across the road from Kempster's is Stanier Street, another narrow road of modest Victorian dwellings. Walk up it until you come to a crossroads. Cross. On your left is a shop dedicated to 'quality smoking accessories' with its side wall covered with trippy street art with an *Alice In Wonderland* theme. The first house you come to, number 16, is a rather nicely preserved bit of Victoriana, with its bay window, sills, and architraves all intact. If you want to see how it could have ended up, you need only look at number 17, next door. Number 16, though, belonged to Dave Gregory, the last piece in the XTC jigsaw. He lived there with his brother Ian, the fourth Duke of Stratosphear, from the beginning of 1979. A great deal of music was made here, much of it released on Andy's *Fuzzy Warbles* series of demos.

Andy has come a long way south. Now he starts the other part of his journey: up. Be prepared for a longish walk, which will catch out those of you who are taking a virtual perambulation on Google Street View. At the top, Stanier Street gets quite steep before seeming to come to a dead end. But it's not. Carry round to the right and there's a lane. You will get a good view of the Brunel Centre tower from here; but then you do from everywhere.

At the end of the lane you meet Deacon Street and should turn sharp left, still going uphill. On your right is a pair of iron gates. This is the back entrance to Radnor Street Cemetery, a pleasantly situated and uncrowded graveyard, built in 1881, with a chapel of rest at its centre. Walk through, taking time to observe the monuments to long-gone Swindonians, most of them departing this world in the last days of the nineteenth century. The grave is one of the few places you are not observed by Mr Google.

Find your way past the chapel to the cemetery's western entrance in Clifton Road. Go through and turn right. This whole area was built on open farmland in the 1870s as part of the rapid expansion of New Swindon. At the time the hope was that the land would be used for spacious villas, so that Swindon's commercial elite would be able to combine business with a little light agriculture. It was not to be. Clifton Road is typical of the area: crammed with terraces with tiny front yards. Most have been 'improved' over the years in ways that make you weep.

At the bottom of Clifton Road is Radnor Street itself. Turn left, past a redbrick building owned by a specialised industrial microprocessor company. People laugh at Swindon, apparently, but it was always early into high technology. The railways were as exciting as the internet, and as profitable. And Swindonians started making semiconductors, at Plessey, not long after they were invented.

Soon Radnor Street turns into Stanmore Street. Turn sharp right and head steeply downhill. A blue sign at the end tells you that you must turn right, but you're on foot, so turn left into William Street. Suddenly there is a mini-roundabout, a wider road, and a little bit of space. This is Kingshill Road. Turn left and start your climb. We are going up in the world.

Kingshill was a main road into Swindon in the days before there was a New Swindon. It was turnpiked in 1757–58 and is still busy. The farmland north and east of Kingshill Road was auctioned off from 1870. At the bottom, where we are, Kingshill is nothing to write home about. As you ascend, though, the houses on the south side are bigger and better, in high Victorian style, with gabled roofs, mock Tudor timbers, and names. In Britain, a house with a name is something to aspire to. One is called YNYSDDU, a reflection, perhaps, of the influx of Welshmen into the Swindon Works into the 1860s.

There are no names on the houses on the north side, which are substantially knocked about. There is certainly no name on 46 Kingshill Road, which is where Andy lived with Marianne when they were first married. There was a name in 1979, though, because it was a shop. Downstairs was the shopfront of Wyborn Signs, Marianne's father's business. The shopfront, and the Wyborn Sign saying Wyborn Signs, has gone. The house has been crudely remodelled into one-bedroomed flats for rent. But there is one remnant of the sign-making days: in the garden is a large, crumbling brick shed, once Wyborn's factory.

It was from 46 Kingshill Road that Andy would contemplate Respectable Street, which is to say Bowood Road, which is opposite. Go and have a wander. In contrast to almost everything we have seen, Bowood Road is made up of postwar suburban private housing: tidy semis on a hillside with trees in blossom, flowers in the front garden, two cars in the drive. No caravans now: one camper van. Andy's satire is affectionate. While he rips into the hypocrisy of the lower bourgeoisie, as was compulsory among his contemporaries, he does so with affection. Is it far-fetched to detect a note of yearning: a young man, newly married, working hard, scorned by his new in-laws, wanting to settle and lead, yes, a respectable life?

Old Town

And now at last we are approaching Old Town, formerly Old Swindon, the little agricultural settlement that received such a rude awakening when Isambard Kingdom Brunel decided to build his railway works a mile or so away down the bottom of the hill. Keep on up Kingshill Road, and cross a mini-roundabout into Bath Road, where the road levels out. Enjoy these houses, big three-storey Victorian villas, with a feature we have not seen anywhere else: rooms in the gables. Somewhere to store all those Victorian children and, of course, servants. These houses were for Swindon's tiny haute bourgeoisie. Being a hard industrial town, it didn't have much in the way of lecturers, lawyers, doctors, bishops, headmasters, and all the rest.

Those people had made it to the top, and so have you. Old Town itself, just along the road, is interesting and salubrious, a place where the comfortably off can refresh and amuse themselves. There's an arts centre, a shamefully abandoned old Town Hall, and a shabby but delightful museum/gallery with a special interest in naïve and folk art: it seems likely that Andy has drawn inspiration here.

Cross the mini-roundabout outside the museum and take a walk down Wood Street, a pleasant old thoroughfare which has plenty of places to eat and drink, and all the quaint, unnecessary things that make middle class life so appealing: an osteopath, a proper hardware shop, a jewellers, a specialist running shop, and somewhere to buy extravagant 'gifts' for adults. It is Swindon's peculiar predicament that, despite its increasing wealth, it has never allowed itself to quite become middle class: Old Town is so unlike the rest of Swindon that it might as well have a fence round it.

Old Town is where Andy's Complicated Game has ended. He has reached the last square on the board. It is where he has made his home for the last thirty-odd years. His house is nice and solid, and thankfully not knocked about. But it's not a big house. There are no servants' quarters, but there is an attic and, in the garden, a musical shed where Andy plots his revolution.

Shall we go and find Andy? No. Unlike him, we're going back to Penhill. Come back out of Wood Street and turn sharp right at the mini-roundabout. You're in Victoria Road. On the right-hand side is the home of the venerable *Advertiser*, as previously mentioned. Keep walking down the hill, past curry houses, charity shops, and the old Swindon College, around Regent Circus, and you'll eventually find yourself in Princes Street, one of Swindon's pointless bursts of dual carriageway. You want Stop B, the number 17 for Penhill. Every ten minutes.

And that concludes the tour. Thank you for visiting Swindon. Please take your baggage with you.

CHAPTER 1

THIS IS POP

FROM *WHITE MUSIC*, JANUARY 1978
RELEASED AS A SINGLE, MARCH 1978

Let's talk about when you were twenty-three, and you were writing this song, and the whole world was your clam, and oyster, and every other shellfish. [*Laughs ruefully.*] Yes. Right.

Can you channel back to those times and tell us what you were thinking? I can, actually! I was thinking about it earlier. This song exists purely as a way of not wanting to be bracketed by music journalists, who were desperately falling over themselves to try to give a name, and build a box, quick, to put all this upsurge of new music into. For my sins, I used to read *NME* at the time— *New Musical Express*—which was very elitist and very snobbish, but it sold you this elitism and snobbery under the guise of insight and new appraisals of things. But it really was just musical snobbery.

'You can pigeonhole music along with us.' Exactly. And they were desperately looking for what box to put this new explosion of noisy music into—which of course largely came out New York a few years earlier, with the Ramones, and Television, and the New York Dolls. I was a huge fan of the Dolls—so much so that you probably know that I penned a letter to actually join them.

No, I don't remember that story! Oh! Yeah, I was such a huge Dolls fan, around '73 or '74 when they first came out, that I thought, 'Wow! This is the band I want to be in.' And I actually wrote a letter—I never plucked up the guts to post it—but I wrote it, and my pseudo-name was 'Lord Andrew English'. [*Laughs.*] You know, along with Syl Sylvain and Johnny Thunders and Killer Kane, I was going to be Lord Andrew English.

I like it!
It just would have put a horrible Mott The Hoople slant on the whole thing.
I can see it now. But I didn't have the guts to post it. I thought, 'Well, maybe
one of the two guitarists is going to die off, what with all the drugs they're
doing, and I'll get my shot in first.'

So, you didn't want to actually post it because you were afraid it might work!
I was afraid they might say, 'Yeah, sure!'

Then what would you do?
Jesus, I don't know. I probably would have felt terribly trapped. You know, the
passing fad of the New York Dolls would have been like some glam, glittery
albatross around my neck forever. It would have gone horribly wrong. But
journalists in England were trying desperately to pigeonhole this new music,
and I really didn't like the phrase 'punk'—it just seemed kind of demeaning.
I didn't like 'new wave' either, because that was already the phrase used for
French cinema of a certain period. I remember going into an HMV store in
Swindon that had not long opened up, and somebody said, 'Oh yeah, they're
showing a video of the Sex Pistols!' They had a video of 'Anarchy In The UK'.
I thought, 'OK, well, I'll go and check what all the fuss is about.'

Had you not heard them before?
Probably not. This was '77, and I walked in this HMV and waited ten minutes
or so, and, in rotation, 'Anarchy In The UK' came on. And I thought, 'Is that
it? Is that what all the fuss is about? It just sounds like a slower version of the
Ramones, or The Monkees with a bit more fuzz.' I don't know, it just wasn't
new enough, you know?

**Yeah, I remember being pretty surprised when I heard the Sex Pistols for
the first time, because I was imagining something far 'worse'.**
They sort of had a modicum of professionalism, and they had a very good
producer in Chris Thomas.

**And I thought the guitars and drums were pretty good—it was straight-
ahead rock'n'roll.**
Yeah! Sure, it was just cranked up rock'n'roll, so I thought, 'What's all the
fuss about?'

Though the vocal-delivery style had to strike you, I'd imagine, because that's the thing that really struck me as being radically different. It was the attitude and the kind of anti-melody aspect of it, during a time where radio was being dominated by disco and corporate rock.

But I didn't even think that the vocals were terribly new. People like Ian Hunter—having mentioned Mott The Hoople—were actually singing with that sort of voice before. I just felt underwhelmed.

That sort of spurred me on—watching this stuff that I thought was rather average, and the sort of thing that I'd been into quite a few years before then. You know, watching the Stooges, and the Dolls, and the glam side of Bowie, especially the more minimal stuff, like 'Jean Genie' and 'John, I'm Only Dancing', or 'Rebel Rebel'. You can see *exactly* where the Sex Pistols were coming from.

I thought, 'I don't want to be called 'punk'—I want to name us before we are pigeonholed by someone else.' Then I thought, 'Well, what sort of music *do* we make?' And once I'd seen the Sex Pistols on this video, I thought, 'Well, it's just pop! You can't call it anything else—it's just pop music.' And that was the revelation. It is just pop music—let's call a spade a digging implement! [*Laughs.*] Let's be honest about this. This is pop, what we're playing.

And that was the purest inspiration for that song. *I* was going to pigeonhole us—or un-pigeonhole us!—before we were pigeonholed by the likes of *NME* and people who would want to put stuff in their boxes, in their construct.

And were you successful in that? Do you think that this song, being on your first album and everything, shaped the critics' assessment of you?

[*Sighs.*] No, because they were going to put their stamp on us whatever we did. But I thought it was almost like, 'Hey hey, we're The Monkees'—it was a case of, 'Hey, hey, what we play is pop.' So don't try to give it any fancy new names, or any words that you've made up, because it's blatantly just pop music. We were a *new* pop group. That's all.

Part of the reason that a lot of musicians in the mid-to-late 70s embraced punk was because of the anti-virtuoso quality of it. Prog rock had emerged, and groups like Yes and ELP were doing side-long songs and really emphasising their musicianship, while punk was a reaction to that—it was the pendulum swinging the other way.

But that had happened before, in the 50s, in England.

With what? Skiffle?

Yeah. I mean, the skiffle thing was acoustic punk, basically. [*Laughs.*] People made their own instruments, like 'tea-chest bass', or rhythm poles, or by blowing on a jug, or scratching a washboard, or beating on oil drums. And then they'd buy a guitar that cost £2, from a catalogue or something—a 'two-guinea guitar'! You know, literally unplayable, but it made a sort of a noise, kind of in-tune, and that was really a reaction to the fact that we couldn't do electric rock'n'roll like the Americans, and young kids couldn't do classical music, and young kids couldn't do the cool jazz thing—and so it was a homegrown, idiot burst of energy, to sweep away the stuff that we couldn't do with stuff that didn't belong to them.

And I think punk was like that as well. Prog rock couldn't be done by most kids on a council estate in England. The classics still couldn't, modern jazz probably couldn't—I just sort of saw it as 'skiffle II.' A way of saying, 'Well, we can't do your kind of thing, so let's find a simplistic, idiot version that gives us a lot of joy, that we can do on crappy, cheap instruments.'

Did you buy into that attitude as well? Is that something you believed, or were you perfectly happy to embrace the concept of being able to play your instrument well?

I loved the energy of it, and I loved, to some extent, the minimalism of it, because that's a place I was trying to go, with wanting to play short songs again, in any case. You know, I'd been through all the noodle-y stuff, and been through the stuff where—you know, you'd go out for the evening to a pub or a club in Swindon, what few there were, and the DJ would be playing Yes, or ELP, or 'Son Of My Father' by Chicory Tip, and it didn't feel like my music, specifically. And then I'd go home and listen to the New York Dolls, and Bowie, and Iggy, and that sort of really stripped-down primal stuff.

So, I loved the energy when punk came along. I thought the 'Year Zero' mentality was kind of necessary, but also kind of stupid—this 'there shall be no music before 1977' approach. That was very Red Guards—you know, smashing up the beautiful culture that existed before them, because there was *not allowed* to be any previous. And the more stupid side of punk tried to do that, you know—to negate anything that was there before. Yet it just sounded like skiffle with the volume turned up, or it sounded like what the Americans had been doing for five years previous.

And you remember thinking that then?

Part of me did, anyway. Another part did feel caught up in the spirit of the time because, generationally, it caught me at the right moment. I hadn't really felt part of any movement before then, so I sort of did get swept up with the optimism of 'Ooh, we're making something for ourselves.'

But I did start to see through it quite quickly. In fact, some of the lyrics of 'Complicated Game' and 'Travels In Nihilon' are me seeing through the fakery of it all, and commenting on how quickly commercial concerns moved in on it. As soon as you could say 'bondage trousers' there they were, at several hundred pounds a pair! And they weren't being made out of your old school uniform at home.

Right, that was the paradox of punk—it wasn't just a reaction to the complexity of the popular music of the day, it also was a reaction to the commerciality of that music. But then it was very quickly co-opted.

Oh yeah! It was a case of, 'Wait a minute, kids want to buy this stuff! *OK.* Let's get in there.' As soon as something gets taken away from you, you start thinking, 'Hang on a minute—I didn't think it was supposed to go like this.' But, at the same time, it was very needed. A lot of youngsters didn't feel that the music of their parents or older siblings was *their* music. You know—it's the gang thing. 'Let's have *our* gang song!' And 'Close To The Edge' is probably not your gang song!

So I guess I just didn't like the attempt by the media to put the new music into a bracket very quickly, make a coffin for it, and nail it down and control it. So, I thought, 'Well, by writing 'This Is Pop,' I'm going to say, 'Don't bother putting this in a box, because I know it's just pop music.' If you listen to the demos we were doing for a year or two before we made *3D-EP*, you can hear that we're playing two-, three-minute songs that are quite succinct, and that we're trying to go different places in the arrangements, and different places melodically and structurally.

Right. Instead of just three-chord idiot songs, which is what a lot of the punk stuff was.

Yeah. I liked the energy of punk, but I didn't need to pretend to be stupid. I could play, to a certain degree, and I didn't see the need for pretending to be unable to play. I think that's not necessary. There's a big difference between 'unlearning' your instrument, and pretending to be stupid for commercial reasons. The process of learning by unlearning—that never stops. But the process of being able to play reasonably well, and then just saying, 'Oh damn, I'll just play E and A all night,' that's not very rewarding.

So we tried to find new ways of constructing what we thought was pop music years before that. Much to the bemusement of a lot of our audiences, when we got live shows.

Why is that?
I don't know! We'd be playing somewhere in 1975, with John Perkins in the line-up, on keyboards, and a lot of the audiences would just be laughing, or smiling and drifting away. I thought, 'Wow, we're getting to them, because they think it's comical!' You know, as long as you're having an effect on someone, at least you're making a difference. They didn't understand what we were trying to do, but a couple years later it was like, 'Wow! Hey, this is new!' 'Yeah—it was new a few years ago for us, but you just laughed then!'

So you don't really feel that there was much difference between the stuff you were doing in 1975 and 1977–78?
Not that much difference, no. It was better-recorded, and it did have more of an energy injection around '77.

With Barry's arrival?
Yeah. And that's also to do with us playing the songs more live. You find that the energy goes over better as a live thing. It's the old Beatles' 'Mach Schau', you know?* Suddenly they're playing everything at twice the speed, at twice the volume. I mean, things like 'Neon Shuffle'—you hear the old recording of that, from 1975, some people have got this demo—it's Steve Hutchins, who was our vocalist then, and myself on guitar, and Colin on bass, and Terry on drums, and it's predominantly the same song, but two years previous. The more we played it live in those two years up to '77, the faster and nastier and choppier it got!

As you got more confident in it.
Yeah! That's the 'Mach Schau' principle—'Make it a show!'

---

* When The Beatles were appearing at the Kaiserkeller in Berlin, the club's owner, Bruno Koschmider, would shout at them 'Mach Schau! [Put on a show!]'

So, you've told me about the inspiration about the song. Do you remember the actual writing of it?

Well, growing up a Beatles fan, I remember thinking of what symbolised pop music to me, what was the start of the 60s—in fact, the death of Queen Victoria!—was the opening chord of 'A Hard Day's Night.' That was the sound of her being stabbed in the back with an enormous sharpened Rickenbacker. 'There! Queen Victoria's officially dead.'

So, I took the opening chord, and thought, 'I want to base my song on a giant, edited collage of Hard Day's Night-ness.' So I tried to write the whole song using as much of that opening chord in different places as I could—in fact, even opening the song with that rather demonic chord. It's actually the 'Hard Day's Night' chord with one note's difference. And the notes are—should anyone out there wish to play it—in ascending order, F, A, D, G, C, G-flat.

It would end on the high G if it were the 'Hard Day's Night' chord. There are two schools of thought on that chord—one school of thought says that it's as I've described it, and one school of thought says it's G, D, F, C, D, G. Of course, now it's all over the internet, and theories abound.

But I took that chord, and I made the whole song out of it. I took it up to D, then down to B, then G, then up a semitone and turned it into a seventh—to an A-flat seventh. So that's the whole song—it opens on the one-note variation of the 'Hard Day's Night' chord, then we have a bit of percussion, then that pattern. So I tried to make a new construction out of a sort of collage of that opening chord.

Right. But then on the chorus you turn it around a bit, right?

Yeah, it goes to C, then D, is it? Then F, G, C, C—and Barry does that *really* florid [*sings keyboard pattern*].* Very nice little melody, that.

Did he come up with that on his own?

I think so. I made a little note that I *really* like that little bit he does there. Would you like to know what my rather minimal notes say? Playing the track today—first time in ages—I'd forgotten the little 'yes' at the beginning of the single version. I'll tell you what it was [*laughs*]. When we were doing the vocals in Essex Studios in London, which is where I think The Clash did a lot of stuff later, I'd said to Mutt Lange, 'Look, I want it to sound really

---

* Barry Andrews, who had joined XTC on keyboards at the beginning of 1977.

cold and futuristic. What can you put on it to make it sound cold?' He said, 'We'll try a flange.' So he actually *recorded* the vocal track with the flanger on. He was committing to it—it wasn't a case of, 'We're going to do it in the mix,' it was a case of, 'This is how it goes down to tape.' It sounded so good in the headphones that I just couldn't stop talking and listening to myself with the flanger. I'm just sort of going [*imitates flanged voice*] 'Helllllllo … Yyyessss'—and, of course, one of them gets left on the tape! Because they're rolling, and I'm supposed to be doing a take, and I'm just listening to myself in the headphones with this fantastic sound on the vocals, making all these sibilant noises.

Tell me a little bit about the guitar lead that you're doing in the intro there. What was going through your mind when you're doing that? It's very dissonant.
You mean the solo-y thing on the album version?

Yeah, that's what I'm thinking of.
That was just me disassembling Chuck Berry, really. [*Laughs.*] I'm pushing Chuck Berry where he didn't ought to go! Playing him in two or three different keys at once, like it's a sort of a bad dream of pop music—it's the sort of phrases that Chuck Berry, or The Beatles would have played, but mashing them up and putting them in wrong keys—you know, the whole song's in D, but I'm playing them in D-flat, and D-sharp, and D. So, it sort of sounds like a bad angular dream of Chuck Berry.

Did that just fall out, or did you do that on purpose? Did you search around to find that?
I'm a great believer in the concept of, you throw your hands on, and what comes out is what you get. Because you've already made the decision in your head that your hands are going to go there, really knowing full well that it's not going to fit, but that there are going to be some great accidents.

Was that this particular take, or was it something you guys had been doing live and you'd stumbled on and decided to keep?
Before the album version, I'm not sure how much we played this live. I think we did to some extent, but I remember it was still quite a new song by the time that we got to be doing it for the album.

I remember playing it a lot in those London clubs and pub venues. But I think it was one of the later ones to arrive for the *White Music* album. We didn't have it by the time we were recording *3D-EP*, because I probably would have put that one forward, you know? So it was probably written, or being written, by the time we did that EP, and then up to doing the album in '77. But the album wasn't released until early '78.

But I like accidents. I like to put myself in the way of musical harm. I like being at the wheel of that musical car, and aiming it at the wall, just to see what shape the car's going to come out. You know, it might come out an interesting shape that would have taken me forever to decide on otherwise. You might as well just drive it at the musical wall and bend it up a bit. That thrills me, you see. I still do that now, with Monstrance.* It's a matter of, 'OK … go!' 'What key are we in?' 'It doesn't matter! Go!'

And music should be that way—there should be the thrill of the unknown. Otherwise it becomes very calculated and it's just another job, right?
I think so. I think if it's all measured and organized, there's no room for the accidental. And the accidental is truly thrilling.

That's where the muse is speaking through you.
There are no mistakes. There are only new ways of doing things.

We were speaking about the album and the single version, and one of the differences is the little bass-and-drum pattern there.
Do you know, I didn't listen to the album version today!

You've got to listen to *White Music* more!
No—that's naked-baby photos! Please. Give me the dignity of letting me put my trousers on.

I know that, in the end section, the intro chord comes in again between each chorus, which I thought was a mistake pretty much as we were doing it. So, as we came to do the single version, that was something that had to get corrected.

---

* Monstrance was Andy's free-improvisation trio, featuring Andrews on keyboards and Martyn Barker on drums. The *Monstrance* album was released in 2007.

Why did you decide to turn that bass-and-drum pattern around between the album and single versions? Was it the result of you guys playing it live and deciding that the pattern you use in the single worked better?
I think so. You're playing it live, and you're thinking, 'Don't you just want that to keep going there?' With everything on *White Music*, after we'd finished it, it was pretty much of case of, 'Wow, why didn't we just put more of a steady rhythm behind it?'

Well, you were talking before about how producer John Leckie would take snapshots.*
Yeah, he would never suggest anything; he would never say 'Do it like this,' or 'Do it like that.' He'd just say, 'OK, everything's ready—away you go!'

So that's where the songs were when you took that 'photo'.
That's where they were, from playing live or even having just been written.

Barry's part—or, his instrumentation—is different between the two versions, too. When you're playing the intro on the album, for example, he plays that sustained chord on the Crumar, while he uses a synth on the single.†
Yeah, he does like a high, tensile, cold string thing on the single. The album is more organ- and piano-based.

So let's talk about the bridge a little bit. You break out of that chord structure you were talking about there, right?
I've forgotten the chords! I'd have to sit down with the song and work it out, like I was in my own tribute band!

That'd be great! You guys should start a tribute band.
Yeah! Think about it—a tribute band to the Talking Heads! The Talking Sheds, from Swindon. I'll be Tina.

---

* John Leckie began his career at Abbey Road Studios, and went on to work with Simple Minds, Be-Bop Deluxe, Public Image, The Dukes Of Stratosphear, The Fall, The Stone Roses, Radiohead, Muse, and many more.
† The Crumar was a cheap Italian organ.

Let's talk about the lyrics in the bridge. They're pretty in-your-face.

Yeah, that's all the criticisms—it takes forever to get a record deal, or to get recognised, or to have people not just flocking away from your live gigs laughing. It did take a long time, we did go the wrong way—we wanted to do it *our* way, we didn't want to do it *their* way. And they thought our way was the wrong way. And yeah, we *did* play the songs much too loud! Especially after we had our own PA system built. [*Evil scientist voice*] Mwa-ha! We could be as loud as we wanted!

Did you actually have people looking down their noses at you and saying, 'What do you call that noise'? Was that coming from life at all?

It was just kind of a parental thing. You know, you've got to bear in mind that I'd be at home, living with my parents a few years before then, playing *Trout Mask Replica*, you know [*laughs*]—or my mother turning the power off if I plugged my amplifier in, and things like that.*

Really?

Oh yeah, she'd rather sit in the dark and the cold so that I couldn't make a noise with my electric guitar and amplifier. Or, Colin would come to the door, in the early days of The Helium Kidz, with his bass under his arm.† I'd arrange for him to come 'round, so we could go up in my bedroom and run through the numbers, and she'd deny I was in! She'd go to the door, and he'd ask, 'Is Andy in? I'm here to rehearse.' 'No, he's not here, love.' You know—knowing full well that I'm waiting upstairs, thinking, 'Why isn't Colin coming up?' [*Laughs ruefully.*] My mother was an *enormous* influence on me! So, if she *would* let Colin in, then she'd turn the power off.

Nice. [*Laughs.*] So that's where you got the idea for doing the unplugged sessions, right?

Well, I was still plugged! But un-volted—or whatever the phrase would be. My father was quite musical, and it was his crummy old guitar leant behind the sofa that got me picking up guitar in the first place, but my mother was decidedly against me making [*Monty Python 'Pepperpot' voice*] 'that 'orrible noise!'

---

* *Trout Mask Replica* is a 1969 double-album by Captain Beefheart.

† Colin Moulding had been playing with Andy since 1972, firstly in Star Park, later renamed The Helium Kidz.

In any form at all, huh?
Yep.

Were there any songs that you could play that she did like?
No. The standard parental thing was, 'C'mon, play us a *tune*, then.' And if it wasn't 'Wheels Cha Cha', they didn't want to know. * 'Hey Mom, I've worked out 'Dachau Blues'! Wanna hear?' † [*Laughs.*]

What about The Beatles or something like that?
They liked The Beatles up until they grew moustaches, and then certainly my mother claimed, 'They've spoiled themselves *and* their music.'

'Those nice young boys.'
While I thought, 'Wow, they finally got *really* interesting!' So that's the generational thing. When I lived at home, I showed my mother the sleeve to *The Spotlight Kid*, by Captain Beefheart, where he's got the Nudie suit on.‡ It's a *really* tacky kind of country & western Glen Campbell outfit. And she said, 'Ooh, who's that? He looks nice. I bet that sounds *lovely*.' [*Chortles*.] And I thought, 'Jesus—do you think I should lock her in my bedroom and force her to listen to "I'm Gonna Booglarize You Baby"?'§

It would serve her right, after everything she'd done!
It would serve her right, yeah.

When Dave joined the band, did you change the live arrangement of this song much?
No, we still kept the same arrangement, but we shared duties a little more evenly, I think.

He played this mostly on guitar, right? Did he even play keyboards on it?
He played a few little key bits, if I remember correctly. I'd have to listen to a live version to say for sure. But he would play within the chord structure, and

---

* A British hit for the Joe Loss Orchestra in 1961.
† From *Trout Mask Replica*.
‡ *The Spotlight Kid* was released in 1972. A Nudie suit is a flamboyant rhinestone-covered outfit designed by Nudie Cohn (1902–84), a Ukrainian-born tailor working in Los Angeles.
§ The opening track of *The Spotlight Kid*.

I could play the little solo section, or whatever, so it would sound a little bit more like the album. But it sounded pretty beefy with two guitars playing it live. And a little bit of beef is a good thing!

It's interesting that you didn't even consider listening to the album version of this in preparing for this interview. You only pulled out the single version.
Yeah, because the *White Music* version was sort of like trying it out. It wasn't quite right. Whereas the single version is much more right.

It wasn't for many years after I'd heard the album version that I heard the single version, because it wasn't as widely available here in the US.
Ahhh! And what did you think? 'Oh, they've spoiled it by playing it too regularly'?

I liked it, but it was a shock hearing it so much more … swish, I guess.
Produced. Yeah. Well, the sounds on it sound more high-quality. I think the engineering has more weight to it. It sounds terribly dismissive of John Leckie, and I don't mean it to be, because John's a wonderful engineer, but the album version sort of sounds thinner and more demo-y. But on the single version, the drums sound deeper, the guitar sounds more chiming, and the keyboards sound more sparkly.

Well, certainly, in the drums and bass, it's a glimpse of the sound you'd eventually develop with *Black Sea* and *English Settlement.*
Yeah, I think so. It's a nod toward that sort of thing.

Interview conducted October 28 2007.

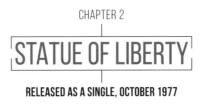

CHAPTER 2

STATUE OF LIBERTY

RELEASED AS A SINGLE, OCTOBER 1977

Let's talk about 'Statue Of Liberty'.
Do you know what I heard today? I hadn't heard it for many, many years, but I heard 'Made in Heaven' by Be Bop Deluxe. They were quite a sort of a template for us—well, sort of a template for *me*—pre-*White Music*.

What did you find compelling about them?
I liked the succinctness of them. I could see what they were aiming for, and they were obviously aiming at and hitting it much better than we could. I think things like 'She's So Square' sound almost like ersatz Be Bop Deluxe, but not played as well, or as tight. But what they were aiming for was a noble thing. It was almost like all the good parts of Yes condensed down to a few drops. Whereas Yes were a little long and flaccid in places, Be Bop Deluxe had the best, tight side of Yes, and distilled it and squished it down. And I thought, 'Hey, that's not a bad template.'

So, 'Statue Of Liberty' almost has Be Bop Deluxe in the back of my mind. I also think I wanted to write a Lou Reed *Rock'n'Roll Animal* thing, like 'Sweet Jane'—the very simple [*sings pattern*] three-chord thing. It was a matter of, 'Well, if Lou Reed can do something great with three dumb chords like that, I'm sure I can.'

It would have been 1977 when I wrote this. Marianne and I had two very cheap rooms next to the shunting yard at Swindon Station, in Swindon's red-light district, which is sort of all around the Manchester Road area. I was living in Number 7 Gladstone Street—there's a Victorian-sounding street for you! They were tiny Victorian houses, but they'd been split up into two two-room flats. You shared the lavatory with the people downstairs.

We both worked at McIlroys department store, and we stole—excuse me, 'borrowed'—a role of blue felt, which was ostensibly used for window dressing.* The flat was disgusting, so we covered everything in it with blue felt. We stapled it all over the sofa, which was rotten and decaying. We stapled a load of blue felt over the grotesque table. We made blue-felt curtains, blue-felt carpet—I mean, everything was covered in blue felt.

So, this was your Blue Felt period!
This was my Blue Felt period, yeah! We made a bed cover—actually, it got so damp in the bedroom that we ended up living in just one room. We'd lay in sleeping bags, and stick our feet in the oven to warm them up, then turn it off and fall asleep with our feet in the oven, because it was that cold. [*West Country accent*] But 'ey, we were 'appy!

We had zero money. I remember that, while we lived there, the band auditioned Barry Andrews—which really was just a drinking session, to see if he could drink as much beer as we could. If he could, he'd be in the band! [*Laughs.*] Very musical audition, as you can see. He could indeed drink a lot of beer—more than me, apparently, because I remember puking into the sink in the front part of the flat, with Marianne pushing bits down the drain with a plastic Chinese takeaway spoon, and me looking up at her wistfully in between hurls, saying [*drunk and miserable voice*], 'I think we found a keyboard player!'

I also remember that I spray-painted some Stuka dive bombers on the wall! It was just white walls in there—except for the blue felt on the furniture—and I thought, 'We've got to put some décor up.' I started by getting bits of posters from hoardings—what you call billboards in the US—I'd go around to these places that put them up, and I'd ask if they had any spare. They'd say, 'Well, we have half of one here that you can use,' or whatever, so I started by putting these pieces up as wall coverings. When these pieces of random cigarette ads, or whatever they were, kept falling down—or maybe we got bored with them—I decided that I'd paint some Art Deco-looking palm trees, which I did every couple of feet. I then got bored with those pretty quickly, so I decided to add some Stuka dive bombers bombing them. [*Laughs.*] I made a stencil of a Stuka about a foot long, and spray-painted multiple blue Stukas attacking the palm trees—which, I remember, the landlords weren't too happy about!

I was going to ask if you were allowed to decorate!
Not really, no. But it was dull looking at those white walls. I had a fantastic

---

* Then in Regent Street, Swindon.

collection of tin badges, or buttons—including some porn ones that I made myself—stolen when we finally moved out, to a place around the corner. We put our few belongings out on the pavement, loaded them into the car, and went round to drop stuff off. I left the cork notice board with all these badges on it outside, and of course somebody took it.

Tell me about writing the song.
I remember thinking, 'If Lou Reed can write these powerful songs with moronic repetitions of three chords, why can't I?' It was a case of saying to myself, 'You don't have to write stuff with incredibly odd changes or 'new' ways of forming songs—there's still some juice to be wrung out of three chords.' So, I found a pattern of C, G, A-minor, back to G—a real Lou Reed kind of chord change. You can almost sing 'Sweet Jane' over it!

What's the chord that you drop down to when you sing, 'You've been the subject of so many dreams'?
E-minor, then going to an A, then G7—to build it all up …

Going to the G7 is very Beatles-esque …
That's true, yeah. But it gets you right back to the chorus, which is the same chords as the verse! I just set it up with that little ramp section.

What about the end, where you seem to play a descending pattern? Do the chords actually change there?
It's still pretty much C, with a descending bass part. On the recorded version we get into all those dubby echoes on the vocals, then the song ends on a B-flat—it doesn't resolve.

So I was sat there, banging around these three chords, and I remember Marianne was ironing—she used to love ironing for some reason, I don't know why.* She got the ironing cable all tied up, and she was holding it in the air, sort of trying to let the cable unwind itself. And her hair was—I don't know if she'd just washed it, but it was sticking out all over the place, and I looked up and thought, 'Jesus—she looks like a weird, futuristic version of the Statue of Liberty, holding this hot iron with her arm up in the air like that and a handful of washing in her other arm, like the book or something.'

---

* Marianne Partridge, née Wyborn. They married in 1979 and divorced in 1994.

I thought, 'Wow! Statue of Liberty!' And *bleaargh!* that was it, that just became the lyric. No more, nothing deeper than that. It was just one of those things you fall into. [*Sings*] 'Whoa, whoa, whoa, whoa-ah, whoa, my Statue of Liberty, boop boop!' Like a sort of Steamboat Willie tugboat there. [*Laughs.*]

So, there's not too much to tell you about this. It came very quickly. It doesn't particularly mean anything—it was just the idea that I thought she looked like the Statue of Liberty untangling the flex from the iron.

At the same time, you take a step further. It's one of the reasons I liked you guys from the beginning, because you were a little smarter and funnier than the other bands out there.
[*Yogi Bear voice*] Smarter than your average band! Yeah, we had all the pick-i-nick baskets from the other bands …

Exactly, you stole them all. But, you know, the whole thing about sailing 'beneath your skirt'—there's a very arch sense of humour to this song.
Yeah. Obviously, I was sailing beneath *her* skirt, but it's the idea of Lady Liberty, and you kind of sail beneath her skirt to reach [*dramatic voice*] the Land of Freedom, or whatever. And it's just a metaphor for pussy, I'm sure of it! But it got the record banned by the BBC.

Which is always a good thing for publicity.
It's great, but it's so stupid. They were playing Lou Reed's 'Walk On The Wild Side', where people are giving head. Obviously, no one knew what that meant at the BBC!

Which is pathetic enough, when you think about it!
It really is. [*Laughs.*]

Looking back at the lyrics—is there more to it than that? Were you writing at all about what she represented to you?
I probably was hankering to go and see New York, and the world in general. Apart from being born in a forces hospital in Malta to a sailor dad and a dutiful mother, then coming back to England when I was very young, I'd never been anywhere else. So I used to fantasise about doing something that would enable me to see the world without having to join the navy like my dad. I figured that the only way I could get to see these places that you dream of—

and New York is one of them, because, along with London, it's kind of the capital of the world—was if I got in a group, got popular, and toured around. So, I do suppose there's some wishing going on there.

So what was it like when you finally did see Lady Liberty?
I actually never went to the island. I've only seen it from the mainland, and thought, 'Oh, is that it?' [*Laughs.*] It was kind of underwhelming. What does it say on the Statue's book? Do you know what it says on Liberty's stony book?

I think it says July 4, 1776, in Roman numerals.
Oh, so it's a finger to the British, is it?

Kind of. Given to us by the French, of course!
Oh, then it's going to be a finger to the British, isn't it? [*Laughs.*] The funny thing is, this song always went down well in France—maybe it was because of 'Liberty'—they knew what that meant.

Maybe! You could have also sung 'Égalité! Fraternité!'
Stick it to the Englishé!

One of the reasons I like this song so much is that it's a great, almost archetypal example of early XTC. It starts off with a very punchy bass/ drum combo, the guitar is skanking against that, then the organ and piano kind of washes over everything.
Yeah, I'm a complete skanker—as many people no doubt mumble as they walk past me. [*Laughs.*] But if the drummer played a straight backbeat, I wanted to play in the holes of that—I wanted to play on the offbeat, so I could be heard, and make that mechanical clock thing.

In this case, the holes are in that reggae offbeat thing, on the 'ands'. By putting my guitar part there, I get heard, he gets heard, and the clockwork is made—you know, the little cogs intersect, instead of clashing or grinding against each other.

I liked funk, I liked reggae. I was drawn to what I now know as guitar orchestration, where even if it's an all-guitar band, it sounds great if they don't play over each other. Instead, they play little parts that are away from and mutually supportive of each other, instead of the moronic bar-band thing where you have three guitarists, and they're all playing exactly the same thing. What's the point of that?

When I listened to the song today, I was reminded that Barry Andrews barely plays his jangly Lawrence piano.* He's playing what appears to be an electric piano—sounds like a Wurlitzer.† I don't know why, but maybe John Leckie was going for a different sound or Barry fancied hitting something different, but it certainly sounds that way to me.

It certainly has a lot of delay on it. I wanted to ask about the 'solo' that he plays, which is this funny, minimalist solo that seems largely based on the echo.

I think Barry was embarrassed by the concept of soloing. It was the years where one was not supposed to do anything that showed off your musical prowess in any way. That was verboten, it being Year One in the Pol Pot—in the Pol Punk!—regime. Solos and musical ability—that's what belonged to history, and everyone was out to start afresh. Which is crazy, because a hell of a lot of babies got thrown out with a hell of a lot of bathwater. But that's a feature of revolutions, isn't it?

So yes, in that part, he's reluctant to take a solo. He's playing like it's an accompaniment piece, as if there should be singing there or something. And that Crumar organ—god, I loved that thing. I just wish he had ditched the piano permanently and just played that organ, because I loved the sound of that. I mean, the whole thing about wanting a keyboard player in XTC was to recapture my kid-brain idea of what the future should sound like.

The future, to me, was a Farfisa organ played loud through a Vox AC30, distorted!‡ It was the sound I heard at fun fairs as a kid—you know, on Johnny And The Hurricanes records. Put a bit of slap-back echo and reverb on it, with a little distortion, and that, to my kid brain, was what Starship Troopers were going to be listening to on their personal stereos. So I wanted that in my future-looking band—even though, I suppose, it was already a dead future by then. It *was* the future in the late 50s/early 60s, though.

---

* Lawrence Audio pianos were made in Ireland in the late 60s and early 70s. Stevie Wonder was one notable user. Their action was mostly made of plastic, and they have consequently disappeared.

† An electro-mechanical piano built in the US between 1954 and 1984.

‡ Farfisa organs were built in Italy between 1964 and 1976. A Vox AC30 is a British guitar amplifier.

Still, you can see why he wanted the piano, too—as a balance to the futuristic organ.

Sure. I know that the previous keyboard player, Jon Perkins, wasn't keen that I kept pushing him toward getting a Farfisa or something similar. He had a Davoli synth, and that to me had a kind of Farfisa-esque sound.[*] But he would mostly insist on playing his Fender Rhodes piano, and, to me, that sounded like the past.[†]

Sure—it's very lounge-y.

But the fact that Barry Andrews had this crude organ ...

So to speak!

Yeah, I recognise the many entendres there! We're not talking about 'My Weapon', though. But the Crumar was an instrument I really loved, and had so much to do with defining our early sound.

This song had a role in getting you signed, right?

John Peel—may he rest in peace—liked the song, and he was very, very instrumental in us getting a record deal.[‡] We played at Ronnie Scott's club in London—they used to have jazz downstairs, and then a scummy bar upstairs where they'd put on rock music. We had sent him a cassette of some demos, and he obviously liked them enough that he came along to the gig. That night, he particularly mentioned that he liked 'Statue Of Liberty'. He gave us a session on his BBC show, because of going to that gig. And then, because we got a session on the BBC on the John Peel show, record companies became interested, more people wanted to book us for gigs—it was like suddenly we had this big rubber stamp of approval. He was very, very instrumental in eventually getting us a record deal.

People can get an idea of what you guys looked like playing this song back then, because it made it on to the *Old Grey Whistle Test* DVD.

That's right. There was also a promotional video made for it, which is just us dicking around in a tiny studio, and I think there's a cardboard cut-out Statue of Liberty that we're probably abusing and mucking about with. But yes, I

---

[*] A crude Italian synthesizer of the 1970s.
[†] An electro-mechanical piano introduced in the 1960s and especially popular in the 70s.
[‡] John Peel was a very influential BBC disc jockey. He died in 2004.

think we did three songs for the *Whistle Test*, and they ended up using one or two. 'Statue Of Liberty' is one. [*Dramatic, sorrowful voice*] And I was thin, and I had hair! Arrrrgh! I was looking a little 'Brian Jones' at that point, with my pudding-basin haircut.

You were all looking younger, and playing well.
Yep. Terry did his good, solid tub-thumping drumming. Barry played great, and I always thought it was very good how Colin fitted his vocal exactly to mine. Those were the days where we didn't always talk about the harmonies—we either felt them instinctively, or there was no harmony. We were still very naïve at that stage.

You were quite the performer, really mugging for the camera.
Why did I sing like that? Desperate to be remembered, that's what it was.

Well, let's talk about that a little bit, because that always struck me as kind of a 50s/60s-type hiccupping vocal.
I suppose I sang like that on purpose, because I didn't know how to sing. I didn't think I had a very good voice, and so I thought, 'I'm going to grab something that people will remember.' I also liked the idea of kind of dubbing yourself as you sing—you're chopping the words up like you're punching them in and out, or something. I think the *Rocky Horror Picture Show* soundtrack has got a lot to answer for.

And that is very 50s-based rock.
Yes. I liked the kitschness of the idea of the rock'n'roll voice, so I thought, 'I can do that.' If you mix that with the need to change vowel sounds to be heard through crap PAs, what you end up with is how I sound for at least two albums.

Speaking of crap PAs and your singing style, your love of percussion comes across in these vocals—'I lean right over to kiss your stony booK.' You're really emphasizing the consonants there.
Oh yeah, if you're singing along with a slap-back echo or whatever, it triggers off another *K-k-k-k*. It's almost that rather trashy kind of hiccupping Buddy Holly, almost 'dial-up a corny rock-and-roll vocal'. You've got your slap-back echo on it, with lots of hiccups triggering off the echo. I guess I found that

easy to do. Plus, the seal-bark bits were easy to get over on shit PAs, where you couldn't sing 'e' sounds—you had to turn any 'e' sounds into 'oooh' sounds, or else you wouldn't be heard, they'd just disappear.

Having sung through my share of shitty PAs, I figured it had to have something to do with that.
There's a practicality to it. It's a mixture of practicality for crap PAs, and the cartoon rock'n'roll voice.

Were you consciously doing that to set yourselves apart from the snarling punk and new wave vocals of the time?
Yeah, I think so. I didn't want to sing in a London accent, because I didn't have a London accent, I had a …

West Country accent.
Exactly. Our managers *begged* us not to tell anyone that we came from Swindon, but it was obvious the second that we opened our mouths. Especially Terry. He was the living Troggs tape! But our managers would sit us down, and say, 'Look, do *not* tell anyone you come from Swindon. If they ask you where you're from, say Mars, anywhere—do *not* say you're from Swindon.' So, of course, immediately we'd spoil that by talking about Swindon in all the interviews. We were proud of coming from England's comedy town! It was like a perverse badge of honour.

You seem to have a complex relationship with your home town—you love it in many ways, but then you talk about it being a comedy town.
We were always compared to Talking Heads in the early days, and people have asked if that grated on us. It did, but it was because, in some ways, they were on the winning streak. I've said in the past that it would have been very interesting historically if we'd swapped places, us from New York and them from Swindon—I think we would have been given much more respect automatically, instead of being treated as council-house kids from England's comedy town.

You could have moved—you could have gone to London, for example— yet you've remained there all your life.
Ah, small-town living is in the genes and in your outlook—you're just happier

with smaller things. I guess it all boils down to the devil you know. I could try and dissect it, but it's always a frustrating thing to do, because there's a hell of a lot wrong with this town. In fact, probably more wrong with it than there is right with it.

It's a tricky one to put into words, this love/hate relationship. It's unfortunate how Swindon is seen by everybody outside of Swindon—if you want a laugh in your show, just press the Swindon button.

The two towns mentioned in *The Office* are Slough and Swindon.
There you go. A new team comes to Slough—which is the other joke town—so where do they come from? Press the laughs button—it's got Swindon written on it.

Yet the people of Swindon are survivors. The town experienced some real urban decline when the rail works closed, yes?
Oh, yeah. The reason for us to exist almost vanished! It used to be a tiny little village that hosted a livestock market. When the railways came along, they found out they were running out of coal and water right around where Swindon village was, so they figured it would be a great place for them to stop: 'We can do repairs here, we can store coal and water. But where will the workers live? Tell you what—this line has to go through to Bristol, and we've got to cut through a few hills to get there, so why don't we use the stone we take out of those hills to build houses for the people who are going to repair and refuel the trains at this point?' That's the reason why the 'modern' version of Swindon exists.

But everyone's proud of their little town. Other Swindonians get worked up when I sometimes talk the town down, but they should be a bit more allowing. They know I know what it's like. They know I grew up here, and still live here, and know it as well as they do.

What do you remember about the recording of this song—John Leckie's role as producer, things like that? For example, there's a handclap that goes along with the 'boo boo!' Would he have suggested that?
I think we probably would have suggested the handclaps, because we liked the insouciance of bands standing and clapping—you know, it's somewhere between the New York Dolls and Slade. It's like a little spice sprinkled on top.

Did you bring this song into the studio fully formed, or did John have anything to do with how it was realised in the studio?

We were pretty much playing it live like that—minus the handclaps. We couldn't stop to do those while playing, of course, and I personally hated bands that encouraged the audience to clap along—I thought that was overt manipulation. I didn't mind subtle kinds of psychological manipulation, but this overt, 'Come on, put your hands together!' kind of shit—I always hated that. And I think we was recognised, even at the time, that the song was going to be a single, even before we recorded a note. I was slightly embarrassed by that—my rock head would have liked something a little more exploratory for a single, or a little tougher.

Well, you also had 'This Is Pop', right?

Yeah—those two were the singles, but I think in my heart of hearts, I would really have liked it to be something like 'Into The Atom Age', or 'I'm Bugged', or something unusual, you know? But that was not going to be. It was like having a kid who was a bit better than the others—who was born with this Harry Potter-esque 'S' birthmark that set him apart as a single.

Well, a lot of times, simple equals single—people gravitate toward something direct and approachable.

Yeah, dammit! But I wanted the more exploratory, artsy side of thing.

That's funny—in many ways, it's the story of your career.

You're right—that's been a constant, all the way through.

Interview conducted February 11 2007 and January 11 2015.

CHAPTER 3

MECCANIK DANCING

FROM *GO 2*, OCTOBER 1978

Let's look at 'Meccanik Dancing'. This is the album opener for *Go 2*, and obviously there was a lot of stuff going on with the album itself.
It was *really* that 'difficult second album'.

Right. You've told me that the living conditions, and how you guys acted, were like *The Young Ones*.*
Yeah, that was difficult! Plus, you know, Barry was trying to—well, let's be frank, I *felt* he was—trying to take my band away from me. I don't know if he was or not.

He was trying to express himself, and his own songwriting, within an environment that you and Colin felt that you'd carved out?
Yeah. See, I had, like, a picture—I wanted the first album to be *White Music* and it was the black-and-white thing, and I wanted to carry on the black-and-white thing with the second one, and then open up on the third. I had the great 'three-album plan'! [*Chuckles*] It sounds vaguely communist, doesn't it? 'Joe Stalin's three-album plan!' So, it was a plan where on the second album it would be my songs, and Colin's songs, but maybe opening up a little more musically, and then for the third one, I was open to different things—it could go a little more multi-coloured, a little more varied. Maybe then, if Barry then brought up stuff, we'd do the best of his songs. But, from out of nowhere, on the second album, he pulled up, like, seven songs!

That many? Wow.
Yeah. And they were *good*, dammit! I got the willies. So, I thought, 'Shit, this

---

* A BBC2 sitcom about young people sharing a squalid house, first broadcast in 1982.

bloke's trying to take my group away from me!' I could see there was kind of an attempt by Barry—and probably an attempt by me, though I didn't realise it, because I was in the middle of it—to sort of hive off the group and bring it my way. And you could see that he was trying to bring Colin and Terry his way.

Sure. That's a fairly well known band dynamic, unfortunately.
Yeah, so we were wrestling for control of the baby. It was a tricky time, that whole album.

Why weren't you threatened in the same way by Colin?
I think we had a dynamic where Colin was more passive, and I was sort of bringing him along. He was like my apprentice or something.

But certainly the quality of his songs was good—I mean, he had many of the early singles, and you've told me that you felt real competition from him.
Oh yeah, I did. He was much more melodic than me, and he got into it very quickly, whereas I had a longer run-up. I'd written at least 300 songs before we got to making an album in the first place, and those 300 songs were really not very good indeed, but Colin was kind of brand-new to it—and, like I say, suddenly Barry, from nothing on the first album, had *seven* songs he brought up for the second album. It was like, 'My Christ!' This could have easily have been a double album, and Virgin were not going to go for that.

So, I really feared that Barry was trying to hijack my group. As I said, I did kind of have this plan for the way we were going to do it, and I could see that that plan was being taken off the rails. Also, I think I felt personally a little bit disappointed that the first album never made—and I can see why it didn't—the [*chuckles*] commercial impact it might, you know? We borrowed a lot of money to make that first album, and it got about no. 28 in the charts, and then off it went—gone! And Virgin immediately turned around and said, 'Well, where's the next one?' We were literally writing it on tour.

So, even with the melodic competition from Colin, you never felt threatened by him?
No, because I saw it as friendly competition. But Barry's got this fierce intellect—you're going to cut yourself on it. You've got to go careful.

Did you guys ever think about writing together, or did you ever? In some bands that I've been in, when you have several strong writers, one of the ways you could get around the competition was by composing together.
No. The nearest I got to it with Colin was the lyrics—I thought his melodies were excellent, but his lyrics might have needed attention. So, I'd try to make suggestions—I didn't even want a co-writing credit. 'Look Colin, you're mixing your metaphors here,' or 'That really doesn't rhyme with that—if you use this word, it'll rhyme.' Or, you know, whatever it was. 'You've posed a question here, and you've not answered it.'

He was making the sort of mistakes that I'd started to already come through, and I could see that they were mistakes, and I wanted to help him out. But I think he thought that I was being the bossy older kid who wanted to mess his songs, you know? So he resented any changes that I tried to make to the actual, physical content of his songs. But for some reason, he would allow me to have quite a big hand in arranging them. I think because he frequently had no idea how they were going to go until they got into a communal work-out setting—everybody putting their five eggs into the basket.

What about co-writing with Barry? Did he have the same attitude?
I've got to say that his lyrics were very good, and also his sense of melody—which I hear he's getting back to, because I know that he's been in the 'melody wilderness' for a long time now. But when he brought up those seven songs initially, they had very interesting melodies and very sharp lyrics to them, so I immediately felt threatened—which is why the atmosphere was strained during the whole making of this record.

Why did you choose this song as the album opener? Is it because of the response you'd had to it live, or something else?
It just kind of felt like a good, kicking-the-door-down, pop, breezy opener. I mean, make no mistake, this *is* the pop song from the album. In my opinion, Virgin missed a trick by not considering this for a single. Because, dammit, you could dance to it! That was a big consideration then. If you had a track that was half-decent, *and* you could dance to it, then that was the one they wanted to think about maybe as the single. I thought this filled quite a few criteria—you could sing it; it was about a subject you kind of related to, if you were English, at the time, and, dammit, you could *dance* to it! It came back to me, as I played it today, what I'd actually based it on. Which famous work song is it based on?

You got me!
OK, just sing the melody to yourself, but sing it telescoped up, so there are no rests between the lines.

[*Sings tune, brings it up to speed, and comes to the realisation just as Andy starts singing.*]
'Mama's little baby loves short'nin', short'nin', Mama's little baby loves short'nin' bread.'

Yeah! Of course.
It's based on that song. I told you, you could hear it! [*Starts singing the lyrics of 'Meccanik Dancing' to the 'Short'nin' Bread' tune.*]

So, where the hell did that come from?
I don't know, it was just one of those tunes that must have rattled 'round my head as a kid. Along with [*sings*] 'There's A Hole In My Bucket'– which I'm sure is going to surface in some song somewhere!* It's one of those tunes that seems to be kicking around in your head forever, and it just seemed to surface on this. I don't know who wrote 'Short'nin' Bread'—it's probably 'trad,' isn't it? That famous writer Mr Trad, who seemed to write an awful lot of the old material.†

[*Laughs.*] So, which came first, the music or lyrics?
I have to be honest, I can't remember. Like I say, it came back to me today that the melody is based on that song. I can tell you what the kind of main impetus behind it was. It's obviously punning, with the way it's spelled, on a chain of dance halls in England, called the Mecca chain.

Explain a bit more about that, for readers outside of the UK.
Well, there was a chain of dance halls where you take yourself on the weekend—they were originally old cinemas or theatres that they'd turned into dance halls, with dim lighting and a big huge bar at one end, and a DJ or a stage with a shell backdrop or something for a band. They were just sort of temples, really—temples of dance and drink. There was a chain of these, owned by a company that call themselves Mecca.

---

* Originally a German folksong; a UK hit for Burl Ives and Odetta in 1961.
† Usually thought of as a plantation folksong, 'Shortnin' Bread' was originally written by James Whitcomb Riley, in 1900.

Are they still around?

I don't know if they are. Maybe somebody who frequents one of these places can tell us, but they seemed to be everywhere in the 60s and 70s.* So, the places where people went to dance in most of the towns in England was the local Mecca. And also, the place where my parents' generation went to dance was called the Mechanics—short for the Mechanics' Institute, which was a kind of a social club in Swindon that was run ostensibly for railway mechanics.† It's pretty much the Mechanics' *Destitute* at the moment—it's just a really smashed-up, vandalised shell of a beautiful old building. They should really try to save it. We used to rehearse in the scenery store of the theatre there.

So, my mother would always talk about 'dancing at the Mechanics', which I thought was an odd-sounding thing as a kid. The lyrics are a cross between the Mecca dance halls, the Mechanics in Swindon, and how we used to hang around in the nightclub that our first manager had.‡ None of us ever would have got in if he hadn't been our manager—you know, we were just scum—but we used to hang around and watch these people getting drunk out of their skulls and trying to dance like robots! I thought that was really weird—I mean, that the mating ritual involved trying to be mechanical. They'd be loose as a goose, yet trying to dance like a piece of machinery. That fascinated me—I liked the dichotomy of it—that these drunken, loose people would spend all week in the factory, and then they'd be there in this nightclub, or in one of the Mecca clubs, trying to dance like a robot.

Was this a result of the music of bands like Kraftwerk, or were they doing that anyway to non-mechanical music?

They'd be largely doing it to that 'das Disco' kind of thing, but it seemed to spill over into lots of songs. This album has got a couple of those sort of observation songs about Swindon—the other one that comes to mind immediately is 'Battery Brides', of course.

---

* The dance halls are gone; the Mecca name now adorns a chain of bingo halls.

† The Mechanics' Institute (technically Institution) at Emlyn Square, Swindon, was opened in 1855 as a social and educational centre for employees in the town's Great Western Railway works. It closed in 1986, and there have been numerous attempts to reuse it. It has recently fallen into the hands of the UK government, which is considering its options.

‡ XTC's manager Ian Reid owned the Affair on Theatre Square, Swindon. It is now a lap-dancing club.

So, what else can I tell you? It was recorded in Studio 3, the *small* studio—although it's still pretty bloody large—of Abbey Road.

That must have been something for you guys—to, at that point in your career, be in that studio.
Do you know, I never thought about it until much later. It never really particularly occurred to me.

Was that a matter of the 'insolence of youth', or did you really not know your history?
I think it was the insolence of youth, and I never realised, at that point, what an enormous impact The Beatles had had on me. I wasn't aware that I loved them that much, if you see what I mean. So, people who worked there would say, 'Hey, this is the "We Can Work it Out" harmonium,' or whatever, I'd go [*blandly*], 'Oh, yeah.' Or, 'This is the piano that McCartney played such-and-such on!' I'd say, 'Oh, really.' Then go plonk-plonk-plonk on the piano, and, 'Oh yeah, quite nice, isn't it. Quite nice-sounding.' It never sunk in!

I do remember John Leckie, our producer, showing us a section of girder that Mal Evans apparently played with a hammer for 'Maxwell's Silver Hammer'.* They tried it on anvil, but it didn't sound right—it sounded much better on this piece of girder! Who knows? Only Mal could tell you the real story there, and I don't think he's going to!

So, a lot of the Beatle thing never sunk in for me. I mean, *now* I'd be ultra-aware of that. And, in fact, with Holly going in to Abbey Road shortly, she's ultra-aware of it, because I've drummed it into her.† When she was a kid, I'd sit her down and we'd watch *Help!* and *A Hard Day's Night*, and stuff. I think she had a crush on Paul McCartney by about the age of eight.

And it's obviously had its effect on her.
Yep. She also has the concise-songwriting gene. Obviously, being sat down in front of those movies as a kid has got to come out somewhere. But I really wasn't that—I shan't even use the word 'enamoured'—I wasn't so *aware* of it. I was too busy thinking about what we had to do there, and not about the history in the place, if you know what I mean.

---

* Road manager, assistant, and friend to The Beatles. Died in 1976.
† Andy's daughter, Holly, was recording Beatles-esque pop with her band, The Shebeats, at this time.

That makes sense. When you're at that age, you think the world's revolving around you.

Around *you*! And you think, 'Oh, that other stuff is the past. Who cares? That's the previous generation.'

'Whatever, gramps.'

[*Chuckles.*] Yeah, exactly.

One of the things that struck me about this song when I was listening to it today is …

I know what you're going to say. Go on.

Let's see if I can fool you, then. [*Laughs.*]

Is it the locked-in groove?

Well, Colin and Terry have got that going, but then the thing that struck me is how syncopated you and Barry are on this.

I'm playing that skanking, off-beat guitar—F6, and B-flat6, if you want to play along!—and they're locked into that [*sings bass and drum pattern*]. In fact, they're pushing the 'ah-one'—they're really laying that heavy push on that. They're not on the one, they're before that—they're on the 'wuh' [*chuckles*]— of W-U-N. That's a very odd groove. I vaguely remember them kicking this around for quite a while to find this funny, locked funk that they got into. Colin's literally playing 'Short'nin' Bread' on the bass. And I just love where the bass drum's put on that pattern. Because if he'd have just put it on the 'one', it just wouldn't have had that jump.

It's a cool part—I love what Terry does with the hi-hat there.

Yeah, because he's getting into that big, aggressive disco thing. I think we mentioned it before, but disco records were an *enormous* influence on us. He really loved that whole 'pea-soup, pea-soup, pea-soup' kind of drumming.

This is when he was first starting to show it, then it became very dominant on *Drums And Wires* and *Black Sea*.

Yeah, you get to peek at it on 'Meccanik Dancing'.

Right. But in the very beginning, where you're playing that odd guitar

figure, Barry's being very percussive too, in that organ part he's playing during the intro. And then, you guys are doing a call-and-response type of thing.

Yep. And then he does that little thing after the first chorus, where—I was aghast that he'd done this—'What? He's *rented* something!'—he'd rented a clavinet, and you can hear him playing that there. There was one laying around the studio when we did the single version of 'This Is Pop'. So once he played one there—it was a case of, 'Ooh, I like this!' When it came time to do the second album, he very craftily said, 'Look, rent me a clavinet.' I think he also rented a couple of swish synthesizers—which, for me, that was out of the purist bag, because I just wanted to stick with that Crumar organ, and his ropey old Lawrence piano—those were his colours, you know?

And that was your sound.

Yeah! I didn't want him spoiling the sound. 'What? He's rented a clavinet? That's not our sound!' So, I was getting a little needlessly reactionary.

What else do you remember about the recording of the song?

Well, it was good old John Leckie again. He's just the nicest bloke you could be in a studio with, I'll tell you. He's so fatherly to young musicians.

Which is important—I remember what you've told me about being a producer, about how it's too much …

Too much social work! Too much like being some sort of marriage guidance counsellor.

Too much fighting between band members.

Yeah, you're the probation officer, or something.

So, he's well suited for that role?

He's perfect for that. A couple of years ago, when we were talking about who he'd worked with lately, he told me that he doesn't like working with older bands, because they just don't have the kind of stupidity and energy and naivety, and the general kind of 'up' thing that younger bands have. He said younger bands *really* want to be in there, they *really* want to be working at it, and they *really* want to be sounding great. He said older bands just don't care enough.

Yeah, I can see that.

So, he doesn't like older bands. He much prefers kids, you know? I think he meant that in a musical way. [*Laughs.*]

Let's hope so! But yeah, I see what he means, because there's so much unfettered energy and optimism that you feel when you're that age. As we were saying, the world's at your feet, right?

Yep, the world's your lobster! You can do anything.

Right. So, he was providing you guys with good, solid support.

Nothing fazed him! You know, if a piece of equipment broke down, it was [*mellow voice*], 'Hey, that's all right, we'll just get another one, and look, we'll just use this instead.' His whole temperament was really very good. And Haydn Bendall was the engineer!*

Oh! That's funny. A name that has resurfaced in more recent times.

Yeah, he resurfaced for *Apple Venus*, but he was an in-house engineer at Abbey Road, so he was our Norman Smith or whatever on that album, and John was the producer.† Although he couldn't resist twiddling knobs or setting up microphones, either.

Do you remember any arranging or musical ideas he might have contributed?

No, he never did anything like that. He would never suggest anything other than stuff like, 'Give it one more shot, lads! Try to get the middle bit a bit tighter,' you know.

So he wouldn't say anything like, 'Well, you should double up the chorus at the end of the song,' or something along those lines?

No. He would never do that. Never anything like that. His strength was sort of winding you up and then letting you go, like a great little mechanical toy or something. And then he would take a photograph of you doing your thing, and that sonic photograph became the record.

John was not a 'mess with it' kind of producer. He was a 'let you do exactly

---

*   Haydn Bendall was an engineer at Abbey Road from 1974 to 1991. He would go on to engineer and co-produce *Apple Venus Volume 1*.
†   Norman 'Hurricane' Smith (1923–2008) was the EMI engineer on nearly 100 Beatles songs.

what you're going to do, and he'll make it sound as good as he can make it sound' guy. And, do you know, I have a lot of respect for that. I mean, sometimes you need an arranger, sometimes you need an outside voice saying, 'Hey, that's too long, can you chop that out and get rid of that,' but John never did any arranging, John never did any structural changes or anything like that. He would sometimes say, 'Do you know, that would sound good if we put it through this little tiny speaker,' or 'That would sound really good if we tried it through this piece of equipment, because I know that screws the sound up in a really interesting way.' His suggestions would all be to do with sonic quality. And I liked that a lot. You could always rely on John making it sound good. So, he was at the controls, and everything was all right with the world. I was so wound-up about being in the studio that when that red light went on, you know, it was like 'Ohhh, my god!' Very nerve-racking.

So, were you guys recording pretty much live?
Yeah. It was pretty much live, and then if anybody messed up really badly, you'd drop their part in, or have another go at it, or whatever. But it was mostly live—you all played the take, and that was it! The take without any mistakes on it was the take.

Let me look at my notes. Oh yeah, I was reminded, during the bit where I say 'helps you unwind', I think that's one of the first times we'd used a harmonizer. Was it the first? We'd probably used it on some of the dub stuff at the end of *White Music*, at the end of the session. Anyway, the bend down at the end of 'it helps you unwind', that's just dialling a harmonizer down. It may have been at John's suggestion. I was asking, 'Can we make it sound like it's actually unwinding?'

And what about the octave jump right before that? That's always struck me as very Beatles-esque, but you weren't thinking along those lines then?
No, I'll tell you, The Beatles were the farthest thing from my mind! I don't think The Beatles came back into my mind musically until *Black Sea* or *English Settlement*, where I thought 'Knuckle Down' sounded a little Beatle-esque. And then it really wasn't until *Mummer*, on that middle section of 'Ladybird' that I thought, 'Shit, this sounds a bit like The Beatles! Ahh, what's wrong with that?' And that, for me, was a big moment. But they weren't consciously in my head up to that. I wasn't going to admit to an influence as square as that, you know?

Part of the whole punk movement, of course, was the rejection of all that.
Yeah, there was no past. It was Year Zero. A real Pol Pot kind of thing, which is ludicrous, and rather nasty. Because everybody is, of course, the sum of all their influences.

Of course. But at the same time, you can kind of understand what they were reacting against—overblown 70s acts like ELO, ELP, and Yes, and what had happened to music at that point.
Yeah. And I did the same at the time! But hell—now I really appreciate what some of those bands did.

Really?
Yeah, Dave just gave me about three or four Yes albums, and said, 'Here, get into these.' I never asked for them, he just delivered them, and said, 'Oh, you'll like this.'

Oh, what did he give you?
The first four albums. I really used to like—what album's got 'Roundabout' on it?

That's *Fragile*—their fourth album. And that's the first one with the real classic line-up—Howe, Bruford, Squire, Anderson, Wakeman.
Because I like things like 'Roundabout', and I like 'Yours Is No Disgrace'.

That's on *The Yes Album*—that's their third album, the first one with Steve Howe on it.
I like that one about the chess game—what's that called?

'Your Move'—it goes into 'All Good People'.
I think Yes were melodically a really good pop group, but they just had this thing where every song went on twice as long as it should have done.

On the early albums, that's not the case as much. They were more of a singles-type band then, so I'll be interested in hearing what you think of what Dave handed you!
It was funny—out of the blue, he just delivered these four albums, and said, 'Listen to these.'

So, let me look at my notes again—I noticed that there are a lot of backing vocals and counter lines and stuff. And real *yob* choruses on this song. I was reminded how somewhat brusque some of those backing vocals were!

Well, it's a bit understandable—this was a song that was born while you were playing live, and it was meant to be an audience pleaser, so why not have rabble-rousing type choruses, right?
I think audiences got into it. Oddly, I remember playing it more once Dave joined the band. Of course, it had an outing with Barry, because that was the line-up that made the album, and then we toured the album, but not long after that, Barry left. So I actually remember playing it more with Dave in the band.

The cut that is on *Coat Of Many Cupboards*—that's Dave, right?
That's Dave, playing guitar *and* keyboards.

That little monophonic synth, right?
Yeah, that little Korg keyboard we had. So yeah, there are lots of little backing vocals and counter lines. I quite like the little breakdown section, where it's just drums—that rather spastic kind of drum rhythm he falls into. And we're just doing these very close-sounding, dirty-sounding harmonies—they have a lot of rub, and a lot of dirt, to them.

And that was a result of, what—you guys sitting around and arranging that together?
Yeah! Basically, because I didn't have any demo facilities, I would just bring the song up in its rawest form, and just tap my foot, and we'd just try stuff out, you know? Up until '82, all songs were built in a rehearsal-room situation, or even sometimes just in a recording studio, because there wasn't time to sit around in a rehearsal room. Or at soundchecks—that was another opportunity.

So, is there anything about the lyrics that sticks out for you? As you said, this is kind of along the same theme as 'Battery Brides'.
Yeah, I sort of have the two as a pair, really, which is maybe why they had to be close together on the album. I think of me walking from the Affair Club, which our manager ran, past Woolworth's—they were, like, 200 yards away from each other, so it was that observational thing. But no, there's not much otherwise I can tell you about the lyric. I like the simplicity and the

shortness of the lines—that '1-2-3-4 … 1-2-3' thing. I like the almost haiku-like shortness of the lines. I was a bit miffed it wasn't a single, I have to be honest. They never entertained it as a single.

That's where 'Are You Receiving Me?' came from—they sent you guys back into the studio to create a single, right?
Yeah, they said, 'You don't have a single on this album.'

And then it got shoehorned into subsequent releases?
Well, we did actually record 'Are You Receiving Me?' for the album, but we considered it not quite good enough for the album.

Really? It has such a different sound from the other songs, I just assumed that you only recorded it at a different time.
No, I think we originally recorded it at the same session, but thought, 'Ah, well, that one didn't come out quite as good as it ought to, so let's leave it to die,' you know? And then Virgin got to hear everything, and it was a case of, 'Well, we quite like that one, but we think you can do it better, and we'd like you to try another producer.'

So that's why you did it again.
Yeah, that's why we did it with Martin Rushent, and re-recorded it. * Of course, we'd done the same thing with the *White Music* album, with 'This Is Pop'. Virgin saw that as a single, but they didn't think it had been recorded tough enough, or strong enough, or [*chuckles remorsefully*] *expensively* enough. Certainly expensively—Mutt Lange was not cheap!†

Well, when you're lending yourself your money, what does Virgin care?
Oh yeah. I mean, we were getting something like eleven percent, and we had to give four percent of that to Mutt! So, we'd share seven percent between the four of us. So, Mutt took more royalty on that than any of us individually did! Of course, since we never saw any royalties until 1997, it's a moot point! He got paid, but we didn't.

---

* Martin Rushent (1948–2011) was a producer best known for his work with The Human League, Stranglers, and Buzzcocks.
† Mutt Lange is a producer and songwriter known for his work with AC/DC, The Boomtown Rats, Def Leppard, and Shania Twain, to whom he was once married.

I know some of your lyrics are better known than others for having misheard lines in them, but looking at the lyrics now, I can see that I'd misheard something. I'd always thought it was 'to a disco track from Germany'.
No, it's a 'disco trot'!

And then 'I'm under a fluorescent light'—I know lots of people have had different interpretations of that. Is that something you tried to do on purpose, just to try to obscure things?
No! Do you know, I thought the lyrics were pretty easy to hear on this.

You do kind of slur your words there. [*Sings caricatured version of line.*]
Well, I *am* singing it in my theatrically drunk voice! You know, I'm trying to paint the picture for you here that these are people who work in the factory, and they've had too much to drink, and they're under the fluorescent light, and they're just thinking 'I'm going to hit that dance floor, and *dance like a robot!*' [*Laughs.*] I enjoyed doing the dub of this song, actually. We included it on *Go+*, which came with the original LP.

Which one did this turn into? 'Dance With Me, Germany', right?
Ah! The harmonizer! Yes! That *was* the first time I had heard a harmonizer, because we did the dubs *after* we did the *Go 2* album.

That's what I thought! I didn't think you did any dubs after *White Music*.
I got John to do 'Fireball XL5': that was done in the *White Music* sessions. [*]
Listen to the version on *Coat Of Many Cupboards*, where the song starts all tinny, and then it goes into the big fat dub version—that was done at the *White Music* sessions. But all the dub stuff that came out on the *Go+* EP was done afterward. So the first time I was exposed to a harmonizer would have been the *Go 2* album. Mystery solved!

Interview conducted August 5 2007.

---

[*] The theme from the animated science fiction series, created by Gerry and Sylvia Anderson and first screened in 1962.

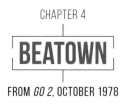

CHAPTER 4

BEATOWN

When I brought this song up, you seemed a little trepidatious about discussing it—why?
Good word! Yep, trepidatious about talking about it. Because it was a long time ago, and while some songs are really clear—where they came from, and what the sentiment was behind them—others kind of get lost in the fog. Maybe the sentiment behind them was kind of just something very slight.

I've got to say, that's one of the reasons I want to talk about 'Beatown' in particular—I've always kind of wondered [*laughs*] what you're going on about in this song.
Yes. OK, you got me bang to rights, Guvnor.

So, what are you talking about? What are the lyrics about in this song?
[*Cockney accent*] I never done it! I swear I never done it, Constable! It was that Colin Moulding—he made me go over the wall and nick them apples!

I was listening to the thing two or three times through today and frantically making notes and spinning back and checking it out, and I thought, 'Why the *hell* did I write this song?' I think that the title came from the onomatopoeic sound of the chord I'd just discovered. I shall reach over and pull up a Martin [*chuckles*] from a pile of discarded Martins—no, from a pile of one!—and it was this change [*plays the chords behind the word 'Beatown'*].

Ah—it sounds vaguely *Tommy*-esque when you play it on acoustic over the phone.
Tommy-esque? Hmm. I don't know about that, but when I blundered into it, I thought it was the type of chord that Todd Rundgren's Utopia might use.

Sure, I can see that.
The chord is the chord of D, right up there on the top, so it's nice and tight, and then you slam on a chord of A, with your little finger, so the resulting chord is these notes: D, A, E, A, D-flat, G-flat. And then you move it down to B, and do the same thing, so it's B, G-flat, D-flat, G-flat, B-flat, E-flat. For me, the chords sounded futuristic and medieval at the same time! They sounded like some big cityscape—you know, it could be [*chuckles*] London in the eleventh century, or it could be Brasilia 200 years from now. It sounds big, and it sounds urban and, like I say, it sounded like it was futuristic and archaic at the same time.

I thought, 'Wow, that sounds like a big town, a big city' and for some reason a 'beat town' just came into my head. I don't know why. It sounds really cheesy, like it ought to be the title of a film from 1962, with lots of beatniks on the beach having some sort of kinky barbeque. *Beat Town Blanket Bingo!* Lots of bongos, beer, and other stuff beginning with 'B'.

The lyrics contain lots of commentary on our manager at the time.* He was always moaning that he couldn't get us on the phone, and it hadn't occurred to him that I was so poor I didn't *have* a phone! [*Laughs ruefully.*] I had to walk about 200 yards to the nearest phone box to call in, to find out what was going on that day or what was happening on such-and-such an issue. [*Imitates annoyed manager*] 'I can never get you on the phone!' 'Well, I don't *have* one.' [*Pissed-off manager*] 'I can never get you!'

He seemed to not be able to grasp that I didn't have one. So, there are little things like that. And 'it's a capital city'—'capital' is the sort of word he would use. [*High-pitched, whiny-yet-posh voice*] 'Absolutely *capital*, chaps! Capital.' And so there are lots of little private in-jokes about the group at the time, and our manager.

Also, it's a song about positive violence, if such a thing exists. It's like a *Monkees* theme tune. It's sort of about us—I know this sounds crazy—'Beatown, yes we're the XTCs, we're coming to your town, we're just XTC-ing about.' You know, it was just one of those rather silly, self-manifesto songs. [*Bad Swedish accent*] 'Hello, we're The Trousers from Sweden, and our song is 'Hey Hey, We're The Trousers', from our album *Meet The Trousers*.' My god, this is bringing my brain to a halt even explaining it! One thing I do remember is, Barry Andrews said, 'I *love* that line, "We use the head and not the fist."'

---

* Ian Reid.

Yeah, tell me about that.
Well, you know, it's how you get things sorted out. You don't just attack. You think.

But there's a conflict of sorts that you're talking about in the bridge. You're saying, 'He says … he says …' and then you say, 'I said they beat you fair and square sir / They use the head, and not the fist.'
Yeah. It's about thinking things through. Use your brain—don't resort to flailing and kicking first. Use your brain if you want to get things sorted out. I suppose if it was The Monkees, it'd be, 'Hey hey, we're quite intelligent, we think things through. We're coming to your town to think things through with you.' [*Laughs.*]

And it rhymes!
There you go. So, what a slight, silly reason to write a song. But I love the idea of that epic rock-y repetition—the opening and closing sections are almost like Philip Glass was in a rock band, or working with music for guitar, keyboard, bass, and drums, you know? Because there is that great, nice, violent repetition to it. I love all that stuff!

It's a pretty powerful song. I was struck by that this morning, as I was really concentrating on it, listening on headphones—it's big. It's one of the bigger songs on the album.
It is, and when John Leckie's three-machine tape phasing kicks in—whoa. You know, I'd forgotten all about that!

How did he do it?
It's the best-quality way you can approach phasing. You have two copies of the tape on two different machines—one copy on each machine—and then you have a third machine to record the results. You play the first two machines, and make one of them go slightly out of sync.

So you're literally phase-shifting!
That's right, rather than using an external effect. So, you drive machine number one against the sound of machine number two, and as you drive it slightly out of sync, the whole track goes [*imitates effect*]—you know, it combs through the phasing, and you capture it on the third machine.

Is he only doing it on some of the instruments? I don't think the bass is involved in the phasing at all—it sounds to me as if it's drums and the high-end, trebly stuff.
I think you don't have to do it 100 percent—you can do different degrees. I'm pretty sure that everything went through it.

OK, so maybe you only apply it to certain frequencies?
Maybe certain frequencies, or possibly it was not done to such a deep degree as, for example, on 'Jason And The Argonauts'. The phasing on that is actually mechanical—it's a device called a Bel flanger.* The whole track went through that 100 percent. But on 'Beatown', I seem to remember it being tape phasing, but you can obviously do different depths, you know? I'm pretty sure you can. Now you've got me thinking! Yeah, I swear it was tape phasing, because that was a trick that John showed us how to do, and boy, were we impressed.

We did this in Abbey Road Studio 2, the Beatle room. But, as I've said, that was of no importance to me at the time, because I was in Beatle denial! And, oh boy, have I got a punky voice on this—have I got a silly, yelping voice.

It's funny—you do, on the studio version, but then I was listening to the live version, and you're actually singing quite clearly on that. You aren't 'barking' as much.
With *Go 2*, I was starting to wonder, 'Should still be doing that silly voice by now, or should I relax and be a bit more *me*?' you know? So, by the time we got to playing it live with Dave, I was getting more relaxed and being a bit more myself, I think.

Yeah, that version is on *Transistor Blast*.
Sure. There's also an Australian live version.

Which was on the 'Love At First Sight' single. I don't have that, but there is a version on *Transistor Blast* that was done at the Paris Theatre in London.
And that's with Dave, is it?

From the timing, I'm not sure. It's January 17, 1979.
January 1979?

---

* An electronic flanger made by B.E.L Electronics in the UK.

Was Barry still with you then? Because though it's keyboards throughout, it's a different tone, so I thought it could be Dave.

Was he still with us in January '79? He may well have been. Do you know, I can't remember. Jesus, I've got to get that out and find out! It doesn't sound like two guitars to you?

No, it's keyboards throughout the song.

Oh, that's Barry then.

Dave used to do this on guitar?

Yeah. If you listen to that Australian version, from wherever it is—the Marconi Club, I think—that's Dave doing some luscious Ernie-ing over the end there.[*]

So, what are you saying at the beginning of the song? You're spelling it out, but not exactly.

I'm just phonetically spelling it out. It's like teaching sounds: 'oh', 'eh', 'ah'. I don't know why I decided to do it like that. I guess it's the teacher in me! [*Laughs.*] 'Gather round now, children!' It's probably my hang-up about being the last to read in my class, actually. For some reason, I was slow with reading. I may have been mildly autistic.

Well, Einstein didn't speak until he was four, I think.

And what was the first thing he said? [*Little kid voice*] 'E=mc^2, Mommy!'

'Eureka! I have found my voice!'

So, he didn't speak till he was four, eh?

Yeah, I believe that's the story. They all thought he was a dope. So there you go, Mr Genius!

    Let's talk about the drums. First of all, Terry's stamina on this song is just unbelievable. Having just gone through a little *Go 2* party with other fans in the DC area, I had to get my forearms back in shape, and realised what a young man's album this is!

Oh, yeah—don't you love it when he does that roll right before the end-

---

[*] 'Ernie-ing' is Andy's favoured term for the string-bending that features at the climax of most guitar solos.

repetition part—both hands, both toms, simultaneously. No overdubs, of course—all one take.

And it's one of the few songs that he plays a ride cymbal on.
That's right! Yeah, he was a hi-hat man.

Did you ask for a ride cymbal on this song?
Do you know, I cannot remember. In my minimal notes on this song, I've written 'Terry workhorse'. He *really* is a workhorse on this track. We did some of the album in Studio 3, but I think John said, 'If we can get Studio 2 for a week, we can do a lot more live-sounding backing tracks.' I've got a feeling that this was a Studio 2 recording—the drums sound somewhat better, but they're still relatively close-miked. That was John's sound—he didn't like ambience too much on the kit. Which led us to seek out Steve Lillywhite and Hugh Padgham.* But yeah, Terry's really sweating away on this one.

Let's talk about the bass line a little bit.
It's very good! It's kind of minimal, but it really works.

The end part is minimal, but he has some quite complex runs in the chorus.
Yeah, it's very much that kind of music—I don't know what it's called—that you'll hear when someone's trying to evoke a cityscape, taxi horns, and things like that. You know, scurrying city sounds. So, maybe Colin was getting that out of the chords, too, because I don't remember saying to him [*chuckles*], 'Try a scurrying, cityscape, workers-hurrying-to-the-office bass line, please'! He just kind of got it, you know?

Right. And this would have been one of those songs that you'd worked out in rehearsal?
In those days, it was just, 'OK, I kind of want something a bit like this—go!' And off we went. But yeah, it's very melodic. I also like the intro, where he plays those big accents on the 'two', you know? I think it's a chord or something.

---

* Steve Lillywhite produced *Drums And Wires* and *Black Sea.* He would go on to produce albums by Peter Gabriel, Big Country, U2, Crowded House, Joan Armatrading, Morrissey, Simple Minds, The Rolling Stones, and many more. Hugh Padgham engineered *Drums And Wires* and *Black Sea.* He went on to produce or co-produce Phil Collins, The Police, Sting, The Human League, Split Enz, and many more.

He also shows a lot of stamina in that end part. That's not easy, to just keep doing those two notes over and over again.

No, not at all. But these were the days where Terry and Colin would *really* challenge each other to lock-in to what each other did. You know, they would have these kind of *duels*—you'd see them going at it in rehearsals or soundchecks. Terry called everybody by their last name—it was like an Army thing. So, it was never 'Andy'—it was [*barks*], 'Partridge!' Or, 'Andrews!' Or, 'Moulding!'

So, Terry'd yell out, 'Moulding!' Colin would turn round, and Terry'd be *going* for a rhythm and Colin'd have to be on it in a nanosecond. They were always trying to catch each other out. And 99 times out of 100, they'd be on it together within a fraction of a second—whatever the other one was going to pull out of the bag as a challenge, you know. There was a kind of roughhouse camaraderie. A *brotherhood*, dammit.

I remember you telling me, when we spoke a long time ago, about the different drummers you'd worked with, and how you thought that Terry had the most musical dialogue with Colin out of anyone in the band.

Absolutely. I mean, the pair of them came along together as a unit. It was like, 'I know this bass player,' and 'I know this drummer,' and it was them two. They'd played with each other before then—not for very long, but they did have a bit of a background together. They were looking for guitar players, singers, whatever, and I was kind of a guitar player, and a reluctant singer.

Let's talk about the keyboards a little bit.

Oh yeah, I *love* that organ! That's the very pinnacle of the Barry Andrews organ timbre—you know, the tonal quality he could get out of that Crumar.

It just swirls throughout the entire song.

Oh, I *love* it. I love the bit on the outro where he's playing those dissonant, clustery, swirly things. They are just—oh, it's *sex*, made into a cheap organ. That was *his* keyboard sound; yet, for the *Go 2* album, he borrowed some rather swish synthesizers.

Right, he'd rented out a Clavinet.[*]

He uses the clavinet on the middle section. He's mirroring the bass line, I think.

---

* An electrically amplified clavichord made by Hohner in West Germany.

Is he using any synths on this?

I don't think he is. I think it's all Crumar, otherwise. You know, I'd see this synth lurking in the shadows or whatever, and I'd think, 'Oh shit, I don't really want that, because that's not the sound of the band. The sound of that band is that Crumar, and his fuzzy Lawrence piano.'

I think that, at that point in our career, a band's musical identity was *very* important. If you went veering off track too quickly, you ran the risk of losing people who'd just got on board, you know? Which was probably why I felt so threatened when Barry suddenly brought up seven songs for this album. [*Sings, imitating John Shuttleworth*]* 'Seven songs by sunset!' Sorry, what a strange coincidence! Ooof!

'It can't be done, Ken!'†

'It can't be done, Barry!' [*Imitates Barry*] 'Oh yes it can, matey, and I'm gonna do it!' So yeah, I love the sound of that Crumar. There's something about it that is better than other cheap-sounding organs that I've heard. And at the time, I didn't like the Hammond organ sound. I love it now, but at the time I associated it with the sort of people my dad used to play with. He'd go out playing with these combos—playing dance-y, jazzy, classic stuff. And it'd always be a Hammond, so I just seem to associate it with the cheese of easy listening. But the Crumar keyboard sound, to me, that was the wet dream of the kind of psychedelic bands from the late 60s that I really liked. It was embedded in my psyche, you know?

Very spiky and angular.

Exactly, and especially the way he played it.

Let's talk some more about your guitar—you talked about those chords, but what else?

I'll tell you, another important guitar thing for this song is—and I don't know how you're going to write this up—but this figure of [*grabs guitar, plays intro to verses*]. I stumbled on to this figure, and again, it's that repetition, that mechanical playing. You know, it's related to 'Battery Brides', it's related to 'Day In Day Out', it's related to all that kind of, 'Aren't you the band who

---

* John Shuttleworth is a fictional singer/songwriter created by English writer/performer Graham Fellows. He has been a staple of BBC Radio since the early 90s.
† Ken Worthington is John Shuttleworth's next-door neighbour and sole agent.

play guitars like they're sequenced?' So, you can hear that over the intro, and before the verses. And in the middle, I changed to the very thin, out-of-phase tone—my Ibanez guitar has got a little phase switch that you can flick to put the pickups out of phase, and I used that for the very scrubby kind of tone I have during the bridge. You can also hear that on the rhythm guitar of 'I'm Bugged,' if you want further reference of that sound. That very thin, insect-legged [*imitates guitar part*]. That's the Ibanez flicked out of phase.

Until today, I'd forgotten all about that phased ending, which is a little more Dukes, actually, than I would liked to have admitted at the time. But I was obviously getting a hankering to do the Dukes, because it was around this time that I met with Dave and said, 'Do you want to do a psychedelic record?'

Really? Before he was even in the band?
Yeah, before he was in the band. I think I'd gotten back to Swindon with either some rough mixes or finished mixes of *Go 2*, and when I came back, we were living in a different bedsit—the new address was no. 12 Manchester Road. Dave came to see me there, at a house-warming do. I played him the mixes, and I said, 'Look, do you fancy doing a psychedelic project, where we're a band from the late 60s?' I was probably as keen on doing that as I was [*laughs*] on the album we were working on at the time, so yeah—that phased ending of 'Beatown' may have been a subliminal bursting-through of the Dukes.

I didn't realise this had formed in your head this early on. What brought this up in your mind? I have a theory—probably not original—that pop culture repeats or references itself every twenty to twenty-five years. When you guys did come out with the Dukes, it was kind of in line with this twenty-year cultural cycle, if you know what I mean, but you were ahead of your time on this one.
Well, I guess it was because it'd made such a big impact on me as a schoolboy. You know, 'Arnold Lane' and 'See Emily Play' had damaged me more [*laughs*] than I would like to admit, and how do you get that out of your psyche? How do you use it?

At the same time, with punk and new wave reigning supreme, for you to think about psychedelia was …
I know, it was the *wrong* thing to think about, during the whole punk explosion!

Although, I must admit, it was one of the reasons you guys stood out for me—there was something different about you. I could tell that from the very beginning. You weren't just another punk or new wave band.

[*Imitates old, stodgy gentleman at the club*] Good grief, no, man! I actually disliked a lot of the music of punk, and I thought a lot of the attitude was forced and strained. And the political side of it was just complete bullshit. Kids of that age aren't interested in politics—they're just interested in beer and tits.

'Titties & Beer', as Frank Zappa would say!

Exactly—there you go. That's all you're interested in at that age. But I *loved* the energy—so why can't you just put that energy into the music? You don't have to be a bad player—you can be a good player! Don't pretend to play rubbish, just to snag some fashion points this week.

Back to the vocals, there are some are some harmonies I wanted to ask about—I think Colin's way above you, on lines like 'You won't even get them on the telephone,' but then he drops below you, on the repeating 'Beatown' part at the end.

Yeah, that's me and him doing those close harmonies. It's pretty much identical live, as well. Colin and I would work hard to try to stay as tight as possible on the harmonies. Even if there were bends in what we were singing, like at the end of this song. We'd try to stay on with each other. It was a pride—regimental pride!

I've always thought your voices complement each other well, and this is a good example of that.

These are still the days when I think he was trying to sing a bit like me. Then we made the mistake of touring with the Talking Heads, and suddenly Colin started singing a bit more like David Byrne [*chuckles*], and then, by the time he'd got through that, he was just singing more like Colin. But initially, around the time of *White Music*, he was doing sort of ersatz Andy.

A final quick question about the lyrics—when you mention, 'It's a capital city,' there's a pun there, right? You mentioned that your manager used to say, 'Capital!' but at the same time you're talking about how it's all based on money—on capital—right?

Um, no, not so much! You're being very creative in reading into that there, but

I think I was thinking more that it was a capital city as in the central place. Capitol—'t-o-l,' rather than capi-*tal*, right? Which one's money and which one's central government?

Well, in the US, according to various styles, it's 't-a-l' for everything except if you're writing about a building where government takes place, which is a 'capitol'. But the city is 'capital'. I've had to deal with that as an editor. How confusing! I'll leave that one to you, then, because you've confused this little old anorexic—anorexic? No!

I hope you're not!
[*Laughing.*] Anaconda? Anne of Green Gables? What am I? That's why I was slow reading at school—I was Anne of Green Gables! And no one knew! [*Laughs.*] Yes, I was agnostic at school. I couldn't understand all the Biblical stuff we were reading. I was Agnes Moorehead.* Sorry, I'm going off on one. God, I fancied her in *Bewitched*!

[*Incredulously*] Agnes Moorhead?
Yeah, she played the mother.

Yeah, but by that time she was getting on a bit, wasn't she?
She was, but it was that filthy, slutty eye makeup! I have a real thing about makeup. And Agnes Moorehead in slutty eye makeup. I think this is probably a perfect ending to this interview.

All female fans should note this when thinking of approaching Andy!
Uh oh. We'll have that carved on my tombstone, I suppose.

Interview conducted July 20 2008.

---

* Agnes Moorehead (1900–74) was an American actress who played the mother of Samantha (Elizabeth Montgomery) in the 60s sitcom *Bewitched*. She was seventy-one by the time the series ended.

CHAPTER 5

⌐ROADS GIRDLE THE GLOBE¬

FROM *DRUMS AND WIRES*, AUGUST 1979

Let's talk about 'Roads Girdle The Globe'.
Well, I've done some research for you! [*Fake German accent*] Jah! It vas fun sewing together ze twins, but zen I had to put zem down and start the correct research!

Good, you can be our Rhodes Scholar.
Ouch. OK, well, I knew you were going to ask me why I wrote this song, but I needed to find something out before I could answer.

Right after the *Go 2* album, I lived in a couple of rooms at 12 Manchester Road, in Swindon—which is I think the nearest Swindon gets to a red-light district, actually—with my girlfriend at the time, Marianne, who later became my wife. I was staying up late one night, and I saw a foreign film on television, which was the main spark to writing 'Roads Girdle The Globe'.

For years, I haven't been able to identify what the film was, but I did some research yesterday, and I identified it. It's a Finnish film from 1970, by a filmmaker who also wrote it. His name is Risto Jarva, and the Finnish title of the movie is *Bensaa Suonissa*. The English title was *Gas In The Veins*. I can remember very little about the film, other than it's about a car-crazy couple, I think. I think it's a bit of a proto-*Crash*—which I never saw, but after you read so many reviews of a film, you almost feel like you've seen it.*

Anyway, watching this Finnish car-crazy couple film—car equals sex, you know—something clicked in my head: *wouldn't it be greatly cynical to write a hymn to the motorcar?* Because a lot of people treat cars like a religion.

---

* Andy is referring to the 1996 film by David Cronenberg, based on a novel by J.G. Ballard, about people who are sexually aroused by car accidents.

They have to have the correct car, all they talk about is their car, they watch car programs, they get car magazines …

They wash it, they polish it …
Oh yeah, they *adore* it. It's the altar of the garage. For some people, it's really a religious experience—but I never got that, because I'm not interested in cars one jot. A car is a car! I'm almost like that with guitars—whereas Dave, for example, is kind of guitar-crazy. He'll try to talk to me about guitars, and I can almost feel myself closing down, because it's just a plank with wires that helps you write a song, you know? It's the same with cars for me—it's just a thing that gets you from A to B.

Now, the thing about guitars can't be completely true, because you have to have some amount of anthropomorphic love for your Ibanez, I would imagine. It's been with you a long time.
I have a nostalgic attachment to it. I mean, if that got stolen or broken, I'd feel a little upset. But the level I'm talking about with cars—you know how crazy it gets. People lose all sense of proportion when it comes to cars, and car worship. So, with that car worship, I thought, 'OK, let me write a cynical hymn to the motorcar.' It's really the car saying, 'Oh, thank goodness there are roads everywhere, and thank goodness it's all been sacrificed for the road, and for *my* benefit,' you know? The holy trinity for the car is …

Oil, iron, and steel.
Yeah. 'Hail Mother Motor, hail piston rotor, hail wheel!' It's one of these weird sort of holy-trinity things. [*Adopts whiny pedantic voice*] 'Well, the Trinity is three things, but it's really one thing.' [*Laughs, adopts his own voice for reply*] 'So, what do you mean—is it three things or one thing?' [*Whiny voice*] 'It's three things *and* one thing.'

'It's a mystery.'
'It's a mystery! Nobody understands it. Just shut up, send me your money, and believe it.'

Exactly. You have three verses in this song—did you do that on purpose? Was that part of the whole trinity thing?
No, I think it just probably felt too long with more! I was reading a lot about

the Futurists at the time—you know, the Italian art movement?* The sort of thing they would write would be in praise of speed, and motorcars, and machines. I think there were big dollops of that in there as well—so, the lyrics are quasi-Futurist.

I wanted to ask you about the syntax you use in the lyrics.
It's like badly translated Italian Futurist manifestos! That's the syntax.

You do this on later songs, too, like 'Shake You Donkey Up'. Here, you say things like, 'you every race', or 'we all safe in your concrete robe'.
I guess I just like that disconnect. It's like you've already put the lyrics through a translator.

You want to have some fun? Take your favourite lyric, put it into an online translator tool, then translate to Japanese, then to Finnish, then to Italian, then back to English and then read it. It's *great* fun. It gets so removed, you know? Chinese whispers to the nth degree. I like that disconnect! I wanted it to be like some of the Italian Futurist manifestos about speed and cars and mechanical things. Because *that* was the future in 1913—it was speed and cars and aeroplanes.

All the potential that technology presented.
Sure, and you can see why it would have been exciting! Of course, you read them now, and they're very naïve. It's that kind of naïve praise of cars and concrete that I was lampooning.

It's the pre-World War I view of technology, I guess—after the war, everyone looked more at the dark side of technology.
Yeah, the mincing machine.

There's a little difference between the printed lyrics and the sung lyrics that I wanted to ask about. You seem to switch around 'sacred' and 'holy'—so, the lyrics say, 'Am I tied in / Or do I turn / Your sacred incense / You tyre burn.'
Yeah, that's like the dream sequence. I'm thinking about things like turning in

---

* Founded by Filippo Tommaso Marinetti in 1909, Futurism despised everything old and worshipped technology, speed, youth, and violence.

my sleep—it didn't come out very well, but it was the idea of a wheel turning, and turning in your sleep, and turning your vehicle.

Yeah, I get all that, and I do think that came across well—your puns in this song are very funny. I mean, 'Am I asleep / Or am I fast?'
No one ever says 'slow asleep'! What's fast about being asleep?

It's probably the same sense as something being 'tied fast'.
Yeah, it's held and locked and in there.

But in that part above, even though it says 'Your sacred incense', you sing 'Your holy incense'. And later, when it says 'Am I get there / When is A, B / Oil, iron, steel / You holy three', you actually sing 'You sacred three'.
So, the written lyric is different to the sung one—I probably let them have a lyric that wasn't quite right. I'd written it out one way, but then sang it another way. That happens quite a bit—you know, where stuff has gone off to get typeset for the sleeve art, yet when you actually do the vocal, you something a little different. Because—like most of our early albums—this whole album was done pretty damn quickly. The longest we spent was on 'Making Plans For Nigel'. We spent five or six days on that, because Virgin had already decided that it was going to be a single. And then everything else got banged out pretty quickly. It was only a few more weeks after that.

Yet there are significant differences between this album and *White Music* and *Go 2*. Those two first albums are very straightforward and simple, but as I was listening to this song today, I was thinking, 'Wow, there are a lot of layers to this.'
Well, the instrumentation is quite simple—it's basically two guitars, bass, and drums—but I wanted it to sound like metal and cars. Like, musically, if cars were making the music. So the chords do crash and grate against each other.

Yeah, I think this song is a really great first glimpse at what's going to happen on *Black Sea*. You and Dave come up with very dissonant yet very complementary guitar parts.
It was something that I was particularly thrilled by on this song, because everyone's part sat together great. I'd forgotten the bass and drum parts until yesterday, when I listened to the song on headphones. I thought, 'Wow! That

bass part is really good, too! Not only do you have two complex guitar parts crashing and colliding and scraping together, but you have this lovely cyclical drum part and a very snaky, melodic bass line.' Colin's probably being more melodic than Dave or I are.

And he's got a really cool, biting tone on this, too. Was there anything special he did on this song that you remember?
I don't know what instrument he's playing. I don't think it's the Newport, because it sounds too metallic. Maybe a Fender bass? I was playing a Fender Bronco, which is a poor man's Stratocaster. I think I swapped that guitar for a bass, so I could potentially do some bass playing on demos. I'm on the right channel, with the slightly wiry sound, and Dave's on the left-hand channel. Let me see what I'm doing here [*grabs acoustic guitar, starts playing*]—I'm playing a high thing in B, with open strings ringing in the middle. It's rather dissonant—it's like an exotic B-minor, with a C and G thing in there. Difficult to describe.

It's funny that when you play these parts for me over the phone, on acoustic, by itself it's very pretty and jazzy sounding, but when you and Dave are banging against each other on electric guitars, with bass and drums in there, it's something else entirely. You wouldn't think it had any relationship to jazz, but it does.
Right—when you pull the actual pieces apart, they're quite nice things. Because the main motif—[*plays the part underpinning the 'Roads girdle the globe' part*]—if you played it with a samba or something behind it, it might be quite pretty! But, instead, Dave and I are purposely crashing into each other with a couple of stock-car guitars. 'Wow, isn't that great, the way that Fender tore up that door!' We wanted it to sound metal-y and car-y—as if cars could play guitars. But, returning to my notes—it's the closest we ever got to Captain Beefheart, I think. Because of the orchestration of the guitars and bass.

I could see that, except for the fact that the rhythm is so regular.
It is a very regular rhythm. I actually really like the tempo of it—I used to love playing it live. Plus, listening to it yesterday, for the first time in ages—when the first few bars came in, I thought, 'Bloody hell, it's a bit like the Talking Heads for the first few bars!' You know, you sort of expect me to twitter on [*high, David Byrne voice*], 'I'm cleaning! I'm cleaning my car!'

You know, there was a thing in some newspaper in England recently, about their album *More Songs About Buildings And Food*, and the fuckers didn't mention that I thought of the title! Bastards. Oh, and I did something stupid—I did that thing where you sort of check your credentials. There was a Sunday supplement in the cafe where I went and had a coffee—'England's 50 Best Songwriters'. I thought, 'Ooh, I've got to make the Top 50, surely!' I sat and read the supplement, and was I in the Top 50? [*Chuckles ruefully.*] Fuck it, no. And yet, some of the people that were in there—'What's *that* person doing in there? What the fuck is *Pete Doherty* doing in there?' He's one of England's Top 50 shitheads, you know?

'One of England's Top 50 Heroin Addicts.'
Yeah, it just goes to prove you shouldn't check your own credentials, because you're going to be in for a slap. The really annoying thing is, the second I die off, people are going to go, 'Hey, do you know, they were quite good!'

'I'm going to buy lots of their albums!'
Exactly. 'It's a shame he died!' You just *know* it's going to go like that! *Bitches.* [*Laughs.*]

So, I wanted to mention that, for me, this song comes closest to what you guys achieved in terms of the mix on *Black Sea*—the Big Sound.
Yeah, at the time, this was my favourite track on *Drums And Wires*. I thought that, if you cut that album down the middle, this was sort of at the core of it. It is very drum-y and very wiry!

Were you the one who came up with the album title?
Yeah. It was celebrating the guitar line-up, you know? Plus, we knew we wanted more of an emphasis on the drums, because we were a little frustrated that we didn't get that so much with John Leckie. The couplet 'drums and wires' is out of an earlier song that was never recorded, called 'Jazz Love.'

Drums were obviously a big part of your sound live.
They were a *big* part of our sound. It was like, 'Why can't we get that on record? Let's try to find somebody who can get this on record.' This album was a big jump toward it. We wanted to celebrate the move away from keyboards back to the primitive twang and thump.

I also like the title because it boils it down to what every band is—even if you're using keyboards, it's still wires, you know? Everything is drums and wires.

We were going to call the album *Boom Dada Boom*. I'd been reading about the Futurists, I'd been reading Dadaism*, because I liked the mischievous nature of it, and then, in *The Beano*, a kid's comic, I saw a picture of Dennis The Menace's dog—this is the English Dennis The Menace, who's very different than the American one. He's much more Satanic—he's got dark, spiky hair, and he's got a dog called Gnasher, and I think he's got a pig called Rasher who was a later addition. In one frame of the comic, Gnasher was playing a drum set, and just smashing the shit out of it, and it said above it, 'Boom Dada Boom.' I thought, 'We've *got* to have that as the cover.' But then someone said, 'Oh no, *Beano* won't let you use the drawing' and all that, so it was a matter of, 'All right, we'll come up with something else.'

You were talking before about how you viewed this song as the core of the album—is that why it ends side one of the LP?

I tend to think in terms of openers and closers. That's how I'll put an album together—'What's a great opener, what's a great closer?' When it was vinyl, I could do that for each side.

And you have two great closers on this album, because 'Complicated Game' is also a great one.

Yeah, we got lucky on this one.

So, tell me about the 'Vernon Yard Male Voice Choir', which sings the 'bo-bo-bop-bo-bo' part.

That was everybody we could rustle up at the time. We were being visited by two A&R men from Virgin—the legendary Al Clark, and an Australian chap called Laurie Dunn.† They're on there, plus all of the band, our two roadies—Steve and Jeff—and I've got a funny feeling that Hugh Padgham's in there as well.‡ Either Hugh's in there, and Steve Lillywhite is working the

---

* A short-lived art movement that began in Europe during World War I.
† Al Clark was a Virgin press officer before becoming a film producer and moving to Australia. Laurie Dunn was head of Virgin Publishing and later head of Virgin Records in Australia.
‡ Steve and Jeff are Steve Warren, Andy's childhood friend, and Jeff Fitches. Both are still living in Swindon.

tape machines, or the other way around. So, there are nine people, and we may have even tracked it up a couple of times, because I wanted it to sound moronic. 'Don't sing too in-tune.' It's one of those.

I wanted to ask you about your own vocals on this—it sounds as if you're doubling up, and there are times where you're trying to sing a little out of tune with yourself, to 'broaden' the note, to make it a bit dissonant.
Do you know, I never twigged that from listening yesterday. I just thought, 'Jesus, this is the epitome of 'seal bark' in places!' Johann Sebastian Sealbach! Sorry. But I think I wanted it to have a desperate edge. I didn't want it to sound comfortable.

Why?
Because they're killing machines! They're stalking the planet, like modern, mechanical wolves, and destroying it. How many people do they kill each day?

[*Sarcastically*] Oh, cars don't kill people, people kill people.
OK, well, you get out of the car, and let's see how many people you can kill then. If you put that gun down, let's see how many people you can kill. So, yeah, I wanted it to sound scary, frightening. I wanted it to sound like the uncomfortable thing it is. I mean, how many lives—and how many towns, for that matter—have been sacrificed to the car? English towns have been gutted—they've been filleted—all for the sake of the car. I'm on my high horse a bit at the moment, but England has been sacrificed at the altar of the motorcar, and I'm sure a lot of other countries can claim the same thing as well.

Certainly in smaller, older countries, I think it's felt more. I know in the US, if you're in a newer city, everything is so spread out that there's not as much 'community' to lose. Also, most of the newer cities were developed with the car in mind—there's no cohesiveness to it at all. It's not like a New York or a Boston or even a Washington DC, for example—cities that were developed well before the automobile.
I don't like it. This marks me down as an old fart, but recently I bought a set of DVDs of old English documentary films, from the 30s and 40s, and a lot of it shows English towns, and there's absolutely no traffic on those streets! It feels *great*! You look at it, and you think, 'Wow! How fresh is *that*?' There are trees and houses, and there are roads, but someone on a bicycle, and the occasional

car, but that's it. Even as a kid, we used to play in the road, and once an hour a car might come by. Now, you can't cross the road. But that's my old-man rant finished, I guess.

You've got to wonder what's going to happen to the planet as the less-affluent counties like India and China start getting as many cars per person as we have.
Yeah. But, you know, we mustn't get too precious about them polluting, because we've been polluting for long enough. You know, we've got to give them at least 100 years of car pollution, because that's what we took. Then again, maybe not!

Let me ask you about the volume change at the beginning of the song. Why did you do that?
That was me saying, 'Look, can we have the intro low, so when we get to the 'Roads girdle the globe' motif, that really crashes?' You know, you get comfortable with it during the intro, and then it's, whoop, up the fader comes, and the whole track kicks in a bit more for that motif.

The song is mostly guitars, bass, and drums—but there is a keyboard part during the bridge.
Yeah, that's our little monophonic Korg, which we put in for a *slight* change of atmosphere.* That's the 'Steer me, Anna' bit, which was for my ex-wife, Marianne, whose name is really Mary Anne.

Did you know this song is made up of major sevenths, which are immensely cheesy chords? But they're an inversion of major sevenths that seem to bypass—good car analogy there, 'bypass'—the cheese! Because major sevenths are—you know that group America? 'Horse With No Legs' and all that? Their songs are full of that stuff. I hate those cheesy chords! 'Roads Girdle The Globe' is full of those chords [*plays underpinning of verse*], but I stumbled into an inversion that just seems more linear, and not as sickly. It's got more bite to it.

Given that you and Dave are also creating one über-guitar part with your two guitars, that help reduce the cheese factor a bit too, I'd think.
Yeah, you're right. It's totally burned off any cheese. I'll tell you the notes—in ascending order, it's A, D-flat, A-flat. So, it's one of the few times I ever used

---

* A Korg MiniKorg 700s.

a major seventh, but I didn't realise it was. I don't know much about music theory, really. It's all naïve art for me.

This song strikes me as a good example of the difference between you and Colin at this point. As I was listening to the album before this chat, his songs struck me as very melodic and pop-y and single-y, and your songs are more complicated, more dissonant, a little darker.
Yeah, I'm just an art whore, that's what it is.

You and I were laughing about the critic who wrongly pegged 'Complicated Game' as a Colin song—because anyone who really knows your songs and songwriting styles would know it's not. Was this a choice? Did you guys ever talk to each other about your songwriting approaches? Were you consciously trying to contrast yourself to him?
Before he was really writing, he saw me as the template for how to write. So, you look at things like 'Crosswires' or 'I'll Set Myself on Fire', they're like ersatz Andy songs. But then he got more into his own style—and I was envious of his melodic touch. I liked the way that he could find such appealing melodies. That was his strength. My strength, I think, was lyrics.

On this album, it almost seems like you're purposely being—I wouldn't say anti-melodic—but you seem to be going to the dissonant side.
I think it was a matter of, 'Wow, we can do this! Let's go there, it feels good.'

Because you had a second guitar at your disposal?
That, and also this thing where …

You were getting comfortable with it?
Exactly! 'Let's push it a little! Let's do something that's a bit more thrilling to hear.' You know, I never wanted to go safe. It just felt like we had the capability to push the envelope a bit more. That feels good—it's thrilling to push the melodic and chord envelope.

Anything else you remember about the song?
Do you know Dave Stewart and Barbara Gaskin's version of it?*

---

* Available on the *As Far As Dreams Can Go* compilation.

Yep, I do.
I don't think it was exactly a hit for them. Their hit was with 'It's My Party'. But I was really shocked when they covered 'Roads Girdle The Globe'. Of all the songs to pick! And it was in an interview with Dave Stewart, where he was talking about this song, that I first found out that it was major sevenths, which I'd never realised—I mean, at that point in time, I *really* didn't know what the hell I was playing. He said, 'Oh, I love the fact that they've done these inversions that don't sound cheesy.'

And I quite like the cover of their single—he made it much more like the plush interior of a car. I think we were doing the metal door panels, while he did the nice, comfortable seats and things. I was very pleased that he did it, I was really flattered, but the end product was a little bit like that group Dollar—they were an early Trevor Horn-produced Pop group thing, all very lush synthesizers and programmed songs. It was unusual to hear Dave Stewart take this big, clangorous, industrial Futurist song and make it more like Dollar.

He's quite a musician, and a very nice guy. I was a big fan of his because he'd played with Bill Bruford, and I was happy to get to hang out a bit with him and Barbara when a band of mine opened for them back in the early 90s.
Ah, so you didn't come at him from the Egg angle, then?

No, I found out about Egg because of the Bruford/Stewart connection, then listened to them afterward. Actually, Bruford enlisted Stewart's help on his initial solo albums because Stewart is so knowledgeable about music theory. So, it's interesting to hear you say that it's through him that you found out about the theory behind your own chords!
Yeah, I had to read it in an interview with somebody else! 'Oh, is *that* what I did? Oh, he's right, I *did* do that!' How degrading. [*Chuckles*.] That's another thing you shouldn't read your own press about.

Interview conducted May 18 2008.

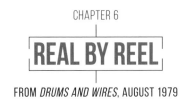

CHAPTER 6

REAL BY REEL

The next song I'd like to talk about—'Real By Reel'—has one of my favourite guitar solos by Dave.

Yeah, he's doing that lovely guitar solo. In fact, I made a note of that when I was listening to this earlier—that's a *great* solo by Dave.

He sure made his entrance into the band in a big way with a solo like this. It's brilliantly concise and constructed, and technically quite stunning. I mean, that little run in the middle of it is so fast and precise.

Oh, I know. The precision of it—I couldn't play that precisely. I'm pretty sloppy, you know. Dave likes to work everything out, and write it all down, and rehearse it. It's the complete antithesis of what I do—with me, it's 'Roll the tape, and I'll just shoot from the un-hip, and see what we get.'

That's one of the reasons why you guys are such a good pair. You complement each other quite well that way—it's almost a right-brain/left-brain thing.

Yeah, we were quite a pair! I must say, it's a great little solo. I think he plays it on his Gibson SG. It sounds like an SG to me, because it's fat but nasal-sounding.

You have said you used to open shows with this. You'd think you'd give yourself something easier to start with, but …

Well, believe it or not, once you get past the intro, the rest of it's pretty easy, apart from Dave's solo. But hopefully two minutes into the song [laughs], his hands would have warmed up a bit.

Would you all warm up before you went onstage? Would you sit in the dressing room and play?

A little, but not much. You'd mostly be having a last crap, or a last few dozen pisses, or trying to stay awake—the thing is, before you went on, you'd get immensely drowsy, and sometimes you would actually go to sleep, just on a bench or something. That's very common, apparently. I remember thinking, 'Is this weird of me? Why am I yawning? We're due onstage in two minutes, I'm yawning and I can hardly stay awake.' Then I read somewhere that Pete Townshend is like that as well. He said he always wanted to yawn and curl up to sleep minutes before The Who would be onstage. I'm sure there's a doctor out there that can tell me the reason for it. I read somewhere today that yawning is a way bringing more cool air to the brain, and the body's way of alerting itself.

It brings in additional oxygen when you yawn.
Yeah, so maybe I was trying to make myself more alert for the experience! I thought the song was a great intro for a performance because you have that melody [*sings guitar part in intro*]. But what I really loved was the drumming, the snare hit on each beat—that was a great, live, sort of rabble-rousing opener. [*Laughs.*] Not to insinuate that everybody in the audience was *rabble*! But that sort of constant Tamla-like snare on every beat—it was a great call to the audience: 'Come on, get up, get into it *now*!' It's a real 'We're on, wake up!' opener. But it was tough to play that intro guitar figure when you've got extremely frightened hands!

When you played this live, you did yelps and screams, rather than the keyboard whistle that you did in the studio.
That's actually not a keyboard, it's me whistling!

Really?
Yeah, I think I grabbed it in the studio, and said, 'Look, can you put an echo on the intro, and I'm going to whistle.' So it's me just going [*whistles up, then down*]. And where it drags in the echo, it makes that little spacey sort of sound. That was great to do live, because Steve Warren on the mixing desk—or Gary Bradshaw, who took over for Steve when he dropped out of the American tour—would put the echo on the vocal mic, and I could do the whistling with the echo dragging, or yelps, or whatever. *

---

* Gary Bradshaw graduated from guitar tech to front-of-house mixer with XTC. He went on to work with Kylie Minogue, Roger Waters, Take That, George Michael and others.

This whole song is kind of like 'dub rock' or something. It's got a very stepping-reggae feel to it, especially in the bass line, which has a lot of triplet patterns [*sings bass pattern during verse*]. The dub elements of it, with echoes and everything, were just completely where our brains were at that time.

When I played this today, and heard the singing—I haven't heard the song for ages—I thought, 'Oh god, the singing is sped-up!' I recorded the singing at a slower speed, and then the tape was put back to normal, so that my voice on playback is slightly higher.

Because it wasn't in a good key for you?
It was in a key that was just *slightly* a stretch. We hadn't bashed it about live, and I hadn't gotten into the muscularity of it—my voice hadn't learned the kind of gymnastic of it, if you see what I mean. That's very much part of the whole body memory—the muscles of your throat have got to *learn* how to sing something. I'd just literally brought this out of rehearsal, and I think I'd pitched it slightly too high.

So I said to our producer, Steve Lillywhite, 'I'm having trouble getting this.' He said, 'Tell you what—I'll slow the speed down a bit, and you sing it, and then we'll put it back to normal.' I asked, 'Will that sound weird?' and he said, 'No, it shouldn't do, if we don't do it too much.' But today, after not hearing it for ages, I thought, 'Shit, that vocal is obviously sped up!'

But, you know, it's no shame. Listen to 'When I'm Sixty-Four'—I think they sped that song up a whole semitone. McCartney sounds about nine inches high on that song.

He was going for that 'vo-doh-doh-dee-oh' kind of effect, so why not?
Right. So we didn't feel too bad, just speeding it up a little bit. It's not a semitone—it's probably just a quarter or something.

Tell me about the lyrics.
It's a very paranoid song. I was looking in my little black lyric book here, and I wrote it originally—it had the title 'Real By Reel,' but original lyrics were about the *people*'s paranoia, and I was playing the part of the eavesdropper.

What prompted you to write a song along those lines?
Do you know, I've no idea! I guess it was a new way of writing a paranoia song, where *I* was the eavesdropper. 1984 was on the horizon, and people

became very aware of how much information on them was being stored, or snooped—I mean, in *this* day and age, Christ, they've got *everything* on you! But then, it was a new thing, and with 1984 approaching, there was a genuine 'ooh, Big Brother is growing' feeling, you know? But these are the original lyrics:

In this day and age
There's no such thing as privacy
I'll tantrum, I'll rage
If my toys are taken from me
I pick up tips from the Six-Million-Dollar Man
We hunters keep all the data we can
We guns may be fake, but we fantasies real
by reel
I'm storing facts about you
Every move, every ounce
I'm storing facts about you
My heart is in the cupboard, waiting to pounce
I stalk and I hide
Under cover and under your bed
On tape and I slide
I collect what you discarded [*awful rhyme!*]
Pick up tips from Flynt and James Bond
We hunters using science from now and beyond
We disguises fake, but we fantasies real
by reel.

And then, the next draft in the book is totally flipped on its head, where *I'm* the subject of the prying.

Wow.
There, that's stumped you, hasn't it, Dr. Freud!

[*Laughs.*] One of the things that struck me, listening to that, is that it reminded me of the lyrical thing that you did on 'Roads Girdle The Globe' and 'Shake You Donkey Up'.
Yeah, you make a kind of primitive Pidgin English.

Were you doing that for metrical reasons, or what?
Sometimes I like the primitive-meets-modern thing. You know—in some forms of Pidgin English, for example, the words for telescope are 'bamboo belong look look'.

'Box belong look look,' which is Pidgin English for television, was the original title for XTC's video compilation, *Look Look*. Of course, the executives at Virgin thought no one would get it, so I said, 'Fine, let's just shorten the title to *Look Look*.' 'Kill him stinkfellow' is disinfectant. I remember these from a Pidgin dictionary that I once saw in a second-hand bookshop—I've kicked myself to this day that I didn't buy it, because I think there's a weird primitive-meets-modern thing in languages like that. So yeah, I've been known to throw those kind of 'bring the sentence to a halt' Pidginisms in there.

Looking at the lyrics on the song as they ended up, you're talking about tape. Were you going for the double meaning there? Tape was how you recorded music, of course, but back then it also was the principal way of storing information on computers.
Yeah, everything was tape-recorded—music, speech, data, whatever.

What prompted you to flip the perspective and make the song from the perspective of the person being watched?
I think I probably thought about it a bit deeper, and thought, 'No, it's *me* that's feeling paranoid, so I'll write it from the way I feel,' rather than projecting me as the Big Brother character—that was stupid. Who have I ever done that to? Nobody. But I felt that that had been the case with me.

So you didn't feel comfortable with the other perspective.
No, I didn't feel comfortable. I felt it was too pretend, so I decided to write it as what it really was—my paranoia.

What do you remember about composing the music itself? Did the music or lyrics come first on this?
Do you know, I can't remember how exactly it was written. I think it fell out from the easy hand-shapes of the chords. You're playing a part-chord, and you're moving your finger, and making the melody as you move these sort of part-chords around, in an easy shape, in C on the guitar, way up the neck. In those days, I used to write songs pretty damned quickly, generally.

Well, you were forced to.

Yes, I had to! 'OK lads, you've got three or four weeks to write an album!' And then the studio's booked, and you'd be in there. 'Whaaaat? I've got no songs! I've got to find sixteen songs in three weeks?' It's amazing that I could do that. Now I can't find sixteen lines in as many years.

I bet you would, if you were put in the same position, where it was your livelihood at stake, and you were given a great opportunity.

Or, if you're inspired by something, like the Disney things. Because, up to about the mid 60s, the best Disney songs were really excellent. So, when I had the opportunity to write for *James And The Giant Peach*, it was like, 'Wow! I'd like to be in that company!' Doing those songs really inspired me, and I did actually come up with four or five pretty damned good songs in one week.* So, yes ma'am—it can be done!

[*Dramatically*] And will be again!

And will be again! Well, hmmm, harrumph. Let's not get into that one.

Let's talk about how the song came together, in terms of parts and all that.

As I said earlier, it's kind of based on that whole rocking drum kit, and that dubby, reggae bass line. I turned my original guitar part around, so I'm skanking in the holes, really. I think Dave's following the vocal line. And then you get into the studio in the Townhouse, and you've got that big stone room for the drums, you know.

When I listened, I was reminded of that beautiful push that Terry does on the 'and' before the 'one', when he hits the snare and the cymbal.

Yeah, I was going to ask about that—who came up with that?

Do you know, I can't remember, but it certainly as hell helps kick the song along. I mean, maybe he did it once, and it was a case of, 'Wow! Do that again! That's great!' Something that just inspires you, so it's like, 'Go back to that.'

Yeah, it's definitely one of the things that sets the drum part apart.

It's a pairing of snare and cymbal, which is always much more vicious than

---

* Andy failed to agree terms with Disney for the use of the material. Four *James* songs, written in 1994, ultimately ended up on Andy's *Fuzzy Warbles* compilation.

pairing bass drum and cymbal. Did you ever realise, that you hit a cymbal on its own, it sounds rubbish?

Sure—it was one of the first things I learned when I sat down at a drum kit. You almost always have to back up a cymbal up with something.
Yeah, it either needs a bass drum behind it, or a snare drum.

There are times, if you're doing something atmospheric or want an accent, when you can hit a cymbal by itself. I sometimes like the wash of a nice cymbal by itself, but it's got to be the right situation musically.
Yeah, but if you're punctuating, you really need either a bass drum under it, or, for a more vicious approach, a snare drum. So when Terry does that on the 'and-one', it's like a kick in the ass to say, 'C'mon, get to that microphone! Get singing!' It's a real good motivator, that snare and cymbal there.

I've just got a load of random notes written down here—the feedback at the end is Dave, overdubbing. That's one of the few times we do a *ritardando*, is it called? A retard dildo? It's one of the few times we ever used one of those, where the song slows down at the end.

And the laugh at the front—I mean, there's all sorts of crap at the beginning of our songs, because we were just too busy joking with everybody in the control room when we were doing vocals, you know. So, obviously, somebody said something that made me giggle, and that little giggle was left on. It was a case of, 'Oh, let's just leave it on, it's a good little way of kicking off the side.'

There's a little bit of that monophonic Korg, the old funny noisemaking thing, in the sort of ramp into the chorus. Oh, and Dave does his best Hank Marvin impression on the run-up to the guitar solo! It's very glorious-sounding, and reminds me of Hank Marvin from The Shadows. You get the vocals doing the very dubby 'Now I lay me down to sleep' pieces, and the guitar's doing this [*sings line*]—which is almost like a little Shadows song or something.

I realised, looking through my little black songbook earlier today, that this was the last song written for *Drums And Wires*.

Ah—so that's why you were saying you brought it into the studio very quickly, and hadn't really gotten used to the vocal line?
That's right. The one written after this was the one that became some of the

lyrics to the thing on the *Take Away* record—one of the poem things on that.* It was a poetry-type thing called 'Renaissance DuBop'. Then 'Leisure' came next!

Really? That early?
Yep. Then the idea after that is what became 'Paper And Iron'.

Did you pitch 'Leisure' for *Black Sea*?
I wasn't sure if it was good enough. I remember bringing it up when we were touring *Black Sea*, and we were actually kicking it around during soundchecks. By then, I suppose I thought, 'Maybe I can tweak the lyrics a bit more, and I've got some better music for it now.'

It's interesting, the order in which things are written. After 'Leisure', there are just a few lines here: 'Slaving for a few iron coins / Think my fingers to the bone.' So that eventually turned into 'Paper And Iron'. Lots of poetry stuff after this—wow, I should read this more often!—and then there's 'Respectable Street'.

There's a BBC version of this song that you did, on *Drums And Wireless*. Do any memories of doing that version stand out?
Not really. I just used to like doing it live, pretty much. It was a good, strong, roaring opener.

The version for the BBC—is that actually recorded live, or did you do the vocals later?
Well, there were several versions. There were live broadcasts done for the BBC, where you hear the audience at an actual show. But if we did it in session for the BBC, that means you have to go into a BBC studio …

Right, that's the version on *Drums And Wireless*.
… and it would have been, you set up two guitars, bass, and drums, and they put some mics around, and it's a case of, 'Go, we've got to get four tracks done before tea-time.'

---

* *Take Away / The Lure Of Salvage*, an album of dub mixes, attributed to Mr Partridge and released in 1980.

So, you'd record the instrumental tracks, and then you'd go back and do vocals? Or were there some where you actually played live and tried to keep as much as you could?

You usually would do the instrumental tracks as strong as you could, and then you'd go out there and, while the others might go off to the pub, whoever was involved in the singing would hang around and do all the vocals in one take, usually. There just wasn't time for more than that.

You recorded a single version of this song, correct?

Yeah, we did, in [*Cockney accent*] Dick James's studios!* He was a very lumpen-looking man. He looked like one of the people in *The Dick Van Dyke Show*. Is it Morey?

Morey Amsterdam.†

Was he the fellow in the office with the bald head?

No, that was Mel!‡

Mel! That's right. Yeah, so Dick James looked like Mel! Imagine a more Cockney Mel. Dick James actually had a hit record in the 50s singing the theme from the Robin Hood TV show. Which he sang in a very kind of swish American accent [*imitates him*], 'Raabin Hood, Raabin Hood,' and then in the middle he's extolling all the kids to join in [*reverts to Cockney accent*], 'Come on children, sing along with me!' He slips back into his obvious real accent, you know.

But we're getting off the track there. So Dick James had a studio called DJM—Dick James Music—and we went to DJM after Virgin said to us, 'Well, what's the follow-up single to "Nigel"?' And we didn't have one!

Why didn't they think there was already a follow-up single on *Drums And Wires*? Why couldn't you just use the version of this song that was on there already?

They said it wasn't 'tough' enough—not strong enough for a single. So we took 'Real By Reel', 'Difficulty', and 'Helicopter' into Dick James's studios

---

* Dick James had been a dance-band singer before going into song publishing. He established Northern Songs with Brian Epstein to publish The Beatles' output.

† The actor who played the character Buddy Sorrell.

‡ Mel Cooley, played by Richard Deacon.

and pulled them apart. Kept the bass and drums, re-recorded some of the guitars, and re-recorded all the vocals. And then we added a few percussion things, and a few more ideas, and then Virgin said, 'Mmmm, no. Still don't like 'em.'

And that's when you re-did 'Ten Feet Tall'?
No, I think that's when I came up with 'Wait Till Your Boat Goes Down'. Is that right?

I thought that was later, but I'm probably wrong.
I may be wrong. I'm going to get slapped down terribly if I am wrong. I always laugh when I watch the *Beatles Anthology*, when Ringo goes, 'Oh, is that on that album?' You think, 'Doesn't he *know*?' But I'll tell you, after a time, you start losing track of stuff. It's not important what song was where, and what order it came out in, you know? It's just music.

Interview conducted July 4 2007.

CHAPTER 7

COMPLICATED GAME

FROM *DRUMS AND WIRES*, AUGUST 1979

Let's start at the beginning with this one. There's a demo of it on *Fuzzy Warbles, Volume 1*—it's basically you and an electric guitar, and you're kind of mumbling the words, making them up. The melody line's there, the guitar part is pretty much there, but the bridge is different. The demo is pretty much full-length. You obviously wanted to get down the structure of what you thought was a completed song.
Yeah, there was more of a folky swing there. Kind of Dylan-esque, though like a foetal Dylan—not quite formed.

Good name for a punk band!
'Foetal Dylan'!

[*Laughs.*] Listening to the words you're working out here, you can tell that you want to use the words 'left' and 'right' at the end of each line, and then 'same' and 'complicated game'. You know where you want the rhymes to go, but that's about it.
Yeah, I'm feeling it out.

Now, let me jump ahead to the bridge. It's very major and optimistic compared to the studio version.
Well, the other one's also in a major key, but it's got some intervals that sound much tenser. You know, like an A to an F is tenser. They're the sort of intervals that Nirvana used to deal in.

I was thinking about why this song came up, and it is a great futility song. By that, I mean it's a reasonably good example of how strong and important futility is.

What do you mean by that?
Because a lot of our lives, or virtually all of our lives, are controlled by things we have no input in. We *think* we have input, but we're fooling ourselves.

OK. But at the same time, you said something interesting there—you said how 'important futility is'. You think it plays a positive role?
It can do, yeah.

How?
Because sometimes we overthink and try to over-manage everything. It'd be better if we just relaxed and let life take us along, because we'd probably end up in a very similar place, without punching ourselves in the face and in the soul continuously. So I think futility can play an important role in life. I'm not sure I've written any other futility songs like this. Possibly bits of 'This World Over', but this is the big one.

Yeah, 'This World Over' is more political.
And more reflective, on the imagined holocaust.

And I was thinking maybe 'Train Running Low On Soul Coal' would also qualify, but that's not really quite as …
No, that's about ageing, really. This one is about 'the futile years'—the Futile Crescent! [*Chuckles.*]

I like the way these lyrics build on this.
They build from absolutely the most minimal, sort of unimportant thing— you know, whether I put my finger *there*—or *there*. What I'm trying to say is, it's kind of like that thing where the butterfly sneezes in China and eventually there's a hurricane in Chile. Wow, we're getting into fractal land here! It's one of those things where you're not sure how important any *minor* action is going to be. Is it going to be incredibly important, or is it going to be futile? It's the little cross on the voting paper—you know, should I put it on the right or the left? This person or that person?

At that time in my life, I think I was starting to feel a sense of futility. It had to do with being in the band, and being stuck on the touring trail, and seemingly not having any control in my career. In fact, I didn't have much control in my career at all.

Interesting, because at that point, you guys were on an upward track.
Sure, an upward track in terms of public awareness and things like that.

But you were already beginning to see underneath the veil?
I could see underneath the dustsheets, and it was *filthy* under there! It was
like, 'I can't get off of this treadmill! Nobody's going to *let* me get off.'
I started to get a sense of futility about lots of things—whether it's your
small hand movement, or parting your hair, or voting, or God and religion.
Even God's thinking, 'Well, it doesn't matter if I do this with it, it's going
to change in some way. Somebody else is going to change it!' So, I guess it's
where the meniscus of futility meets the atmosphere of human interaction
with it.

**I also like the circular logic here—you go from yourself and the littlest
movement to a girl and her hair-part, to a boy and his vote, and then to
God—and then, who comes back and talks to God? It's you. It's back to
you again—not only is there a progression, but it circles in on itself and
starts again. So, what about the lyrics in the bridge?**
I was feeling kind of futile in my musical career—I wanted to go *this* way
and they were pulling me *that* way. I wanted to do this, and they said, 'No
no, you've got to do that.' I didn't think it was going to be like that. So,
I began to wonder, 'Is this happening to other people?' Contemporaries
of mine—was this happening to them as well? I wanted a couple of short
names for the lyrics, and thought they should actually *be* somebody as well.
Then I remember opening up a *Melody Maker*, and there was an article on
Tom Robinson and Joe Strummer.* I thought, 'Great! Those are two short
names—Tom and Joe—and they sound kind of average.' It was like Joe
Soap or Joe Public or Tom Tom The Piper's Son—you know, they're just
real average names. I thought, 'They're people in a similar situation, and I
wonder if they feel this frustrated, and pushed and pulled from one post to
another.'

And, also, people had some funny ideas about those guys. You know, Joe
Strummer—the punk—had a public school background, from a rather sort of
middle-class, upper-class family—then went and killed himself with a cocaine

---

* Tom Robinson came to fame with the Tom Robinson Band, celebrated for its hit singles
'2-4-6-8 Motorway' and 'Glad To Be Gay'. Joe Strummer (1952–2002) was co-founder
and leader of The Clash.

rock'n'roll heart attack. And then there's Tom Robinson—gay activist—getting married and having kids.

It's a complicated game!
Sure is! Who'd have thought, if you'd looked at those two characters, and taken a snapshot of them then, how it would have gone, what their backgrounds were, and how they were changing, and how it would have ended up for them? So, my god, it *was* a complicated game.

And you know, I was game-obsessed when I wrote this.

Why was that?
I spent an *enormous*, an *inordinate* amount of time in my waking hours thinking about strategy problems, or thinking about game design, or moving pieces—'If I move that piece *there*, what else can interact with it, that can affect it to do that?' I was just obsessed with the idea of board games.

When did that start? You've designed several games, correct?
I have. I haven't done anything lately with that sort of thing. But around about then, and a bit after, was the height of my obsession with games. I had it as a kid, and in my late teens I started to design games that were more for the look of the game than the actual mechanics of it. Then, when we were touring, I'd be sat in a bus, rumbling around America or Europe or wherever we were, and I'd be off having these unusual little strategy battles, or trying to figure out if this piece took that piece, could that turn into something? How is there a way of making the piece so it becomes part of the board? Could you do something where the board changed identity while you were playing? I was just obsessed with the idea that *everything* was a game, and *we* were the pieces. Everybody was a player and everybody was a piece, at the same time.

What was it about you and your personality that you were doing this while most other people in your position would have been thinking about where they were going to get their next drink or smoke or groupie?
I don't know! I'm just a nerd *par excellence*, I guess. [*Laughs.*]

[*Laughs.*] Yeah, but at this time you guys were touring with Talking Heads, and you would think there's nobody nerdier than David Byrne ...
Oh, I'm sure I could out-nerd him!

Were you getting interested in toy soldiers at that point, too?

No. It was all art and music. And the two were totally intertwined. Art, music, and design—it was all linked together in one big silvery, exploding mess. Visuals were sound, and sounds were visuals. As I got into my twenties, I became kind of obsessed with the mechanics and the look of board games.

The toy soldier thing happened in about '80—I was going past a shop in Bath, and they had some toy soldiers in the window. There was a little running infantryman, with his rifle 'at the trail'—which means his legs are running, but his arm is hanging down, holding the rifle. It's actually a position in the drill manual.

I saw him, and I thought, 'Wow, I had one like that when I was young!' The one I had probably had no head, and no paint left on it, and came from an uncle or an older relative who had re-attached the head with a matchstick, and all that kind of thing. When I saw this as an adult, I thought, 'Wow, that would be fun to own.' And bought that, and another one in the window, and that was it. My finger was out of the dyke, and *booof*, the North Sea came in. I suddenly became very, very aware that, my god, I *loved* toy soldiers as a kid, and just getting one back in my possession again—that was pulling the pin out of the hand grenade.

I just remembered—when we were working on *Go 2*, I was walking to Abbey Road Studios one morning and there was this young kid with his dad selling some figures from a cardboard box in a street market. I think I bought one from him—a 'toy' soldier, as opposed to a war-games figure, which I was already interested in. So there must have been something under the surface for a while.

Were you trying to make up for something that you felt you didn't get enough of as a kid?

My relationship with toys is totally and utterly formed by the fact that my mother, with her cleanliness and order neuroses, was constantly throwing my toys out or giving them away. She didn't want them to be cluttering up the rooms in any way.

Ah. So, as an adult, you had the opportunity to do whatever you wanted.

I thought, 'Now I can buy toy soldiers and old toys and stuff, and they're not going to get given away, or thrown out after a couple of weeks.'

Yeah, my relationship with toys as a kid was very odd. I had a lot of second-hand toys, because we weren't very rich, so for Christmas I might get a second-hand fort, or a second-hand bike or something like that. And I was fine with that—I didn't care that anyone else had owned it, because it was new to me, you know? But then, a few weeks later, it'd be, 'Mum, where did that box of figures go?' or 'Where did those cars go?' And she'd say, 'Oh, you silly thing, where have you left them?' 'Well, I haven't left them anywhere, Mum, where are they?' Knowing very well that she'd given them away or thrown them out because she didn't want to think they *might* be cluttering up her house, because that would mean she wasn't in control. We're talking about a woman who wouldn't allow waste paper in her waste paper bins. She had to keep control.

Which must have made you feel horribly out of control, I would think. You didn't have a sense of permanence about anything that was yours.
I had no sense of permanence about anything. None at all. And that was on top of my dad being away at sea for the first part of my life, and my mother going out to work to earn money to keep me, and dumping me with different people. That was *hugely* traumatic.

How long did that last?
Five years, at least. As I said, we didn't have much money, and when my dad came out of the Navy, all he had were these fetching-and-carrying jobs, which were pretty menial. Like, he'd be a chauffeur, or he'd be a messenger delivering papers around the villages in a van. My mother always had part-time jobs—which, ironically, she was always losing because of her over-emphasis on cleanliness and order. I remember she lost a long-term job at a chemist's dispensary, because the chemist would get halfway through fulfilling the order, turn away to open another bottle, and she'd put all the tablets away! He couldn't take it anymore. She was beginning to clean away stuff that he was halfway through doing—such was her desire for order and control.

That's too bad. You'd think she could have harnessed that, and gotten a job where it was an asset.
Well, my poor old mum had a lot of mental problems. You know, I guess that's what made me a bit sensitive, which ultimately made me kind of topped up with ideas about stuff. That, and being an only child—you've got to amuse yourself, so you get good with your imagination.

I was going to say—you were probably on your own a lot, living the 'life of the mind'. So, let's get back to the lyrics of the bridge. What did you mean by 'They were arrows in a very bad aim'?

It was the sense that management and record companies and the corporate forces getting the artist to do what *they* want, and not what the artist wants to do.

I must say, even when I wrote that line, I was a bit disappointed with it. I thought, 'I've not said that very well. I'll change it later'—and do you know, I never did.

Back to the beginning of the song—if you listen to the guitar on the demo, you're strumming this, but on the record it sounds as if you're tapping.

No, I play more of a faucet style than a tap style. It's a great sound, rubbing that faucet up and down those strings. [*Chuckles.*]

I like the tension of what I did there—I was actually pulling the strings, though, not tapping.

Oh, really?

Yeah. I'm pulling as many strings as I can get my hand on—probably about four strings. For people who've tried to work the chords out, I can tell you what the first two chords are. You cover the top four strings at the octave, the four highest strings—so that's basically a G6 going on there.

So, at the octave, you mean at the twelfth fret? Remember, I'm primarily a drummer!

[*Laughs.*] Yep. Then, a tone down, you cover the E string and the A string at the position so they register a D and a G. Then, you keep the barred top four strings the same, but move those two notes down a semitone. That's the change. There's a nice tension with that. I just blundered into it, and I thought, 'Ooh, that's really nice and tense. I like that—it's like indecision and tension, and that's perfect.'

So, did the lyrics flow out of the chords?

I've got a feeling they came out of the chords, because of that tension. And if you want to know a sick little secret here, when I was looking for songs for *The Big Express*, I had my guitar in open-E tuning, and I played those two chords, and I came up with 'This World Over'! They're the same chords, just a different tuning!

Well, if you're going to steal, you might as well steal from yourself!
Yeah! *I* don't mind. [*Laughs.*]

So, you're pulling those strings at the beginning.
And it has to be very small and personal to start with. So that's where you get that sort of broken whisper. I found this song immensely difficult to sing, actually, because my voice was really shot.

Because you had been touring?
Touring, and rehearsing, and then straight in the studio, and performing this stuff. I don't know if I was coming down with something, but I can hear my voice cracking and breaking all over the place when I start to get louder on this.

At the same time, I think that's perfectly appropriate for the song.
It does kind of make it sound a bit more desperate. But that's not so intentional. It's because my voice was really *done*. It was one of those things where I don't think I could have sung it again. It was probably a first or second take, but I don't think I could have done it again. But, as you said, it kind of adds to the air of futility and desperation. What really pissed me off is, when the album came out, they credited the song to Colin!

Really?
Yeah, on the original vinyl, and I think it might still be that way on the CD.

I've never seen it credited to him on CD, and not even vinyl, for that matter—though there are lots of different vinyl versions of *Drums And Wires* out there.
I'd forgotten this until last week, when I was in Bath doing a bit of Christmas shopping. I was in Waterstones, a big bookshop in Bath, and there were a couple of those books—*The History Of New Wave And Punk*, that kind of thing. One of them was one of those *1,000 Tracks You've Got To Hear Before You Buy The Next Book On This Shelf* books—this one was about albums, and they had a couple of our albums in there. I think it was *Skylarking* and *Drums And Wires*, and I thought, 'Well, let's have a peek, then.'

I had a look at the *Drums And Wires* one, and the vast majority of this write-up was about how *great* 'Complicated Game' was, and how wonderful it was for Colin to have written and performed it. *God*, do you know, I'd just about buried, over the years, all the annoyance of that happening, and then this chapter in this book, several pages long, is virtually all talking about how great Colin's 'Complicated Game' is, and how *I* never would have done that, but it took somebody like Colin to.

Which is absurd! It just shows what an idiot whoever wrote that is, because it's so obviously one of your songs.
Well, yeah. But like I say, for some reason, Virgin thought that was one of Colin's songs. And that's how it got credited, and there are obviously still people out there in the world who think that is the case. Harumph, huh?

Unbelievable! It's funny, too, because—to me, anyway—on Drums And Wires the contrast between your songs is very clear.
Yeah, I think so. I think you can see the contrast between our songs almost from *Go 2* onward.

Right, where was I? Hey, you know the guitar solo on this?

Yeah. That's you, right?
Yep. I played this guitar solo without hearing the backing track!

Really? Why did you do that? Did you do it on purpose?
I did it on purpose. I thought, 'I want it to just crash across the track.' I'd read somewhere about how Captain Beefheart did the vocals for *Trout Mask Replica* with no headphones on. They just pointed to him from the control room when the track had started, and he just sang. I thought, 'Well, if it's good enough for the Captain, it's good enough for me!' So I said, 'Look, I want to do the guitar solo on this, but I don't want to hear the backing track. Just point to me when it should start.' So, I cranked up my amp to number 11, and put the guitar through my little MXR Flanger, which, if you fiddled with it, it didn't do a flanging thing but instead created a kind of metallic halo around the sound. And that's why the guitar sounds so metallic, basically.

So, everyone was in the control room—our producer, Steve Lillywhite, was sat there, with the rest of the band stood up with their arms folded behind him, looking at me. He just pointed at me, and it was a matter of, '*OK!*' I crashed into this no-key, no-time solo, and Dave practically was pissing himself with laughter. I mean, he was slapping his own legs and guffawing in there.

But he was laughing with you—he liked it, right?
He liked it, and he liked the idea of me not knowing the tempo of the track, or what the hell was going on. I wasn't responding to the track, I was just making 'a mess of noise' that became a solo. I just remember looking up as I'd finished it, and Dave was in hysterics. So I guess it was a big hit.

Speaking of Dave, what is he doing on this song?
He's very understated on this. I think he's playing stuff an octave down from me.

Is he also pulling on the strings, or is he strumming?
I think he's strumming. I was listening today, and it's very blended in the mix. I get the feeling that he's just playing stuff an octave down. I'm not sure whether he's playing keyboards or not. I'm thinking probably not.

Yeah, I was hearing only guitar in there.
I'll tell you what there *is* in there—a drone supplied by Colin's electric shaver! We had a drone part in there—I don't remember how it originally was played, or who played it—and he said, 'That sounds like my shaver!' I think Colin might have been joking, but Steve Lillywhite said, 'Go and get it, we'll record it,' and I enthusiastically agreed. So he brought his shaver in the studio, turned it on, and it was like, 'Wow! That's nearly in the key of the track! Why don't we put it on there?' He went in the vocal area, we put a mic on it, and had to move the speed of the tape slightly one way or the other—it was slightly flat or sharp—and got his shaver to play in tune.

I'm looking at the CD now, and I don't see him credited with 'shaver'! [*Laughs.*]
That's true! But he did play his shaver on it, as well as some very nice, very tight bass guitar.

Yeah, let's talk about that. I love the pattern that he and Terry have going there.
It's the bass drum, isn't it? That bass and drum pattern is kind of unusual. I don't know how they came up with that, but I like all the holes in it.

That's what I was going to point out, too—you would expect it to be much more regular, but it's the kind of stutter in there that makes it special.

While he's doing that nice stiff hi-hat, which is the constant. It's like me pulling the guitar. He's not accenting it, with a loud-soft-loud-soft kind of feel—it's all on-on-on-on-on-on-on. It's rather mechanical. But it does seem to suit the song. And then he brings in that great bass drum with those two little pushes.

And the snare is also very regular. So, do you remember them working that out at rehearsal, or …?

No, but you know, sometimes you'd go out and get a sandwich or something, and they'd still be working it together. Or he'd say, ''Ere, Moulding, come in with me.' Terry would drag him off, and they'd sit there together. In fact, when we were recording, Colin would usually sit there in the stone room with him, because he liked to see the foot and feel the drums. The bass amp would actually be in another room, but Colin would play in there with him.

Yeah, they were really musical partners back then, weren't they?

Oh yeah! Very tight players. And that's the way a rhythm section should be.

There was a connection between the two of them—they saw themselves as a team within the unit.

Oh yeah, very much so. Except nobody wanted to share a room with Terry, because of his appalling feet. He had the worst-smelling feet. I mean, seriously, like someone had thrown up in his shoes!

Poor guy!

If anybody shared rooms with Terry, they'd say, 'Look, leave those outside. I can't even—they're asphyxiating.' [*Chuckles.*]

Let's talk about the end of the song.

I loved all the echo stuff, because that really helped the kind of dub-y feel at the end.

So, you were playing this song live, and really working against that echo?

Yeah, exactly. You can hear that I was having some fun with that.

You guys were listening to a lot of dub music then, weren't you? Because you do the same thing on the live version of 'Scissor Man' that's a B-side on the Love On A Farmboy's Wages EP—it's called 'Cut It Out'.

Yeah, *Take Away* was just about to come up, and all the stuff I had to play with was from the first three albums.

But on that B-side, you seem to really work the echo and rhythm of it, and scat with it, just like on 'Complicated Game'.

Yeah, I like that. I still think echo is important, and still love it—I was mixing some rejected *Monstrance* stuff today …

Yeah, you do some of that on there as well—that's a good point, because there are some songs on there where you play against yourself quite beautifully.

Thank you! Playing with myself beautifully.

No, you'll notice that I said 'against'!

Yes, playing *by* myself. Much better.

Interview conducted December 16 2007.

CHAPTER 8

RESPECTABLE STREET

FROM *BLACK SEA*, SEPTEMBER 1980

When I was first discovering XTC, 'Respectable Street' made quite an impression on me. It really sets the mood for this muscular album.
I saw Respectable Street the other week.

You did?
Yeah, I was visiting Stuart Rowe, who's building a nice little home studio.*

I've been enjoying the podcasts that you've been doing with him. He's a nice guy.
He is, he's very pleasant indeed. And he's not the one who deafened me! For the record. I wouldn't be hanging around with him and allowing him near controls in a studio, if I thought it was him.†

He's working with Barry now?
Yes, he's mixing Barry's new album!‡ Anyway, I was visiting him, and was reminded that Respectable Street is actually a street in Swindon called Bowood Road that was diagonally opposite where I lived when I wrote the song.§ I used to stand in the front room of the two-room flat where we lived at the time, which had a lot of heavy traffic going by.

---

* Stuart Rowe is a well-known Swindon musician and the man behind Lighterthief, who signed for Partridge's Ape House label in 2009.
† During the recording of *Monstrance*, an inept engineer sent a blast sound through Partridge's headphones, giving him a bad case of tinnitus that persists to this day.
‡ Shriekback's *Glory Bumps*.
§ Andy and Marianne were living in a flat above the Kingshill Road shopfront of Wyborn Signs, the business started by her late father and run by her brother. The shopfront has since been replaced by a ground-floor flat.

Was this the same two-room flat that you and Marianne were in when you wrote 'Statue Of Liberty'?

Oh no, this was another one—three places later. This was actually above an old shop, which has now been converted to several flats or one house. I used to stand in the front room, in the area where I used to do most of the writing—it was a little space where I could lay out my amplifier and a cassette player and a microphone and a few effects, or whatever—and I'd stand there looking out the window, and there was Bowood Road. I noticed that several of the houses had this very English thing: a caravan—a trailer, for the Americans in the audience!—in the front garden. And I thought, 'I've *never* seen those move! They must be like status symbols, telling people, 'We could go away, if we *choose* to."

It's like the Monty Python skit in *The Meaning Of Life*, where the uptight Protestant tells his wife, 'I could use a condom—if I chose to,' in response to the 'Every Sperm Is Sacred' song …

Right. 'Could you? *Please*?' Anyway, back then, I'd be thinking, 'The caravans in those front gardens never go anywhere.' At the time, while I was living in these really wretched little flats, that sort of normal middle-aged life in those sort of houses seemed a thousand miles, a *million* miles away from me.

I'd found a nice, rather kind of jagged chord change—the opening B, and then the really strange-sounding D-flat7. So, I was working on this song, and I was kind of annoyed that the woman who lived next door to us at the time was always banging on the wall if I had my stereo system on, just even barely audible. It *really* annoyed me, because we weren't a noisy pair. We called this woman 'Mrs Washing', because she washed *everything*. You know, you'd look out on the clothesline, and you'd see shirts, and then you'd see mats, and then you'd see *shoes*. We said, 'One of these days it's going to be small pieces of furniture, or the dog.'

Or children …

Exactly! So I guess the song grew out of the annoyance with her, and the million-miles-away respectable people living on Bowood Road opposite, and the hypocrisy, the *veneer* of respectability, of the 'curtain twitchers', as they're called. They get behind the lace curtains and have a look—down their nose—at what's going on. And I was in my mid-twenties, and people were decidedly looking down their nose at me. [*Jive voice*] I was poor, man!

You were not just poor—you were a rock'n'roll musician, too!

Yeah! I was either a 'jumped-up, tuppenny, ha'penny ticket writer', as Marianne's parents used to call me, or I was a long-haired layabout. [*Chuckles.*] A cut-purse! A lie-a-bed! A ne'er-do-well—and obviously doing that horrid, *horrid* rock music.

Although, for a lay-about, you were working very hard at that point.

At the point when I wrote that, we were touring ourselves stupid. It was in the midst of touring hell. They'd give you a few weeks off to write an album—I don't know *how* I did it! I guess I must have had some mental process of shuffling away songs in the back of my head or something, and they all spewed out the moment I got home from a tour—because I knew, within a matter of weeks, we'd be in the studio working on that next album.

So, you wouldn't actually write while you were on the road? You wouldn't sit in your hotel room and mess around with ideas?

Occasionally, but not much came out. We did a lot of travelling around, just in a little van, and I remember stopping off at these service places in the States, for example, and buying what I thought were quite swish plastic folders that contained yellow lined paper—I'd never seen yellow lined paper before! I'd sit and just write phrases or ideas, or design games and all sorts of stuff like that. Just doodling.

Right, just language-based stuff. Not music.

It was all words—ideas for lyrics, or just odd words or phrases that I liked, where I'd think, 'This is either a song title, or it's the springboard to push my brain toward a song idea.' But I don't think I ever wrote one whole song. Sometimes we'd run through ideas in soundcheck. But mostly it all came out in one kind of mass vomit after the end of the tour.

Do you think that the touring could have helped with that? You would have been so immersed in music and in being a working, touring musician—perhaps by the time you got home and had a bit of leisure, and were able to focus on something else besides just performing that night and making it through the day, it allowed the creativity to flow a little more easily?

Maybe! Maybe I was just in a constant musical place. The deadlines were insane, but it never worried me, and I don't know why. I think the longest we ever had to work on an album was about five weeks.

Was that to write and rehearse, or just to write?
We'd usually get about three weeks of peace, and then it'd be, 'Have you got the new album yet?' [*Laughs ruefully.*] And of course there'd be no demoing, other than just strumming it into a cassette player with an electric or acoustic guitar, and stomping your foot, or with a little Hammond drum box bonking away, you know. All those little loungey 'tock tock' sounds. And then you'd get into rehearsal, and you'd still be squeezing them out during rehearsal time as well.

Of course, every time I moved to a new place, I'd have to be like some kind of dog, and scratch and make the surroundings my own, you know? And along with that, it was a case of, 'I wonder if any new songs are going to fall out when we move to this new place.' But they did—sure they did, tons of them did.

Moving probably helped with that, I would imagine. Being in a new context kind of shakes you up.
Yeah, maybe it had a good effect! But I remember being concerned about it, thinking, 'Ooh, I just got cosy in no. 12 Manchester Road.'

A lot of people would argue that cosiness is almost the death of creativity.
Oh yeah, I think it is. I mean, I'm feeling a bit squashed by cosiness right now. So I've got to do some stuff to shake me up, I think. But once I wrote this song, I remember thinking, 'This is kind of English. It couldn't be any other nation I'm talking about here.' So I decided it should have kind of a Noel Coward-esque intro. [*Posh voice*] You know, short of me actually singing it like Noel! I can't remember what they used to call it—it had a name in old musical terms—I think it was known as the verse. Where it was the actual funny little bit of the song that is sort of the preamble to the real song. It was very common at one time. I think it was called the verse! I may be wrong on this, but I'm sure somebody can correct me.

And what you're using in this case is actually the bridge.
Well, it *became* the middle. And that's a trick I've used a lot since. It's a case of 'Well, we've already heard it once—we've had a prequel! Now we can have the

actual thing in the middle, in the same tempo, with the same music bashing away.' But I quite like the idea of giving it this Noel Coward-esque beginning, because of its Englishness, you know.

And it makes it a great album starter as well. Was there ever any question that you'd start the album with this song?

I don't think we knew whether it was going to be an album-starter. When we gave it that messed up, telephonic-sounding, old-78 beginning, with the scratch sounds on it, I thought, 'Ooh, is this going to be a starter or not? Is it going to give people the right idea? Because it doesn't go *crash* straight away.' But I think it was a good way of easing people into the Englishness of it.

Oh, and I think it makes the crash—when you *do* crash into it—more effective!

It's the contrast of it, yeah. The scratching was done with a Peter Gabriel album that Steve Lillywhite had. I said, 'Look, wouldn't it be great if it sounded like an old 78?' We first narrowed the EQ so it sounded much narrower, but then it was like, 'No, this is too clean, we need some scratches.' So, I think Steve Lillywhite had a test pressing of the Peter Gabriel album that he'd finished not too long before, and I think we actually messed it up on the run-out groove, or on the intro groove—we sort of scagged it about a bit, so we could have some damage. So I sometimes wonder, did Peter Gabriel know that we damaged his as-of-then unreleased album.

Or that you owe him royalties for the sample!

For the sample of normality that we fucked up to get the scratch! Yeah, the sample of silence …

Maybe the estate of John Cage is going to come after you.

That's right, yeah! 'You stole my idea!' Quite frankly, I'm surprised Cage didn't go for John Lennon, about his 'Nutopian International Anthem'. It's on one of his solo albums, and is made up of this period of silence.*

Anyway, Virgin quite liked 'Respectable Street' when we delivered it, but they said, 'You're never going to get it played on the radio, with words like

---

* John Cage (1912–92) was an avant-garde composer famous for his silent composition 4'33". 'Nutopian National Anthem' is a three-second silent track on Lennon's 1973 *Mind Games* album.

"abortion" and "contraception" and stuff like that.' So they made us go in and do a cleaned-up version, which I rewrote—I changed 'abortion' to 'absorption,' and 'contraception' became 'child prevention'. Pointless, really. Totally and utterly pointless, it turns out, because even though we did a different vocal take—and a *much* better mix, I think …

Really? You like the single mix better?
Yeah, I think the single mix is much punchier. But even with all that, the BBC still wouldn't play it. For many years I didn't know why, and years later, I found out the reason they wouldn't play it was because of the phrase, 'Sony Entertainment Centre'.

Because they were worried about you saying a trademarked name?
Exactly—it was a trademarked name. It was the same reason The Kinks had to change 'Coca Cola' to 'cherry cola' in 'Lola'. And interestingly, when we did the remix for the single, each time we got to the last verse I could hear this backing vocal, it was like a high-pitched note. And it's Terry! Terry had made some sort of mistake, or maybe he *thought* he'd made a mistake, but he got to the last verse, and he was actually yelling in anguish. The note he arrives at is kind of in tune with the track!

During the 'Sunday church and they look fetching' part, right?
Yeah! He's not singing along backing vocals—because he's no Don Henley, you know? [*Laughs.*] But he was thinking we had to do another take or something, because we used to do pretty much everything live then.

And it can be hard to punch-in drums.
Right! So we went in the studio, and we doubled up on Terry's cry of anguish. It was a great little accident that became a feature.

Let's talk about the music a little bit, and who's doing what. One of things I've always thought about the difference between *Drums And Wires* and *Black Sea* is that, on the latter, you found your 'sound.'
Oh, it's *much* more muscular. We took *Drums And Wires* and increased it to the nth degree, if you see what I mean. The drums got boomier and bigger and more gated and more aggressive, and the guitars got slashier, with more punch to them.

This was Hugh Padgham and Steve Lillywhite refining their trade, finding out how to get a certain sound and then taking it on until they could go no farther with it, you know? They were doing a lot of their experimenting on us! Or, we'd ask them, 'Can you make the guitar sound like this, or make the drums sound like that?' And they figure out how, and think, 'Hey, that's great!' Then people like Peter Gabriel would benefit from them, because they went on to work with him and other people, of course.

Although it probably ended up benefiting you, too, because they went from *Drums And Wires* to *Peter Gabriel III*—you know, the melting-face album—and then back to Black Sea. And they had learned a lot of things on the Gabriel album about gating the toms.
Sure—the thread was Hugh Padgham and Steve Lillywhite. Whether they were requested to get sounds, or they pushed to get sounds, they were then taking that between all the different artists they worked with, you know. I also like the push/pull—the chopping—between the two guitars on this album.

Was this a matter of you and Dave getting more comfortable with each other—given that you already had an album under your belt—or was it a case of you realising what you could really do with another very good guitar player in the band?
I think it was the latter. We had narrowed the palette. There was no keyboard player as such, and the variety of sounds from keyboards is infinitely bigger—I mean, a keyboard is like an orchestra, whereas a guitar is pretty much one colour. No matter what you do with it, it's one colour—or it's one strain of colour, where you can have a dark version or a light version.

So we said, 'OK, let's really work with that.' Dave and I worked to not tread on each other's toes musically, so we played in the holes left by the other. There's that constant push/pull—if I'm on the downbeat, he's on the upbeat, or vice-versa. And he would play the snappier parts, the more complicated parts, because these songs had to be performed live, and I was a stickler for it sounding as close to the record as we could get it. So, if I had to do the vocals, I usually gave myself a simpler part that I could play and sing with.

And if it was one of Colin's songs, did you then consciously grab back the more-complicated parts? It seems that you play more solos on his stuff.
Yeah, I tended to play more adventurous things on Colin's songs, because

I was not doing the lead vocal. For example, 'Love At First Sight', there's a sort of mechanism going between the two guitars—their own internal little logical funk—with the patterns we're playing. I don't think I could have done something like that and sung a lead vocal. People think we recorded 'Respectable Street' at the Manor, because they associate it with that film, *XTC At The Manor*, but that was us running through it live for the benefit of the camera crew there. They'd asked, 'Can you do some more songs, so we've got some more songs to cut-in in other places?' But 'Respectable Street' was recorded at the Townhouse.

Dave plays piano on the intro?

Yep. Because neither Colin or I could. You know, we can work out chords on the piano, but we can't change from one chord to the other quick enough. But Dave can, of course, so any keyboard or piano duties would fall to him by default, because we weren't good enough.

You mentioned earlier that you didn't have keyboards in the band anymore, but Dave is quite an accomplished keyboard player.

Yeah, but if you asked him what he was, he'd say, 'guitar player'—without hesitation. He plays the keyboards very well, I think, but he plays them under protest. That said, I thought Dave and I made a good team of two guitar players. In fact, I think there was a book called something stupid, like *The 500 Best Guitar Players*, and the two of us were actually in there as a team. I thought that was very astute of somebody, to pick that out. Because I think we played best in and around each other—you know, using little bits of rhythm and little single lines together. Almost like one entity, an interesting little guitar machine.

Precisely. You complement each other so well, and a lot of the reason for that lies in the difference in your approach—for instance, Dave is very schooled, while you've admitted that you're not.

I'm a bit more feral!

Exactly! But, you know, it's almost a right-brain/left-brain thing. You've got this pure, raw creativity, and are more comfortable improvising, while Dave would rather take the time to work out a part, and is more precise, with impeccable technique …

He's Yin to my Yangeccch! [*Laughs.*]

Well, I'm sure you'll get some people who'll disagree with that, but at the same time, the two of you guys are a really interesting combination, and I think that's why a lot of people were so disappointed, of course, when he left. Let's talk about the drums and bass. Did you write the bass part?

Do you know, I don't think I did! I think that's pure Colin.

Really? It's a nice counterpoint to the guitar parts.

And it goes along very well with that very thuggy, lumpen drumbeat there, especially at the beginning—or 'wombat,' as Terry and Colin insisted on calling it. 'What song are we going to do?' 'Oh, Wombat'—you know, since that was their opening phrase on the bass and drums. And that's what it does, if you listen to it! 'Wombat wombat!'

[*Laughs.*] One of the nice things about Terry was that he was willing to be simple in his playing and leave you guys the room to find holes and play against each other, instead of him stepping all over it.

True. He wasn't one of those 'Mr Giant Rolls' everywhere. He knew how to punctuate—listen to the end of the song, where we sing 'Respectable Street!' and Terry stamps it out with us at the end. Bang bang bang bang bang!

You know, I don't think Terry had much concept of how to tune his drums.

Really? So, when you got to the studio, would a tech help him?

No, not really. I mean, I may be wrong, but I don't remember him ever talking about tuning his kit. It was always a case of just putting a new head on and tightening it up until it felt about tight enough. I don't think there was any kind of specific drum tuning that went on, but I'm sure he tuned them so they sounded good in relation to each other.

Exactly—he probably wasn't doing it to the degree that you and I have talked about when we've discussed other drummers you've played with. He didn't approach his kit as someone like Dave Mattacks would, for example.*

Maybe he was doing it in a kind of naïve, unknowing way, yeah.

---

* Dave Mattacks, most famous for his work with Fairport Convention, played on XTC's *Nonsuch* album.

I'm sure he had a clear idea of what sounded good and what didn't. But he probably wasn't doing the kind of thing you've done on recent records, where the drummer tunes the toms to the song.

Yeah, I don't think there was much of that going on. The drums do sound great on this album, though.

Oh, they absolutely do. This and *English Settlement*—they're just so big. I mean, you guys really defined drum sounds for a lot of people throughout the 80s.

Yeah. It's tough to go back. Once you get the drums that big, where do you go?

Well, you go small—which is kind of what you did on *Mummer*, right?

You go tiny again, yeah.

Tell me about the guitar parts that you and Dave are playing.

It's just that thing of not treading on each other's toes, really. If one person was on one beat, the other person would automatically go to the other beat, to make the funk. Or, one person would play in one octave, and the other person would pull away to a different octave.

Would you tell him, 'I've got a second part in mind, and here's what you should play'?

Sometimes I would, but mostly it just felt right. If you were both playing the same thing, it was boring, and a mess, and there was no width to it, no epic quality. But if you were both playing from different ends of the spectrum, or different ends of the octave, or one was playing block chords and the other one was playing single-note bits and pieces in a different octave threading in between that—it's so much more textural, you know?

So, maybe that would be part of rehearsal, when you would work out arrangements?

Yeah. Mostly we went for what felt organic, but occasionally I'd say, 'Look, can you try playing up here,' because at the time I probably didn't know so much that that was what you had to do. I was much more naïve then about arrangements and ideas. So they would have come from the gut, and not from the head.

During the bridge, there's that *great* guitar line from Dave—that cascading countermelody to the vocal. It's really good. Then, right after the bridge, there's that funny little dead bit. That's me, doing that muted, looking-for-another-tone thing. That's a strange little area, actually.

It's like an anti-solo.
Yeah! You can *rest* for a while in that back room, you know, before you're thrown into verse three.

It seems like you were doing that a bit on this album—I'm thinking of 'Love At First Sight', where you do that one-chord solo.
Oh, the little one-chord steam-train solo, yeah. Expect the unexpected!

Anything you remember about doing the vocals on this song?
I think on the vocals, we have the chorus from the Roland Space Echo, which was in the studio at the time. We liked it so much we bought one and took it out on tour with us. There's a slap-back on that vocal as well. Otherwise, this is one of the straighter things we ever did. There's even the ghost of The Beach Boys' voices in there, in the high backing vocals. I love that stuff.

Did the lyrics come quickly, or did you have to work at them?
They came quite quickly, actually. I felt a good deal of disgust at the kind of hypocrisy, the fake respectability, of my parents' generation. It seemed they had one side of them that was quite clean and upright, and then they could do the most awful things behind closed doors. That fascinated me.

I also like the rhyme scheme in the verses. In the last line in each verse, it's like you don't even care about rhyming—it shows how fed up you are.
[*Laughs.*] Yes. There are a lot of internal rhymes going on, but by the time you get to the end, the rhyme scheme is dead, and you're going downhill there.

Was this the type of thing you consciously thought about, or did it just fall out?
I think I put more thought into it now, but at that time it just seemed to fall out. It was just more naïve, and just felt right.

And you liked the sound of it.
I liked the sound of it, and I liked giving the middle classes a bit of a kicking.

Poor old middle classes! I think the upper classes and lower classes deserve much more of a kicking, personally. But the middle classes get blamed for everything, while all of the problems seem to stem from the upper or lower classes.

You did a video of this song, right?
Oh, Christ—yeah, the video! Jesus. I don't remember who did the video for us, but they'd hired these two houses, and I think it was the filmmaker's concept that we—the band—were the respectable people, doing our string-quartet rehearsal, while the family next door were noisy, and punky, and playing loud, awful records, and we were screaming at them to turn down. Turning the tables, I suppose. And my hair was probably at its most Sting-esque at the time!

I just remember that the little old fellow that they hired to play the punky dad next door—a little bald fellow in his 60s—was actually [*posh voice*] very, very well-spoken, in a sort of Shakespearean way. He never drank—he was a teetotaller—and of course they gave him real tins of booze, with real booze in them. He got out of control! This little, bit-part-playing Shakespearean actor, who wouldn't have said boo to a goose, was on Planet Gone during the filming of this video, because he never drank!

He never had, or did you ruin his years of work battling his alcoholism?
Wow, I never thought about that! We thought he was great, because he was just falling all over the place, and yelling, and crashing around—you know, it was just fun to see somebody who was a teetotaller just totally and utterly off the leash! I remember, when we first arrived there, he asked, very nicely, 'Are you *punkers*?' And we said, 'No, not really, no.' [*Laughs.*]

He was just trying to get into his role!
He was trying to understand where we were coming from. But I think what confused him was the name, and the fact that, when we met him, we'd put on these tuxedos. [*Laughs.*] Dreadful video—it looks so cheap and video-y now.

Well, you're not a fan of any of your videos, are you?
No, I hate every one of them. Well, apart from The Dukes' 'Mole From The Ministry'. That one's OK.

Interview conducted February 18 2007.

CHAPTER 9

NO LANGUAGE IN OUR LUNGS

FROM *BLACK SEA*, SEPTEMBER 1980

Let's talk about what, in my opinion, is one of the Great Pop Songs.
'No Lampreys In My Lunch'!

[*Laughs.*] I was looking at the entry in Neville Farmer's *Song Stories* about this song, and you said it's ironic—that even though the song is about the inability to find the words to say what you really want to say, you think that you pretty much did say what you wanted to in these lyrics.
Well, knowing that you wanted to talk about this song, I remembered that, somewhere, I had a notebook with the first scribblings of this song in it. So I dug it out! It's this little tiny pocket-sized notebook I used to carry round with me on tour. I found the first jottings in here.

So this is from when you were touring for *Drums And Wires*?
Well, I shall tell you [*leafs through pages*]. A couple of pages before are the lyrics to 'New Broom'.* And then it's 'Outside World'. Then 'Millions' got written— all I've written is 'Chin' above it, because that was short for 'Chinese', which reminded me what the guitar figure was.

Yeah, you'd written that originally for Barry's 'Things Fall To Bits', right?†
Exactly. And then there was a song called 'Under A Microscope', which didn't get done.

Meaning you didn't even write music for it?
No, not that I can remember. Then there's another song that didn't get done,

---

* From *Take Away / The Lure Of Salvage*.
† An outtake from *Go 2*, available on *Coat Of Many Cupboards*.

called 'Pretty Precious'. Then, here's a song that was going to be titled, 'I Have The World In My Mouth'. And the lyrics I wrote down are, 'I have the world in my mouth / I can say what I want to say / I have a sword in my hand / I can slay what I want to slay / For a minute I became a crusader / Lionheart, a Holy Land invader / I have the world in my mouth.'

That's funny! So it became the bridge.
And it became the contrary to that! Because when I came to looking through the book for ideas I'd written down, I started kicking this around, and the more I thought about it, the more I thought, 'Christ, I *don't* have the world in my mouth! I *can't* say what I want to say!'

When I worked on it, I realised that what I really wanted to say was the exact opposite of the first sentiment. [*West Country yokel voice*] 'Ooh, in't that strange! Ooh, oi wonder if George Formby ever 'ad that problem!' *

So, yeah, it was originally called 'I Have The World In My Mouth', and it was about how you *can* say what you want to say. Of course you can say what you want to say, but that doesn't mean you're communicating well. Because communication isn't *just* words—it's about all sorts of things, isn't it? It's about every sensory input you can imagine. It's not just sounds of things.

Right. There's intent, for example.
Yes. There's tone, your body language, your inflections, the actual language that you're using—you can raise an eyebrow and it means something totally different, depending on how and where and when you do it. There are so many subtle but powerful variations of communications.

The more I thought about it, the more I thought that most people are totally impotent. I think *everybody* is, when it comes to putting their ideas across. You know, because they face the constriction of society, and the constriction of not wanting to upset people. That's very English, after all.

Was there something definite going on in your life that was frustrating you, that prompted you to flesh this out, going in this direction?
No—I think that, the more I worked on this song, where the idea was that you can say exactly anything you want to say, the more I thought deeper about

---

* George Formby (1904–61) was a ukulele-playing English singer and comedian of the 30s and 40s.

it. I thought, you can use words, and you can say what you fancy saying, but we're *not* communicating. And, like I say, that's an English thing, an English hang-up. The English will say anything they can, other than what they're really feeling. Or, that might be a human thing, generally.

As far as the music goes, it's probably the nearest we ever got to one of my favourite bands—and Colin's and Dave's—which is Free.

Oh, really?
Because it had a Free tempo.

Interesting. I've heard you talk about the similarity to the Beatles' 'Rain', but I didn't consider Free.
The musical template that I had in my mind, I think, was something that Free would have done. I liked their languid, sexy, slow grooves, which seemed to lend a gravitas to some of the crasser things they would sing. Because a lot of their lyrics—let's be honest about it—were not good. With them, it was more the overall thing—the great sound of Paul Rodgers's voice, the beautiful holes in their playing, and the funk that they had.

Speaking of lyrics, let's talk about them a little bit more. Did they just flow out intuitively, or did you really work hard on constructing them?
I really constructed them. But I was very lucky to find 'lungs' to rhyme with 'tongues'. Because it's great, it's all connected. It's all part of the same process of speech. How jammy is that? [*Chuckles.*] It's like the ex-filmmaker who reviews food for one of the magazines here in the UK, Michael Winner.[*] Of course, his column's called 'Winner's Dinners'. That's a great bit of happenstance, you know? If his name had been Michael Eckfast, he wouldn't be reviewing dinners, would he? It was just a great piece of happenstance that 'no language in our lungs' and 'no muscles in our tongues' work great together. That said, I always do work hard on a song. I always take the screwdriver to it over and over again, and tweak and twork—is 'twork' a word?—until it's as tight as I can make it by the deadline of when it's got to be recorded. By the time we did this album, I was starting to get quite serious about lyrics.

---

[*] Michael Winner (1935–2013) was the British director of numerous films, and restaurant critic of the *Sunday Times*.

Looking at these lyrics, too, and thinking about the other songs on *Black Sea*, I sense a sense of frustration. That's why I was asking if there was a specific event in your life that maybe had prompted this. 'Living Through Another Cuba' has an element of political frustration, and 'Sergeant Rock' is about romantic frustration …

I guess I'm just a frustrated individual. I'm a rather tame person who doesn't say what I really mean, and—probably because I'm faint-hearted—winning Lady Fair was difficult for me.

I think it was probably the thought—I know this sounds weird, but I've got to sort of tune in to the state of mind I had back then—maybe I was frustrated that I had an hour and a half to talk to thousands of people onstage, and sing to them, and I found myself not expressing what I wanted to express. That *may* have been some of the motor behind writing this song—where you find yourself in the position of having that soapbox …

Yeah—you have the opportunity, but are you taking advantage of it?

Exactly. And do people *want* you to take advantage of it, or do they just want that little performing monkey on the barrel? 'Oh yeah, get him to do that funny little dance where he jumps backward over his own head while you're playing that tune on the barrel!' That's what they want. They don't want the monkey to throw his fez down and say, 'And I'll tell you what really pisses me off!' You know? So I couldn't communicate onstage. I was too intimidated. I wouldn't wear my glasses, you know, so I couldn't see the audience. Even so, I still felt very intimidated—'God, how many thousands of people are hanging on every word?'

I did have the wrong frame of mind to be onstage. Some people say, 'Oh, it's great when you go on stage, because you know they all love you, and they're willing such great stuff out of you,' but I never found that. I always found it was like a battle. I felt it was me against the world, and that's probably not the right state of mind for a communicating entertainer, if you see what I mean. I felt like it was a war when I went out there, and it shouldn't have been. It should have been much more 'receiving the love' vibes. Because a lot of it was love vibes. A lot of the people who came to the gigs already had the albums or singles—that's the majority of live shows. You're not winning converts, you're rewarding people who bought the record. That's by far the greatest majority of people in the audience.

But for some reason, I would see it as a kind of a war, and I would feel frustrated that I wasn't really saying what I was thinking. The other thing I wondered was, did they really *want* to hear what I was thinking? So, it was a kind of double-barrelled frustration, really.

And did you feel that people were not understanding what you were trying to say? Did you have problems with the critics, or would you talk to fans who would say, 'Oh, that song is about this,' while you knew in your heart and your mind that it wasn't?

No, most people kind of got the gist of what was going on. Although, to make more magic in the songs, I kept hiding behind a persona—I've said this quite a few times, but instead of 'me' I'd sing 'they' or 'she' or 'he'. But really, mostly, I meant 'me'. And that's one of those conventions where you get to sort of say the truth, but you're hidden behind a mask. It's easier to be naked if you've got a mask over your face.

Exactly. So, let's talk about the music a little bit. You said the words came first on this, but I was wondering if you'd fleshed out all the words before you started on the music.

Do you know, I can't even remember! I know it started with that idea about— let me look in the book again—'I Have The World In My Mouth'. Yeah. And then I finished off 'Millions'. What did I write next? Oh, wait a minute! After I wrote 'I Have The World In My Mouth', do you know what I wrote?

What?

'Roads girdle the globe / black belt around the mourning robe.' That's all I wrote! So, there you go, that's the first glimmer of 'Roads Girdle The Globe'.

That's funny. So, this was written as a *Drums And Wires* song, in a way. Because it's in the midst of all those songs that ended up on that album.

Yeah! The first intention of it, yeah. The first inklings of it came out in the *Drums And Wires* material.

Musically, as I mentioned, Free was a kind of a template. I wanted it to make it feel stately and *proceed* through the song in a measured pace, because it's about communicating and I didn't want to rush it.

There are quite a few things in this song that I'd never done, a few chords that I'd never used. [*Picks up guitar.*] I don't know how you're going to do this, because I don't know what the intervals are. I was playing this earlier on.

I hadn't played it for years, but you sort of don't forget it, because it's bashed into your brain through hundreds and hundreds of live shows.

Sure. Muscle memory, burned into the synapses.
Yeah. [*Plays intro.*]

That intro, did that come later?
Yeah, I think that was pinned on, to make an 'event' to start the song.

We're in the key of B, which was good for me to sing relaxed or loud in—and, coincidentally, is a key that Free used to play a lot of their stuff in. [*Sings vocal line*] 'To tell the world just how we'—it goes into half-time there. Then I used to like it when it went to the G-flat7, because I could twinkle around on that chord.

And then there are these chords [*plays 'no bridge of thought' part*]—I mean, they're very strange, almost like jazz chords or old kind of songwriter chords. I don't know where they came from, and I don't even know what the shapes are, to tell you.

Is this because you had the melody in your mind already, and you were just building chords to go with it?
I was just trying to find what would work. I was looking for that [*sings melody line*], and these just seemed to fall easily into place.

And then there's the [*sings and plays the 'no letting out just what you think'*]—which is another old sort of Tin Pan Alley-type chord. You know, it's that [*sings augmented feel*] 'something's about to happen'. And then what happens is, it resolves into the title line.

And then we have that thing that somebody's mentioned, 'Ooh, that's just like "I Want You (She's So Heavy)"'! You know, that [*plays descending arpeggio*]—actually, that little chord change, it's almost like the entire *Abbey Road* album in one little four-bar sequence, you know? Because you've got bits of 'Because' …

There's even some White Album on there, too!
Yeah, probably!

You and Dave worked very closely on this one.
Yeah, I think he enjoyed this song. He got to dig in, and he did a great little

succinct, concise solo in this, which is very well thought-out. I think he really enjoyed it because it tapped into a lot of musical things that were influential for him. It touched on the Fleetwood Mac thing of the twin guitars, or triplet guitars—I'm talking about the original blues band, not the modern Fleetwood Mac—or people like Wishbone Ash, with the two duelling guitars. Whenever there was some sort of sniff of duelling guitars in the air, Dave came to life, you know? So, he took to that like [*pauses*] a member of Fleetwood Mac to an obscure religious cult!

Yeah, so Dave really warmed to digging in to this song, and making that making very concise, wailing solo.

You had written the song before you brought it to the band—did you have ideas for Dave's parts, or did you work them out together?
It was a case of, 'Dave, why don't you stick a solo in here, and give us a little breather?' In those days, I think the demos were extremely primitive. If there was one at all, it would be me either thumping on the floor of the front bedroom of 46 King's Hill Road, or if it was a more-regular rhythm—something like 'When You're Near Me I Have Difficulty', or something else, like 'Rocket From A Bottle'—I'd have this old Hammond drum machine clattering along. So, the band would get the most primitive demos. For this one, it was probably me just thumping on the floor and playing on a very turned-down electric guitar.

Even beyond the solo, the guitar interplay is very tight on this song.
Yeah. It's that sort of precise clockwork thing …

Was that a result of you guys sitting down together and banging things out? Or did it arise more naturally?
I guess we just kicked it around until it yelled 'Kamerad!' and waved a white flag in rehearsal, you know? We knew when we had it on the ropes. Because we'd rehearse things, and it was serious. We were a professional band, and it was a matter of, 'This is serious shit now. We're going to be playing this in front of thousands, this is going on albums. People are waiting for this album.' So, it was a case of putting our serious, 'C'mon, let's get down and work this out' heads on.

What else can I tell you? The middle section has got a rather sort of daft Korg [*sings dissonant keyboard line*] line in it.

And it gets sort of skanky there, with the guitar rhythm.

Yep. It lifts up into that sort of Beatle-esque skank. And then you get that long build-up section. I don't know where that came from, that long build-up piece, where Dave is inverting upward. It's almost like a homage in a way to Free's 'Mr Big' or something.

You say you don't know where that came from, but it was something you worked out before you went in the studio, correct?

Yeah, we had all the shape of it and everything well before Steve Lillywhite or Hugh Padgham came along. As I said, we would really try to nail things down in rehearsal as tightly as possible. Because the thought of being in the studio, with the red light on, and the clock ticking, and everyone going, 'Well, I'm not sure what I'm playing'—that was like a horror scenario.

I still have nightmares now where I'm onstage, and the house lights are on, and the audience are going, 'C'mon, what's the matter with you?' And I'm turning to people, saying, 'I'm not sure what I'm playing here.' Or them saying, 'You aren't in the band! You don't know the chords to this song, do you?' So it's obviously a deep psychological worry. We didn't want to waste time in the studio, and we wanted to be perceived—and perceive ourselves—as very professional, and very 'let's bolt this thing down' watertight.

Toward the end of the song, there's some backward reverb on the vocals, and then it ends with Terry doing the funny, sort of spastic drum groove on the out.

Yeah, that's one of the few times that he actually plays a ride cymbal.

There you go! He was not a ride man. He loved that hi-hat.

And there's a sort of babbling inanity, which we'd taped off the television— which was set in the wall above the mixing desk—at The Townhouse. I think the program that we taped the conversations off of was a show called *Whicker's World*, with Alan Whicker.[*]

Which I know just because of the Monty Python spoof![†]

[*Chuckles.*] That's right, yeah. He'd go round the world interviewing people on

---

[*] Alan Whicker (1921–2013) was a popular journalist and television presenter during the 1960s.

[†] 'Whicker Island', *Monty Python's Flying Circus*, series three, episode one, first broadcast on BBC1 in October 1971.

various themes, you know. But we taped a load of stuff off of *Whicker's World*, and just had it very subliminally quiet, like babble—the sound of humans speaking, but not communicating.

So let's talk about the recording of this song a little bit. The drums are huge on it.

Well, we recorded them in the stone room at the Townhouse in Goldhawk Road, London, which was the old Goldhawk Film Studios. We were in the studio in the back—can't remember which one that was, but it was where they'd built stone room purposefully, to make the drums sound live and kicking. Colin would usually be sat in there with Terry.

So they would track their parts together?

We all used to play live! Dave and I would be in the carpeted area while, through a couple of glass doors, in the stone room, there would be sat Colin in a chair, with Terry crashing away on his kit.

Were you just providing reference chords for him, or were you actually trying to get your parts down?

Some tracks, we'd keep what we played. And then other tracks, it'd be, 'Ahh, that was crap. Can I re-do it?' So, pretty much, we were still playing things quite live then.

That said, you've also told me about songs where Terry would tell you guys to piss off and just let him do his part alone.

Oh yeah. Sometimes, if the drumming was something that he was a bit worried about, or if it was tricky, he would just say, 'I just want to play this with Partsy,' you know. So I'd just stand in front of him, nodding where the changes were, and just playing rhythm guitar. And some things, he didn't want anybody there, like with … oh, which one was it?

Probably one of the really cyclical ones, like 'Travels In Nihilon' or 'It's Nearly Africa'?

Yeah. I'm going to have to think about which one, but he just didn't want anybody. He would just say, 'Give me the tempo, and then nobody play. I don't want to hear anything.' So, it was a case of giving him the tempo, and then he *went* for x-amount of minutes. [*Laughs.*] Which is freaky, you know?

So sometimes, he'd just want me to play with him, but usually it was all of us playing pretty much live. I don't know if I can tell you much more about this song. It was really a case of heads-down, no-nonsense, let's get this album done as best as we can. It was the height of our tooled-up-for-live muscle, so I suppose we were 'live buff'. [*Laughs.*]

[*Laughs.*] How much time did you actually have to write and record this album?
Oh, no time at all.

Was this one of your 'write an album in three weeks' deals?
It was, probably [*sighs*]—it was getting a bit longer for each one, but it still was probably only about three or four weeks. During this time, you had to get together all your ideas, and then get into rehearsal, and then book the studio, and then in you went, you know?

So there was no time off. You didn't get time to, you know, do nothing at all. You were always doing something. I snuck my marriage in, because I came back a few days early from Japan, on tour. So that was the only way I could cram a marriage in.

[*Laughing in disbelief.*] And no honeymoon, I presume …
Nope.

[*Sarcastically*] That must have pleased Marianne.
Well, you know [*archly*], there was nothing *new* to do on the honeymoon, really …

Given that you'd been living in sin.
Yeah, we'd been living in Sin, which is next door to Swindon. A little village, Sin. 'You're now entering Sin.'

This was the second album you did with the Lillywhite/Padgham team.
Yeah. Because they did such a good job on the first one, it was like, 'Wow, we'll go for those two again. That was an exciting sound.' Of course, they were refining their technique all the time, getting into those punchy, gated, ambient drums, and getting the guitars to sound more and more biting all the time.

Lillywhite was starting to bring along his favourite new toy at the time, which was an Archer amplifier—a little tiny Radio Shack amplifier and speaker the size of a box of cook's matches, which he'd seen Peter Gabriel's keyboard player, Larry Fast, using to tune his synth.

He thought it sounded great, and you can hear stuff going through it on the *Black Sea* album. You can hear the little drum machine on the fade-out of 'Living Through Another Cuba'. That's going through the little Archer amplifier.

Really? And it's literally the size of a big box of matches?
Yeah, he used to put it on the mixing desk. They'd get a mic on a boom stand, and they'd shove that right up so the mic was touching the grill of the little one-inch speaker, and then, through the input socket, they'd send whatever they wanted to 'Archer up' out the channel from the desk. And that's the sound.

You know the version of 'Towers Of London' that made it on to *Coat Of Many Cupboards*? The first attempt at a single version?

Yeah ...
This very, almost backward-sounding guitar in the verses—that's through the Archer. I don't know whether you can still buy them, but they were about the size of a box of cook's matches or something. Radio Shack made them. Maybe they're still out there—if any readers can find one, they should let us know!

Interview conducted May 26 2007.

CHAPTER 10

TRAVELS IN NIHILON

FROM *BLACK SEA*, SEPTEMBER 1980

Let's talk about 'Travels In Nihilon'. Where did this song come from?
Well, the title came from the title of a book by Alan Sillitoe that I bought in the mid-to-late 70s.* I was still reading novels at the time, and this is a novel about a non-existent, vaguely communistic-type dictatorship somewhere deep in Europe called Nihilon, which was run by a fellow called President Nil.

Here comes President Nil again!
There you go! So, I borrowed two things from the *Travels In Nihilon* book—the actual title, which refers to nihilists and nothing, and I nabbed the title of President Nil for the *Oranges & Lemons* song, 'Here Comes President Kill Again'. If I remember correctly, you never get to see President Nil. Whenever a photograph of him is put in the paper for some reason, it's always a different person, and/or sometimes an animal, like a gorilla or something like that. [*Chuckles.*] You never really know what this supposed President Nil looks like.

So, it was a great book, but the actual song isn't about the book—the song is really about traveling through the land of nothingness. It's a song about a con—that enormous con of pop culture and the con of religion.

What brought that out of you? Why were you feeling bitter or betrayed?
I was at an age where I did rather get swept up in the whole punk/new wave movement. I foolishly thought, Hey, this may be the turning point for music! Maybe this is truly where *everyone* can be involved—it's like a democratising or Year Zero thing. Everyone can make music if they want to! There are no preconceptions, you don't have to be a great musician. Fashion is blown out of the water because you can wear anything you want.

---

* Published in London in 1971.

It was the last time I think I truly got swept along by my optimism. It wasn't the optimism of the movement as such. It was a time in my life where my optimism was being mirrored by these new possibilities. I was in a band that was starting to go places, the world was looking up for me, I was at a good age, I was experiencing a kind of a movement where I actually felt like this might be my *gang*, you know?

Then very, very quickly, I could see that people were using it for the same old reasons—the same old, selling-you-the-dumb-clothes thing. Punk was about you *making* your own clothes, but very quickly it became about how you had to have just the right thing to wear, and the right thing was *expensive*. I saw through a lot of the fake political stuff, too—which is one reason I never got into The Clash. I just found them hokey on the politics front. At least the Sex Pistols were just having a mess about. They were just having fun—but with The Clash, it was this forced street politics, and I never took to that. I'd much rather have a band like the Ramones, which were more like a 'happening' or something. That's not the right word, but you know what I mean.

So, this was at a time where I did actually get swept along with it, and I quickly saw that it was extremely cynical, and it was exactly the same as what it was supposed to be replacing. There was too much industry involved—too fake, too controlling. It was so commercially driven. So I actually think this song is about my enormous disappointment and my feeling that it was all a con—the music, the fashion, and hey, let's throw religion in there as well, while you're at it! There's no Jesus come and gone! There may not have been one in the first place. It's just a con, and it's time for us to wake up.

You remind me of the old saying: 'a cynic is a disappointed romantic'.
[*Laughs.*] Yeah, there you go! I've never heard that before, but that's bang on.

Looking at the lyrics here, and at the last verse in particular, is there any resolution to this? Or are you leaving it open on purpose?
I'm leaving it open on purpose. It's a real heavy disappointment of a song—it's an oppressing feeling, and I wanted the music to feel oppressive as well. Which it is—I think it's the most bleak thing we've ever recorded. [*Laughs.*] It's a sort of negative 'Tomorrow Never Knows'.* But tomorrow *does* know—it's just going to be more con! You've just got to be alert to that. But yeah, it

---

* A song by The Beatles on the *Revolver* album.

is the bleakest thing we've ever committed to recording. It even includes our own loop of 'monks' going [*deep guttural tone*].*

How did you write the song and present it to the band? Did you demo it?
I did actually! Because I didn't have multi-track facilities of any description at home—I couldn't afford them, I was well and truly on the bread line and below it—I went to this small studio, which a couple of people we knew in the town had set up in the basement rooms of Swindon Town Hall, the old Victorian town hall in the New Town. It was a little room that had terrible acoustics—it was just a little tiny box of eight-by-eight or something, maybe a coal store for the heating?—and then in another couple of rooms down the corridor they had a load of cables trailed to a four-track tape machine, a little mixing desk, and I think they had a Vesta Fire spring reverb, which is about the cheapest-sounding spring reverb you've ever heard. Literally a bed spring in a box, and that's it!

One of the fellows down there was called 'Bubble'.† I don't know what his name was, but that was his nickname—it was because he had a very silly perm, nice bloke though—and there was a local musician who's still on the scene now called Dave James.‡ We originally went down there to demo some material—the whole band, squashed into that eight-by-eight cube—that went on to *Drums And Wires*.

All four of you? Plus instruments?
Yeah! But later I went down there on a few occasions on my own, just to improvise. Just to see if I could vomit out any ideas in a multi-track facility, much like I now do at home. One day I went down there, and I stumbled on this riff—the basic ascending and descending riff of the song. I improvised this idea over the top, based on a lyric I'd been thinking of called 'Jumping The Gap'. It was supposed to be about the synapses in your brain, and signals jumping the gap—you know, when you get a great idea. But I never used the demo—I umm'd and ahh'd about putting it on the Fuzzy Warbles, but the quality is so awful that I thought it was too bad.

So, I had this thing tentatively titled 'Jumping The Gap', which was the 'Travels In Nihilon' riff, but I didn't like the lyrics. They were just improvised, they weren't very good, and I wasn't crazy about the subject matter. But we

---

* John Lennon asked George Martin to provide the sound of 100 chanting Tibetan monks.
† His real name was Gordon Driscoll. He now lives in Appledore in Devon.
‡ Dave James (born 1949) is a well-known Swindon musician and personality.

started kicking it around in rehearsals for *Black Sea*, just playing it round and round. Suddenly, very quickly, this idea about the con spewed out. I think it was the oppressive nature of the way we were playing—Terry with that continuous, rolling rhythm ...

Tell me where that drum pattern came from.

Do you know, I can't remember! The version I demoed had a really nasty old pokey Hammond organ rhythm box [*imitates cheesy beat*]. The essence of it was a rolling rhythm, so I guess I asked Terry to just roll around the tom-toms to establish a pattern that fits the guitar part. So he's playing 'a-lump a-lumpy-one a-lumpy-one AND lump a-lump a-lumpy-one'. He does different amounts of snare hits—one, or two, or three.

God, I listened to it on headphones yesterday, and those are some of the most compressed drums I think I've ever heard! They're totally punching themselves out. Which I never knew at the time—I just thought, 'Wow, they sound great!'

Now that I know what compression is, I can really hear that. But I love that rhythm—and do you know what, I've got a funny feeling that might have been one take.

Was this one of those situations you've told me about, where he would just tell all of you to go away, and he'd just focus and do the part?

Well, he didn't usually use the phrase 'Go away'. [*Laughs.*] I think this was just a case of us just riffing it around until we had enough, because we didn't know how long the song was going to be—we knew there were X amount of verses in it and X amount of other little pieces, but it was a case of, 'Well, let's just keep rolling this around and use it by the yard later.'

Right—because it fades in and fades out.

Exactly. And Terry does a great job! His timing's pretty immaculate on this. He never drummed to a click track or anything like that. It's a great-sounding, brutal, rolling thing. And very dark. But if you're talking about the con and how you've been taken in by it, it's not going to be jolly, is it? It's 'Tomorrow Never *Fucking* Knows'. [*Laughs.*]

So, you had demoed this, and brought it into rehearsal, and it fell together from there ...

Yeah, the lyrics came pretty quickly, I think. I felt much better that this dark, rumbling riff and drum groove—it's the sound of rejection and disappointment and betrayal. I just felt betrayed by the whole musical movement that we were on the edges of.

Funny that this song is on the same album as 'Burning With Optimism's Flames'.
[*Laughs.*] Yeah. Same coin, two opposite sides. Though 'Burning With Optimism's Flames' is a personal optimism, whereas this is more a case of, 'the Organization has had you'. It doesn't matter if it's the music industry, the fashion industry or the religion industry—they've had you in the ass with a steel pineapple. Sideways.

There's an image I won't lose anytime soon! Let's talk about the arrangement.
I was trying to pick out who was doing what. I know a lot of the melody is underpinned by me sliding around octaves on the guitar.

Plus you do the solo on this, right?
Yeah, that's me. It's all based on that drone around E. There are a lot of dissonant intervals. I can't remember what the hell Dave's doing. He's probably playing the Korg, our little monophonic synthesizer, but I can't remember what's he's doing on guitar. He might even be just doubling the riff with Colin.

I think he's also doing some clashing chords in the background as well.
Yeah, I'm doing the octaves that are chasing the vocal melody—some of the intervals against that E are great. For example, 'travels' is B and C, then it goes down to B-flat, which is pretty funky against an E.

Right, you're getting diminished there.
It's a sinister-sounding combination. Real 'Indiana Jones And The Crystal Guitar'. [*Chuckles.*] 'The Mystery Of The Lost Guitar Of The Covenant'—you open up the guitar case and all those roadies' faces melt!

[*Laughs.*] In the beginning of the song, is it just drums and the drone?
Yeah. The actual drone is me just going [*holds low note*].

Is there any keyboard behind it?
There's probably some Korg keyboard in there. It also comes in during the

second chorus, like an octave up. Plus, we could set it up to do these great white-noise sounds, so we programmed this whip noise. I thought, 'Well, if we're going to be slaves to the pop industry, fashion industry, religion industry, we've got to have a whip in there somewhere.' I think this one of two songs we have a whip in—there's one in 'Shake You Donkey Up' as well.

But no other instruments come in until the first chorus of the song?
Drums, and drone, and vocals. And the whispered vocal is very important.

I wanted to ask about that, because it starts off just in the chorus, but then you start bringing it in during the verses as well.
Yeah, more and more. It's the 'nagging paranoia' voice. 'Am I making a mistake here?' [*Evil whisper*] '*Of course you are!*' It's that little demonic voice in your head.

Do you remember which guitars you and Dave were using? I'm impressed by the biting tone of the guitars.
I'm probably playing a Les Paul, actually. Or my Ibanez, but I seem to remember that I was playing a tobacco-y sunburst Les Paul on our records by that point. I don't know which guitar Dave was playing, but I'm sure he knows—he was reading some stuff down the phone to me the other day, and I was amazed by how much he's got written down.*

When you guys were doing this recording, were you going direct to the mixing board, going through amps, or a combination of the two?
We'd be playing through amps. Usually they'd be set up in the larger room to the side of the studio—this was done at the Townhouse.

Because you got a more ambient sound that way?
The main studio was not ambient, actually. It was so carpeted and padded that it was pretty dead in there. The only ambient room was the Stone Room, built for the drums and percussion. Colin would sit in there with Terry—he would have his amp in the larger dead room with us, and he'd wear headphones so he could hear his amp and us. Terry would be thundering away in that live room, with Colin sat in there with him, and Dave and I would be in the larger, dead area peering through the big glass doors at the pair of them in there.

---

* Dave was playing a '65 Gibson Firebird III through an H/H Performer rig.

I guess they had the larger room dead to control the sound?
It was the hangover of the 70s thing where you've got to make everything totally acoustically dead.

And then they'd control the sound with electronics.
Yeah, which is not always so great, because you've got to let instruments breathe. I think a live area and a dead area is probably a good compromise—some instruments you've got to close down, and then others really need to open up.

Did you guys ever play this live?
I don't know if we did! Could we get that giant drum sound live? I don't remember playing it live. Of course, *now* somebody's going to say, 'I saw you in Belgium, in the Sports Hall—here's this bootleg, don't ask me how I got it!'

That'd be great if they did!
It would be, yeah. It wouldn't be the first time—I don't remember playing 'Life Is Good In The Greenhouse' live, but we did, because somebody sent me a recording of it. So, there is hope. [*Chuckles.*]

I also wanted ask about the 'world's longest piss' at the end of the song.
Well, there's a story behind that!

I thought there might be!
Because we've got the Korg doing its desolate wind at the end—'the bleak landscape of disappointed youth'—I thought, 'OK, we need some rain.' There was no tape library of sound effects there in the studio, so it was a case of, 'Well look, why don't we make our own rain? How hard can it be to make the sound of rain?' So we plugged in cable upon cable upon cable, till we had hundreds of yards, with a good-quality mic on a boom stand, and we put it in Steve Lillywhite's room, which had a shower in it. We recorded his showerhead spraying water on to the shower curtain. And it sounded nothing like rain! We got it, and were playing it back, and people were saying, 'That's *nothing* like rain.' Then somebody said, 'It just sounds like somebody taking a piss!' And I thought, 'Ah! That's even *better*! This is the industry—the pop industry, the fashion industry, the religion industry—*pissing* on you, in contempt, for being such a dolt and buying into all their shit!'

We could have gone to a tape library and gotten some proper rain, but it was a case of, 'No, *that* is even better. The fact that it sounds like somebody pissing on you is perfect.' [*Laughs.*]

That's funny, because I thought it was an aural metaphor for your life going down the drain.

No, it was just the realisation that these industries have conned you, and how bleak and desolate and lonely you'd feel.

In a way, this song is like 'River Of Orchids'—there's a lot of repetition, and it gets thicker and thicker and thicker.

Oh yeah, it's a repetition song, like 'Battery Brides' or 'River Of Orchids'. It's the sort of thing that radio stations would never play—it's just too desolate sounding. Too dark.

I think this song convinced me to go with the title *Black Sea*. The album originally was going to be called *Work Under Pressure*, but our management objected. So, it was a combination of a couple of things. Terry and Colin went to this discount bookstore and bought these 'Faces of Death'-type books, with lots of incredibly gruesome photographs. They'd open these books and say, 'Wow, look at that!' For me, it was, 'Oh god, how *black* is that?' Then we decided that we were going to finish off the album with 'Travels In Nihilon' and, given that we needed a sea theme—because there we are, *in diving suits*!—and given that we were ending with this dark theme, the words 'black' and 'sea' came together for me. So, the title meant something to us at the time, but it probably meant nothing to anybody else. It really should have been *Work Under Pressure*.

Dom Lawson, a friend of mine who is a musician and music journalist, has told me that this is the song that convinced him that you guys were, in essence, a metal band.

Well, we were pretty metallic, certainly on that album! There's a lot of cranked-up guitars and drums. Also, you have the clash of those notes against the E drone. You're not supposed to put some of those notes there! It just sounds a bit *ouch*. It sets up one scale and then grinds into another area.

So, was there any question at all that this would be the album closer?

I don't think so. I think it was a matter of, 'Well, follow *that*.' [*Laughs.*]

Interview conducted June 27 2008.

CHAPTER 11

SENSES WORKING OVERTIME

RELEASED AS A SINGLE, JANUARY 1982
FROM *ENGLISH SETTLEMENT*, FEBRUARY 1982

You've said that your choices for singles rarely were released as singles. Is that true for *English Settlement* and 'Senses Working Overtime'? Wasn't that your choice from that album?

Yeah, I think it was the obvious choice for the single. And I must admit, I was trying to write a single when I wrote it. I knew it was going to be a single when we recorded it, but I wasn't too embarrassed about it being crass, because it wasn't. I did feel a little embarrassed—oh hell, my entire *life* is one giant embarrassment!—because there was no discussion about it. Everyone knew that this was going to be a single.

You told me that you were recording *Drums And Wires*, the band spent more time recording 'Making Plans For Nigel' than other songs on that record, because you all knew it was going to be a single. Did that happen with this song?

I don't remember that being the case, no. We had to get an awful lot of material recorded, because everyone wanted to hear what all the songs that we had sounded like. That's why it ended up as a double album—it was a matter of, 'We've got so much material, let's just record the whole lot.'

The other three might have a different take on it, but I don't remember it being a case of, 'We really must concentrate on this song.' It seemed to get just a similar amount of attention to any other track—in fact, some other tracks seemed to get more attention. For example, I remember fussing with 'Melt The Guns' or 'Jason And The Argonauts' more than I do with 'Senses'.

You said you were trying to write a single—tell me about that.

I remember going into the front room where I lived at the time, which was a couple of rooms above an empty shop, an old Victorian shop front, on

Kingshill Road in Swindon. I used to write in the front room, which had nothing in it other than a sofa and a black wicker-work table with a telephone on it, because it was sort of quiet. [*Chuckles.*] Well, I say it was quiet, but it was on a busy main road. All you could hear was the rumble of traffic in there. In fact, there's an early demo of 'Senses'—I think it's on *Coat Of Many Cupboards*—of me trying to grasp the structure of the song, and all you can hear is traffic. That was my 'quiet' writing room!

I thought, 'Well, okay, what were immediate great singles that had you singing them within ten seconds?' And literally the first one that popped into my head was [*sings*] '5 … 4 … 3 … 2 … 1' [*imitates beat*], you know, the Manfred Mann thing.* I thought, 'Okay, 5-4-3-2-1, I'll go 1-2-3-4-5!' So, I thought, '5-4-3-2-1 was like a count-down to something; 1-2-3-4-5 is like adding up—what are there five of? There are five fingers—no, really, there are four fingers and a thumb. There are [*dumb voice*] five seasons! *No.* There are five *senses*! Right!'

I worked for a while on this kind of stomping, idiot pattern, thinking about the five senses. Then I thought, 'Well, everyone has five senses, what's great about that? Well, they're not just working, they're going crazy! They're working overtime! They're taking all of life in, and it's too much!' Because life *is* just too much. It's amazing, you know. Dave, still to this day, thinks I've rewritten George Harrison's 'All Too Much' by the Beatles. [*Laughs.*]

I began to piece it together. I had the '1-2-3-4-5', and it was going to be about the senses, and these senses were just going to be going crazy at the fantasticness of the world. Then I thought, 'Well, I'm going to need a verse.' The chorus is in E, and I remember I was playing the chorus, not looking at the guitar, and I stumbled and inadvertently played a part of an E-flat. I thought, 'Fuck, that sounds great! What is it?' I looked down, and saw I was playing the E wrongly, playing it like a messed-up E-flat, and I thought, 'Wow, that sounds really medieval! Let me find another chord that fits with that.'

I messed around until I found two chords that seemed to go together. The first chord is basically an A-flat minor, I think, while the second one might have something to do with D-flat. I thought, 'Yeah, this sounds great—it's medieval, it's like pictures from illuminated manuscripts of peasants tilling the soil, and wow, how hard life was in those days. So, I know—I'll make the verse

---

* Their hit single from 1964, written as the theme tune for the pop music TV series *Ready Steady Go!*

kind of like these little figures tilling the land, and cutting hedgerows, and stuff. I'll make it as if it's *their* woes, and *their* worries, and the things that *they'd* be singing about—or the things they'd be fantasising about.' About how the clouds were all made of whey, you know, while worrying if there was enough straw for the donkey, and all that. After I blundered into this sort of medieval thing by accident for the verse, I thought, 'I'll roll with it. I'll write kind of medieval words to it and, for the rhythm, we'll go with a sort of medieval tight little drum.' But I didn't know how to join the half-time medieval bit to the great big stomping bit in E, the moronic backwards Manfred Mann bit. I had a song called 'The Wonderment'—some of the lyrics of which went on to become 'Tissue Tigers'.* I took part of 'The Wonderment', which was the A to the A-suspended part, and then the B to the B-suspended. Ending up on the B was a great way of getting into the chorus, because that's the set-up for E, you know. So that was it—I nabbed a piece of that song.

Listening to it today, I was reminded that the song also has a sneaky little key change—when it's coming out of the bridge, into the chorus, it changes into B-flat. So, instead of the chorus being in E, it's now in F.

So, in essence, you've done a modulation—which is a well-known production trick to take a song 'to the next level'—but you've done it in an unusual place.
Yes, so it's not as noticeable. I don't remember anyone pointing out, 'Hey, they did the cheesy key-change thing!' In fact, I only just realised it as I was listening to the song today—I thought, 'Oh, you crafty little beast! You slipped a key change in there!'

Did you bring that with you to the studio as part of the song, or was that something worked out during production?
It was already part of the song. I've got a feeling that I got myself slightly lost in the middle, and it was a consequence of that—I just ended up coming out in a different alley.

A happy accident?
Yeah. And I came up with the words pretty quickly—about the world being biscuit-shaped, or football shaped.

---

* 'Tissue Tigers' appeared on the B-side of 'Senses Working Overtime'.

Once you had the song structure together, the words just flowed out?
Yeah, I got the chorus first, and then I blundered into the medieval verse, which I kind of went whole hog into—even down to, in the studio, doing some plague-ridden backing vocals. I said, 'Look, can we sing these backing vocals like we're really suffering? Like your youngest has got the plague.' [*Laughs.*] They were known as the 'Lady Di vocals', because Colin said, 'Are we singing, 'Lady Di Di'?' And I said, 'No, it's just like [*sings vocals*], it's like 'If I Was a Rich Man' or something; just kind of wretched land-people noises, OK? It's the sort of thing you'd sing under your breath if you were trying to get your plough kick-started on a frosty morning!'

You have a lot of opposites in the lyrics—the innocents can live slowly, the guilty ones can die slowly. It sounds as if you're working something out.
Wish fulfilment, I think. I'm wishing the world was more just—but it's not, because the guilty ones *can* sleep safely, and there *is* fodder for the cannons. Every time there's a war, there are always plenty of people who will go. But life *is* fantastic—even the crap stuff. The busses skidding on black ice and the bullies beating you up—if you weren't alive, you couldn't experience that.

So, you're comparing and contrasting extremes.
Or even subtle differences between similar things, like lemons and limes. And, as I say, a wish for natural justice—the same natural justice that I was probably wishing for when writing 'Scissor Man'. [*Laughs*]. It's never going to happen, that this figure with scissors is going to come and lop bits off of you because you've been bad, and there are plenty of bad people out there who deserve it!

But life is not fair. It's got bad stuff and good stuff. I'm saying, 'Isn't it great that at least we can experience it?'

The bass part on this song is really distinctive and quite brilliant. Did you work it out beforehand and bring it to the band, as you did with songs like 'Mayor Of Simpleton'? It's such a great counterpoint to the other parts.
Colin was playing fretless at the time—I can't remember the make of it. When he bought it, Terry and I said, 'Oh no, he's got another fretless!' He used to have a fretless Danelectro in the very early days of XTC, and eventually he came to me and asked me to paint frets on it so he could see where he was, because Terry and I used to call out, if there was any out-of-tuneness in the bass department, 'Get a *fretted* bastard!' [*Chuckles.*] But he wouldn't, of course.

So when he bought another fretless, just before *English Settlement,* Terry and I said [*in anguished tone*], 'Oh Moulding, why didn't you get a fretted bastard?'

Anyway, I remember talking to him about medieval ploughing and playing something that would evoke the drudgery, the physicality of picking something heavy up and dropping it again. So I think that's how he came up with the little counter-melody he plays.

After all, those were the days when you'd only have the idea in your head— we didn't have multi-track facilities to sketch these ideas out. You'd come to rehearsal, and just have to explain your ideas to people and give them some vague impression of how it was supposed to go.

Did you rehearse this album a lot?

Yeah, pretty intensely. It was written in quite a short time, and we didn't have much time for rehearsal—we'd finished a tour, and then we only had a matter of weeks to write and rehearse the next album. We did have a couple of numbers already prepared—'Snowman' and 'English Roundabout'—that we'd been playing live on the previous tour.

Would you have rehearsed this at the Manor?

No, we *always* rehearsed everything as tightly as possible *before* anyone ever stepped foot into the recording studio, because of that big clock wiping off thousands of pounds as it went round. I even used to feel bad about changing strings in the studio—you'd look at the clock and ten minutes had gone by, and you could figure how much you'd just spent on those strings!

When we were recording *White Music,* I had a huge stack of old Helium Kidz fliers printed on golden-yellow paper.* On the back of them, I would measure off the sections with a ruler, in different-coloured inks and stuff—here are the lyrics, this is the shape of the song, there's going to be a verse here, and these are the chords, then a chorus, and these are the chords, and all that. Everything was mapped out, because I knew once we got in the studio, it was *very* expensive. These were the days where we tried to have no uncertainty in the studio.

So where *did* you rehearse these?

There was a local musician named Terry Alderton, who everyone just called

---

* Partridge, Moulding, and Chambers played in The Helium Kidz, who subsequently changed their name to XTC.

'Fatty', because he was rather large.* He opened these studios in town. Essentially, it was a large old store that had been sectioned up with plasterboard—a bit of a bodge job, but that's England for you [*chuckles*]. I think our management probably did a deal with him so that we could get either free or cheap rehearsal time if he could use our gear. It was a bit disturbing when you came in to rehearse, because you'd say, 'Hang on a minute—isn't that our mixing desk? Hey, that's our echo unit!'

So, we'd get together and talk about the songs. You'd either have a primitive cassette, or you'd strum through the song and say, 'I'd like the drums a bit like this, and can you keep the bass really low here, because I'm going to be playing up high. And Dave, can you stay down with the bass or maybe repeat the figure I'm doing,' or whatever. We'd really discuss what was needed, because it couldn't come out of our brains onto recorded demo. That didn't start until *Mummer*, when we first got Portastudios or other small multi-track recorders.

Anything you remember about the bridge in particular? Speaking of the bass again, that seems to be another place where it changes, and the whole band kind of kicks everything up a notch.

It's almost as if that middle section is a whole other song. It's probably the closest we ever got to being prog [*chuckles*]—because the thing that annoyed me about prog was, 'Why do a nine-minute number when you've got three great three-minute songs there that you've stitched together? Why don't you just leave them as three songs?' But I suppose that we're guilty of that to some extent with this, because this whole middle section kind of grew in intensity from a vague idea during rehearsal.

And the song grows in intensity after the bridge, too—you have the modulation you mentioned, then the final choruses are more intense and arranged. I'm thinking of that triplet pattern that Terry does in particular.

Oh, yeah—that's a great fill, that. I don't remember exactly how that came about—I don't know if it was requested or Terry saying, ''ere, fucking try this out, you bastards!' [*Chuckles.*] He had a way with the English language! It was *vigorous*. So, it might have been something he did, then we said, 'That's

---

* Fatty Alderton's Tudor Studios closed in 1981. Its site, in Fleet Street, Swindon, is now occupied by the Sir Daniel Arms pub.

great—let's keep that and do it together.' Terry wasn't an improviser—he was the human programme. You'd request the most ludicrous thing, give him five minutes, he'd get it in there, and that'd be it. But he was not the sort of person who would just sit and fire some strange things off the top of his head. Only in his humour did he do that.

Which actually ended up working very well for you guys, because it enabled you to keep the songs tight and focused. A lot of bands struggle with drummers who focus on the flashy, 'look at me' stuff, and end up messing with the music as a result.

The thing was, none of us wanted to be guilty of playing *dull* things. If Terry just had to sit and play [*mocks standard rock drum beat*] all day, I think he would have gone crazy. He liked things that were unusual to play—and so did we! It's what we liked to *hear* as well—unusual conversations between the drums and guitars. It was always a case of, 'Yeah, what you're doing now—try it on those other drums,' or, 'What's it like if you play that all on the offbeat?' or, 'Try it double-time,' or, 'Try it half-time.' Or, 'Don't play any cymbals on this one,' or, 'Don't go near that hi-hat.' And once he got himself programmed, it was great. For this song, I asked Terry, 'Can we get a little medieval drum thing going here?' So he used a roto-tom for that verse rhythm, and combined it with that one-drop kind of reggae bass-drum thing in there, too.

Going through the Snyper drum synthesizer, no doubt.

Yep. And that was an odd little mixture—the reggae one-drop drumming with his foot and the boom of the Snyper, combined with thirteenth-century England with his hand! Altogether, it came out pretty well.

Everyone was in a love affair with their new instruments. I'd bought an acoustic guitar—I'd given my previous one away on a kids' TV show. Dave says that's when I got the Martin—he helped me find it. I think I might have written the album on a cheaper acoustic, and then someone said I needed a better one to record, and that Martin was the thing to get. I didn't know about Martin guitars at the time, so I took their advice. Dave went and picked one up—'Here's your acoustic guitar from now on.' And he did a great job—Martins are beautiful instruments, they sound fantastic. Every acoustic guitar I played on record from that point on was that Martin.

Dave had just gotten his twelve-string Rickenbacker, which he had always wanted. Colin had his new fretless bass, and I had my Martin. I don't think

Terry had anything new, though—he had gotten the Snyper and the roto-tom before *Black Sea*. But I'd say that 'new instrumental love' is the sound of *English Settlement*.

Dave adds some great flourishes throughout the song. I'm thinking of that high guitar pattern that comes in during the second verse, for example.
Verse two is always the place where, if you're going to add something, that's where it starts. 'OK, they're going to be bored, because they've heard this through in verse one. So in verse two, we can be a little different.' Dave was always very good at that. He felt that naturally—I didn't have to say to him, 'Can you just add something different in there?' He'd *know*. He's very talented, and can naturally orchestrate guitars. If I played a G in one position, for example, and wanted him to play a G, he'd find another position, or he'd pick out a figure while I strummed, or something like that—the more twinkly stuff to go between what I was playing. He's very good at that.

Did your co-producer, Hugh Padgham, bring anything to this song? Do you remember any suggestions he may have had?
I remember him bringing more things to other songs, actually. His style of engineering is, 'Get the best, the nicest, sounds you can get on the instruments.' It's kind of an old-fashioned way of thinking, but that was his style. His production style, as an engineer, is not to mess too much with those sounds once he's got them. In fact, the nearest we got to an argument while doing the album—and Hugh is very easy-going!—was, I wanted him to put a lot more compression on the sound of 'Knuckle Down', which he really resisted, because he had recorded these beautiful sounds.

This is why engineers can be reluctant mixers, because they never want to mash up or do anything to the beautiful sounds they've recorded. You know—a million-dollar engineer makes everything sound like a million bucks, and then you say, 'Now, can you make it sound tiny, squish the shit out of it and echo it?' [*Anguished voice*] '*No*! I recorded that acoustic guitar! You can't possibly do that!!' They're really protective, you know? So, they don't always make the best mixers, because they don't want to mess with their pristine recordings.

Anyway, I think there was a compromise on 'Knuckle Down'. No doubt he went and turned down the compressor when I wasn't looking! And I forgive him for that. We all got on splendidly well doing the whole album. There was a lot of camaraderie. Most of the tracks were played live—we'd capture the drums, and keep as much of the other instruments from that initial take as we could. But that was the case on pretty much everything up until then.

You guys were a pretty well-oiled machine at that point.
Yeah. We were the live machine. Once we had the facility to make home demos, there was a lot more careful building of sounds. You become more aware of the arrangement of the whole thing.

You take a more compositional approach at that point, and you have a reference that you're shooting for—the demo.
Yeah. But with this song, I wasn't sure once we'd finished recording it whether it *was* a single. I actually thought that it came out a bit too complex, once we'd finished it, for it to be a single, because of that middle section.

Which Virgin cut back for the single …
They did, yeah. They hacked a few bits of that out.

Did you have anything to do with that at all, any input?
No, it was Virgin saying, 'We're just going to cut some of this out, because it's too long, and radio won't like it.'

I read somewhere that the imagery of 'and buses will skid on black ice' was too scary for them.
No, I think it was a case of how they could make it shorter, to not upset DJs in the time stakes. I don't think they needed to cut anything out, but they did like to meddle in our songs continuously. I mean, look at 'Life Begins At The Hop'—in the radio version, they cut out every fourth line! So nothing rhymes in it! [*Laughs.*] How's that for great record-company interference? So, they chopped that out of there. Later, I heard that somebody had played the song on some speakers that were out of phase, and all they could hear was me doing the sort of contrary vocal interjections about the matches, England's Glory.

What prompted you to put in those interjections? Free association?
I love matchbox art. In fact, matchbox art has occurred in several songs—that one, and also 'River Of Orchids'. The Peckham Rose is a brand of matches.[*]

---

[*] 'Rose Of Peckham' matches were imported by D. Rose Ltd of Peckham, south-east London.

And 'a striking beauty' is England's Glory's tagline?*

That's it. One of them, anyway. I was just being a little English there, sticking in a little bit of English trivia. But because this character played this on out-of-phase speakers, the only thing that was really clear to him were these words—but he got them wrong! He thought it was something like, 'Striking at me!' And then he theorised, 'This is why Andy isn't touring anymore—he's been *murdered* in the studio! Someone has struck at him.' Yeah, sure! So, I'd sing that—'Help, I'm being struck, I'm being murdered right now!' And then I'll go on to sing the last choruses, then I'll be around for the mixing, and then I'll die. [*Laughs.*]

How polite of you! How veddy English.

Yeah, I know, I know. Speaking of being English, I like the crows on the song, too. We got them off some sound-effects record. I wanted it to be very English, and I thought, 'What's the sound that you hear in your head when you think of the ploughing medieval serf? The sound you're going to hear is the jingle of harnesses—and crows cawing!' So, we had to get some crows. I think they're crows, anyway. Maybe some ornithologist out there will write in and say, 'No, they're rooks, actually.' But, to me, that was important to put the final full stop of the medieval thing we had going on there.

Tell me about the video.

That one was done really quickly, in Shepperton Studios, while we were rehearsing for the *English Settlement* tour. And so that's us rehearsing. I can't remember the name of the filmmaker—somebody Grant, John Grant?†—but he said, 'Look, I've got an idea where we play you the song at twice the speed, you mime it at twice the speed, and then when we slow the film down to normal speed, all of your motions will still be in sync, but you'll be [*slowly*] *much more graceful.* And that's been used a hell of a lot since then, but I think we were the first ones to do it.

Interview conducted December 10 2006 and January 11 2015.

---

* England's Glory matches were made by Moreland & Sons of Gloucester. They are now manufactured in Sweden by Swedish Match.

† Brian Grant.

CHAPTER 12

JASON AND THE ARGONAUTS

FROM *ENGLISH SETTLEMENT*, FEBRUARY 1982

Let's take a look at 'Jason And The Argonauts'.
Or, 'Jason And Chintzi', as it became known in the band.

[*Laughs.*] Why was that?
Because there was a porn magazine floating around in the band van that had a middle-aged couple who were pretty grotesque—Jason and Chintzi—having sex. He was fat and moustachioed … and so was his wife! So, it was like, 'Where are we going to put Jason and Chintzi in the set tonight?' Or, 'You messed up that change in Jason and Chintzi!' [*Laughs.*]

I was playing the song recently—haven't heard it in many years—and I'd forgotten the little intro with all the cymbal work. It's like a musical equivalent of the sunshine sparkling on the sea. Just all those different cymbals tinkling and glittering—and of course it's on the outro as well, because the intro becomes the outro. I think I never got over 'Tales Of Brave Ulysses', by Cream. I thought, 'If *they* can do a song about Greek myth, then so can I!'

Did you read mythology as a kid?
Not so much, no. I used to get a comic called *Boy's World*. There was a fantastic artist called Ron Embleton who drew a strip in the centre that was a lot of Greek mythology all sort of mashed up. It was called 'Wrath Of The Gods'. The drawings were so beautiful—the illustrations were just *so* good—that I couldn't wait to see it each week. Then, as a kid, of course, one of my favourite films was *Jason And The Argonauts*.

The Ray Harryhausen film?
Yeah. Most people's favourite scene in the movie is when the hydra's teeth become the skeleton army. That wasn't my favourite, though. My favourite bit

is when they go into the base of the huge bronze statue of Talos, and steal stuff from in there—you know, they grab something they think is a javelin, but it's actually a gold pin or something, or what they think is a shield is actually a gold button. Of course, Talos knows this, and comes to life.

But they really mess up the scale, because sometimes Talos is about 40 feet high, then in a few scenes he's about 100 feet high, and then in a few other scenes he's almost 1,000 feet high. It's like, 'C'mon, how big is he, fellas? Get your scale right!' But I love that film, which I originally saw in the cinema. It's one of those films you can watch again and again.

Absolutely. So was that your basis for the song?
Well, I'll tell you what started it. The actual song came out of finding the main, propelling [*sings ascending/descending guitar pattern*], which just fell into my hands. It was almost like a twitch—it just fell into them so easily.

I mean, it's just a one-note figure, with another note in constant harmony, and it felt so good. I thought, 'Wow, that's almost like the sound of travelling across the sea.' And then of course, it's, 'Who travelled across the sea? Jason and the Argonauts!' And *bleargh!* this whole idea came out.

It's interesting how your mind comes up with these associations.
You can play a little figure or a chord, and as you're telling yourself what it sounds like, that frequently becomes the lyric. This little figure just sounded like travelling across the sea, and then for me it was a very short step to Jason and the Argonauts.

You know the actual motif of [*sings, emphasising the high note in the pattern*] 'Jason and the ArGOnauts'? I took a long while to find that, because I wanted something that suggested antiquity. And I'll tell you where my brain was headed—the music to that film with Kirk Douglas and Tony Curtis called *The Vikings.** The theme for that movie has, you know [*sings dramatically, going up and down*], big leaps in it!

It sounds like something being blown by a distant horn, summoning you. And I thought, 'How can I find a motif with a big leap in it?' Not that I wanted it to sound like the music in *The Vikings*—I just had that in mind— but I was looking for the big dissonant jumps, like somebody blowing a ram's horn or something.

---

* Released 1958.

And I imagine that the lyrics were driven by the fact that you guys were touring your heads off.

We were touring our heads off. But it was the only way I was going to see the world, I thought. Previously, I'd thought I was going to have to be in the navy if I was going to see the world, but I've probably seen more of the world than my dad did, because of all the touring and promotional trips we did. You do get to see a lot of stuff that you've never seen before, and you start to try to want to make sense of it. And you start to see people behave differently as well.

You sound very disappointed with people in this song. It's a very cynical song. Was that a result of touring, or was that something that was building up in you anyway?

I think it must have been something that was building up. I guess it's one of those 'life metaphors'—it's the journey of life. It's not just about journeying around the world, it's also about growing up and journeying through life, and the stuff you see while doing it. That does make you cynical.

You seem to be a bit prescient in your lyrics sometimes. All throughout *Nonsuch* there are songs containing lyrics that made me wonder if your marriage was breaking up at the time—songs of jealousy and rejection—but in fact you didn't find out about your wife's infidelity until later.

Much, much later.

With 'Jason And The Argonauts', it looks like you are presaging what you would soon be going through with your manager and the music business.

Yeah, I guess I was the process of 'un-naïving.' You know, unravelling. This was also written by me at a time when I'd decided I didn't want to tour anymore.

You knew at this point?

Yeah. I knew that I didn't want to tour. I did actually spend quite a bit of time in the studio trying this concept out on the others—getting them one at a time and saying to them, 'What do you think about not touring this album?' Just testing the depths, you know. But the universal message was, 'Oh, it'll be great! Let's get out there.'

It was going to be your first stadium tour as headliners, right?

Yeah, it was the one where we finally got our own big bus. We didn't have to bunk up with another band, or travel around in a little van, you know? But yeah, this was written from a perspective where I *knew* I didn't want to tour. I *knew* I was not enjoying the treadmill. I was beginning to feel *really* like a prisoner. And that's not a good feeling. Yes, you're getting to see and experience the world—yet, inside, the bars are closing in, you know? That's a *very* strange mixture of feelings.

Although at the same time, the image is, if you *are* Jason and the Argonauts— which a touring band could be cast as—you have this opportunity to go out and do and see amazing things—as you say, 'human riches you'll release'.
True.

Is there a paradox here? You felt trapped but released at the same time?
Hopefully you're bringing joy to others, but paradoxically you're feeling more and more trapped by each tour you go on.

There is no golden fleece.
No, none at all. 'There may be no golden fleece, but human riches I'll release.' You can make people feel happy. It's nothing to do with money or riches or anything.

Let's talk about the structure of the song. Anything in particular stand out to you?
I like the little stagger in the melody—[*sings verse vocal pattern, made up of slow and fast triplets*]—don't know where the hell that came from.

Well, it's a very percussive thing. Did you write the lyrics, and then fit them into the 'box' of the music you'd created?
I probably had one or two lines. Once I get that, I usually kind of know where that part of the song is going to go, and then can sketch in the 'What am I trying to say?' part. But the intuitive stuff, the stuff that gives you the framework of the song—that usually falls out pretty quickly.

So, if you come up with a line that has more syllables than you need to keep going with the rhythmic pattern you've set, you do a fast triplet or something like that, to shoehorn them in?
Sometimes. I also like to tweak things, adding a syllable here, or taking a

syllable away, or using an old way of saying something—an old word that hasn't been used for a while that says the same thing but maybe is fewer syllables. You can plunder any language to make it say what you want to say.

You know the bit that goes, 'Seems the more I travel'? I always thought, for some reason—and I annoyed myself when we did it—that we sounded weirdly like the Talking Heads during that little bit.

Yeah, I'd read another quote from you saying that, and I guess once you say that, I can see it, but I didn't really hear it at first.
Do you know, the second we started kicking this around in rehearsals, I thought, 'My god, that bit sounds like the Talking Heads. Don't tell anyone—let's see if *they* notice. But I'm surely noticing.' I don't know what it is, it's just the percussive way of playing that little piece.

Is it the melody that you're singing, or is it the fact that the music gets relatively more straight there?
It's straighter and more percussive, and momentarily goes into a kind of dancey sort of backbeat disco-y thing.

Speaking of which, tell me about the drums on this one.
You know the strange push on the snare drum all the way through this? Terry keeps a steady four-on-the-floor with the bass drum, and plays the snare on the 'and' before the one. I seem to remember vaguely at the time liking the spastic propulsion—and I don't know whether it's a mistake or not on the original—of 'Street Fighting Man'. Because during the first quarter of that song …

You don't know where the one is.
Exactly. Charlie Watts is putting that snare beat on the 'and' before the one. You know, it's 'push-one'. I really remember liking that sense of dislocation. I think I got Terry to play that because in my head I wanted to use that dislocation on top of the straight four-on-the-floor bass drum. I think it worked great.

Sure, because the steady pulse is already there.
Exactly. You just have that little thing kicking it along—like kicking a can down the street or something. And, do you know, once he programmed himself to play that rhythm, he played it really well.

Oh yeah, it's like a prototypical song for him.

Yeah. I also like the '1-2-3's on the roto-tom—we put a little flutter echo on them in the mix, to add just a pinch of psychedelia to them, I think.

The liner notes credit you with keyboards on this.

On the outro, the little monophonic Korg does sterling service as a pretend woodwind. That's buried deep in the mix there, because if you have it too high, you're going to know right away it's a synthesizer.

You were playing a Prophet V on this, too?

I think the Prophet V was the little scrape of tiny bells, in the 'all exotic fish I find' part. I think the ersatz woodwind at the end was the Korg. I seem to recognise the timbre of the Korg. It does have a woodwind-esque [*makes nasal 'hawhhh' sound*]. I don't know how you're going to write that noise down!

How about the bass?

I think Colin's playing fretless on this.

Really? It sounds very punchy and fretted to me.

Yeah, that's true. I know his favourite at the time was the fretless.

And on other songs on the album, you can definitely hear it.

Yeah, it may be the Newport. I'm going to take that back. Let's see, what else can I tell you? The big long middle section is that joy of repetition, just a case of, 'OK, well, they're going on their voyage, so let's go on the voyage.' Actually, I think we chopped out a section. It was even longer in the original recording. I know that we did some editing on that album—we took out a big chunk, a couple of minutes, of the end of 'Melt The Guns'. I think we took out a couple of minutes from the middle of 'Jason And The Argonauts' as well.

On this album you tend to stretch out in the middle of a couple of the songs. You also do that on 'It's Nearly Africa'.

Yeah. What we did with this one involved sort of minute differences in the guitar figure—that ascending and descending pattern. You try to set yourself a little task of seeing how you can play as many little minute differences in that over the space of a couple of minutes, you know? [*Sings variations on the pattern.*] Using the same notes, but just trying to splice it a different way each time you do it.

And you and Dave are both doing that?
Yeah—it's a case of us making the ocean surface or something. It's human fractals!

Did you double-track as well on that?
I think it's just two guitars, Dave and me.

So you're playing an acoustic guitar with a pickup, and he's playing twelve-string?
I think I'm playing the Ibanez, just with a very particular tone. And Dave's playing his twelve-string. And then you get those little vocal parts—I'm sort of fading myself in, plus they're being faded on the desk as well. Little 'memories of the song', if you see what I mean.

The whole thing is almost as if you're in an incredibly fast boat, and you're looking over the prow just staring into the sea for a couple of minutes. That's the whole essence of the song, really. It's almost as if the little vocal motifs that come up are like dolphins jumping by the prow or something.

Have you ever been on a sailing boat or out to sea at all?
I have, but, being scared shitless of water, it's a different experience for me!

Because, when you describe that, having sailed myself, it is very evocative of that experience—standing there, and feeling the wind push you.
You've got to eat less curry, if you're feeling the wind push you! Well, I was guessing at that feeling, I suppose—looking over the prow and staring into the moving water. I try to make our music as pictorial as I can. But you knew that.

And you know the big flange throughout that part? A lot of people out there think that was done the classic way, with a couple of tape machines—in fact, three tape machines, you have to do it with—but this wasn't. This was actually done with a tiny little device about the size of a box of cook's matches called a Bel flanger.*

---

* An electronic flanger made by B.E.L Electronics in the UK. It also came in a rack-mounted version.

Really? I had assumed it was a rack device there in the studio, but nothing that small.

Yeah, it's pretty small. I've read people say, 'Wow, that is the best analogue tape flanging I've ever heard! They really did it properly, with three machines and all that'—which we've done in the past! The Dukes' flanging was all classic tape flanging. But this one was, I don't think we had the machines around, so it was a case of let's use the Bel flanger. It was great, because you could control where you were in the wave. So that's why the wave comes to its conclusion just at the right moment, into the next section. The 'manimal' section. That's from *The Island Of Doctor Moreau*. Who wrote that, H.G. Wells?* The half-animal, half-human creatures he experiments with are known as 'manimals'.

I believe so. Speaking of that section, I remember—when I was first discovering you guys—being especially struck by the line about being in a land where men forced women to hide their facial features, and how we in the West do that through makeup. I was impressed by your ability to use that kind of cultural magnifying glass, or mirror, to show us ourselves and reveal something about our attitudes.

I'm glad to hear that. In England, we were talked down by a lot of critics for being smart-arsed. Things like the lyric you mention didn't constitute observation or astute lyric-writing—it constituted being smart-arsed.

Why would people think you weren't coming up with a helpful observation?

At that time in England, politics—or fake politics—in lyrics was still very much the thing. People seemed to think there was an 'authenticity' in idiot lyrics, or an authenticity in political or politicised lyrics.

A result of the punk aesthetic and its reaction against overblown music?

Yeah. I mean, singing about Jason and the Argonauts—'What are those fellas trying to do?' I was just trying to describe this process of travelling the world, and growing up, opening up, seeing things. The critics weren't interested, though.

It sounds, from our conversation, as though you were able to realise your 'vision' with this song. There have been very few songs that I've written where the recorded version came out sounding exactly like what I heard

---

* It was indeed by H.G. Wells, and published in 1896.

in my head. How is your success rate on that? Do you think, because you've had a longer career and know the studio pretty well, that you've come closer?

Yeah, it gets easier. When you first start, you're not really able to crystallise your thoughts so easily. You don't get such a strong picture in your head, and you can 'go with it,'—you know, 'Oh, we went *that* way with it, I'm kind of happy with that, it's kind of thrilling, I didn't envisage that.' And, to some extent, that still happens. There is perhaps five or ten percent of some unforeseen 'wowee' that can happen in the studio with a song—even though I know all the parts that everyone is going to play, and I know the shape of the song, there still can be a moment where someone says, 'Hey, try this', or someone makes a little mistake, and you say, 'Ooh, what's that?' It can even be a little sound you dial up, or a little mixing decision, and you think, 'Oh, I never really quite heard that in my head, but that's great. That's even *better* than what I hear in my head.'

I was always prepared, although my ego is very strong and precise about what I want on my songs, usually. That said, if somebody else comes up with an idea that I think is better than the one I had, great! That can go in. I have no problem with that at all. When it's a case of, 'That thing he's come up with is so much better for that song,' then it's going in. So there is that element of surprise that you can never account for. The great generals in history try to account for this, and it's certainly there in the studio.

So, you've made a conscious decision from the beginning to try to be open to accidents, or better ideas?

Well, I think I'm just as smart as your average bear. My job is to recognise that if somebody comes up with something that's giving me goosebumps where previously I had none, then it should be part of the song. *Whatever* it is, and whoever suggests it. It can be a little bass run, or a harmony, or a little guitar figure, or something on the keyboard, a mixing decision—anything. It's the thrill of the unknown.

Interview conducted March 28 2007.

CHAPTER 13

NO THUGS IN OUR HOUSE

FROM *ENGLISH SETTLEMENT*, FEBRUARY 1982

'No Thugs In Our House' strikes me as a very angry song.
I don't know if it is, actually! I think it's more of a genteel morality play. It's a real *Threepenny Opera*, but delivered over some rock'n'roll. To me, it's almost Dickensian in its morality, with ironic little twists.

[*Mock snort*] Dickens? Twist? I get it!
Oh, ho ho ho! 'Do you like Dickens?' 'I don't know, I've never been to one.' But yeah, it is rather archaic in its structure.

Sure. It's got three acts—four, if you count the bridge.
Right. That bridge is like an interlude. Funnily enough, I was looking through some notebooks yesterday evening, and I found one I didn't even know I had! There wasn't much in it, but I'd jotted down, around the time of *English Settlement*, lots of ideas and connections and bits and pieces.

I'd had a video idea for this, which eventually became the sleeve to the single—that is, to make it like a toy theatre. So, I was obviously seeing it as the sort of play you'd put on in a Victorian toy theatre—you know, a penny-plain or tuppence-coloured kind of thing.

You say you don't think it's angry, but for me, it comes across as very angry. I mean—guitar and drums, bang-bang-bang-bang, and then you go, 'Rwarrrrr!'
[*Laughs.*] Well, that's my Johnny Winter yell you're hearing there.* It was one of the things we'd do in the dressing room—I was always being provoked, because I had, like, the loudest yell in the known universe. It'd be, 'Oh, c'mon

---

* Johnny Winter (1944–2014) was a blues guitarist and singer.

Partsy, do your Johnny Winter yell. Give us all a laugh.' So I'd yell like a wounded mountain gorilla or something, which would cause great mirth and merriment amongst all company gathered therein. I thought, 'Well, I've got to throw this into a song somewhere,' you know?

You set the stage very well that way. To me, anyway, it sounds like you're about to sing about something you're indignant about, or angry about.
Well, I could never stand parents who didn't bring their kids up properly.

Was there a particular situation for you that brought this to mind? What prompted the writing of this song?
I think it just was a desire to write this rather old-fashioned/modern morality tale—you know, to bring it up to date. At the time it was written, there was an awful lot of awareness of the National Front in England—we'd done at least one Rock Against Racism festival by that time—and at that point in England, there was an awful lot of anti-right kind of feeling, because it seemed like they were growing in prominence.* It was probably more to do with the paranoia of the time rather than their actual prominence, if you know what I mean.

'Knuckle Down' draws on the same sentiment.
That's the one that got me the nasty letter from somewhere in Arizona. If we do an interview about that song, I'll have to try to dig that letter out. Some right-wing knucklehead—[*sings the word to the tune of 'Knuckle Down'*] knucklehead—didn't like me saying that we should be nice to all other races. Wrote me a very heavy letter chiding me. And yet I remain 'unchidden'. Go figure.

Anyway, for this one I decided not to be as direct as 'Knuckle Down'. I made up this character, Graham, who basically is asleep all through the story! Because he's been out drinking all night.

And beating up Asians.
Exactly. So, you never even get to meet the main character in the story. He's offstage. He's ob-scene. I thought that was quite a nice mechanism.

---

* The National Front is a far-right British political party that reached its height at the end of the 70s and then declined sharply.

Because the lyrics are just a reflection of his actions, rather than actually looking directly at them.

Right. It's the young policeman reporting his actions, or his parents saying, 'Oh, our little angel couldn't possibly have done this!' And there are a lot of word games in there, obviously.

Let's talk about that—there are some phrases I'd like to ask about, because I've always wondered about them. Why is it an 'insect-headed worker wife'?

Well, we lived next door to this woman whom we dubbed—we never knew her name—'Mrs Washing'. She would wash *everything*. One day she was hanging out underwear that could best be described as 'waspies'. They were corset-type things—to give you a wasp waist.

So, she was hanging these out one day, and it was like, 'Oh, she's hung out her waspies, I see, so she's like a worker in a wasp hive or something.' It was that kind of word play—who would hang out waspies? Well, it'd an insect-headed worker wife—there's that alliteration. It's a little word-circle thing there, something that sounds [*chuckle*] very surreal. People think she's a normal person, but why does she have an insect head? It's just so that the word circle feels complete.

'The husband burns his paper, sucks his pipe while studying their cushion floor.'

Yeah, that cushion floor was sort of a [*salesman voice*] *luxury vinyl flooring* that, to my parents' generation, was the height of success. If you had cushion floor—and I think it was probably spelled 'Cushionflor' [*chuckles*]—if you had *that*, you *really* had made it.* I think we even had that in our kitchen for a while when I was growing up, and you know, my parents felt like they were royalty. Just because of this *padded linoleum*.

And yeah, he's got his pipe at the kitchen table, and he's reading his paper and absentmindedly setting fire to his paper with his pipe—I'm just trying to set the scene here. A little poetic licence.

'His viscous poly-paste breath comes out.'

It's the sort of a breath that a lot of that generation seem to have, which kind of

---

* Nairn Cushionflor flooring is still in production.

smells like wallpaper paste. It also symbolises a kind of claustrophobia, where you feel the entire world is wallpapered over. All of their world is covered in wallpaper and Cushionflor, and so it's natural that his stinky breath would be reminiscent of wallpaper paste.

Which of course makes sense when you're talking about 'their wallpaper world,' and is a great image, because at first glance, wallpaper could look like a solid barrier, but there also could be nothing behind it.
Exactly—there's nothing to it. You can poke your finger through it, because it's all surface. At the time, I detested wallpaper. For me, it symbolised an older, dead generation. But now I actually have a grudging respect for it. I really like French pictorial wallpaper of the 1800s; in fact, I treated myself a couple of years back to a large-format book called *French Scenic Wallpaper, 1795 To 1865.** The wallpaper in it is beautifully printed, sort of classical scenes. So, I've grown a grudging respect for wallpaper, but hopefully my breath doesn't smell of poly-paste!

[*Laughs.*] And then, 'A boy in blue is busy banging out a headache on the kitchen door.' So, you're setting that up …
Yeah, and the snare drum is reinforcing it! Bang-bang-bang-bang, while Graham is offstage there, snoozing.

People have asked, 'Why 'Graham'?' Well, there is a bit of mischief behind choosing that name. [*Chuckles.*] He's going to hate me for saying this, but Colin has got a mystery brother called Graham. Colin and Graham never see each other. I mean, Colin's reclusive enough, but Graham is *reclusive*, to the point of being like Howard Hughes.

In fact, in all the years that we were playing live, all the years we were in the studio or doing videos or whatever—all our friends would turn up, everybody would come along, relatives would look in, but I *never met* Graham.

Have you ever met him?
No. I've only seen one blurry photograph of him. Colin's mystery brother, Graham—I never saw him in thirty-something years. So, that was the mischief of making the Graham the National Front thug, because Graham is

---

* Edited by Odile Nouvel-Kammerer. The English version was published in 2000 by Flammarion.

completely the opposite of a National Front thug—he's so timid and shy that it's almost like he's only rumoured to exist.

But at the same time, he was someone you never see, just like the Graham in your song!
Exactly.

So, then the second act opens, after you've set the scene.
Yeah, you pull off your little cardboard characters and get your next set of characters ready.

'The young policeman who just can't grow a moustache.' I've always loved that line—why did you write it that way?
Because young policemen always try to grow moustaches [*deep voice*] to give themselves authority!—and they never can! It's like three or four wisps, and it's blond and ineffectual, and you want to walk up to them and say, 'Look—for Christ's sake, shave that off, because the very fact that you've brought that out into the open air says to people, 'I'm so concerned that you might not take me seriously that I've grown a moustache! Look! *Respect it.*' Can't you see how stupid you're making yourself look?' So, young policemen should never attempt to grow moustaches.

We'll add that to the *Partridgean Book Of Rules*.
Exactly. Like Confucius. [*Bad imitation of Chinese stereotype*] 'Partridge, he say—Young policeman never try grow moustache. Never ever ever. It totally right out. It wrong.'

This second act is a little more straightforward—you're not as surreal in your imagery. It's the conversation between the policeman and the parents.
Yeah, I need to tell some story. It's that device in film [*laughing*] where they cram in all the story; you know, you've had all the action, and then forty minutes in, you need to have two people at a table talking, in essence telling you what the film's all about. That's the equivalent of this in the song.

Then to the bridge, which, as you said, is a bit of an interlude. The narrator steps in to talk about what the parents have overlooked.
Yes, this is the point where the spotlight turns to the narrator in a separate box

off the side of the stage. He's filling in anything that you haven't grasped so far. It hints that there's something sinister in the lad, because his parents think it's a boy's club badge he's wearing. But it's not, of course. It's from one of these right-wing groups.

And then, in the last verse, you bring things around full circle. She's out there hanging her waspies on the line again, but now everything's OK. Let's talk about the music and the recording of the song.
Actually, the whole song fell out as a result of me messing around with 'Summertime Blues'.* It's not the same chords—I'm not sure what key that's in, but if it were in E, then it'd be E, A, B. But I messed around and stumbled on a chord that I'd never found before, which I realised has something to do with D, but I still don't know the name of it. The song starts in E, then the notes of the second chord are, in ascending order, G-flat, A, D, A, B, E.

I thought, 'Ooh, that's interesting—that has an unresolved lift.' You're settled on E, but then you're momentarily lifted up and hanging on that second chord, then you drop to E again. It's a very bumpy rhythmic ride, and I thought, 'Ooh, this is good. Have I found a chord that nobody else knows about?' So that's where it came from—dicking around with 'Summertime Blues'.

I'm assuming this is one of these songs that you guys developed and arranged in rehearsal?
Yeah. It was very tightened up in rehearsal. You can tell that—it's *so* steady. Everyone's completely integrated with each other. There's not a beat or note out of place on this. It was bashed to death at rehearsal at Fatty Alderton's Tudor Studios in Swindon.

Great performance by Terry Chambers, actually. He's on the button there, all the way through.

Oh yeah. Rock solid.
Yeah, really. And how he does that *strange* mid-section …

I wanted to ask you about that, because it's very 'Nigel'-esque.
It is—if you listen, there's a very dead floor-tom on one side, very clicky-

---

* By Eddie Cochran, released 1958.

sounding. And then he's playing this triplet counter-rhythm on the hi-hat against that. I'm not sure what his foot's doing.

He's doing four-on-the-floor with his kick drum.
Right. I don't know how that all came up—it's completely spastic, but completely perfect!

So, that wasn't anything you suggested?
Well, he and I always worked really closely on what the drum rhythms for any song were going to be. That was my closest relation to Terry. That, and humour. We didn't have a lot in common outside of him drumming, even though we were from the—god, I hate to say it, but it's important in England—the same class. Now, it's different—I spoke to him two or three days ago, keeping him up on stuff. He calls every six months or so, and we have a chat.

The credits list Colin as playing Fender bass on this. You and I recently talked about how you and Dave sometimes wished he'd 'just play his Fender'.
Well, if he *did* just play his Fender, then we obviously thought it was weird enough to mention that it's a Fender! Perhaps we were trying to suggest that he should *stay* playing that Fender, and stop picking up his cartoon novelty bass of the week. [*Chuckles.*]

It's very punchy.
Oh, it really is. It's very punchy, and he does put some rather seasick-sounding semitonal runs in there, which add to the queasiness of the scenario.

I like the passing tones that he does in the chorus, where you guys are all banging on the A-G-F chords, and he descends to each one.
Yep, that slipping-between-chords thing. Oh yeah, he's a great bass player.

And you're only playing acoustic on this?
I think so! I think Dave's doing all the electric guitars. Dave's doing that ferocious kind of rock'n'roll meets Stax thing—like Booker T & The MGs. You know, that Fender guitar and four-beat snare punching along together. And it's definitely related to 'Life Begins At The Hop'. It's very Dave Gregory in that respect.

He also plays that rather 'Holly Up On Poppy'-esque keyboards in the middle section. That's the Prophet-5 synthesizer, which I would take home and try to program, to create sounds that I knew I would want to hear on tracks. Because you had to build the sounds and then save them in memory. There were some pre-programmed sounds, but it was a great delight to try to build your own. I had a notebook where I had all the sounds notated, just for that reason: 'this is how to dial up a flute' or 'how to dial up a calliope' or something.

And you were really *were* dialling up things on that, because it was an analogue synth.
It was, and it was the old attack-decay-sustain-release approach—ADSR. Which is I think is a porno expression as well.

I'm a little afraid to ask what the letters stand for.
[*Laughs.*] I think the last word is 'Roebuck'—just to give you an idea of how wrong it is.

[*Laughs.*] Is this just you singing? Are you overdubbing your voice?
Do you know, I never twigged that. I know I asked Hugh Padgham to give me a kind of rock'n'roll slap-back vocal effect, to help the 'Summertime Blues' feel.

And that is one of the big differences I noticed between the studio version and the BBC version of this song: the BBC version is much drier.
Yeah. You have to kind of knock the songs out at the BBC, and it's a case of, you know, 'The thing to make echo—we're using that on the guitar, so we can't possibly put it on your voice.'

Was it that primitive?
No, probably not, but it *is* a case of you've got to get so much recorded and mixed so quickly—you've got a couple of hours to do four songs, and it's got to sound presentable. The best thing that you can hope for is that there's more nervous energy than there is on the album.

And I think it succeeds on that level. It's interesting to listen to it; because there's not such a wash of reverb, you can hear other things going on more

easily. For instance, you're doing lots of percussive strumming accents on the acoustic.

Yeah. Well, this is the most rock'n'roll XTC have ever been, I think.

You mean, like classic rock'n'roll?

Yeah, with the almost kind of 'Rock Showband' kind of feeling, you know?

What was the recording situation for this song like?

The *English Settlement* sessions were pretty rushed. We did a double album's worth, and a bit more, all recorded and mixed very quickly. There were some late nights, and there was also the thrill of the stone room at the back of the Manor studios there.

You've described to me how Terry would be in there, often with Colin, and you and Dave would stand in the room outside while you all played together. Was this like that?

That definitely was the situation at the Townhouse studio. I think it was the situation at the Manor as well. The stone room at the Townhouse was such a hit that they decided to add a similar thing to the back of the Manor, which didn't originally have one.

Was it big enough for a whole band, or only big enough for the drum kit and maybe one other person?

Potentially big enough for the whole band, but you wouldn't want to make everything sound so harsh and ambient. It would be appalling for separation. It was very complimentary for a rock drum kit, or to make anything sound more live, like to brighten a trumpet or give extra sparkle to an acoustic guitar. It was great for that. But if you'd put amps in there as well, it would have just turned into a gooey mess.

When we did *White Music* at the Manor, they didn't have that room, and in fact the only supposedly live area at the Manor prior to that was a little corner section, about six-foot-by-six-foot, that had a little wooden floor. That was their concession to live, but it was only about two per cent more live than the rest of the heavily carpeted room! They definitely needed to do something there, to put a bit of spark in, so adding that extension of a stone room was great.

Let's talk about the coda at the end, if you could call it that. Just when you think the song's going to end—rwarrr, it comes back with a vengeance. Was that something you planned from the beginning, or did you say later, 'Wouldn't be great if we just fooled people this way'?

It probably grew out of enjoying playing it in rehearsal. You kind of don't want to stop, you know? The song would stop, and Chambers would probably look over, and we'd be off and running again. 'Ooh, that feels so right!' A case of, 'Well, why stop? This is great fun, let's do some more.'

I also really like the false start, with the quiet drums. I don't know where that idea came from, but I was reminded of that, listening to this yesterday. I think that's a great way to bring the listener into the song.

Yeah, you kind of do that on 'Roads Girdle The Globe', too.

Yeah, but for that song, we moved up the whole track up a couple of dB when it came into the motif part. With this one, the drums were made to sound very thin and quiet—kind of like a drum version of that thin acoustic guitar, and then suddenly, when the rest of the band kicks in, you get the proper drum kit. And it sounds great. Because you think, 'Oh, well, that's it then, here we go,' and then suddenly, *Pow!* Sucker punch.

One more question—there's a video out there of you guys on *The Old Grey Whistle Test* doing this song. Any particular memories of that? I think it's a great performance.

I was exceptionally nervous. I did *not* want to be touring. And it was like, 'Oh no, this is the tip of the iceberg of touring, and what's the first thing we do? *Live television* to the nation!' You've been writing and rehearsing and recording an album, and you don't want to go back on the road, and what do they do? They put another worldwide tour in, and they start you off with live television.

So the *Whistle Test* was live?

It became live after a number of years. Not very many people realise this, but earlier, bands would mime to backing track, and either add a live vocal in, or they would just sing along with their record. For example, when the New York Dolls were on there, with the track 'Jet Boy', they're just singing along. They've got the mics in the studio, and you can hear the clumping of their stack heels louder than you can the actual tracks. They're obviously miming.

When David Bowie was on there doing 'Five Years'—and people say, 'Oh, that's the greatest performance!'—he's singing to a backing track, for Christ's sake! Anybody can see this.

But then, as the years went on, they would insist that bands really did play live. When we did our appearance doing 'Statue Of Liberty', that was totally live. So was the 'Yacht Dance' and 'No Thugs' appearance.

Was it going out on to the airwaves live, or were you performing it live in front of a audience?
It was a performance, one take, and then they'd put it out the following week, or whatever.

I thought maybe it was actually streaming out live to TV sets across the nation.
That would be the worst! No, in this case, you got the one shot at it, and that was it. So, I guess, that was second worst. [*Laughs.*]

Interview conducted August 21 2008.

CHAPTER 14

BEATING OF HEARTS

Let's talk about the album opener for *Mummer*, 'Beating Of Hearts'.
It's going to be tricky for me to come up with much about this, but you, being the chief inquisitor that you are.

I'll get it out of you. [*Laughs.*] Time to go on the rack! Bring out the comfy pillows!
You're gonna Guantanamo me, baby!

Wait, I've got to put on *Loverboy* at volume 11, to truly torture you.
Yeah, put on 'The Final Countdown' by Europe. What music *do* they use to torture the prisoners?

Apparently death metal, or anything that has a lot of bass and drums, and sinister, choppy guitars.
Does it come out on the GuantanaMotown label?

All the greatest hits!
Greatest hits, greatest punches, greatest waterboarding in the world!

Strangely enough, that's a good segue to talk about this song—because it's against violence and talks instead about the power of love.
Right on.

Let's start off by talking about the history of this song. This is one of the last, if not the last, songs that Terry drummed on.
That's right. It was a pair that we did as a kind of audition for Steve Nye, the engineer, and also auditioning Genetic Studios, which belonged to Martin

Rushent, who produced 'Are You Receiving Me?'* He had his own studio complex, up in the woods in Reading. He must have bought these buildings off the army or something—they were these weird bunkers up in the woods.

So, we said, 'Let see what these studios are like—it might be good to do the album there—and we'll also do two tracks, because Virgin are talking about a double A-side single.' That translates to, they can't decide, and they don't want to upset the songwriters. [*Laughs.*]

Talk a little bit about your relationship with Virgin at the time—this was right after you'd said, 'No more.'

The relationship was not in a good place. It went very bad from '82 until the late 80s. It was going way down the slippery slopes, because we were getting ready, with the *Mummer* album, to make the album that would sell almost the least of our career, I think.

Really? I thought *The Big Express* held that dubious distinction.

I'm not sure. I think it's [*laughs*] kind of a photo finish! Or no, it wouldn't even be that fast, it'd be a linocut finish with these two poor-selling albums. I think they've sold a lot more since, but at the time, they probably sold about 30,000 or something each, and I think Virgin were very upset, because they wanted mega-millions.

And you were poised for world domination after *English Settlement*.

Well, we were certainly poised for English domination, because the *English Settlement* album had been top 5, and the single was no. 10—that's the highest we've actually been in the English charts, disgraceful to say. Until *Top Of The Pops* finished on television, I'd always watch it and see what was at no. 10, because that was supposedly culturally comparable to where we were! God, that's a shock—some of the shit you've got to share your number in the charts with.

So we were trying out Steve Nye, because we liked the sound of the *Tin Drum* album.† I didn't like the singing; I actually found it slightly comical, to be honest. It was sort of like somebody taking the piss out of Bryan Ferry. But I love the actual sound of the record—it was beautifully recorded.

---

* Steve Nye co-produced *Mummer* and went on to work with David Sylvian, Clannad, and the Penguin Café Orchestra.
† By Japan. Released by Virgin in 1981.

So that's how you hooked up with him—it was you being proactive?
I think somebody at Virgin gave us the *Tin Drum* album. 'Oh here, try this band, you might like them.' Because when you walked into their offices, they'd give you stuff.

Right. And then charge the artists for it.
Or charge *us*! We'd be looking for beer in the fridges of the A&R people, or something like that, and they'd be foisting these albums on us that we didn't particularly want.

So they gave me this, and I really, really liked the sound of it. So, it was a case of, 'Let's try the potential of a double A-side single, and let's try Steve Nye, and let's try Genetic Studios.' It was kind of a gamble, which didn't start very well, because on the first day of the session, I think Steve Nye turned up about 4:00 in the afternoon, and I think we'd been there since about 10:00 in the morning. I did not feel kindly to him when he walked through the door, and was just like, 'All right lads?' It was a matter of, 'Where have you been?' He'd failed test number one, which in my book is punctuality.

The engineers, presumably, had been there?
Well, the in-house person from Genetic Studios was racing around trying to get a load of microphones ready, not knowing which ones the Steve Nye would want to use.

Oh, so it's not even like you were filling the time getting a sound or anything?
No! I think we were just sort of jamming, and messing around, and saying, 'Where the fuck is he?' He arrived very late, and that was a bad start to me. And I think it was kind of an omen about his personality. He's a wonderful engineer, but he's possibly the grumpiest person we've ever worked with.

That said, we did choose to work with him. He did pass the audition purely on the beauty of his recorded sounds, but he was tricky to work with.

I think that, for an 80s album, *Mummer* has aged quite well, because of its overall sound.
That's because, apart from rather subtle synthesizers, there's nothing too artificial on it. I mean there's probably more synthesizer on the *Abbey Road* album than there is on *Mummer*! But that's Steve Nye. When he records things, they are very subtle and they do have a quality. Even when he records

fake things, synthetic things, they do seem to have an analogue beauty, or almost a living, breathing kind of quality. That's an amazing talent, you know?

But you'd work with him, and arrive at, say, ten in the morning, and he'd be hunched over the mixing desk putting a mix together or getting some stuff ready, and it'd be *hours* before he'd talk to you! He wouldn't even say good morning. It might be two or three hours had passed before he'd say 'uungh' [*grunts*].

When you've talked about the role of the producer, you've emphasised how important it is for them to have strong interpersonal skills.

Oh, they're midwives! They have to have a great bedside manner, and if they don't, you're thinking, 'Well, I don't want to pop my baby out for *you* to pull it! You're not going to put your hands around the head of *my* baby! Get me someone else.' But Steve Nye is as grumpy and tricky an individual to get on with as he is marvellous as an engineer. His engineering is truly beautiful. Really platinum-quality recording. I mean, things like the drums on 'Ladybird' are just totally three-dimensional. That's how to record a kit, you know?

The drums on 'Beating of Hearts' also are quite focused and nice. Is there anything that you remember particularly about recording the part? The toms are very *tuned*.

I think Terry was probably bullied by Steve Nye into tuning them up. I realise now the importance of well-tuned drums. I mean, after you've worked with people like Pete Phipps and Dave Mattacks and Chuck Sabo—people whose kits are so beautifully tuned that they sound musical when they get played, and you think, 'Oh, that's a delight to your ears!'—you appreciate it.* But I don't think Terry particularly tuned his drums. As long as they felt kind of tight enough, and sounded about right, he was OK with them. But there wasn't any particular thing he did. I don't remember his drums sounding particularly musical—if anything, they sounded kind of box-like. They did sound musical when he *played* them, though.

But the idea for the drums for 'Beating Of Hearts' was based on a kind of buoyant Indian rhythm. You know, [*sings*] *boom*-badap-bom, *boom*-badap-bom, *boom*. I don't think Terry actually plays it as buoyantly as I would have

---

* Pete Phipps of The Glitter Band and Random Hold played on *Mummer* and *The Big Express*. He has also played with The Eurythmics and Boy George. Chuck Sabo played on *Wasp Star* and has worked with Elton John, The Pet Shop Boys, and many more.

liked. He doesn't *quite* put those accents in the sort of *micro*-metre place that gives them the buoyancy that beat has when Indian drummers play it.

Yeah—it was interesting even to hear you sing that, because there is a very subtle difference.
He's a little bit more linear in his approach. The difference is tiny, but important.

Then there's the fast triplet pattern on the high drum.
Oh yeah, that was overdubbed later.

And that was what, a roto-tom?
Yeah, I think it was, sort of tuned up and played to match the guitar during that one pattern.

And then there's a tambourine on the 'one' that was overdubbed later?
That was added later, yeah.

But otherwise, that's pretty much it for the drums, right?
Yeah, it's very minimal! He just cycles around that rhythm all the time. Good sense of timing—I don't think he played it to a click track, because Terry didn't like click tracks.

Yeah, he told me that he never played with a click while with you guys.
He would just sit and get in the groove. It feels good, time-wise. He played with a click on 'Melt The Guns', but only because it was integral to the rhythm of the song.

Was this one of those things where he told you guys to go away and get a cup of tea, while he locked himself into the track?
I think it was either me and him, or Dave and him. Certainly I don't think he would have benefitted from Colin playing along, because Colin's just playing 'bomp' on the one—there's nothing really flowing to glue Terry to the bass.

Was he fine with just having that very spare, repetitive pattern to play?
Yeah. He certainly liked repetitive patterns. That was Terry all over. I did as well. I mean, the pair of us would be egging each other on.

We always talked about me drumming on stage with him, actually. Having a set of toms or something set up, and we would do something where maybe Colin would be singing, and I'd be drumming a tom-tom pattern, and Terry'd be playing a counter-pattern, to get a really good groove going, but we never got round to it.

We had a lot in common in the rhythmic side of things then. We had nothing in common socially—you know, you couldn't talk to Terry about books or theatre or anything like that. But if you wanted to get on about drumming or share a curry or a few beers, he worked on that level.

You were talking about how this has kind of an Indian rhythm—what prompted you to do that? Was this the backbone that you built the song from?

Well, I always wanted to do something with that buoyant, bobbing rhythm, but the whole song really came from the guitar tuning. I'd read somewhere that the Glitter Band had got the sound on their guitars by tuning every string to the same note, which they then played through a distortion pedal with a bottleneck. So, instead of chords, you had six notes [*chuckles*] sort of overdubbed simultaneously, if you see what I mean. I thought, 'Well, that's a fantastic sound! I wonder what it's like to mess around with.' So I just tried it—I tried tuning every string to the note of E. I'd heard that they tuned to the note of A, but I thought I'd try it with E.

So, I was dragging the plectrum across the strings, and it sort of made a rhythm as you played—drrrr-lang, drrrr-lang. Because it was all the same note.

Right, but slightly different timbres, because you have different weights of strings.

Different weights and thicknesses of strings, yeah. And then you just throw your hand on, in a straight barre, and you're playing—well, not quite chords, because at best they can only be octaves of each other. So, they're not chords, and they're not single notes—they're something else.

I was just moving my finger around in a straight barre on the guitar [*sings 'Beating Of Hearts' guitar pattern*], and very soon a song came out. That almost chime-like, or bell-like, guitar pattern suggested ethnic instruments to me—certainly somewhere east of Dover, like India, or the Middle East, or maybe the Balkans or something. And I thought, 'Well, if the song is growing the way it's coming out now, we'd have to make the drums fit with that as well.'

Then, in the studio, we had the Prophet 5 synthesizer imitate—I don't think we knew about sampling at the time, and there was no way to play samples on a keyboard, I don't think—a kind of orchestral bowed bass and/ or cello thing, and we knocked up an accordion patch. I would actually do that—I would take the Prophet home, and sit there and build things I knew I might want in the future. It was like a hobby, you know? 'Hey, let's see if I can make an accordion!'

So, we fleshed out the east-of-Ipswich [*chuckles*] sound, with our fake instruments, Terry doing his curry-flavoured best on the drums, and Dave and I, with these jousting, six-stringed, one-note guitars.

I remember reading that one of the ways you got the distinctive sound of the guitars on this song is that you played electric guitars but instead of amplifying them, you miked them, and played them as if they were acoustic.

That's right. We did that a lot—the first time we did it was 'Pulsing Pulsing', and I really liked it.* I could hear it at home, because I'd have an open mic on a cassette machine or something, and would be just strumming an electric, and I thought, 'I like the acoustic quality of when you get the mic near the guitar—you get these super highs that don't go down the pickups.'

So, we did that from 'Pulsing Pulsing', which was *Drums And Wires* time, onward. It's all over *English Settlement*, and from then on, really. It's even on *Wasp Star*.

But on most other songs you'd just use it as a type of sound reinforcement, right? Whereas on this one, it's very prominent.

It's prominent, yeah. Usually, we'd have the electric signal go out to the DI port on the mixer board, and/or an effect or amp somewhere, and then we'd put a mic about a half-inch away from the strings, so you had to sit very close and not move, you know? Then it would capture those super-highs, and you'd blend them in with however you'd process the electric side of the signal, and you either have that as one sound, or you split them across the stereo. You'd have, say, the acoustic side to the left, and the electric, treated side to the right.

A great example of that is 'I'm The Man Who Murdered Love'. You listen

---

* The B-side to 'Making Plans For Nigel'. Also released on *Rag & Bone Buffet*.

to the rhythm guitar, and it's an electric guitar done in that way. It seems to play across your head, because you have the acoustic side of the electric on one side, and the treated side of the electric on the other.

So, on the guitars on 'Beating Of Hearts'—Dave's playing a twelve-string, I think …

[*Chuckling*] And all twelve were tuned to E?
Tuned to E, yeah. He may contradict me, but I think it was a twelve-string. But we miked it up and blended it with the electric side of it, and the same with my guitar.

You were playing the Ibanez on this?
I think so. I'd say the acoustic side of it is heavier in the mix. Because it sounds very thin and brittle. I love that sound, actually.

It's funny—you've talked to me before about the fact that your guitar chord shapes or patterns are easier than people may think, and this is one of those cases where I thought you guys were doing something exotic.
No, I think they're mostly just straight-barre patterns, but across all those strings—it's like a rolled *R*, you know?

So, there's a call-and-response thing you and Dave are doing? Is that how it worked?
I'm playing on the intro, where you hear two guitars, and all the middle sections as well. Then, we're sort of jousting against each other. You know, I play the pattern, then he would do it—it's sort of like a canon effect.

Let's talk about the lyrics a little bit. When in the process did the lyrics come in?
I think the musical side suggested the lyrical side. This is really corny, but it's probably that, for me, the Indian-type sound equals 1967 or '68, which to me means love, and that led to the whole thing about the human heart being the strongest rhythm, the most powerful thing. It really is one of those rather corny, 'there's nothing greater than the power of the human heart'-type songs.

So, like I was saying, it's kind of tricky for me to come up with anything to say about it, other than it's made up of descriptions of the power of emotion. Human emotion and love, good; war and war equipment, bad.

Why did you build the lyrics around the whole concept of sound and loudness?
I guess it's the thing of, however loud you can think of these loud war noises—explosions, rifles, screaming war lords, tanks, bombers—you know, the most awful sounds that man can make, probably topped off with an atom bomb—sure, they can blow people to bits, but human emotion and the human heart makes a subtle, very quiet noise that is stronger than all of those.

So, the difference is inside versus outside.
It's inside versus outside, it's the beating of this little motor that keeps you alive, and helps you make decisions *for* good, and make decisions *not* to kill, and *not* to destroy. It's far more powerful. I guess I'm just a soppy old pacifist at heart.

The lyrics are full of idealism, but the music is kind of dark.
The music's dark, and some of the sentiments—certainly those that describes some of the negative aspects of human behaviour in there—are rather dark.

'Tanks on the highway' is a pretty grim image.
Yeah, that, and 'bombers in flight'—that sort of thing. My state of mind was very fragile at this point—as in, 'Oh my god, what's going to happen next?' Because Virgin didn't seem to want to talk to us anymore, you know.

Were they really that cold with you?
They were. It was a matter of, 'Well, that's all over, then. That's all finished.' They couldn't imagine that a band could work in the studio and still sell records.

Even though Steely Dan was already a shining example at that point?
Well, The Beatles were an even more shining example!

Sure, exactly.
I think they were just set on the thing that you *have* to go out and tour—that kind of thing. As you say, Steely Dan—or even a thousand bands that are

made up of session players or faceless people that play in the studio—still have huge hits, right? But they couldn't see that. They were still stuck on the whole 'you've got to go out and play live' thing.

And, of course, we never saw any money from any of the tours we ever did. And any time we tried to talk to our manager about what was happening to the money, we were fobbed off with, 'Oh, well, you know, we'll have a meeting,' or so and so. Of course you never had time, because we were either in the studio or we were on tour. Or we were writing and rehearsing to go in the studio, or go on tour. So there was no spare time to do anything.

But with this album you were able to break away. Tell me more about writing this.
All I can remember was, it was written in the back bedroom of our brand-new house. Well, not brand-new, but brand-new to us—it was the first time we'd ever had a house, because we'd just lived in flats before that.

And that's where you're living now?
Yeah. We moved here in '82. I got a mortgage using my Performance Rights Society money.* I'd saved up £8,000, which was a *phenomenal* sum to me then.

The demo for this is on *Hinges*, part of the *Fuzzy Warbles* series, right?
Yeah, I think it is!

You've got a little beatbox going on there.
A little beatbox thumping away—poorly recorded. Very badly recorded demo.

Were you even using a multi-track recorder then, or just singing into a cassette recorder?
It was a four-track cassette machine. It was the first album that I had any facility to record in multi-track, and I wasn't very good at it yet. I was really learning the trade as I went.

Tell me about the vocals.
You know the bit that goes 'buoya-dada, buoya-dada, buoya-dada'? The bit that sounds like a Popeye vinyl record stuck in a groove? [*Laughs.*] That came from

---

* The PRS collects fees from those who play copyright music publicly.

a TV programme I saw, where I saw this Indian tabla player explaining that, during the kind of classical regimen they go through to learn the instrument, they have to learn to sing all the patterns they play. You know, 'dah-dah dikki-dah dikki-dah dikki-di dahdahdah.' That sort of thing. So that was my intent on that part—to sound like a tabla teacher. I don't think I pulled it off—as I say, it's more like broken vinyl Popeye.

Well, I think the intent came through. It's a very percussive vocal part.
But it's a bit silly! Whenever I hear it, I end up thinking that. 'Why do you want the sound of an ersatz tabla teacher on your record?' [*Laughs.*] I do remember that I'm harmonising with myself on this.

Yeah, I've always liked the harmonies you did there, and kind of had a feeling that it was all you.
I wanted it to be really snaky and tight, and it's difficult for another person to get exactly the timbre and the same melodic line as you.

And to feel the rhythm in exactly the same way—the same phrasing. You take an interesting approach to the harmonies there, where you split apart, and one part will go down while another goes up, and then you come toward each other again, then split back apart. Was that all thought out, or just an in-the-studio thing?
If it's on the demo, then it would have been thought-out pretty early on, but if it wasn't, it was a later, 'Ooh, let's try that!' type of thing. Because, as I've said, usually there's at least ten percent of stuff that rears its ugly head in the studio while you're playing a song. If you're lucky, even more.

Sometimes, when you're knocking a song through in the studio, you can find some things that you just never foresaw, and it can really make a song. And, conversely, it can break one, because sometimes you put a song under the magnifying glass, and rather than magnifying and apparently becoming bigger, the sun burns it [*chuckles*] and it sort of shrivels and dies.

You also mentioned synthesized accordion sounds and bowed instruments.
It was a case of, 'Well, we can't really afford a bowed double-bass, or a couple of cello players, so maybe we can just knock something up,' you know? The sounds are OK, but as I say, they're much saved by Steve Nye's engineering, which is beautiful.

I remember the first time I played this song. I had a nice stereo with speakers that had fifteen-inch woofers, and the first time I heard 'bombers in flight' the house shook.

'Bombers in [*sings it very low*] fliiiight.'

Is that the lowest note in your catalogue?

I think it is, actually! I know when we were mixing 'Wonderland' initially in AIR Studios with Steve Nye—the mix that we didn't use, because we used Alex Sadkin and Phil Thornalley's mix—that George Martin was hanging around, because Steve Nye had requested an sub-octave device.* We were looking for something to make the 'booping' keyboard go down lower than the bass drum. So there was George Martin, setting up this sub-octave device for us and dialling that up—and so we got to work with George Martin for five minutes!

Did you get to pepper him with questions?

Hey, nice! [*Laughs.*] We *Revolver*'d him.

You Taxed him, Man.

It was taxing, man—yeah. No, unfortunately, we only saw him a very short time, and then we ended up not using that mix.

Interview conducted April 20 2008.

---

* Alex Sadkin (1949–87) remixed most of *Mummer* with Phil Thornalley engineering. Thornalley later became frontman for Johnny Hates Jazz, and has written two hit songs for Pixie Lott. George Martin, legendary producer of The Beatles, was the founder of AIR Studios in London.

CHAPTER 15

LOVE ON A FARMBOY'S WAGES

RELEASED AS A SINGLE, SEPTEMBER 1983
FROM *MUMMER*, AUGUST 1983

Let's talk about 'Love On A Farmboy's Wages', one of my favourite songs from one of my favourite albums.
I'm ready—I'm sitting here in my old rocking chair. Although it shouldn't be.

Your chair is not supposed to rock?
Yeah. This one's rocking, though.

But is it rolling?
No, it's just the Majesty of Rock. No Mystery of Roll is involved.

[*Laughs*.] Back to the song, you mention that the middle part has a jazz feel, and I'd go even further and say it even has a slight latin feel.
Hmmm!

I've always felt, when playing drums along with it, that there's kind of a double-kick pattern—and-one, and-two, and-three, et cetera—that you can put in there that reminds me of a samba.
I really enjoyed coming up with the drum patterns on this song. I was really sick of big drums by this time. You know, sick of that massive drum sound.

The whole album seems to be a kind of reaction against where you had been heading as the big touring machine.
Yeah. I could see other people kind of taking off with that sound as well. I thought, 'Ohhh, we're being followed here, so I'm going to drop the trail.' I had a funny little drum machine—I can't remember the name of it, but it was sort of programmable. It was one of those things where you had to sort of follow the flashing lights or whatever—'1-2-3-4-5, HIT that button there'—

so it'd hit beat five out of eight. So, you could kind of program it, but all the sounds were tiny and they sounded like little clay pots. You can hear it on the demo version. I liked the smallness of it. It suited where I wanted to go—I wanted to get away from giant drum sounds, and I wanted to get away from big, noisy *ROCK*.

The gated toms ...

Yeah, the gated ambient sound, cranked-up guitars, and all that stuff. I just wanted to take a break from that.

Acoustic guitars were a big part of that—I was well in love with my Martin acoustic, which was a fairly new acquisition, by this time. I think I got it as some point during *English Settlement*, or as we were starting doing that album. I think we'd already started it, and Dave saw it in a paper advertised. He said, 'Oh, someone's selling a D35—you should really get one of those.'

Yeah, because there's quite a bit of acoustic guitar on *English Settlement*.

It was one of those things were you get an instrument, you fall in love with it, and it has to be on everything. I really wanted to go more acoustic. It was being threatened on *English Settlement*, you know, but came more into force on *Mummer*.

So, here we have this lovely little cyclical drum pattern—which we actually rehearsed with Terry, but he was trying to think of a way of telling us that he was going to leave the band. I don't know if he was purposely struggling with the song as a way of vindicating what he was about to say—'Look, I'm off'— but he couldn't seem to grasp this pattern, which normally he wouldn't have had any trouble with. I mean, it was right up Chambers Street—a repetitive little cycle pattern. But he said, 'Ah, you know, I'm having trouble getting this. I can't play this, I can't do it.'

He actually walked out on this song?

Oh, yeah. It was a case of sticks-down halfway through. The cymbals were still swinging, and he's saying, 'Look, I'm off. I've got to go.' He couldn't really explain why, but he was getting a lot of pressure from his brand-new Australian wife, who was pregnant and didn't want to live on a shitty brand-new estate where the rooms were so tiny that they had to put the bedroom furniture out on the landing!

They put a double bed in the room, and they had about six inches to walk around the edge of the bed, to get out the room—and that was the master bedroom! She didn't want to live in all that mud and filth. You know, it was like she found herself living on the Somme! [*Laughs.*]

She'd flown over from Surfers Paradise, in Australia, and found herself living in a box on the Somme, and being pregnant as well! She may have even had the kid by then, I can't remember. And, understandably, he felt bad for her. He knew we weren't going to be touring anymore, so it was like, 'Oh, OK.'

How did you guys take that, when he made that announcement?
I felt a little stunned, but not as stunned as I should have been. I kind of knew something was coming—I knew that his head was in a funny place, because when I stopped the tour at the start of the US leg of the *English Settlement* tour, and flew home just to think what the hell I was I going to do with myself, he went to Australia to visit Donna. He was there for quite a while, while I was sat in the back garden writing the material that was going to go on *Mummer*, and I knew that something was amiss. Otherwise, he would have come back to England, and said, 'OK, what are we doing? Let's get into rehearsals! What new material have you got?' But there was absolutely no champing at the bit.

And he normally was like that?
Well, he'd be keen. He'd usually take himself off to go on holiday while you were writing an album, or he'd go work on a building site, or hang around with his friends drinking, or all three. But with this one, he just shot off to Australia, and was obviously soaking up the sun and the 6X—sorry, the 4X—over there.*

[*Laughs.*] Right. The 6X is where you are, right?
6X is where I am, yeah. They can only afford 4Xs. [*Laughs.*] So, I sensed something was wrong, you know. And then he made a big palaver of not being able to grasp this new material, which was too poncey for him.

---

* 6X is the famous ale produced by Wadsworth's Brewery of Devizes, near Swindon. Castlemaine XXXX (pronounced 'Four X') is a brand of lager originating in Brisbane, Australia.

I suppose you had the usual band meeting, where you discussed what was going to happen—did you decide at that point that you didn't want to bring a permanent fourth member into the band?

Yeah, it was a case of, 'Well, we don't know where our next dinner's coming from, because we're not on tour now.' We were still paying ourselves quite a small amount, and to put somebody else on the wage roll when you didn't quite know what your future's going to be might have been a crazy move. So, it was a case of, 'Let's get somebody in who's a good drummer, and they don't have to be permanently waged.'

We were rehearsing in the scenery store of the Mechanics' Institute, which was where the railway workers would go for their entertainment. There's a beautiful theatre up there—or it *was* beautiful. It's probably completely derelict by now. There were rooms where you could play cards, and a library. Basically, it was kind of a Victorian entertainment complex.

And the scenery store was … ?

The scenery store was on one side of the stage of the theatre—it was where they slid and stored all the scenery. We rehearsed the whole album there.

That's not where you did the videos for the songs from that album, is it? That space looked tiny and atmospheric.

Actually, that's about 100 yards away from where we rehearsed. It's one of the original railway cottages. When Brunel drove the railway from London to Bristol, he found that the trains ran out of everything by the time they reached Swindon. So it was a case of, 'Well, we better put facilities here so they can re-coal and water, and we better have repair stuff here, and we might as well have a station here. And if we're repairing trains, you know, we might as well put in factories, so we can build them as well.'

It was the practicality of trains running out of things, and people needing to get off and have a piss, and people needing to get a sandwich—do you know what I mean?

It was just one of those natural progressions. [*Dreamy voice*] 'By the time we got to Swindon.' And Joni Mitchell never even came here, as far as I know! She never went to Woodstock, either! Wrote that song in a hotel room. Cha! My hippie dreams were shattered.

So, yeah, the little piece of video thing for the *Play At Home* series on Channel 4—the inside scenes were filmed in one of the original railway worker's houses, which were built of stone that was taken from the tunnel called the Box Tunnel—they had to cut through the hill to get to Bath, on the way to Bristol. So, instead of throwing the stone away, they used it to build the workers' houses, in the back of the line in Swindon.

Back to the drumming pattern, which you said was the genesis of the song—you started with that and an acoustic guitar?
Yeah, I found that little kind of drone-y riff, the [*sings pattern*]—the one you hear in the verse. And I had this little cyclical drum pattern going around, talking to it, and that was all the conversation needed, really.

And then we were talking about the bridge and its feel—why did you go in that direction?
I just wanted to get away from the key. The song's in E, basically, and in the middle section I lifted it up to something like F-sharp, and used open strings, so you still have the droning thing, but it kind of went into a—I don't know, it just fell into more of a jazz place. I don't know why that would be—maybe it's the choice of chords or the accents in it, but it kind of naturally felt like it wanted to do that, so rather than say, 'I'm going to stay on the farm here, stay rustic', it just wanted to swing a little bit more in that section.

Was this an instance where Pete Phipps's ability to play that kind of feel further inspired you?
Oh, Pete Phipps was great. I think it was Dave who suggested him, because, after being in the Glitter Band, Pete Phipps had drummed in a band called Random Hold. They'd supported us on an English tour, so we'd be sort of staggering down in these cheap hotels, having hungover breakfasts with Pete Phipps and the rest of Random Hold, and then watching them occasionally in the evening, thinking, 'Ooh, he's a good drummer, isn't he? Make a mental note of that.' And then Dave said, when Terry left, 'I wonder if we can get Pete Phipps's phone number—track him down, and ask him to come along.'

He was perfect. I was a little worried that he was just going to be thump-crunch—you know, more like the Glitter Band and the more brutal side of Random Hold's thing—but he also had a great light touch. He could really click into a light, jazzy feel, which he showed on things like 'Ladybird'.

Let's talk about the bass on this song a bit.

In the choruses, I asked Colin, 'Can you get any more *cow* out of your bass?'

Cow?!

Yeah, in the chorus, where it goes 'Shilling for the fellow who milks the herd,' you have this [*imitates bass part*]—it 'moos'.

Well, that's appropriate for the subject matter, right?

It's perfect! We wanted someone to think, 'Wow, what are they doing there? They're squeezing a heifer there. Squeezing a Jersey.' No, it's really the bass, trying to get it to sound more like a cow. It's all down to the stage-setting, you know? You've got to have the correct scenery. I also really like that counter line he does at the end of the chorus, under the 'love on a farmboy's wages' lyric.

Was that something you came up with and asked him to play, or did he come up with it on his own?

I think he came up with that. It's very pleasant. I also like the way the song appears to change key as it moves into the chorus, but it actually just goes to the root key of the verse.

As far as guitars go, you and Dave are both playing acoustic.

Yep, we start on acoustic. And when I start singing, I'm trying to sing like a French horn. I know that sounds a weird thing to say.

No, given the way you fade-in your voice, it makes total sense.

It sounds more English, and more out-in-the-field, you know. Then, as the song progresses into the 'we will borrow your father's carriage' part, Dave adds an electric guitar, too, underpinning things. And I think there also may be ersatz French horn in here—Dave on the Prophet V.

As you move into the bridge, there's more percussion: wood block, cymbal bells …

The sheep have entered the picture! [*Laughs.*] There's a wood block, and I think there's a cowbell in there as well.

And you've got a vibraslap in there!

Of course, everyone's vertebrae sound like one of those. If you're going to 'do vertebrae', you've got to have a vibraslap. The section after the 'breaking my back' line, that's actually the verse pattern, using the same open and closed notes, but the closed notes have been moved up a tone, so the open notes are slightly dissonant against them, if you see what I mean.

I do. Lyrically, this is one of your 'Holy shit, I'm not going to make enough money to support my family' songs.
You know, I still worry about that. It's still a big threat for me. [*Laughs.*] I'm obviously bitter about not getting the money I thought I ought to deserve or something. I look around, and I see people like Elvis Costello, or other contemporaries, and I think, 'Jesus, they're so much richer than I am!' You know, 'I wrote songs as good as he did!' I can say that, not facetiously or boastfully. I think I've written songs as good as Elvis.

And from what I've read in interviews with him, I think he thinks that, too. He admires your songwriting.
But when I see him on the *Sunday Times* Rich List …*

Oh my. I didn't realise he was that wealthy.
Oh yeah. I don't know, I think his last count was something like twenty million. But I never made the money, or a fraction of the money, in this game that I thought I would. And I guess that, even by that age, I was thinking, 'Grrr, grrr.'

This is really the first articulation by you of that, I think. I can't think of any earlier songs where the theme is quite so obvious—maybe 'Paper And Iron', but even that is almost as much of a socialist statement as anything else.
Yeah, and it's also about the pride of working—and the fact that my dad would never let me know how much he made. I don't think he ever let my mother know, either! You know, he gave her x-amount per week, and there was no conversation about it. But, needless to say, I've never really worked on a farm. The nearest I've ever been to it is helping my father out a few times collecting milk churns from farms. He used to work for Latton Creamery,† I

---

* An annual survey of Britain's wealthiest individuals.
† Latton is a village nine miles north of Swindon.

think, and go around with a truck to pick up these full or empty milk churns from farms. I'd help him do that occasionally. It was tough work, but I have never been a farmboy. It's merely allegorical.

There's something about that allegory that seems to draw you, though. When we talked about 'Senses Working Overtime', you mentioned that you were channelling medieval farmers in that one.
Yeah, well, you write these little playlets, or something. It's the same as if you were writing a script or a book. You put yourself in the place, and if you can draw on any of your experiences—I mean, I *did* paint pictures, I *did* carve wood, and the parents of my girlfriend, who then became my wife, *did* tell me I was no good. In fact, they used to call me a 'jumped-up, tuppenny, ha'penny ticket writer'!

Really?
They probably called me a lot worse when the doors were closed.

Undoubtedly. What is the significance of that lovely phrase?
My last job I had, before I gave it up to be a professional musician, was painting posters in a department store.* That was known at the time as being a ticket writer. So I was a jumped-up, tuppenny, ha'penny ticket writer. And I think her father called me that because *he* was the owner of a professional sign company.†

Oh, I see. Charming. He was a *full-fledged* ticket writer—a pound-note ticket writer.
Yeah, exactly! [*Laughs.*] And he certainly could not have jumped up, because he was *vast* and *round*.

One of the reasons I love these lyrics is that there's the whole push and pull between the obvious angst of feeling that you don't have enough resources to support your wife, but then there's the very beautiful yearning of, 'We will borrow your father's carriage / We will drink and prepare for marriage.' You know, you can feel the warmth and the love there. It

---

* Andy worked at McIlroys department store in Regent Street, Swindon, now demolished and replaced by a branch of fashion chain H&M.
† Wyborn Signs.

provides a backdrop for the anxiety about finances, and the reality of the world.

[*Pauses.*] Yep.

[*Laughs.*] So I got it, eh?

That is a very 'Italian interview' question! That's the sort of thing they do—they spend a quarter of an hour, saying [*Italian accent*], 'And I feel like-a you are saying … the metaphor of the … the allegory and … the way you are expressing it'—and then there's a big gap after that, and all you can say is, 'Yep! Ya got it, Luigi.' They're notorious for those kinds of questions.

Thank you-a very much!

It's-a nice!

Well, what was the thought process as you were working out these lyrics? Did you try to do the same thing as you were doing musically—you were saying that you had the little stuttering guitar-and-drumbeat thing, and then you wanted to do something different for the bridge, to change things up. Do you think about this when you write lyrics? Do you also say, 'These lyrics are too flat, I need some dynamics'?

On this song, the first thing that fell out lyrically was me just gibbering idiotically over one of the guitar patterns. I do this a lot. I think the first actual lyric that came along was [*sings*], 'Shilling for the fellow who brings the sheep in,' because that sounded onomatopoeically like what I was playing on the guitar. 'Shilling for the fellow who milks the herrrrd'—you know, that was where we were saying, 'Oh yeah, we've got to get the bass to be part of the herd!' But the first line that fell out was 'Shilling for the fellow.' And that really is the tagline of the song. If the whole song was a film, it'd be the tagline on the poster.

So, the chorus came first, and then I think I found the verse.

You mean the lyrics?

I think musically as well.

Really? I thought you'd said you started with the verse pattern, with the drum pattern behind that.

Yeah, but now that I'm thinking about it, I think the first thing that came out—as I start to dig into my brain—was the 'Shilling for the fellow' section. *Then* it was the verse pattern. So you're going to have to go back and rap me on the knuckles! I've got it out of order there.

That's OK, it's the songwriter's prerogative. Let's talk about the single of this song. I remember buying this EP.
Ah, yes—the single for this song came out in a gatefold sleeve that looked like a wallet—and it really was my wallet! I came up with the design, and when I talked to Design Clinic* I said, 'Look, instead of putting lettering over the top of the photograph, why don't you actually go to one of those places that emboss leather goods, and just get the title embossed into my wallet?' Which they did, and they put a few bits and pieces in the wallet, to suggest I wasn't well off—there was an old ten-shilling note, which of course was defunct currency by then, and there was a photograph of some cheeky-looking girl—who everyone at the time thought was my wife, but instead was just a 1950s beauty who Design Clinic selected and slipped in the little clear holder in the wallet.

Of course they sent me the wallet back after the photo session, and I thought, 'Oh no, of course—now I've got this all over my wallet! If I go in the pub and take this out, people are going to think I'm a …'—you know, why would I have the name of my band embossed on my wallet? *And* the name of the latest single? So I had to buy a new wallet. [*Laughs.*]

The sacrifices you make for your art!
Exactly. That cost me a new wallet, that cover session did.

Interview conducted January 21 2007.

---

* Virgin's in-house design department. Rejected the name 'Virgin Design Clinic' for fear that it would be shortened to 'VD Clinic'.

DRUMMER

MOEBIUS MOOD / JUST KEEPS ON COMING
IN OEBIUS ~~BEBUS~~ / KEEPS ON DRUMMING
MOEBIUS INGUNS / JUST KEEP ~~ING~~ ON
WE'RE MICE ON A TREADMILL EATING
JUST EXCRETING

ROT AWAY WITH ME
MY FELLOWS
ROT AWAY WITH ME

FROM POLES NORTH WEST SOUTH AND
EAST

FEET BY

IN THIS DAY AND AGE
THERE'S NO SUCH THING AS
PRIVACY
I'LL TANTRUM, I'LL RAGE
IF ~~DAILY KEPT BACK~~ FROM ME
MY TOYS ARE TAKEN / I'LL UP
~~WE ~~ ~~WE TEENAGERS MISSED~~ THIS
~~WE~~ THE SIX MILLION DOLLAR MAN
WE HUNTERS KEEP ALL THE
DATA WE CAN
WE GUNS MAY BE FAKE
BUT WE FANTASIES REAL BY
REEL.
I'M STORING FACTS ABOUT YOU
EVERY MOVE EVERY OUNCE
I'M STORING FACTS ABOUT YOU
MY ~~HEART~~ IS IN THE CUPBOARD
WAITING TO POUNCE.

I STALK AND I HIDE
UNDER COVER AND UNDER
YOUR BED

ON TAPE AND ON SLIDE
I COLLECT WHAT YOU HAVE
DISCARDED

PICK UP TIPS FROM FLINT AND
007 JAMES BOND
WE HUNTERS USING ~~IN~~ SCIENCE
FROM NOW AND BEYOND
WE DISGUISE IS FAKE
BUT WE FANTASIES REAL BY
REEL.

REAL BY REEL

IN THIS SECRET TIME
INVADING ON OUR PRIVACY
UNKNOWING WE MIME
TO ~~SEE~~ ~~THE JOY OF~~ THE MINISTRY
WE'LL PLAY FOR
THEY CAN FILM YOU BED OR WHEN
YOU TAKE A BATH
THEY CAN TAPE EVERY CRY THEY
CAN TAPE EVERY LAUGH
THEY CAN STEAL YOUR SOUL ~~THEY~~
SO YOU WON'T KNOW WHAT'S
REAL

BY REEL
BUSY LITTLE BEES RECORDING
EVERYTHING YOU FEEL ON
REEL BY REEL

DOCUMENTED DOWN LIKE
RATS ,
THEY'LL GET YOUR ~~AS YOU~~ SQUEAL
~~EVERY~~

IN OUR HIDDEN TIME
IGNORING MAY HELP YOU TO
COPE
REHEARSING FOR CRIME
AS EXTRA'S IN GOVERNMENT
CINEMASCOPE

THEY CAN FILM YOU AT WORK
OR WHEN THEY LET YOU PLAY
THEY CAN TAPE WHAT YOU THINK
THEY CAN TAPE WHAT YOU SAY
THEY CAN BLURR YOUR I.D SO YOU
WON'T KNOW WHAT'S REAL

BY REEL

THIS WORLD OVER

SLEEVE IS PACK/PACKS OF POST CARDS FROM AROUND THE WORLD, FAMOUS CITIES BUT PHOTO IS ALL THE SAME PILE OF RUBBLE WITH DIFFERENT NAMES ON

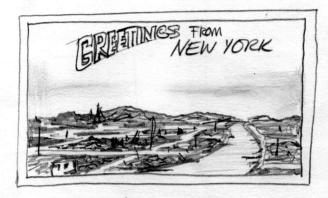

LONDON
NEW YORK
MOSCOW
PARIS
ROME
PEKING
BERLIN

MAYBE USE HIROSHIMA PHOTO WITH A LITTLE TOUCHING UP AND 'NICE' POSTCARD SKY ADDED.

PUSH ME

(PUSH ONCE)

NUCLEAR 'BUTTON' AS SLEEVE MOTIF/BADGE

ALL YOU PRETTY GIRLS

PORTHOLE CUT IN CARD SEA HORIZON PRINTED ON RECORD LABEL GIRLIE PICS ON CABIN WALL. (PLASTIC WINDOW?)

TROMPE D'OEUL (?) STYLE SAILORS CHEST WITH TATTOO OF BEAUTY. EMBOSSED OUT NIPPLE AND ST. CHRISTOPHER

XTC

ALL YOU

Pretty Girls

HAVE you got your master
RACE THE BIGGEST SON WHO'LL
~~strike~~ WHEN ~~strike~~
RAISE ~~HOLD THE TORCH~~ ~~F~~ FATHER
NOT SO MUCH A SON MORE OF
A STORMTROOPER ~~to~~ TO CARRY
ON HIS DADS CRUSADE
            H F

NOT SO MUCH A SON MORE OF
A STORMTROOPER TO ~~carry~~
~~on~~ WHEN DADS NOT HERE
HOLD THE
TORCH   H F

HAVE YOU GOT YOUNG MASTER CHARLIE
THE BOY WHO'S LIVING WELL BEYOND
HIS WORLDLY MEANS
            H F
SEE HIS PARENTS KILL THEMSELVES
WITH WORK TO KEEP THEIR
DANDY IN ITALIAN JEANS.
            H F

THE ~~BEATING~~ OF HEARTS.
~~DO YOU KNOW HOW YOU ARE~~
~~WOKEN~~

DO YOU KNOW WHAT NOISE
AWAKES YOU
EVERY MORNING FROM YOUR
BED ~~...~~
~~...~~
~~...~~ ~~TEAR~~
~~...~~

YOU HAVE HEARD
YOU HAVE HEARD THE LOUDEST
SOUND IN ~~...~~
                    TANKS
LOUDER THAN ~~...~~ ON
THE HIGHWAY
LOUDER THAN BOMBERS IN
FLIGHT
LOUDER THAN NOISE OF HATRED

THIS AND EVERY WORLD YOU
CAN ~~...~~ THINK OF

COMING FROM THE ~~FARTHEST~~
HILLSIDES
COMING FROM INSIDE YOUR HEAD

~~...~~ LEADING
~~...~~ US
~~...~~ FROM ~~...~~
DARKEST NIGHT
IS THE RHYTHM OF LOVE
POWERED ON BY
THE BEATING OF HEARTS

                    YOU MAY
DID YOU KNOW ~~FEEL~~ THIS
POWER   IT ALWAYS
DRUMMING ON ~~...~~ IN
~~LOUD~~ SCALS
NEVER TRY TO USE IT
BADLY
TUNES OF GOOD ARE ALL
IT PLAYS

YOU HAVE HEARD
YOU HAVE HEARD
THE LOUDEST SOUND IN THIS
AND EVERY WORLD YOU
WILL VISIT

~~...~~
LOUDER THAN...
        THORNS
~~...~~ OF DICTATORS
RATTLING SWORDS
~~CRACKING~~ OF RIFLES
SCREAMING WARLORDS

~~...~~
~~...~~ FOR
A HEART WITHOUT LOVE IS A
SONG WITH NO WORDS OR ~~...~~ A
TUNE TO WHICH NO ONE IS
LISTENING
                    GIVE
SO YOUR HEART MUST ~~...~~ LOVE
~~AND~~ YOU'LL FIND THAT YOU SHINE
~~THEN~~ AND
LIKE THE RAIN ON THE LEAVES
YOU'LL BE GLISTENING

(THE EVE~~RY~~DAY ~~STORY OF~~) SMALL TOWN

SMALL TOWN
SNORING ~~LIGHTS~~ UNDER BLANKETT
    WOKEN BY THE CLANK
    ITS JUST THE MILKMANS DAWN ROUND
SMALL TOWN
    HIDING UNDER COVERS
    THE LODGERS AND THE LOVERS
    ARE ASLEEP DOWN SMALL TOWN

    SHINY GREY/BLACK SNAKE OF BIKES
    HE SLITHERS
    BEARING IN THE MEN AND BOYS
    TO ~~WORK~~ WORK (POPULAR)
WE' ~~THEY~~ 'LL STAND IN ~~ALLOTMENT~~ LINES   OUR
    MAKING ALARM CLOCKS THAT'LL WAKE ~~THEIR~~ WIVES UP
    DONT ASK ~~THEM,~~ ~~THEY~~ HAVENT THE TIME
            US   WE
    ~~SO~~ WE'RE RACING THE HOOTER THAT'LL SIGNAL, LIFES UP!

    SMALL TOWN
    CROUCHING IN THE VALLEY
    WOKEN BY THE SALLY
    ARMY SUNDAY ~~WEEK~~ ROUND   DID YOU HAVE TO
    SMALL TOWN   MARCH TOILET
    COUGHING IN THE ~~BATHROOM~~   WHO ON ~~EARTH~~ ~~COULD~~ SPOIL IT
    ~~DIDNT WE HAVE A LAUGH~~
    ~~ON FRIDAY NIGHT ROUND SMALL TOWN~~   ~~LEVEL~~ ~~THEY~~ PULL DOWN SMALL TOWN
                                        WORDS   YOU

    IF ITS ALL THE SAME TO YOU
    MRS. PROGRESS
    THINK I'LL DRINK MY OXO UP
    AND GET AWAY
    ITS NOT THAT YOUR REPULSIVE TO ~~ME~~ SEE
    IN YOUR BRAND NEW CATALOGUE ~~RAYON~~ NYLON NIGHTIE
    YOUR TOO FAST FOR LITTLE OLD ME
    NEXT YOU'D BE TELLING ME ITS 1990
                I'VE
    AND, ~~I'VE~~ LIVED HERE FOR A THOUSAND YEARS OR MAYBE MORE
    AND, I'VE ~~SHELTERED~~ ALL THE CHILDREN WHO HAVE FOUGHT MY WARS
          SHELTERED
    AND AT A PAYMENT THEY MAKE LOVE IN ME
    IN BYCYCLE SHEDS
    ~~AND~~ AND SQUEAKY OLD BEDS
    INSIDE OF THEIR HEADS
    AS ~~THE~~ TORIES AND REDS
    AS SINGLES AND WEDS
    AND THATS HOW I'M FED

MAYOR LOVING

the

ARMBANDS

MILITARY EQUIPMENT

BADGES

PLAYING CARD PACK OF ONLY HEARTS SUITE

FLAGS/BANNERS.

PRODUCT
DRINKS
SOAP POWDER
BOOKS

POPPY

WORLD FLAGS

GREAT BRITAIN

FRANCE

JAPAN

UNITED STATES OF AMERICA

USSR

ISRAEL

LONDON TRANSPORT

FROM POOLS OF XYLOPHONE CLEAR
FROM CAVES OF MEMORY
I CALL ~~THE~~ CHILDREN ~~GATHERED~~ AT HEART
THAT WE ONCE USED TO BE
FULL REIN
~~GIVEN~~ IN FOAMING SEA HORSE HERD

TO GLIMPSE IN MIRROR ~~TIGHTEST~~ HAND HELD
~~FOR~~ ~~SHIMMER SHELL~~ ~~CHEST~~ IN CATHEDRAL SHELLS
A SIGHT AS NEW AS NEWBORN
~~OR~~ OLD AS SOLOMONS WELLS

FREED TO ROAR AND ROLL ~~IN~~ ~~THE OCEAN~~ ATLANTIC WILD
GROWN THROUGH CHILD
SINCE MERMAID
SMILED

DEAR GOD, HOPE YOU GOT THE LETTER AND...
I PRAY YOU CAN MAKE IT BETTER DOWN HERE
I DONT MEAN A BIG REDUCTION IN THE PRICE OF BEER
ALL THE PEOPLE THAT YOU MADE IN YOUR IMAGE
SEE THEM STARVIN ~~IN THE STREET~~ ON THEIR FEET
'CAUSE THEY DONT GET ENOUGH TO EAT FROM
GOD, I CANT BELIEVE IN YOU

DEAR GOD SORRY TO DISTURB YOU BUT, I FEEL THAT I SHOULD
~~BE~~ ~~THAT THIS~~ BE HEARD LOUD AND CLEAR
WE ALL NEED A BIG REDUCTION IN AMOUNT OF TEARS
AND ALL THE PEOPLE THAT YOU MADE IN YOUR IMAGE
SEE THEM FIGHTING IN THE STREET
'CAUSE THEY CANT MAKE OPINIONS MEET ON
GOD, I CANT BELIEVE IN YOU

YOU SURE WORK IN A REAL MYSTIC WAY
WHAT USE DO YOU HAVE
FOR THOSE WHO DIE YOUNG?
YOU SURE WORK IN A SADISTIC WAY
NO PERSONAL APPEARANCE
~~YOUR~~ ~~VOICE~~ ~~GAME~~ JUST GUESSING GAMES

T ABOUT
~~BANG~~ BY ~~LITTLE AID~~ PRIESTS PREPARED TO MURDER
~~TO~~ SPREAD YOUR NAME?

= TO

URGH!

YOU MAKE DISEASE   DON'T KNOW IF YOU'VE NOTICED BUT
THE DIAMOND BLUE   YOUR NAMES ON A LOT IN ~~THAT~~ BOOK
                                                          THIS
YOU MAKE MANKIND

~~SING SURE MADE YOU~~ AFTER WE MADE YOU

THE DEVIL TOO!   OUT.

2 GOD   HOPE YOU GOT THE LETTER AND
RAY YOU ~~CAN~~ ~~BREAK~~ YOUR FETTERS AND CHAINS
E BACK ~~SOME OF OUR~~ ~~GUILT AND~~ GIVE A LITTLE BRAINS
                SUPERSTITION

AN THE PEOPLE THAT YOU MADE IN YOUR IMAGE
ETWEEN RECITING PSALMS
ARE BUSY STOCKING UP THE BOMBS FOR GOD
                PLEASE FORGIVE ME TYPING THIS
2 GOD ~~SORRY TO DISTURB YOU BUT~~ HYPE
E YOU EVER READ THE ~~BLURB~~ IN YOUR BOOK
CRAZY HUMANS WROTE IT YOU SHOULD TAKE A LOOK
— AU THE PEOPLE THAT YOU MADE IN YOUR IMAGE
U ~~BELIEVING~~ BELIEVING THAT JUNK IS TRUE
U ? KNOW IT AINT AND SO DO YOU
AN GOD, CANT BELIEVE IN, CANT BELIEVE IN

T   BELIEVE IN HEAVEN AND HELL
SAINTS NO SINNERS NO DEVIL AS WELL
PEARLY GATES, NO THORNY CROWN
R ALWAYS LETTING US HUMANS DOWN
E WARS YOU BRING THE BABES YOU DROWN
THE LOST AT SEA AND NEVER FOUND
M ITS THE SAME THE WHOLE WORLD ROUND
E HURT I SEE HELPS TO CONFOUND
T FATHER SON AND HOLY GHOST
JUST SOMEBODY'S UNHOLY HOAX
M IF YOUR UP THERE YOU'D PERCIEVE
T MY HEARTS HERE UPON MY SLEEVE
THERES ONE THING I DONT BELIEVE IN
    YOU
R GOD.

GRASS
MEETING PLACE
ANOTHER SATELLITE
SUMMERS CAULDRON
BIG DAY
EARN ENOUGH FOR US

① GRASS

XTC·GRASS

GREEN SLEEVE WITH DEBOSSED IN WORDS IN LIGHTER/SOIL COLOUR, AS IF WORN IN GRASS.

② GRASS

VERY WELL PHOTOGRAPHED CLOSE UP OF FEMALE (REVERSE) MALE PUBIC AREA INTERTHREAD WITH SMALL WEEDS/FLOWERS, OR DAISY CHAIN

③ SUMMERS CAULDRON

CLEAR PLASTIC BAGS WITH WORDS BEING DRAGGED INTO CENTRE HOLE OF DISC. LABEL IS COLOURED LIQUID SPIRALLING DOWN HOLE, WITH FLOWERS DROPPED IN.

④ ANOTHER SATELLITE

CLEAR BAG WITH NIGHT SKY BACK CARD. PICTURE DISC OF EARTH IN CENTRE AND SPUTNIK. ALL VISIBLE TITLE COULD BE ON MOON STICKER ON OUTER.

ALBUM TITLE :—

SKYLARKING
ALL DAY LIFE
SUMMERGOOD
RITE
RITE THINGS
LEFTOVER RITES
PINK THINGS SING

⑤ BIG DAY

XTC
BIG
DAY

DRAMATIC LIGHTING MAN IN SUIT BOUND AND HOOD OVER HEAD. BLACK AND WHITE PHOTO BUT TARGET/HEART PINNED ON BRIGHT RED.

⑥ GRASS

XTC
GRASS

PAIR OF WHITE JEANS LABEL ON BACK IS XTC. GRASS. JEANS CLEAN EXCEPT FOR GRASS STAINS ON SEAT

⑦ GRASS

GRASS

XTC

LEAVE LETTERS ON PATCH OF GRASS OVERNIGHT THEN 2 DAYS/ NEXT DAY PHOTOGRAPH WHERE GRASS HAS YELLOWED.

MAYOR OF SIMPLETON

THE CIRCUS IS ~~STATE~~ SAD
WITH ITS ACROBATS AND JUGGLERS
BUT THE CIRCUS OF ~~THE~~ HEART
IS THE ONE ~~THAT~~ THAT HIRES US ~~AS~~ CLOWNS   FEEL OR
~~AS BLACK AND FUN THINGS~~ YOU THINK OF ME AS JUST A FUN-THING
~~BY THE KNOW ONE THING~~ I DON'T KNOW MUCH BUT ~~TO~~ TELL YOU ONE
I'M MAY BE NOT AS BRIGHT AS THE RISING SUN 'CAN   THING
OF WORLDLY MATTERS I KNOW NONE
AND I MAY BE THE MAYOR OF SIMPLETON
BUT I KNOW I LOVE YOU

I MAY NOT HAVE MUCH OF A BIG HIT SONG
MY ARMS AND LEGS ARE TO SKINNY AND LONG
AND I MAY BE THE MAYOR OF SIMPLETON
BUT I KNOW I LOVE YOU

I HAD ~~MY~~ MY BOOK FUL OF SEA
~~HAD A CLUMP OF STING~~ HELD IN MY ~~FEW FEATHERS~~ HAND
I CRIED YOU INTO MY EYES   SCHOOLBOY
WHEN YOU RAN THROUGH MY HANDS

ALL THOSE WAVES TO TUCK ME IN

LITTLE LIGHTHOUSE

          A LITTLE
SHE'S ~~A LITTLE IF~~ LIGHTHOUSE
WHEN SHE OPENS UP HER HUGE EYES
AND ~~THEN~~ STREAMS OF DIAMONDS SHOOT OUT
'TILL WE'RE WADING ~~OFF THE~~ WAIST DEEP
IN ~~HER~~ HER BRILLIANT LOVE

SHE'S A LITTLE LIGHTHOUSE
WHEN SHE OPENS UP HER RED MOUTH
AND ~~AU GER~~ GOLD WORD RIBBONS ROPE AND RODEO
~~AU~~ THE DARK CLOUDS ~~LEAVE THE SCENE~~ ABOVE
          IN BOUQUET

HIGHER AND HIGHER
DARING AND DRIVING DEEP UP INTO THE WILLING BLUE BLANKET BEYOND
DENTIST THE YAWNING SKY
NEEDLE

IM FLOATING OVER CHALK HILLS
OLDER THAN THE MATRON MOON
IM FLOATING OVER CHALK HILLS
THE STRANGE THING IS IM HAVE NO BALLOON
WHEN I FEEL LIKE IM GETTING HIGHER
OVER EVERY TREE AND SPIRE THEN
CHALK HILLS OF ENGLAND ANCHOR MY FEET
CHALK HILLS OF ENGLAND BRING ME BACK TO BED
FROM ERMIN STREET.

CHALK HILLS AND CHILDREN

IM FLOATING OVER STRANGE LANDS MOON
IM FLOATING OVER STRANGE LANDS   THE SHOWBIZ DEEP
STRANGER STILL NO BALLOON   ITS A SCULLETS   MOON
THEN THERE   SEQUINS SHOWBIZ

BUT IM GETTING HIGHER FICKLE   'TIL THE...
WAFTED UP BY TAMES FIRE
CHALK HILLS AND CHILDREN ANCHOR MY FEET
CHALK HILLS AND CHILDREN ME TO EARTH
ETERNALLY EVER ERMINE STREET BRINGING BACK

                    TO KNOW   / EVEN I NEVER KNOW WHERE
     WHEN MY EYES ARE CLOSED   I GO WHEN MY EYES ARE CLOSED

IM SKATING OVER THIN ICE   CHALK HILLS AND CHILDREN
UPON BLUNTED BLADES OF METAL SOFT   ODDLY COMPLEAT
IM SKATING OVER THIN ICE
NONESUCH NET HOLDS ME ALOFT
     WHILE SOME

BUT IM GETTING HIGHER
LIFTED UP ON LUCKS CIRCUS WIRE 'TIL THE
CHALK HILLS AND CHILDREN ANCHOR MY FEET
CHALK HILLS AND CHILDREN BRINGING ME BACK TO EARTH
ESSENTIAL KISS OF FAMILY SWEET
     SOUL AND
EVEN I NEVER KNOW WHERE I GO
WHEN MY EYES ARE CLOSED
EVEN I NEVER SPIED THAT THE SCENE WAS ACTED
EVEN I NEVER KNEW THIS IS WHAT I'D BE
EVEN EYES NEVER MEAN THAT YOURE SURE TO SEE
STILL IM GETTING HIGHER
ROLLING UP ON THREE EMPTY TYRES TIL THE
IM SOARING OVER CROWDS
 CANNONBALL IT SEEMS
IM ROARING OVER INISHED CROWDS
PROPELLED UP HERE FROM LONG DEAD DREAMS
STILL IM GETTING HIGHER
ICARUS REGRETS AND RETIRES ... PUZZLED

BUBBLEGUM   ELBOWS - ESQUE

LOLLY (SUCK IT AND SEE)

I'VE GOT A GIRL CALLED LOLLY
A MICRO MINI SKIRTED DOLLY
SO I CALL HER ON THE TELEPHONE
AND ~~CALLED IT~~ I ASK HER IF SHES ALL ALONE
THEN I TELL HER THAT I KNOW A GAME FOR TWO TO PLAY

LOLLY, SUCK IT AND SEE
SEE IF YOU CAN MAKE IT CHANGE ITS COLOUR FOR ME
LOLLY. "   "   "   "
SEE IF YOU ...   "   "   "   ..

I'VE GOT A GIRL CALLED LOLY HER
WE GO OUT WALKING WITH ~~MY~~ BROLLY
RUN FOR SHELTER WHEN THE RAIN COMES DOWN
HOLD HER TIGHT WITH NO ONE ELSE AROUND
THEN I TELL HER THAT I KNOW A GAME FOR TWO TO PLAY

LOLLY . . . . .

LOLLY LOLLY
GET YOUR HANDS AROUND THE STRIPEY STICK
LOLLY LOLLY
TASTES SO GOOD THAT YOU JUST HAVE TO LICK . . .

LOLLY . . . . —

ITS ALL IN YOUR IN YOUR BACKYARD
UNDER CANOPY OF AIR   WHEN ITS DRAWN
THE GRASS IS GREENER   WITH LOVING CARE
ALWAYS

RIVER OF ORCHIDS WINDING MY WAY
WANT TO WALK INTO LONDON ON MY HANDS ONE DAY
RIVER OF ORCHIDS READS OVER GROWS
WANT TO WALK INTO LONDON SMELLING LIKE A PECKHAM ROSE

I HEARD THE DANDELIONS ROAR IN
PICCADILLY CIRCUS

75

YOUR DOOR
YOUR WINDOWS
YOUR ATTIC FULL OF PAINTINGS

ROOK ROOK
AND ~~SPEAK~~ FROM ~~IN~~ YOUR BOOK
WHO MURDERS WHO AND WHERE IS THE TREASURE HID?
CROW CROW
SPILL ALL YOU KNOW
IS ~~THAT~~ MY NAME ~~AND~~ ON THE BELL?
   THAT

ROOK ROOK
E~~XPLAIN~~ IN THE BROOK   CAN BE
IF THERE'S A ~~TREASURE~~ ALL I ~~A~~ PART OF IT
           SECRET   BEFORE I'LL LET ~~YOU~~ GO, SAY
CROW CROW
O PLEASE WAIT, DON'T GO ~~HAVE TO KNOW~~
IS ~~CLEAR~~ MY NAME ~~AND~~ ON THE BELL?
     THAT

~~BEAT YOUR WAXEN WINGS~~
~~SOAR UP HIGH 'BOVE THE WASHING LINES~~
~~CHIMNEYS WHISPER YOUR FOUL CONFESSIONS~~

           SEE THE SEMAPHORE ~~OF~~ FROM THE
                                  WASHING LINES
SOAR UP HIGH ~~ABOVE~~ ~~BARKING SHEETS~~
~~ON THEIR WASHING LINES~~
BREAK THE CODE OF ~~THE~~ THE WHISPERING
CHIMNEYS AND TRAFFIC SIGNS
        WHATS THE MESSAGE THATS
~~THERE'S SOMETHING~~ WRITTEN UNDER
THE BASE OF CLOUDS
PLANT ETERNAL, ~~HELP US~~ I KNOW YOU KNOW
SO ~~BUT~~ DONT BLURT OUT LOUD

ROOK ROOK
BY HOOK OR MY CROOK
I'LL MAKE YOU TELL ME
WHAT THIS WHOLE THING'S ABOUT
CROW CROW
WHY CANT YOU SHOW
IF THAT'S MY NAME ON THE BELL

            ON THE WINGS OF NIGHT
~~FAST~~ ASLEEP AND
~~I HAVE DREAMS WHERE~~ I'M FLYING ~~TOO~~
ABOVE ~~HILL~~ FIELD AND ~~TOWN~~ STREAM
MY HEAD BURSTING WITH KNOWLEDGE
'TILL I WAKE ~~AND~~ ~~COME~~ ~~DOWN~~ FROM THE DREAM
          THEN
IF I DIE AND I FIND THAT I HAD A SOUL
INSIDE THAT
PROMISE ME YOU'LL TAKE IT UP ON ITS FINAL
                                    RIDE.

NO MORE WAR
CLEAN THE SMOKE
HELP THE POOR
HUMANOSAURUS.

THE LAST BALLOON

THE LAST BALLOON IS LEAVING
THE LAST BALLOON FROM ~~THERE~~ FEAR
THE LAST BALLOON IS LEAVING
~~AWAY FROM~~ FROM SHAME AND FEAR
AWAY ~~FROM~~ ~~THE WEIGHT OF FEAR~~

FORM THAT LINE RIGHT HERE
LINE UP AND DRY YOUR TEAR

CLIMB ABOARD CLIMB ~~ABOARD~~ ABOARD YOU MENFOLK
~~BUT~~ YOU WON'T NEED ~~DON'T BRING~~ ANY GUNS OR KNIVES
CLIMB ABOARD CLIMB ABOARD YOU MENFOLK
THEY BELONG IN YOUR ~~FORMER~~ LIVES — DROP ~~THEM~~ ALL
~~PAST LIVES~~
FORMER

WHEN THE WIND OF CIRCUMSTANCE
BLOWS ME OFF MY COURSE

SAFE HARBOUR

THE LAST BALLOON IS LEAVING
THE LAST BALLOON OF ALL
THE LAST BALLOON IS LEAVING
DISCARD ~~UNDRESS, DISCARD,~~ LET FALL
UNDRESS

CLIMB ABOARD CLIMB ABOARD YOU WOMEN
LEAVE BEHIND YOUR GEMS AND FURS
CLIMB ABOARD CLIMB ABOARD YOU WOMEN
THEY BELONG TO ~~THE~~ BAD OLD YEARS
DROP ~~THEM~~ ALL

CLIMB ABOARD, CLIMB ABOARD YOU CHILDREN
MOVE YOU ~~MUST MOVE~~ WHILE YOU'RE FLEET AND FAST
ALOFT CLIMB ABOARD, CLIMB ABOARD YOU CHILDREN
WE'RE WEIGHED DOWN BY OUR EVIL PAST

DROP US ALL
'''
FREE YOUR HANDS ~~AND HEAD~~
DROP US ALL
'' ''
... LIKE SO MUCH SAND.

THE LAST BALLOON IS LEAVING
THE LAST BALLOON THEY'LL FLY
THE LAST BALLOON IS LEAVING
AND WE ~~DROP~~ QUALIFY

≥119

XTC + APPLE VENUS VOLUME 2

XTC + APPLE VENUS VOLUME 2

XTC + APPLE VENUS VOLUME 2

CHAPTER 16

SEAGULLS SCREAMING KISS HER, KISS HER

FROM *THE BIG EXPRESS*, OCTOBER 1984

Let's talk about yet another one of my favourite songs of yours, 'Seagulls Screaming Kiss Her, Kiss Her'. First thing I've got to do is ask you a question that a friend of mine posed. He's an avid bird watcher and protector.

[*Laughs.*] You're not going to ask me what sort of seagull it is?

No! He wants to know about the role of bird imagery in your music— there seems to be quite a bit of it, and he wants to know why that is. You know, you have *Skylarking*, you have 'Rook', you have this song …

They're one of those forms of life that are just everywhere. You know, I sit in my kitchen, and they're wandering around on the skylights. Or I'm sat here at the computer, and four or five feet away, every ten minutes, there's a blackbird with a mouthful of worms flying into the nest right next to the window and feeding its young.

One of the most appealing sounds is birdsong. They're all over my demos, because the Shed is not soundproofed!* You can't hear them because of the other sounds, but if you isolate the tracks you can hear them.

Do birds represent any particular thing to you? Do they represent freedom, or … ?

Well, they represent a lot of things. They represent dreams, because you imagine yourself as a bird flying over the town, for instance. Or being carried up by a bird in some way—that's like 'Rook', you know. Or *Skylarking*, the skylark—which is almost extinct now in England—is such a representation of the freedom and joy of a summer's day out in the fields. It was also a navy

---

* Andy has been recording in a small wooden shed in his back garden since 1990, having been forced out of his attic studio when the floor beneath it collapsed.

term for messing about in the rigging—or 'frigging in the rigging', as the song would have it! If I was messing around, my father, an ex-sailor, would say to me, 'Hey, cut out your skylarking!' So, that's why that album was called *Skylarking*—it's just us messing around.

And there's 'Liarbird', of course.

It's a lyrebird, yep. It's spelled differently—that's the pun, arf, arf: Cheap Puns R Us. So yeah, there's quite a bit of bird imagery. Maybe my mother was frightened by an archaeopteryx when I was in the womb!

Actually, when I was a kid there used to be a woman who lived next door to us who was so petrified of feathers that if a bird came near her, or entered her garden when she was hanging out the washing, she would run screaming. If you showed her a feather, she would just freak right out, she had such a bird phobia.

Was it the birds, or the feathers?

I was too young to ask her. I was five or six, you know.

You were having too much fun torturing her, running up to her with feathers.

I was just puzzled! She'd scream and throw her washing basket down and run away if a blackbird came. I thought, 'What's she afraid of? Is she afraid it's going to peck off her nose, like in the nursery rhyme?'

Exactly. Maybe she'd been watching too much Alfred Hitchcock, or reading too much Du Maurier.*

[*Laughs.*] Yeah. Maybe it makes sense—you know, birds *are* the last surviving relatives of the dinosaurs. Pluck all those feathers off, and you've got a little dinosaur there.

So yeah, there's quite a bit of bird imagery. But then again, there's lots of sea imagery. And *this* is a song where they come together. In fact [*German mad-scientist voice*], let me pull out my notes, Herr Bernhardt!

I've just got a load of random stuff written here, so I'll just dive in. This was my first keyboard composition *using more than one figure at the same time.*

---

* Daphne Du Maurier was the author of 'The Birds', a short story in which flocks of birds attack a village, subsequently made into a film by Alfred Hitchcock.

[*Laughs.*] I know that sounds laughable, but before then I'd had written a few things on keyboard, but I'd only done them one note at a time.

Such as … ?
'Bushman President'.* You know, it was all done on a monophonic instrument, with *the index finger.* Or 'Somnambulist'.† That was all monophonic, single lines.

So, your more atmospheric, avant-garde stuff.
Well, I guess our early keyboard stuff. If it was me writing it, it had to be monophonic, because I couldn't get the concept of the two hands obeying, you know. It was too much to think about, for some reason.

For example, there's that crazy keyboard part during the bridge of 'No Language In Our Lungs'—was that something you wrote? I'd always assumed that it was something that Dave had added to the arrangement, given that he was the keyboard player.
I can't remember how it came up. We would talk about a lot of stuff in rehearsals, and say, 'Well, we need something to sort of lift that piece there—a little counter-melody, or whatever.' We always had this little monophonic Korg keyboard standing by—it was the 'goofy noise generator', you know. I think Colin's still got it, actually. It's a lovely little thing, a real museum piece now. And then later on, we treated ourselves to a Prophet-5, which could play *five notes* at the same time!

But, at some point, Dave said, 'Look, we've got to get a Mellotron for *Mummer.*' He noticed that there was one was for sale, so we bought it. You can hear it all over that album.

Oh, sure, yeah. 'Deliver Us From The Elements' …
And 'Human Alchemy'. It's all over. We can't wait to get psychedelic, basically. And the Mellotron *is* the psychedelic sound machine.

It's interesting to hear you say that, because on these two albums—*Mummer* and *Big Express*—I thought you guys were creating a new niche that I called 'prog-pop'. What you guys saw as psychedelic elements, I saw

---

* Part of the 'Homo Safari' series and a B-side to *Making Plans For Nigel.*
† B-side to the US version of the 'Ten Feet Tall' single.

as progressive, because the Mellotron is all over early Genesis and Yes and King Crimson, for example. I guess it all depends on your point of view.
Yeah, the proggers tended to have longer, more involved things, with more passages in them, whereas I was still very much a fan of the succinct pop format. It's like a tennis court, or something. 'We're going to play tennis, and it's going to be on that-sized court.' We could go to a football field, or an airfield, but that might be a bit stupid, because it would break the tension of the game, which has to do with the size of the place you're in.

Right. It increases your focus.
Absolutely. That's why table tennis is so damn manic! So yeah, we had a Mellotron, and we finished the *Mummer* album, and I said, 'Bagsy the Mellotron!' Do you have that phrase in America?

No. 'Bagsy'?
Yeah. That means, 'I'd like that! Gimme that.'

Oh, so like, 'Dibs!'
Yeah. 'I got first dibs on the Mellotron.' I had a house then—in fact, the house I'm in now. So, I wrestled the bloody thing up the stairs …

Don't tell me you got that in your attic!
No, not in the attic! It went in the back bedroom, which was empty at the time. It just had one little washbasin in the corner, on which the tap dripped all the time. I remember coming up with 'Seagulls' in that back bedroom, with the Mellotron on the bare floorboards and the old dripping basin going there.

I found the sounds so inspiring. I don't know if you know, but with a Mellotron, you can have three sounds on one tape bank at the same time. It was the old American three-track format, which was the format that Phil Spector did a lot of his recordings on. The Mellotron was originally an American idea—I think it was called a Chamberlin in the States. Todd Rundgren actually had one full of dead mice.[*]

[*Dramatic voice*] He killed them with his music!
He bored them to death! He sarcastic'd them to death! They couldn't take

---

[*] Todd Rundgren, writer, performer, and producer, produced XTC's *Skylarking* album.

it a day longer. [*Laughs.*] Anyway, when they started making the Mellotron in England, they were still using that American three-track head format. So the sounds that they recorded on to the tapes were split into three tracks. You could combine three instruments. We had things like brass, strings, and something else on one set of tapes; then we bought another set of tapes as we did *25 O'Clock* that had flutes in it—because, if you're going to be psychedelic, you have to have the 'Strawberry Fields' flutes, you know.

It was very, very inspiring to sit and struggle with this thing. And I found that I could actually manipulate three fingers at once! Two on one hand and one on the other hand—and I had a sort of a semblance of a song going!

For a long time, it remained a little instrumental thing. It was almost like my party piece—you know, when we'd get into a studio, I'd rush over to a keyboard, and say, 'Hey! What do you reckon to this?' And I'd play it, and it was, 'Oh god, Partsy's playing his party piece again.' I think the melody was played with the left hand, which is not usually the case with melodies, but I'm not a keyboard player, so I didn't know that, you know.

So I had this little dreamlike instrumental, basically, that reminded me of the seaside, because—although I think it's a brass tape on the Mellotron—it has an organ-like on-and-off attack and release. And it has that memory of brass in it, if you see what I mean. So, over time, I started to flesh out lyrics to this little instrumental party piece. It grew from that.

So, you had the basic verse structure? That's what came first?
Yeah, because it was the melody in the left hand.

You put lyrics to that, then the rest of the song grew musically from that?
The shape of the song grew from that section. Once I started to put lyrics to that section, it was like, 'Ooh, this is good.' I figured I'd start the song off with an instrumental and vocal noise version of the melody—you know, that very screwed-up, phase-y, flange-y vocal sound—and then repeat the melody with words, but realised that I'd then need something different.

The song has actually sort of got two middle sections, because when it goes into the 'And all the flags that flap on the pier' part, that is purely just added in there to break up the reoccurrence of that continuing melody.

Right. It's not your standard chorus structure.
No—it's very oddly structured, this song. It's rather dreamlike in its

structure. It sort of makes sense, but it doesn't, on the first few listens, if you see what I mean.

Sure. It's not your typical A-B-A-B-C song structure.
No, not at all. But to me it made sense, because I was putting that piece in there to stop having that repetition of the verse melody all the time.

Let me look at my notes again. I just put down things as they occurred to me. It's LinnDrum all the way through.*

So, there's no live drumming in there at all?
No. Because I just wanted the sense of disparate percussion. It's basically LinnDrum bass drum, and tom-tom [*sings pattern*].

Right. There's no snare until the bridge.
Until the bridge, and then a big, fat, tuned-down rattly snare comes in. And then there's also a lot of other disparate bits of percussion that are triggered off by the LinnDrum pattern. On every seventh beat, there's a little composite noise that we made down at Crescent Studios.† We made it with a little thumb piano, and a little wood block or a muted cowbell, and possibly something else, like a milk bottle. But there's definitely a thumb piano and a block.

Yeah, when I play this, I do that sound by playing a flam on the bell of my ride cymbal, but obviously it doesn't sound quite the same. It has way more decay than the sound you used.
Yeah, though we did put some reverb on ours.

And you have hi-hat in there as well, a two-note pattern starting on the 'three'.
Yeah, that's triggered as well. I was LinnDrum mad but I actually really didn't want anything like a conventional drum kit until the middle section. The whole disparate-percussion thing suited it very well.

The euphonium you hear in there is a euphonium [*laughs*]. It's a real euphonium, played by a real euphonium player named Steve Saunders.‡ We

---

* The first drum machine to use digital samples of real drums.
† Studio in Bath belonging to David Lord (see below).
‡ One of Britain's most versatile and in-demand brass players.

actually recorded his part in London—we went up on the train with David Lord, our producer.[*]

This is in the days of two-inch, 24-track tape, right? You weren't doing the stuff digitally, obviously.
No, no. We had to lug the 24-track tape with us.

And went into a studio …
Yeah, Odyssey Studios.[†] It was the same studio we did 'Gold' and 'Great Fire' in.

Did you have to deal with tape head-alignment issues or anything like that when you were moving from studio to studio?
If we did, it was not the sort of thing that we musicians really knew anything about. I mean, I knew *nothing* of that in those days. I was much more interested in: 'How can you screw this sound up? How can you make that sound weird? How can you get this to *thrill* me?' I still believe that every sound should *thrill*—you know, should be so beautifully recorded, or be out of the ordinary, or be in an odd place.

But as you get older, you understand a lot more about what thrilled you sonically when you were younger. You think, 'Oh, that's why it was thrilling me. I *know* now.' Or, 'It's *that* effect, or *that* interval, or it's *that* release of that chord going in to that one', you know?

You understand how the machine works a little bit more now.
Yeah, which does take some of the mystery out of it—but that's the price you pay for knowledge. When logic and knowledge come in, magic and voodoo go out the window, because you know how it's done! You stop being the audience, and you start being the people backstage doing those effects.

'The man behind the curtain.'
Yeah. With a sheet of tin, making thunder! *It's not real thunder, folks!*
I do remember having quite a row with Dave, actually, about the mode of this song. Because the melody goes way out of the scale of the chords—the melody of the instrumental line that the euphonium plays. That went

---

* A classically trained composer and conductor who went on to work with The Korgis, Tears For Fears, and Peter Gabriel.
† Near Marble Arch, London.

all over and all through, and broke out of the key and the chords that were accompanying it.

Which of course is part of its charm. That's what creates the friction, or frisson, of the line.
Right. But Dave didn't like that. He's much more traditional in his compositional sense, and he got David Lord on his side, and the pair of them were saying, 'Well, it sounds wrong. It sounds like a mistake!' I said, 'Well, it's not a mistake! That's how I want it to go. I can *hear* that it goes out of the key momentarily, and I can *hear* that it makes a rub there, but that's what I'm going for.'

They suggested a few changes, but I just held my breath and had a little tantrum, and said, 'No, it's gonna go like that! That's how it's written!' And the pair of them had to back down—which I didn't like. I didn't feel good doing that, but then again, I couldn't figure out why they didn't feel bad suggesting that I change it, because it upset some sensibility they had about key and scales. I thought they were much more open-minded musically than that.

But that kind of perception is a strange thing, too. I'm sure Dave was doing it with the band's best interests in mind, but of course he wasn't inside your head and hearing what you were.
I guess so. But it was frustrating. When you want your art to go one way, and those who wish to straighten you out are saying, 'Oh no, you should really'—that's frustrating. Dave actually did that a couple of other times—one of them was in 'Season Cycle', but that time Todd wouldn't back Dave.

But in this case, yeah, we had a bit of a row about that, but the pair of them did back down. It was like, 'Oh, he's the crazy composer, he must know what he wants,' you know. I don't like having a little tantrum like that, but when people can't understand what you're going for, you just have to beat your head against their brick wall, you know? But in the larger scheme of things, it's amazing that—in all the years we worked together—Dave, Colin, and myself had so few disagreements.

So yeah, where were we? At the time, I thought I was writing 'Marjorine', by Joe Cocker.* In fact, it's probably nothing like that song, but I haven't heard it since it came in out in—what, '68? But in '83, I thought, 'Wow,

---

* Originally released as a single in 1968, 'Marjorine' was then included on Cocker's 1969 debut album, *With A Little Help From My Friends*.

this is just like 'Marjorine'!' So I still don't know whether it is or it isn't. Somebody will have to play that song and say, 'Oh, I can see what he means,' or 'No, he must have got his wires mixed up there.' I may have to go find it myself now, and listen.

What else? I really was very proud of the lyrics to this song.

That's one of the reasons why I love this song so much. I remember when I first heard it, I thought, 'He has just summed up the feelings of every nervous boy sitting next to a girl, throughout history.' The picture of the couple by the seaside, and him imagining the seagulls mocking him, and the delicious tension of wanting to kiss the girl, and know that she *probably* wants you to, but if she doesn't, your world will end.

Yeah, you might as well go and kill yourself! While everything else in the scenario is calling you an idiot. The sea is going [*whispers*], 'Foool … foool.' That's not just the noises of white noise in the waves! And the seagulls are laughing at you because you didn't do it yet! And the flags are saying, 'What's *wrong* with you?' If they're spelling out any messages, it's what an idiot you are for hesitating!

And the similes and metaphors in here are so great—the warship-grey sea, and the black coastline slumbering on …

Well, I thought of it as the English seaside, which is *so* sad and mournful. It *is* a black coastline, the sea *is* warship grey. It's not Mediterranean blue. It's cup-of-tea brown, or mostly warship grey! It's the colour of steel—it's the North Sea we're dealing with here, or the English Channel. It's not the Caribbean or the Mediterranean.

And the lifebelts always look like end-of-the-pier minstrels, you know? You accompany your parents as a kid to a show at the end of the pier, and there are the people in blackface, on the stage, with a white ring around their mouth, and they start singing, and it's, 'Hey! They're like lifebelts!'

The other great thing here is the payoff—you're building up, the circumstances couldn't be more dire, and then you bring it down to, 'I say I like your coat / Her thank-you tugs my heart afloat.' It's the simplest little exchange in the midst of all this drama. It brings it right back down to two little people talking and saying these dumb little things.

Yeah, just stupid stuff, like, 'Oh, I like your coat,' and she says, 'Thank you,' and it means the world. 'WOW! She *thanked* me for liking her coat!' Your heart just explodes with joy at something stupid like that.

So, is this song about anyone in particular?
I think I did write this about Erica.*

Was this after—I know there was an incident somewhere where she tried to kiss you.
Oh no! In fact, I was still putting this song together, and we were in Crescent Studios trying out David Lord as a potential future producer, doing 'Thanks for Christmas'.† Erica was in England, visiting some friends in Oxford, I think. She found out—as she usually did, because she was a fantastic detective—where we would be in the studio, and she turned up. I was in the performance area, and there was a grand piano there in a little side room, and I said, 'Yeah, I've got a new song, and it goes like this.' I actually sat at the piano and played it to her, and tried my best to sing it at the same time.

And she must have thought, 'Well, hell—if *he's* not going to take the opportunity, I sure am!' And she leaned in to kiss me, sat next to me on the piano seat, as I'm playing her this song, and I thought, 'Oh my god!' and just, true to type—and the fact that I was married, and didn't want to fuck up my marriage—I leaned right out, scared shitless, and sort of immediately said [*fast*], 'Oh, well, I've still got a lot of work to do on that, and let's go into the control room, shall we?'

Yeah. And meanwhile, she's thinking, 'He was *just* telling me to kiss him!'
Exactly! I've written a song to her, telling her I'm too chicken to kiss you, maybe you should kiss me, and she tried to, and I just lived out the scenario in the song! And do you know what? Bath, where the studio was, gets an awful lot of seagulls, because they come up the Avon, which opens up into the Avon estuary. So that's one sound you do hear a lot of in Bath.

Where did you first meet her?
Oh, my goodness. [*Sighs.*] This is a long story, but the quick version is, she

---

* Erica Wexler, the daughter of screenwriter Norman Wexler, first met Andy in 1980; they began living together after the end of his first marriage. Erica produced an album, *Sunlit Night*, in 2013.
† Released in 1983 under the pseudonym The Three Wise Men.

had a bit of a crush on me, and saw me playing live in America, and actually borrowed/stole a car—even though she couldn't drive!—and drove it with her friend miles and miles upstate to see me somewhere, just so she could see me again, and watch the show and all that.

At the time, we had done a song, 'Take This Town', for the movie *Times Square*. That was a Robert Stigwood film—a stinking Stigwood film! It was *so* bad—but we'd never seen the film, so we thought, 'Yeah, let's go to the premiere in New York.' Her dad, Norman Wexler, was involved with Stigwood because of *Saturday Night Fever*, so she said to her dad, 'Can you get me some tickets to the after-premiere party, because I'd really like to bump into Andy.'* And she really did!

Enterprising young woman that she is.
Yep!

And the rest is history. So, back to the song.
Back to the song—I think the combination of dreamlike, unexpected song structure, and the pride of being the first thing I could work out with two hands on the keyboard, *and* what I considered to be really, really good lyrics, kept this at the top of the list of my favourite XTC songs for quite a few years. It's been knocked off now—probably by 'Rook' and then 'Easter Theatre', actually.

Oh, you mean it was no. 1 on your list?
Yeah.

So it's still in your top five.
I'd say so, yeah.

Did you do a lot of reworking on these lyrics, or did they come out pretty quickly? Because each line seems very tight and concise.
Tell you what, I've got a big orange sketchbook here with the original things. Let's see—I've the sleeve designs for potentials, if it was going to be a single. No, do you know what, I don't think I have the original lyrics in here. No, in this notebook, I was designing a video for it, where there were masked

---

* Norman Wexler wrote the script for *Saturday Night Fever*, which was produced by Robert Stigwood.

people, who had these big flat semi-Picasso-like masks. They were stood in a big desolate landscape near the sea, and a sort of proscenium across the top was constantly scrolling, changing the different images that were either telling the story with you, or contradicting what was going on. And then there was also the opposite of that, a band across the bottom that was scrolling the other way, which was either completing the imagery or contradicting what was going on.

But it never got to be a single, so I never got to use the idea. And I wouldn't have been *allowed* to use the idea, even if it the song *was* a single, given our shit history with videos! But I still have all the designs for the masks—they're rather odd-looking. But no, I can't find the lyrics in this notebook.

So, what can you remember? Did you really slave over the lyrics, or did they come relatively quickly?
I just think I managed to focus. I can't remember how long it took. I did them in dribs and drabs, but it was one of those things where I was able to make that white-hot focus on them. I've done that a few times, where I *really* concentrate on the lyrics of something, and try to make the imagery as complete as possible in the least amount of words. It's like you distil your intentions down and down and down until each drop of that stuff is deadly, like 100-proof alcohol.

From what you've been saying, it sounds as if you built each section of music and lyrics at the same time, rather than doing one or the other first.
Yeah, and once that was done, there was that joy of getting them to all fit over each other. That's some weird legacy that Bach has left me with—liking Bach when I was younger, and thinking, 'Why do I like this?' I like it because it all fits, like pieces of a great clock or something.

Is there anything else about the music or recording that you remember?
One of the things I remember from time I've spent at the seaside was these almost-random firings of coast guns, either for timing—you know, 'At mid-day, tradition is to fire the coastal gun'—or for other reasons. And so I wanted that kind of coastal-gun sound, which goes into the middle—you know, in between the 'he who hesitates is lost' and the 'if you want her' part. It's also on the outro. That was LinnDrum tom-toms tuned down, with a fuck of a lot of reverb on them.

And Colin's playing his new Wal bass, which I think was the first bass he ever had with an active circuit in it.

What difference does that make?
An active circuit will give a real sharp boost to the sound, but it usually doesn't boost much in terms of bass—it usually boosts the higher frequencies. It was very popular with 80s bass players for that slapping kind of playing that emphasised the highs. That was the active circuit actually boosting the higher frequencies in the pickups.

So he got one of those, and [*chuckling*] he would insist on using it, and of course there wasn't that much bass on it! It was all this high burping tone, you know. And poor old David Lord, I remember Colin saying to him, 'Wow, that bass sound is really good, David, how are you doing that?' And David was turning to me, and saying under his breath, 'He doesn't realise, I've got six compressors chained up to level out that sound, to get some bass in it!' Because it was all burp and no bass.

And Dave was playing the Mellotron?
Yeah, he's much more proficient. When I showed it to him, he was like [*imitates Dave*], 'Oh, is that all it is?' [*Laughs.*] It's three fingers! Melody with the left hand, and the sort of semi-chords on the top with the right hand.

Right, so he added more fingers, I presume.
I think he probably put one or two more in there, yeah. He probably thought what a moron I was for only have two-note chords and a melody line. But to me, that was a *big leap*, you know.

Now, you guys did some other versions of this song, too. You recorded it at the BBC—so it's on *Transistor Blast*—and there's the *Fuzzy Warbles* version, too.
Yep. The *Fuzzy Warbles* one is the home demo, done in the back bedroom, in which the shape of it is all there—kind of how I wanted it to go. It was just refining the sounds, you know.

And then the BBC one was the typical routine?
Yeah, you're given a day to do four songs. We had no drummer, and it would have cost us money to find a studio, find a drummer, pay a drummer, rehearse

for a week or whatever getting the songs down. And then you had to trust that the BBC engineers could get some decent sounds in an afternoon. You'd get all these songs done *and mixed* on the same day.

So, what we did was to basically use the same LinnDrum programs that I'd used on the recording, because they really couldn't fuck that up, could they? But that was in the days when we thought the LinnDrum was going to save us. It was like, 'Wow! We've actually become *modern* momentarily!'

Well, I think it was the first drum machine with real sampled sounds, so it actually sounded like drums, even though the feel wasn't necessarily there. The feel was rubbish, because people hadn't worked out that feel is down to *microscopic* differences—differences you *cannot* program. And they constantly shift and move, which gives you the groove, you know?

Exactly. That's the push-and-pull of the song.
Yeah, that's why, with real drummers, a song becomes more alive, and it's breathing, and it's a work of art. Whereas a machine—it's a dead thing, it's just sort of making these widgets of sound that come out exactly the same every time. There's no passion in that.

Interview conducted July 4 2007.

CHAPTER 17

THE EVERYDAY STORY OF SMALLTOWN

FROM *THE BIG EXPRESS*, OCTOBER 1984

Let's talk about 'The Everyday Story Of Smalltown'. What prompted you to write this paean to small-town life?
I think that at the time of *The Big Express*, part of me wanted to do an out-and-out concept album about Swindon—my take on the town, my life in the town, and the town's life itself. I think that's why the album's called *The Big Express*. It might be a concept album by stealth! That's why there are things like 'Train Running Low'; 'Everyday Story Of Smalltown'; the connection with my father through 'All You Pretty Girls'; there's my fear at the time of nuclear Armageddon, because we were still neck-deep in the Cold War; there was our situation with our manager, which was 'Liarbird', so that was autobiographical …

And 'Red Brick Dream'.
'Red Brick Dream' was out-and-out about Swindon; Colin's 'Washaway' was about life on the Penhill council estate; 'I Remember The Sun' was about the fields that he and I used to play over, next to the council estate. For all intents and purposes, *Big Express* is a lot more a concept album than most people's concept albums! But we never said it was. It's the anti-*Sgt Pepper*, which everyone thought was a concept album, but wasn't. With *Big Express*, nobody thinks it's a concept album, but it *actually might be*.

It's interesting to hear you say that, because I actually did think there was something like that going on, especially when you pair the album with *Mummer*. The two albums together have always been two sides of the same coin for me—one rural, one urban.
Right! Where Colin and I lived, on the Penhill estate, used to butt up next to the countryside. It's not like that now, because it's all been built over, but the

first house I lived in on the estate—which was in Latton Close—I could go
out in my front garden as a kid and twenty foot away was a fence to farmland.
You could just hop the fence and roam off over farmland, streams and stuff.
Colin used to do that as well—we used to go over the fields, and get chased by
farmer's boys who'd shoot at you with shotguns, or rough you up.

Did you actually get shot at?
Well, I personally don't remember getting shot at—I remember getting
threatened and them waving shotguns at us. People have told me, though, that
they had been shot at—you know, with buckshot. These farmer's boys hated
the thought of this council house scum going over their fields. 'How dare they
play in our woods on our land?', you know?

**Right. But it's not like you were doing damage to the crops or anything—
you were just out playing.**
Exactly. We were just snapping twigs to make bows and arrows, and bending
them to make dens and stuff like that. Yeah, den building—that was big as
a kid.

Hence the song, 'Let's Make A Den'.[*]
And hence that song, yeah! We were practising to be grown-ups.

When did you and Colin meet? How old were you?
Well, he was in the same school as me, but because he was in the year below,
I didn't really know him. Everybody knew about the kids in the year above
them, because they might beat you up, but nobody took any notice of the
kids in the year below. So he was in my school and he knew of *me*, but I never
took any notice of him. He might as well have not existed, because he was
younger. So, it wasn't until 1971 that I was aware of this very long-haired
beanpole of a character who always seemed to be paralytically drunk on a park
bench, all covered in vomit or something. He had a terrible alcohol problem.
I think marrying Carol probably saved his life. Because he was going down a
slippery slope. I'd always see him sat there with the down and out's, or with
the drunken bums, and he'd be sat there sharing bottles of cider and shit like

---

[*] Recorded as a demo at Andy's house in 1985 and released as a B-side to 'The Meeting
Place' and on *Coat Of Many Cupboards.*

that with them. Or you'd see him covered in his own sick and stuff, and you'd think, 'Wow, that fellow's a real mess, and he's only young.'

So then, even after that, when you guys were touring, would he make a point of not drinking?
He'd drink after the gigs. We always drank after gigs, never before. But by then he was off the slippery slope.

He knew when to stop.
Exactly.

So, back to 'Smalltown'—it's about Swindon …
'Smalltown' is one of the pivotal points of this album. It's about Swindon, and it's also Swindon singing it. Especially in the middle section, where the singer becomes the town.

That's one of the most beautiful parts of the song for me. I love the lyrics.
This is a lyric-powered song.

You were really coming into your own as a lyricist by this time, I think.
When I heard it today, I thought, 'Shit, there's some ersatz Dylan Thomas in there.' Around about the same time that I wrote this, I vaguely remember reading a Dylan Thomas book called *A Child's Christmas In Wales*.[*] I had an illustrated version by Edward Ardizzone, a famous book illustrator, and I remember enjoying it.[†] I liked how Thomas let strings of words go, so they all reflect on each other. I was trying to do that more and more. So, I think there's a little vein of Dylan Thomas in the lyric of this, if that doesn't sound too pretentious.

Not at all. I've always found these lyrics to be incredibly evocative, and intimate. You and I have talked about this before, but the thing I like about Graham Fellows and his John Shuttleworth character is the fact that, though he is making fun of the characters he creates, he's incredibly sympathetic to them as well.
It's affectionate.

---

[*] Originally published in 1955.
[†] Published 1978.

Absolutely. It's the same thing when you're talking in this song about somebody who's 'coughing in the toilet'. It's like, 'Well, of course they're doing that—we've all done it.'

Yeah. A lot of this is about my grandparents—both of them. I mean, both sets—[*imitates Paul McCartney*] 'Because everyone's entitled to two, aren't they.' [*Laughs.*] Isn't that a line from *A Hard Day's Night*? One of my granddads worked for the Great Western Railway for a lot of his life. The Great Western was kind of the Wal-Mart of Swindon, in that everyone worked for it.

Swindon was a company town, yes?

I think that some crazy amount—like two people in every three—worked for the Great Western. It was behind these great walls, so everyone just called it 'inside'. 'Where do you work?' 'Oh, I work inside.'

So, my mother's father worked for the Great Western for a long time; he's one of the characters in this. And I also think of my father's father with his rolled-up cigarettes in the toilet, coughing and hacking away, in their little bungalow on the Penhill estate. Or where they used to live, near one of the railway lines in Rodbourne. They used to have a tiny house with an outside toilet, with a sort of crescent moon cut in the door, you know?

An outhouse.

He'd be sat in there coughing and hacking away. It's one of the sounds of Swindon for me. Another of the immortal sounds of Swindon was the Great Western factory hooter, calling people to work. We ended up using the recording of the last time it ever sounded, on 'The Meeting Place'.

It's funny that the image you're talking about, of 'coughing in the toilet', is as simple as that. I had always thought, given that you're 'woken by the Sally Army Sunday march-round', that 'coughing in the toilet' was about retching from the after-effects of a hard Saturday night.

Oh no, it's my granddad with his roll-ups in the toilet. That was one of *the sounds*—you'd know where granddad was, because you'd hear him in there with his cigarettes. You'd go in there an hour later, and it'd still stink of his roll-ups.

So, let's talk about the lyrics: 'Smalltown, snoring under blankets / Woken by the clank / It's just the milkman's dawn round.'

'Blankets' and 'clank / It's'—it's very Hollywood, that. That's kind of *Wizard*

Of Oz rhyming. And do you know, the milkman still wakes me up. Even in this age, I can hear the little electric cart going phwizzzzz-BANG. The BANG is every time he takes his foot off the sort of bumper-car pedal—it just slams to a stop. He was a big family friend, actually—the milkman. He was a fellow called Bert, who was our milkman for years while I was a kid. Then he gave up being a milkman, and funnily, he went over to doing a bread-delivery round. So he went from five years or so of being 'Bert the Milkman' to five years or more of being 'Bert the Baker'. Or the other way around, perhaps? [*Laughs.*]

Selling two of the staples of life! Let's see—'Smalltown, hiding under covers / The lodgers and the lovers / Are asleep round Smalltown.'
Ooh, how romantic!

[*Laughs.*] 'Shiny grey black snake of bikes / He slithers / Bearing up the men and boys / To work.'
I think that's one of the better lines, and it comes from hearing somebody say that when it was 'home time' at the Great Western factory, this great mass of bikes would come out, because not many people had cars. I heard somebody say, 'It's like a big black snake of bikes!' And I thought, 'Is it really black? I *guess* so.' But then as I thought about it more, I thought it was more a grey-black, so I literally ended up using the line 'Shiny grey black snake of bikes'.

Which is more like a snake anyway, because of the way their scales are slightly iridescent.
Right. You're not sure if it's black or silvery or grey. And, then after the 'he slithers' line, I think we shake a shaker on the recording, to make a cartoon snake noise. 'Bearing up the men and boys to work'—and it was. You know, young kids worked at this place as well.

'We're standing in poplar lines'—why poplar?
Well, they always seem to plant poplar trees in lines—in straight rows. You can see this on the continent as well—you see it in France, these lines of poplars acting as a windbreak.

Ah, I see. When I first heard this, I thought it was 'popular lines'—I thought you were making a pun that they were making a popular product line.
Oh, no no no. That's kind of interesting, though—I hadn't thought of that!

No, it's 'poplar,' the tree. Some older parts of Swindon do have lines of poplars. And when you see people working in factories, often they're lined up the same way.

So, where were we? 'Making alarm clocks that'll wake our wives up.' I don't think they make alarm clocks in Swindon. I just wanted an image where you're building something small and mechanical and doing this repetitive work, and then the irony is, you end up buying it yourself. So you've got to give me a bit of artistic license there! And then 'Don't ask us, we haven't the time'.

Which is why you used the alarm-clock image—it sets up that line well.
There you go. 'We're racing the hooter that will signal life's up.' You haven't got any time to talk about what life's all about when you work in a factory—you're on your bike, and off you go, and, 'I've got to get there before the next hooter sounds, because if it does sound, they're going to dock my wages, or send me home and dock me a full day's wage if I'm ten minutes late.' Because they used to be bastards like that. But the hooter also signals that work's up, and eventually it will signal life's up, because most people worked at the Great Western—that *was* their life.

'Smalltown, crouching in the valley'—because my first house in Swindon was in an area called 'the Valley'. 'Woken by the Sally Army / Sunday march-round.' A lot of Sundays, the Salvation Army—or the Sally Army—they would have this marching brass band going around. So the *one day* you have during the week when you could lay in and sleep longer, sometimes you couldn't, because [*laughing*] these fucking religious nutcases would be out there parading up and down with this brass band at unearthly o'clock in the morning!

'Smalltown, coughing in the toilet'—there's my granddad—'Who on earth would spoil it / Would they pull down Smalltown?' I don't think I did this well, but I have to explain my intention. Part of me thought you shouldn't spoil this place by pulling it down. That'd be terrible. And, of course, Swindon was starting to be pulled to pieces at that time. At the same time, part of me wanted to say, 'C'mon, pull this thing down, let's start afresh, because it's getting a mess.' I wanted it to be truly taken both ways.

Then we've got verse two—'If it's all the same to you / Mrs Progress'—because that's what was going on. I was thinking of Bert the Baker/Bert the Milkman saying this bit. It's kind of like they're characters in a play, these people. 'Think I'll drink my Oxo up and get away.' Because this is the sort of thing—my mother would get Bert in and make him a cup of tea, and he'd say, 'Oh, I've got to drink this up, love, I've got to be away.'

Why did you use Oxo there?*
Do you have Oxo in the States?

We have things like beef bouillon.
It's the same thing—basically a cube of dried blood. You squeeze it into some boiling water, and mix it up, and pour it on your meat, or you can just drink it, like a sort of savoury tea. I think it was seen as a macho thing, like a working man's 'dead-hard cuppa tea'. [*Laughs.*] 'Hey, I'm drinking bull's blood here!' It's the sort of thing you give someone on a wintry day, to pick 'em up.

'It's not that you're repulsive to see / In your brand new catalogue nylon nightie'—because that's what all the mums wore when I was a kid! They'd be getting their milk in the morning, coming out on their doorstep, and they'd have these kind of cartoon, fluorescent pink see-through layered kind of nightie things on. And Jesus, I still find those erotic now!

My family used to *live* by the postal catalogue. It was a bit of fuss to get into town, so once or twice a year, they'd get this mail-order catalogue sent. If I got it before they did, I'd look at the underwear section! Ohhh, you just wanted to know what was beneath those corsets! You know, that tummy-restraining panel—all of my attention as a kid was focused on what was going on under that tummy-restraining panel.

Anyway, my mother wore a brand-new catalogue nylon nightie, but so did every mother in the row. 'You're too fast for little old me'—because she's Mrs Progress, right? 'Next you'll be telling me it's 1990'—Wow! I mean, as a kid, that was the *future*.

Of course! And it's even better that you're writing this in the mid 80s and saying that, because it shows that you're writing about a different time.
It's me as a kid, thinking about the people around me. For me, in the future, we'd all be living on Venus and having holidays on Neptune and eating dinner pills and wearing jetpacks and a silver suit, you know? And now look at it—it's still 1950 here, except with computers. [*Sighs.*]

---

* A beef stock cube, first marketed in 1910.

Then, the next character onstage is the town itself. 'I have lived here for a thousand years or maybe more / And I've sheltered all the children who have fought the wars / And as payment they make love in me.' And that's all the payment that the town needs.

And there's a long list of where they do it: 'In squeaky old beds / In bicycle sheds/ Inside of their heads /As singles and weds / As Tories and Reds/ And that's how I'm fed / And that's how I'm fed.' That's all the town asks—that people keep making other people in its presence. Which is all a town could want, really—because if you want to kill a town, just take the people away.

Indeed. The music of the song is related to the lyrics, of course—you talk about the Sally Army in here, and there's that kind of feel to it.
Yes.

It's got that march beat, and those faux horns.
Definitely faux horns. I think our producer, David Lord, who was a great arranger, said something like, 'You'll need a flugelhorn, and a trombone or two, you'll need a trumpet or two,' and so on, and we said, 'Well, how much is this going to cost?' I think we were a bit scared off by that.

But then he said, 'Look, I'll tell you what we can do. Andy, you do the thing on the demo, which I really like'—he was talking about the comb-and-paper thing I did on the demo, which was just me showing whoever was going to be our producer that 'this is where the brass band goes'—'and if that's not enough,' he said, 'then I know somebody with some pretty good samples of brass.' And that was Tears For Fears.

Ah, so that's why you credit them on the album.
Yep. We borrowed this emulator/keyboard setup from them.

You used that for 'Train Running Low On Soul Coal', too?
No. Just used it for 'Smalltown'.

Oh, I thought that's where you got the samples of the train noises.
Oh no, those aren't train noises. Those are the LinnDrum turned down as low as it could go. People have all these theories out on the net—'Oh, they're rubbing a wire brush against the snare rim' and all that shit. No, the industrial noises at the beginning and end of 'Train' are a LinnDrum tuned

down as low as you can get it. And all the great drumming is Pete Phipps, not a LinnDrum!

On 'Smalltown'?
On 'Smalltown' and 'Train Running Low'. The stuff that sounds 'drummy'.

So we borrowed this emulator, and knocked up a kind of communal arrangement—Dave would say, 'Try this line out,' and I'd say, 'OK, now put that line in,' and then Colin would say, 'Ooh, try that harmony with it,' and then David Lord would say, 'OK, now try that response line to it.' So, we did an arrangement by committee. Which worked out really well—for faux horns fakery, it doesn't sound too bad at all.

There's a big ghost of Ray Davies wandering around this. It's a big hats-off to The Kinks, and to 'Autumn Almanac' in particular.*

Is it that, or is it more of a homage to the *Village Green Preservation Society*?†
You know, I never heard the *Village Green Preservation Society* album until the late 80s or early 90s. In fact, I haven't heard most of The Kinks' albums. The only one I'd heard until the late 80s was—oh, what's the one about going to Australia?

That's *Arthur*.‡
That was the only one I'd heard, because a friend of mine, Spud Taylor, had it. I knew of The Kinks and their B-sides because of their singles. It was the same situation as The Beach Boys. I knew them because of their singles and B-sides, and I only knew The Kinks because of that, too.

Do you have their stuff now?
Not albums, no. Because I don't like a lot of what I've heard. I think they were a *fantastic* singles band. But I think their albums contain some great tracks, and some filler. But despite that, people get the idea that I was slavering over Beach Boys and Kinks albums—and it's not true. It's not true at all. To me, they were just singles groups. And I still haven't changed my opinion. I think The Kinks made faultless singles, and a lot of faultless B-sides, but their

---

* Released as a single in 1967.
† Album released in 1968.
‡ *Arthur (Or The Decline And Fall Of The British Empire)* was released in 1969

albums are a bit hit-and-miss. I don't know why, but I get the impression that no one wanted to spend the money to get things done properly.

When I first started hearing them, I liked the songs, but thought they sounded pretty bad. I had cut my teeth on The Beatles, so it was strange for me to hear their very garage-y type of approach.
Sure. Sometimes I fantasise—what would it have been like if The Kinks had access to George Martin and Geoff Emerick and all the engineers at Abbey Road and stuff? They would have been unstoppable.* But they didn't. They had cheap-shit studios, and banged it out quick, and the arrangements weren't always there. The Kinks didn't have arrangements—they just had Nicky Hopkins with his Mellotron occasionally!†

So, let's talk about the drumming a little bit—as you said, it's Pete Phipps, not the LinnDrum.
Oh yeah, and he did a great job! We got him to use a lot of ambience, because I wanted it to be really stomp-y. I knew I didn't want to do this song with programmed drums. The only ones I wanted to do with programmed drums were the ones that had to have a mechanical backbone to them, such as parts of 'Train Running Low', where I wanted it to be redolent of mechanical things. And people think it's mechanical on 'Shake You Donkey Up', but it's not—it was Pete Phipps! He was a fucking great drummer.

Oh yeah. Still is, I presume!
It's all that Tai Chi he used to do. We'd come in some mornings, and he'd be there in his gear, doing it. [*Whispers*] 'Don't interrupt him!' 'What's he doing?' 'It's OK—he directs the tides by doing this! That leg going in the air slowly there—he's just getting a tide in the Straits of Hormuz sorted out right now.' [*Chuckles*.] But yeah, he did a great job on this.

He's got a great martial feel on the song.
Yeah, it's kind of a pop version of the march. It sounds sort of corny, but stick with me here—I can imagine some of the other characters in the song joining me in this march, marching around Swindon. You're accruing more

---

* Emerick was engineer on the later Beatles albums.
† Pianist and organist who played on four albums by The Kinks.

and more people as you march through the song. To the point where, at the end of the middle section—which has got a kind of steam-train noise puffing through it, and which I think was a kind of fucked-up snare drum—when it bursts back into the song, there are tapes of children screaming and yelling in playgrounds. Because I wanted people to think that there are more and more people joining the march.

Ah, OK—I'd heard that, and always wondered what it was, and whether or not I was hearing things. People on the XTC fan site, Chalkhills, have complained about modern-day mastering techniques, which push songs to their sonic limits throughout the song, leaving no aural 'headroom'. The reason I thought of that is that this song seems to me to be a good example of making the song bigger and bigger and bigger as you get toward the end. That's not quite as possible nowadays if people are going to be mastering everything big and flat throughout the song.
Well, they also *record* songs like that now, and they treat it like that as they go along, and then they master it so it doesn't move. Which is wearing on the ears, because there are no dynamics.

Exactly. But it seems as if, in this song, you guys were consciously trying to build it.
We were trying to build it, and trying to give the impression that the cast of characters in the song and the town is growing and growing. So, at the end of the middle section, you can hear that sort of steam train, and we do a little mini-fade, where the steam train chuffs away, taking the song with it. Then suddenly, *BAM*, it's back in your face, back out the other side of the tunnel. At the end, there's everyone stamping around in a big parade, you know?

What are you and Dave doing on the song? Colin's part seems to be pretty straight ahead on this.
Yeah. The stomping guitar on the left-hand speaker is all Dave—that sort of chopping, 'Ball And Chain'-type guitar. And the more slightly twinkly, twangier one on the right is me.

Dave's playing keyboards on this as well, right? Is David Lord playing?
Dave plays most of the keyboards, I think. David Lord would usually lean over and say, 'Could you make it a bit more like this?' I think it was only a

mono keyboard, so we would have built up the lines, like actual brass pieces.

I remember that the first part of this that I wrote, apart from having the idea that I wanted to do a song like this, was that motif that you hear before the verse. I wrote that on the guitar actually—it was like a chord thing, where you could hold the chord, and move the root notes around. I remember that quite clearly—that was the first thing that came up.

So the music came up first, and kind of brought the lyrics out of you?
I knew I wanted to write a song about Swindon, this small town. You know, whenever anyone would talk about Swindon, they'd say, 'Oh, it's a small town up the M4.' Which it is, but it has grown incredibly in the last twenty years. In fact, it's a real definition of a doughnut town. It's all around the outside—there's nothing left in the middle now.

Anything else you remember about the actual writing of the song?
One funny thing—because of the subject matter, and because of some of the brass-band-ish nature of some of the melodies, I remember feeling guilty that the verse was in E! The bluesiest key of all blues keys. 'Should I move this to be in another key? It seems almost wrong, to be in E.'

Too ordinary?
It was too ordinary, and too sort of American or something. I wanted it to be ludicrously British.

You were playing in your open-E tuning?
No, not on this track, actually. This is one of the ones that's not in that.

A lot of this album was, right?
Yeah, in fact, most of this album was open-E tuning, but not this song. So, I felt guilty that it was in E, but I thought, 'No, it's got to be. This is how it works, and this is the right tonal change, and everything.' This whole track is a real excerpt from a teenage opera. And, as I said, in my head, even though I didn't say it—because at the time one of the biggest, sweary, cussiest things you could ever say was, 'Yeah, it's a concept album'—to me, we were making a concept album.

Interview conducted January 26 2008.

CHAPTER 18

25 O'CLOCK

(AS THE DUKES OF STRATOSPHEAR)
FROM THE EP *25 O'CLOCK*, APRIL 1985

Let's speak about '25 O'Clock', your first foray into psychedelia.
The only note I made about this song—because I've been speaking so much about the Dukes lately*—is, 'It's a quasi-Eastern, pretentious, doom-laden teenage control song.'

OK, then. Thank you very much! Good night!
Shortest interview ever!

Well, there's a lot of history out there about the Dukes—for example, about how they first met in a tea shop in Twickenham in 1962—but if you could give a brief overview about how the whole Dukes Of Stratosphear project came about, that'd be a good place to start.
In the later 70s, I found myself longing to be doing the music that I loved as a kid of thirteen or fourteen. I'd be listening to the radio then, and there'd be stuff like 'See Emily Play' or 'Strawberry Fields Forever', 'My White Bicycle'—you know, all these great psychedelic singles—and I'd think, 'This is wonderful! When I grow up, I'll be in a group, and we'll make music just like this!' Of course, as a kid, I had no grasp that this was just the whim of fashion, and that this music was going to last only a year or so, and then it would be gone!

But it affected me so profoundly that when I was in a position to be in a group making records, I thought I should say thank you to the people who made *those* records. And the best way to say thank you to them was by sounding just like them.

---

* This interview was conducted right after XTC re-released the Dukes Of Stratosphear albums.

Sure—imitation being the sincerest form of flattery. So, you contacted Dave early on, right when you were in the middle of the punk wars.

The punk wars! Which is a phrase used all the time now, and I started it! And I never get credit for it.

Well, we'll give you credit right now and here.

There you go. I used to use the phrase all the time in interviews, and then I started to see it creep into other people's definitions, mostly by other journalists.

So yeah, even during the punk wars—when we were fighting for *your right to wear bondage trousers!*—I was interested in psychedelia. In 1978, I invited Dave Gregory, with a bunch of other people, to a playback at my flat for the just-finished *Go 2* album. After the beers had gone down and all the people had gone home but Dave, I was chatting to him, and I said, 'Look, do you fancy making an album of songs that sound like they come from 1967?' He said, 'Yeah, I'd love to, but when could we do this?'

We talked about it a lot, but he wasn't even in the band at the time, and really, to be honest, I didn't have *any* spare time at all. I was constantly touring, and it was all I could do to get home long enough to get my underwear clean, and then it'd be back out on tour, or back in the studio, or back at rehearsals, or whatever.

Why did you ask Dave to do this?

Because I knew that he liked 60s music, and was such an aficionado of that kind of thing. I'm *not* going to use the word 'genre'! I refuse.

But you just did! *Too late.*

D'oh! Damn. No, I'll say 'type'—that *type* of music. Anyway, I knew that he was such a big fan of it that he would do a good job.

In 1984, while we were working on *The Big Express* album, during spare minutes I'd sneak off upstairs in Crescent Studios, in Bath, with my cassette machine and whisper these ideas for psychedelic songs into it. I was beginning not to be able to contain the desire to do this. You can see it leaking out earlier—you can see it leaking out on *Mummer*—'Let's get a Mellotron! Let's put some backwards so-and-so on here.'

Yeah, sure: 'Deliver Us From The Elements'.

Right. 'Let's do phasing'—all that. Even on *English Settlement*, during a drunken jam session one night, it was like, 'Hey! Let's pretend we're a 60s band improvising some songs.' So we were struggling, sort of feeling around in the dark, to be the proto-Dukes even then.

But by '84 I could contain it no longer, and was actually writing stuff that could be done in that style, the first one being 'Your Gold Dress'.*

Wait—are you saying the infamous Drunken Sessions were the first appearance of the Dukes?†
Kind of, yeah. There's one called 'Orange Dust', which was just made up on the spot.‡ It took all of ten seconds to make that up. But that wasn't the way to do it, because the songs that I loved weren't the kind of sprawling jams that you often find in psychedelia—they were quite well-arranged and organised little jewels, you know?

Absolutely. If I remember correctly, after *The Big Express* you got the opportunity to produce someone else—Mary somebody?
I was put together by Virgin with a Canadian artist they'd just signed called Mary Margaret O'Hara. The couple of times I spoke to her, the alarm bells were going off, to be honest, and I should have listened to them. I was thinking, 'This is not going to happen. This is not going to work between us.'

I got to meet her in Virgin's offices. I spoke to her for about ten minutes, sat on a sofa outside somebody's office, and she then decided that I was the one to produce her album. So, Rockfield Studios in Wales were booked, and she and her band came over.§ I got John Leckie to agree to engineer it, so I thought, 'That'll be a good team. I'll produce it, I'll do the musical side of things, and John can do the engineering side of things, and it'll be great.'

I went down on a Thursday or Friday night, and John said he could join on the next Monday, so I said, 'OK, I'll go down and start rehearsals—I'll start knocking the band into shape,' you know? The band were there, but for some reason, I couldn't get them to agree to play. I said, 'Look, we've got a whole album to work through here, could we please start rehearsing this stuff, and letting me in on what you're doing?'

Finally, on day two or three, I went to bed at midnight, thinking, 'Fuck

---

* On the *25 O'Clock* album.
† Recorded after a visit to the pub during the mixing of *English Settlement*.
‡ Unreleased demo.
§ The celebrated Rockfield Studios is near Monmouth in the county of Gwent.

it, they're never going to rehearse! I don't know what we're going to do.' I was asleep for about an hour when the phone rang. [*Mimics caller, speaking abruptly*] 'We want to rehearse.' So I got up and got dressed, and went down to the studio.

They started to play through a few things, and I thought, 'Jesus, this is *really* rough.' Their sense of time was not good—it was all over the show. So I said, 'Look, I've brought a LinnDrum down with me. I'll hook it up, and we'll give you some headphones, and we'll put a click in them, because I want to get it more rhythmic.' Then—oh boy, you could cut the atmosphere with a knife. It went really sour, and that was it. They immediately halted the rehearsal.

The next morning, at breakfast, their manager pulled me to one side and said, 'I want to have a talk with you.' He took me out on the long walk, the driveway outside the studio, and said, 'Mary doesn't want to work with you. She doesn't want you producing her album.' I said, 'Oh, is it because I asked them to rehearse with a click track, because of the timing?' He said, 'Well, partly—and she said you're giving off bad vibes.'

Maybe they knew their timing was shit, maybe they knew they were really rough, and I hit some raw nerve by saying, 'Look, you've got to rehearse this more in time—I want a groove out of you people.' I mean, I was trying to be nice about it, but basically I got sacked because my 'vibe' wasn't right.

So I said, 'Well look, John's coming down tomorrow. He's a great engineer, you should start with him. He'll make you sound great. You play it how you want to play it, but work with John. He's wonderful.' But they didn't want to work with him either. John was an 'Orange Person', a follower of the Bhagwan Shree Rajneesh—he's not at the moment, or he's not since, but he was at the time. She refused to work with somebody from a devilish cult.

[*Laughing*] By 'orange', you mean he wore orange robes?
He would wear normal clothes, but dyed orange. I said to him a while ago, 'What was it all about?' He said, 'Well, to be honest, I just used to like to go to the ranch.' Where was the ranch? It was up north somewhere, on the West Coast?

In Oregon, I think.
Something like that. He said, 'I just used to like to go to the ranch for the free sex.'

Who wouldn't?!*

So we suddenly found ourselves with nothing on the books. I said to him, 'Hey, do you fancy making a psychedelic album?' He said, 'Sure,' and that was it. It took about one nanosecond for him to answer. I knew he'd be great for it, because of his credentials. And really, that was it! This was the chance we needed to go and be this 60s band that sounds like every 60s band I ever loved.

I had maybe three songs. John originally tried to get us into Edgar Broughton's studio or use his equipment, because I said it would be nice if we could use period gear.† But then he went to see it, and he said, 'No, it wouldn't be good enough.' He then mentioned, 'Well, there's this funny little Christian studio in Hereford, and they've got some great old gear in there, and they're not expensive'—because the only way we could get Virgin to agree to finance the project was if they'd give us £5,000, which you couldn't really make an album for. And, to be honest, I never had all the songs! I was really winging it. It was just pure intention. I think by the time we went in the studio, I had 'Your Gold Dress', 'Bike Ride To The Moon', '25 O'Clock'—did I have any others? 'My Love Explodes.' I had four songs.

It was originally going to be a full-length album, but time was running out, basically. We did it very quickly—we did all the recording in about five or six days, and did all the mixing in that much time, too. It was all just first takes. We didn't have the luxury to keep going over it. In fact, I think we spent as much time just rehearsing it and bashing it through *in situ* with the mics on us, ready to be rolling at any second.

Did Colin have 'What In The World?' written already?

I think he had it lying around as a song, yeah. Colin was the least interested in the Dukes. That's not quite right—not 'least interested', but it just wasn't his experience. Dave had had very similar experiences to me—you know, psychedelic British singles, and both being guitar players and liking that kind of thing. But Colin was more of a heavy metal kid. He was more into Black Sabbath and Uriah Heep and people like that.

---

* Bhagwan Shree Rajneesh (1931–90) was an Indian guru who founded a commune in America, celebrated for its open attitude to sex. It collapsed after its leadership was found to have launched a salmonella poison attack on local residents. In 1985, Rajneesh was deported, and returned to his original base in Pune, India.

† Rob 'Edgar' Broughton (born 1947) led The Edgar Broughton Band, a psychedelic blues outfit of the late 60s and 70s.

One reason he connected so well with Terry, I guess, given how much Terry loved heavy music.

That's right. But he didn't really have much of a grasp of psychedelia. That said, by the time we got hold of the song he brought up for *25 O'Clock*, and we'd added all these sound effects and tape loops and stuff over it, it blended in perfectly. It's like the great lost relative of 'Only A Northern Song', you know?*

Yeah, very Beatles-esque. So, let's talk about the song '25 O'Clock'.

Although the Dukes are primarily English psychedelia—big dollops of Pink Floyd, and The Move and The Beatles and Small Faces, stuff like that—there's also some American stuff that seeps in there, and I think '25 O'Clock' is the American-sounding one from that disc. It's people like The Electric Prunes— you know, 'I Had Too Much to Dream Last Night'.† I loved the atmosphere on that track. I loved that quasi-Eastern, minor-scale thing.

It's very difficult to talk about the song, actually, because it's more of a sonic intention than a real song. It's taking the sand of psychedelia and trying to make a castle out of it, but there's sort of no reason to do that, if you know what I mean.

I see what you mean by the intention of it, but are you saying you're going more for a moment in time than an actual song?

I'm going for a moment in time, and I'm going for a sort of feeling that— well, the whole Dukes thing is a fancy dress ball, so it's like you're somehow putting history to rights. You're somehow being the grown-up version of you at thirteen, with the music you heard, which turned you on to adult novelty music—which, to be truthful, psychedelia was—but you're rewriting history. You're correcting history by going back and bringing that thirteen-year-old kid forward, and saying, 'OK, I'm the 'older you' now, I can make all this happen. We've got a studio, I can play the guitar, I can write a song, *let's do this*.'

So, that dreaming thirteen-year-old kid was in charge in my brain. He was the one coming up with this quasi-Eastern song. It's very difficult to pin down to it being a parody of one group, because it's not. It's more of a feeling from the time.

---

* From The Beatles' soundtrack to *Yellow Submarine*.
† A single for the band in 1966.

I think that's actually part of the charm of 25 O'Clock—it's one of the reasons I like it a bit more than Psonic Psunspot. For me, 25 O'Clock is much more of a melange—except for 'Mole From The Ministry', which is pretty much a direct lift from *Magical Mystery Tour*—but all the other songs have lots of different influences, and you can play 'spot the bands' throughout each one. Do you know what I mean?

Yeah. It's a real tapestry of influences. Well—not influences as in subconscious influences, but there are quite heavy dollops of, 'Yeah, now we're trying to sound like whomever.' But, in terms of how we've been talking about songs in all our previous interviews, this is very difficult to talk about. Because it's not me being 'real', as such.

Had you ever intended this as anything else but a Dukes song?

No. In fact, it never existed before this overwhelming intention to do this project came up.

Oh, so you did the demo after you'd decided you were going to do the project?

Yeah. The only song that I'd written before we decided to do the Dukes was 'Your Gold Dress'. I whispered that into a cassette machine during the mixing of *Big Express*. I also had one called 'Martian Invasion, 1970'.

[*Laughs.*] Are we ever going to hear that?

[*sings, very solemnly and dramatically.*] 'Martian invasion, 1970—bom bom bom—what will become of the likes of you and me—bom bom bom.' It was all about how the Martians are coming, and they're going to enslave us sometime in the far future—*1970!* There was only a very poor quality mono demo, so if it were ever to see the light of day, I'd have to re-record it, I think. It's so crass. You've heard the best part of it. [*Laughs.*]

Something to look forward to! So, when you knew you were going to do this project, you wrote '25 O'Clock' …

I think we had something like five days while John was trying to get a studio together, and we were trying to get Virgin to agree to pay us some money to do it. I thought, 'Oh Christ, I better write some songs, quick!' So all of the demos that you'll hear on the *25 O'Clock* expanded record—and some of them are on *Fuzzy Warbles* as well—they were all knocked up *really* quickly.

And just as a way of giving the band a guide of what you were going for.
Yeah—really, to show them how the song would go, but knowing that most of the delight would be in the actual production value of it—the phasing, and the reverse guitar, and the tape loops and all that. Stuff you couldn't rehearse.

I wanted to ask about some of the differences between the demo and the studio version, but you've kind of explained the differences right there. For example, in the demo, there's backwards guitar liberally splattered all over the place, there's lots of organ, you repeat the initial lyrics—things that you decided not to do on the studio version.
When we just started bashing it around as a band, it suddenly came to life. It was like, 'OK, we don't need to go back to the demo, because the demo is just the most primitive springboard.' It suddenly had such a robustness in the studio that I wouldn't try to copy the demo, because there was not much there in the way of arrangement ideas. There just wasn't time to think about how to arrange the songs. It all happened so quickly—the whole idea to do it, and then suddenly we're in a studio, and suddenly the red light's on, and it's, 'OK, let's go for it!' There was no time to sit and say [*preciously*], 'Should that be a minor ninth or an augmented ninth?' [*Chuckles.*]

You said that you were looking for a studio that had vintage gear—what about your instruments? Let's start with the keyboards.
We already had a Mellotron, which we'd used on *Mummer* and *Big Express*. We managed, through a friend of friend, to get in touch with Verden Allen, the keyboard player for Mott The Hoople, who lived in Hereford, and he agreed to loan us his Hammond organ. He caught us taking the back off of it, to get access to the Leslie speaker. The organ was his baby—we thought he'd loaned us this organ and then gone home, but he was hovering outside the studio looking in the door and shit.

While you tore it apart!
John said, 'Yeah, wouldn't it be great if we took the back off the Leslie cabinet and connected up a microphone so we could sing though it?' Verden caught us doing this, and he just fucking freaked out—[*mimicking a Hereford accent*] 'Roight! That's it! Oi'm taking my bloody organ, and you're not bloody havin' it, ya bastards!' He and his rather aged dad came and picked it up in a van, and took it away. But when they went off to get the van, we just had time to

quickly do the organ overdub for 'What In The World?' [*Chuckles.*] So, we didn't end up having a Hammond for the entire session, but Dave had this Roland JXP keyboard, I think. We used that to build a little, cheap-sounding Farfisa-type organ-sounding patch with that.

And that's pretty much what you used on '25 O'Clock'?
Yep. It was better, actually, because we got that cheap sound.

How about your guitars? Had Dave started his collection by then?
Yeah. In fact, he wrote some pretty exhaustive liner notes for the re-release of the album—a lovely article called 'Stratosgear' where he describes all the technical side of things. I didn't have any vintage gear. I think I just brought my brand-new, cheap Fender Squire Telecaster—£150 worth of guitar. But it sounded fine. I knew the kind of tones I wanted, and I thought, 'Well, Syd Barrett played a Telecaster, so I can get those sounds.'

It is an appropriate guitar for that time period.
Yeah, it's just that it's a new one, and it's the cheap, kind of beginner model, which a lot of guitarists would sooner cut their own hands off than play, but I don't have any qualms about playing cheap guitars.

Were there special amps that you guys used?
Do you know, I can't remember much about the amp situation. Dave would know. It was such a blur, it was such a fast thing, that I don't remember too much about it. We just seemed to be in there, and threw some microphones on the drum kit, and said, 'OK, Ian, it goes like this!' We got Ian Gregory to play drums because we needed a drummer quickly, and the only one I could think of was Dave's brother!* I knew he'd never made any recordings before— he'd only played at an amateur level, but he was great! He was just right. It wouldn't be the Dukes with anyone else, I think.

John Leckie reminded me that Ian had this great thing about wanting to change the tuning of his drums before each song, so that the kit sounded slightly different each time. That helped, you know—it helped the 'disguise nature' of the quality of each track.

---

* Ian Gregory is Dave's younger brother by two years. He got his first drum kit at fifteen and continues to play semi-professionally today.

Do you remember sitting down and giving him any guidance in particular for this song?

We did, for things like 'My Love Explodes'. I wanted him to drum like Charlie Watts—'Drum like Charlie Watts doing a swing rhythm for "19th Nervous Breakdown".' On a lot of those Stones things, Charlie Watts is playing swing rhythm while they're playing straight. That's where you get the groove from. So I asked him to do that on 'My Love Explodes', and also, from *Psonic Psunspot*, on "Little Lighthouse".'

But I don't particularly remember any specific guidance for this. It was just a case of crashing through it a few times in rehearsals, so any guidance was probably like, 'Give us more bash-bash-bash!' It was all grabbed very quickly, and sort of intuitively, I guess.

What do you remember about the bass part? Colin's playing on this song is very distinctive, very punchy. But, as you say, he was more of a metal kid. Did you sit down with him and say, 'Look, this is the type of bass part that I'm looking for'?

We all agreed to play simple, because in the music that we liked, there were no technical chops going on. I mean, the Beatles were pretty rough players. They just had enough to get through. So did Pink Floyd. None of the records that we liked from the late 60s were particularly technical records. The people who we liked were not great players, it has to be said.

Do you remember if he played the part on this song with a pick or with his fingers? The sound is very distinctive, and obviously some of that has to do with the way you guys mixed it, but …

I know that on a lot of those records—especially the ones that had more of a dreamy, druggy feel—the bass would be reverb'd and echoed, so I think it's probably muted, and probably played with a pick. I think there's probably quite a lot of echo on it as well, so you get that slappy kind of sound.

As for that two-note pattern of the bass part, prog was really born out of the ashes of psychedelia. People were borrowing more and more from classical music, so it was OK to play those kinds of bass lines. Before, if you strayed away from a blues-based bass, people would have thought you were insane.

But I find I almost can't talk about '25 O'Clock' the song. Isn't that weird? It's almost like trying to capture a dream of something. There's very little concrete about it in my head.

But do you feel that you did capture it? Did you realise your intent?

Yeah. When we did this, there were no brakes on ourselves about being stupid. There was no shame. 'Yeah, let's put loads of recordings of clocks on the front. That's really corny, and *they* would have done it in 1967. Let's do that.'

It's kind of like how actors can be more free when they're in a part, because they're not being themselves.

Exactly! But how many musicians are like that? None. We were even playing badly on purpose in some cases. I remember saying to Dave—because Dave plays the organ solo and the guitar solo …

Does he? I assumed it was you on guitar, since he was playing keyboard.

No, they're both Dave. If you listen, I'm playing the little rhythm guitar underneath. Dave is playing the organ solo, and the fuzz guitar, and he's doing all the feeding-back guitar as well. I'll tell you, Dave was born a Duke.

And yet you made him a Lord!

He made himself a Lord! He picked his own name.

Did you guys all do that?

I picked Colin's, because [*laughing*] I think he was not as into it as we were, so I thought, 'OK, I'll find one for him.'

And you went back to when he used to have long hair, right?

Yeah, because everyone used to call him 'Curtains'.

So I said to Dave, 'When you play this lead, can you not play too well? Can you play kind of stumbling and not very fluid, because the players that we liked at the time were not that great.' So, it was a case of acting the role through the playing. You hit the nail on the head with what you said earlier—it was like being an actor. We were acting at being other musicians in another time.

Anything you remember about singing the song?

I'm shamelessly being over-melodramatic with the vocal and the melody. There's also an octave vocal on it—I think I'm doing that. You know, there is a pomp to it. It's a kind of teenage pomp—[*melodramatic voice*] 'I'll control you! How *dare* you run away from me? I'll make you mine, you wait and see!' It's like a real petulant teenage kid, you know?

Yeah—'Every move you make, every breath you take.'
Doo-doo-doo-doo, dah-dah-dah-dah!

What were you thinking of when you wrote this song? What prompted it in the first place?
'25 O'Clock'—you know, a lot of fascination with time was going on. Concepts like time were very psychedelic. The whole melting Dali watch, and time travel. You've got to tap into the subject matter.

Did you sit down and say, 'I'm going to write a psychedelic song' and everything kind of fell out?
Yeah, pretty much. I probably thought something like, 'OK, what would you have? It'd be about maybe an abstract subject like time—and what *isn't* time? There are twenty-four hours in a day, so … twenty-five! The strange time that doesn't exist!' It's all incredibly corny, but so were the majority of psychedelic songs.

Sure—there was this innocence back then, where people could get away with it.
Exactly. It was like, 'Ooh, we can pillage *Lord Of The Rings*—we can write that weird cosmic shit ourselves!' That's how people thought. It *is* quite naïve, and it *is* quite cringe-worthy, a lot of it. So, you have to write in that style. It's sort of opera meets Eastern meets 'What you would try for if you were some spotty geek who was trying to be heavy and meaningful?'

Speaking of a mix of styles, let's talk about the end—there's that Bolero-esque rhythm …
[*Mimics ending*] *Time!* And then of course, you've got to have the scraping of the open piano strings—you put the loud pedal down on a piano, and it takes the dampers off all the strings, then you just rub a coin up and down the strings.

That's very much the thing they would have had on *The Avengers*, when one of them would get drugged and the corridor would start spinning and going at weird angles.* So, we had to have it, because that was a corny way of suggesting the drugs kicking in.

---

* *The Avengers* was a British spy/sci-fi series of the 60s.

What memories do you have of the mixing and the after-effects or processing that you did?

There were some wacky little things—like, I remember saying to John, 'Can we do something with the panning?' He had a great suggestion—when it goes into the solo sections, he changed all the pan pots to the opposite direction. So when it goes in and out of the solo section, everything suddenly pans completely opposite to where it was prior in the song.

Every single instrument?

Exactly. Listen on headphones, and you can hear them all swap around at that point. After the solos we stopped, changed, swapped them all back again, made the edit, and so it cuts back to the original panning positions. It really flosses your head out! It's like having big purple rope going through your ears and flossing your brain through, you know?

As we were mixing this, everyone was working the desk. Everyone was working pan controls and the various effects: 'Great, get that reverb now,' you know. That's what it was like before automation. We used to have to rehearse what we'd do during the mix, just like we had to rehearse what we'd play on the instruments.

Interview conducted April 10 2009.

CHAPTER 19

THAT'S REALLY SUPER, SUPERGIRL

FROM *SKYLARKING*, OCTOBER 1986

Let's talk about Supergirl. Why her?
I've come to the conclusion that DC Comics were much more influential on my thinking than Marvel.

I was always a DC fan. I preferred them as a kid, even though I love Marvel's movies and characters today.
I guess, for me, they just went in earlier. But the memories are very strong. I can't remember who did the song—is it Steve and Eydie? [*Sings*] 'I don't want to go to the party with you / I don't want to go to the dance / I don't want to go anywhere with you / I just want to stay here and love you …' Do you know that song? It's like an old rock'n'roll ballady thing.

Yeah, Steve Lawrence and Eydie Gormé. It's a Goffin/King song called 'I Just Want to Stay Here'.*
There you go! You see, I get this Proustian moment when I hear that song— when I hear it, I am holding the eighty-page giant *Superman* book in my hands. You know how they used to do those?

I can *see* the cover—it's the one with Rainbow Superman, then there's a statue, like an Oscar Superman on the front, he's like a silver statue or something. I was a huge fan of Superman, but I wasn't a huge fan of Supergirl, I must admit.

Well, she seemed like an afterthought, created to take advantage of his popularity.
Yeah, there were loads of afterthoughts. There was even a fucking Superturtle!

---

* A hit for the husband-and-wife team in 1963.

C'mon …

I'm not joking! There was a flying tortoise in a cape! And there was Streaky the Supercat! [*Laughs.*] Because Superboy had the dog, didn't he, so Supergirl had Streaky.

Because chicks dig cats.

Exactly! And she had a Superhorse, too. [*Laughs.*] I'm not sure how the horse got from Krypton to Earth—well, he galloped, obviously. A chunk of stable flew off into space! A chunk of a gymkhana! But speaking of DC characters—well, of course, there's Brainiac's Daughter. She wasn't a DC character when the song was written, but now Brainiac's Daughter is a character there.

Yeah? I thought you'd just made that character up.*

I made her up. Brainiac didn't have a daughter. But *now*, they've incorporated Brainiac's daughter—whose name is XTC, I jest not!—into the DC universe. Isn't that funny—life is imitating art.

See? The effect that your music can have on the world.

There you go. I always wanted to be a DC or Marvel comic artist. So I guess this is how I get to live out that bit of the fantasy—I have created a DC character. There's a little bit of comic book character stuff running through our music. We even had a song called 'Quicksilver', who was of course one of the X-Men.

That was quite an early song, right?

Yeah, very early. There's a demo floating around—the Jon Perkins† version of XTC did a demo session in Reading. A place called Sun Studios—not the Elvis one, of course! But, anyway, I was um-ing and ah-ing about writing a song about a Supergirl.

Why? What gave you that idea in the first place?

Early on, I wanted to write a song about Supergirl—I thought, 'Yeah, great, I can get all my DC stuff into a song, and I'm singing it to a girl.' And then Stevie Wonder brought out this wonderful early Moog synthesizer-driven

---

* 'Brainiac's Daughter' is a song from the Dukes of Stratosphear's *Psonic Psunspot* album.

† Jon Perkins played keyboards in XTC in 1975, before leaving to join another Swindon band, The Stadium Dogs.

song, 'Superwoman', which I think is on the album *Music Of My Mind*, and I thought, 'Drat, I've been pipped to the post.' Of course, he's singing about a super woman, rather than a cartoon character, but that put me off for years. I came back to the idea in the 80s.

I guess I'm singing the song as a typical hurt male, because in relationships I was always the dumpee, never the dumper.

A lot of lyricists or poets will wait for inspiration to strike; that's the only time they can write. But you seem to be able to be able to draw on experience, like most good artists; even when you're not in the middle of it, you can take an idea or an experience, and work with them.

I think it's because I save stuff up. I save emotions up, I save feelings up. I'll get in touch with something, and a little metaphor will hook me, like a fish hook, but instead of blood coming out, all this stored-up emotion will come out. I'll think, 'Oh my god, of course—that's me getting dumped again,' or 'That's me finding out she was fucking another man,' or whatever. Instead of blood and plasma, all this hurt comes out, and you suddenly find yourself giving words to stuff like that.

You work with other emotions, too. The joy of infatuation, for example: 'You're The Wish You Are I Had' comes to mind.[*]

Oh, I do it with joy stuff, as well! I've hidden away good sensations, or confused sensations, or whatever. But in this case, it was not one specific woman. I guess it was a kind of Bride of Frankenstein of all the women who've ever dumped me. You know, they give you a lot of high ideals, like they're dumping you for your own good. They're dumping you to save you from yourself. Do you know what I mean? They give you all that shit. They try and make it more acceptable—they give you some creative lying.

Right—the whole 'It's not you, it's me' thing.

'It's not you, it's me.' Or, 'You're just too good for me. I don't deserve you, so I'm dumping you to save you the pain of …'

'I don't deserve you, so I'm leaving you'!

Yeah! You know, all that kind of shit. But 'Supergirl' isn't one girl—it's an

---

[*] From *The Big Express*.

amalgam of all the women who had better things to do than be around me. [*Chuckles.*] And, you know, the better things they had to do obviously involved saving the planet, and all that—so, there's a facetious part of it, a little sarcasm in it.

The lyrics are very clever in the way they pull in all the superhero imagery. For instance, 'Now I realise you're on a mission saving some other man.'
Exactly. It's one of the few sarcastic songs I've ever written, because I don't do sarcasm very well.

And there you were, recording it with Mr Sarcasm.[*]
And the shame of it is, he has your first name as well, which is really not good for this conversation! So yeah, we recorded it with Herr Rundgren in der Bunker: Utopia Sound. He'd had the demo, which was eminently more bluesy. If you hear the version on *Fuzzy Warbles*, there's a little beatbox going on in the background …

And harmonica all over it! Tell me more about that.
I'd written it with these rather exotic chords, which are sort of sixth chords—a B-flat with an open G ringing—and I thought, 'Oh, that's rather slick and shiny. I kind of fancy playing a blues harmonica all over it.' So, you get the earthiness of the bluesy harmonica against this stainless-steel, *Metropolis*, Chrysler Building architecture of these sixth chords, and I thought it was a nice mixture.

I remember when we were recording the song that Todd was trying to master it on keyboard, and Dave whispered to me, 'He's got the chords wrong!' I think he thought the chords were major, and they're not. If we're in B-flat [*plays chord on guitar*], the actual notes I'm playing in ascending order are B-flat, F, A, open G, F, B-flat.

I think Todd thought it was [*plays major version, which includes a D rather than an open G*], which is much cheesier. But I'm not playing a major, I'm playing an inversion of B-flat sixth. [*Sings the notes behind 'I can't hold you down' and plays the correct chord on the word 'down'.*] But he's hearing like [*repeats, ends on major chord*]—which is like your classic sit-com 'open to living room' chord! I was hearing it a lot more clangorous.

---

[*] Todd is referring to Todd Rundgren.

So, I fancied doing it with a harmonica, but he talked me out of it, because he was convinced that this was the single on the album.

I was talking to Dave yesterday, and he reminded me that, on a supposed day off while doing the album, Herr Rundgren said, 'Let's go to New York and buy some instruments.' So we jumped in his camper van kind of thing—which was like an Ovation guitar on wheels [*laughs*]—really tacky fake wood and fretwork and all that kind of shit—and drove for god knows how long to New York City. We went to these big music places, I can't remember where exactly they were …

Yeah, on 48th Street. All the big music stores are clustered along one block there.

There you go. And of course, they *were not worthy*, these assistants. They were all bowing and scraping to him, and they didn't know who the fuck this bunch of limeys were, just getting in his way. [*Adopts nasal American voice*] 'Can you get out of the way? I'm trying to serve Mr Rundgren!'

He was saying things like, 'Well, that's nice, that's a nice little small-scale guitar'—it was called a tiple, by Martin*—so he said, 'I want one of those.' And he found a Prophet-10 synthesizer, which was basically two Prophet-5's built together in one box, and we had to wheel this bloody thing blocks and blocks to get to his camper van.

So he bought this Prophet-10, and of course he wanted it all over this track. That meant that the idea of using a bluesy harmonica got ditched, and all these Prophet-10 sounds—and there are dozens of them—got layered all over that recording.

So, all the different keyboard parts are that Prophet-10?

Yeah, I think so. Maybe a couple of them were the Yamaha DX7.

Did he and Dave split keyboard duties? I know Todd played some of the parts.

I thought they did, but I rang Dave yesterday evening, and he said, 'No, I'm not playing anything on this track other than the guitar solo.' So, in fact, all the keyboard parts are Todd.

---

* A tiple is a small instrument in the guitar family, native to Latin America. The Martin version has ten steel strings in four courses.

So Dave doesn't even play rhythm guitar?

He doesn't play anything other than the guitar solo, and I'd forgotten that. I do remember that none of the keyboard parts are sequenced—they're all played in by hand.

Even that very percussive part at the beginning?

Right, that bit at the beginning is sequenced—that's the only thing. It's like a little distorted beatbox thing. I've got a feeling that it's probably a programmed Fairlight synth, because he had one there that he was pretty keen on.

In fact, I think that there is a mechanical programmed backbone to a lot of the songs on *Skylarking*. Like, for example, in 'Meeting Place', there are cranky industrial sounds.

Yeah, that was the first one that came to mind for me.

In 'Summer's Cauldron', it's all natural noises—insects and dogs and crickets and god knows what. In 'Dying', it's a clock ticking away. So, the Fairlight is also pretty much throughout the album. But on this one, the only thing that was programmed, that I can remember, was that intro. But all the actual keyboard parts are just played live, and it's all Old Banana Fingers himself.

Yeah, I remember reading that you guys were appalled at what Todd would consider a good take.

Oh, yeah! His keyboard technique was incredibly primitive. I thought mine was bad, but his was on a par with mine. You know, he'd use something like two fingers on his right hand, and one finger on his left, and that'd be it. And I can still hear it—the shoddiness of the playing.

You know, it's fine—it's part of the character of the stuff now, and you can't complain, but at the time, we were all looking at each other and going, 'He's *not* going to keep that take, is he? That is *so* rough.'

But he had this thing where he had to get it finished on time, because it'd be more money for him, since he was earning a flat fee. He could move on to the next project. But we were appalled that we'd only get one or two takes on something, and that'd be it. You know, 'OK, that's good. Move on.' 'Oh, but there are mistakes on it!' 'Doesn't matter! Let's move on.'

It adds character, right? [*Laughs.*]

I guess so. [*Chuckles.*] I mean, I'm not upset about it now. But I think we all were then. 'What, he's going to let that go? No producer we've ever been with would have let that go.' But yeah—that's the sound of the record. So, it's him playing keyboards, and I'm playing the little scratchy guitar on the right-hand speaker. And, listening to the song, I was reminded of the peculiarity of the drums.

Yeah, I wanted to ask you about that.

What you're hearing is Prairie Prince playing bass drum and hi-hat to a sequenced snare drum from a Utopia record.* Todd asked me, 'How do you see the drums on this?' And I said, 'Pretty simple, but I really fancy a kind of clangorous snare drum—very biscuit tin, almost like a kind of beat music drum, with a lot of ring on it.' I said, 'Do you know the kind of sound I mean?'

He said, 'Does it sound like this?' He pulled out the Utopia album *Deface The Music*, and he put a track on—one of their kind of Rutles things—and I said, 'Yeah, that's the sound! That snare drum on that track, that's the sound.' He said, 'I'll tell you what we'll do, we'll just lift one of these off.'

I can't remember if he took it off the album, or if he had the multi-track there. He probably pulled it off the master tape. So, we played to a click track—sort of sketched it out—and when we got to San Francisco to do the drums and other parts, poor Prairie had to sit there, just hitting his leg for a snare drum, and sat there playing the rest of the kit. The poor devil had to play *around* the backbeat. And that's a tricky thing to do.

How about that little drum-roll part before the chorus?

Do you know, I'm not sure whether that's Prairie live, or a little sampled roll off of a record.

It sounds as if it could be a sample.

I've got a funny feeling it was, but I can't remember where that came from. It's like a little Tamla roll—*boomp*-de-le-lap-*boomp*—which is one of my favourite drum rolls of all time. Dave Mattacks, who played drums with us on *Nonsuch*, said there are two variations I've got to listen for. There's boom-de-le-lap-boom, and there's boom-de-le-lap-bom-bom. So, thanks to Mr Mattacks for pointing out the variation there.

---

* Prairie Prince, born Charles Lempriere Prince, came to fame with The Tubes and Journey, and has worked with artists including Chris Isaak, Todd Rundgren, and David Byrne. He is also a graphic artist.

And he would know, wouldn't he?

Yeah, he is a student of the instrument. Anyway, we needed one of those, and I've got a funny feeling that was lifted off of a record.

So, the drums are a strange patchwork of bits of Utopia, bits of god-knows-where-we-took-it-from, and live Prairie.

I was wondering about the snare—it is a sound that Todd is associated with, but I had figured it was just something about the way in which he recorded the snare that Prairie played.

To be smart about it, we should have waited until we got to San Francisco, cut the track with Prairie drumming, and then either tuned the snare drum to be what we needed it to be, or used it to trigger a more-clanky version, so it would have been perfectly in time with it. I mean, we really did it ass-about-face. I also remember, on some of these tracks, that Colin was very upset that Todd was asking him to play bass to no kick drum.

I know that goes against what he likes to do.

Todd said, 'Look, you put the bass guitar where you hear it, and then we'll get Prairie to fit the bass drum to that.' And Colin said, 'No, I just can't do that!' I mean, he's a bass player, and he's got to marry up to where the bass drum hits. He's got to glue that bass into the drums and the whole feel of everything.

I remember him telling me that this was one of the things he started to do once you guys stopped touring—that he liked to lay the bass part down last.

Exactly. You jam along with the drummer, to get the drumming recorded, and then you can take away that guide track—which is probably too busy a bass part—and then, later on, be more selective about exactly what the notes are.

I'll tell you what—I was on the headphones yesterday, and that reminded of what a bloody good bass part it is on this. And it's an unusual tone for Colin—I can't remember how it was cooked up, but it's got a lot of Jack Bruce burp to it. It's not a tone that I would associate with Colin at all.

And the melodic content of the bass is really very nice on this song: you know, the little tumbles he does going into the chorus; and the little tumbles at the end of the chorus are really very attractive. I hadn't clocked it until I listened the other day, because I don't sit and pick our stuff apart, you know? It's kind of freaky to do that. But I'm doing it to talk to you, and I'm sat there thinking, 'Wow! I never really realised how nice that part is!' He is a great bass player.

Was his part something that might have come out of rehearsal? Because I'm assuming you rehearsed this song before you travelled to America to record. Or did you?

If we rehearsed this stuff anywhere, we did it in Dave's living room. It probably would have been us just sat there, running through the chords, and nothing more. So, it was the sketchiest of rehearsals for the majority of this stuff.

Right. Not like you guys had done when Terry was in the band.

No. And not like the vigorous rehearsals we did for pretty much every other album. Certainly *Oranges & Lemons* and *Nonsuch*, where we had weeks of bashing it through with the respective drummers, you know?

We were talking about Dave playing the guitar lead before—why don't we jump back into that?

Oh, yeah. We walked up to that mezzanine section of Todd's studio, and in the corner, on a skinny little rusty old stand, was Eric Clapton's psychedelic Gibson SG, which is *the* psychedelic guitar—I think even Hendrix's psychedelic Strat is not as distinctive as Clapton's Fool-painted SG.

Fool-painted?

The Dutch art group, The Fool, painted it. They're also the people who did the side of the Apple building, which had to get painted over, because supposedly it was too disturbing for traffic.* And they actually designed the original *Sgt. Pepper's* sleeve, which The Beatles thought was a bit cheesy, and didn't go with.

Funny thing is, if you look at the Clapton guitar close up, it's really rough. It's just fluorescent poster paint or something, which was all the rage at the time. But when Dave saw this guitar, it was like, 'Oh my god, can I play this on one song?' So he used it to play the solo—which is beautifully worked up—on this song.

We'd be doing a vocal or guitar or some keys in the studio, and Dave would be off in his bedroom at the guesthouse, noting out and running through and learning and getting this solo down. Because he really wanted to rise to the

---

* The Apple Boutique was in Baker Street, London. It was open for only seven months.

challenge—if *he* was going to play one of his all-time wet-dream guitars, he's going to play something that's just beautiful on it, you know? It's a fantastic solo—beautifully worked out. It's *really* melodically appealing. But I think I can hear Dave's nerves just a little bit.

Really?
Yeah. I can hear him saying to himself, 'I mustn't fuck up! I mustn't make any mistakes, this is my one chance!' I can *kind of* hear a little of that in his playing, but it's a great solo. Just as a melodic thing, as a little piece, it's *really* well thought-out.

What was the processing on it?
I think Dave would have liked to have played it with more of a cranked-up kind of Clapton-y sound, but it's more of a jazzy tone, and he's got a lot of chorusing on it.

I was going to say, it almost sounds doubled.
It's not doubled. I think it has a type of a Leslie effect, or a chorusing effect, and maybe a little slappy echo. But it's only one guitar.

But, as I say, I think ultimately Dave would have liked to have had that Clapton-esque, cranked-up, Marshall/Gibson sound. Instead, he ended up with a sort of space/jazz guitar thing. The amp might have even been the pocket sized Rockman—by Tom Scholz, the guitar player of Boston—which Todd was keen on at the time.

Let's talk about the vocals, which are quite complex and ornate. Todd kind of follows your ideas from the demo, but he takes them to the next level.
Well, I don't know whether if it's because he's got some of the chords wrong, and because of all these layers of very shiny keyboard, it does actually sound more American to me. And more like Utopia, actually.

Well, it certainly sounds more major than what you have on the demo.
Yes. It is. I think, instead of leaning on the G, he's leant on the D in the B-flat, which makes it a little slicker and a bit more lounge-y.

And more radio-friendly, presumably.
I guess so, because he was convinced this was *the* single. If you hear the flavour

of the whole album, this one does have the more-modern ears put to it—you know, just in terms of sound and treatment. There's nothing quite as late-twentieth-century sounding on the rest of album, if you know what I mean. The rest of the music on there is anything from pagan Britain up to Victorian. [*Chuckles.*] Probably about 1930s is the latest sort of sensation on there.

I'd say you'd get well into the 60s with 'Earn Enough For Us'.
Oh, you're right. There you go. But this track came right up to date, and is maybe even sort of 'retro future', with some of those keyboard sounds. Since he thought it was the single, it got the single treatment.

So, who was doing all those high vocal parts?
I can hear Dave in there, but I'm guessing it's a mixture of all three of us. It may be even a little of Todd, too. I know he's on 'Grass'. But I can certainly hear Dave's timbre in there—that wispiness. You know [*imitates Dave*], 'The man with no voice—Dave Gregory.' You know what I mean? He seems have such a pink-noise content to his voice.

And, you've said before, that's an attractive quality—that you would use that to your advantage in your harmonies.
Oh, sure! If you need a little wispy air in your backing vocals, call for Dave. Because that's the tone you get when Dave sings. I mean, Dave is very upset with his own voice, because he swears he doesn't have one. [*Imitates Dave again*] 'What's the point of me singing anything, Partsy? I don't have a fucking voice!'

Then the funny thing is, you listen to the cover songs he does on *Remoulds*, and he does one of the best Jack Bruce imitations I've ever heard! And Jack Bruce has a pretty robust voice.
Well, there you go. Maybe it's Dave's lack of confidence on the singing front, you know. But I can hear him in the backing vocals, and I'm guessing it's probably Colin and Dave, and/or Dave and myself.

How would Todd end up doing vocals with you guys? Or keyboards, for that matter? Was one of you at the board?
One of us might be at the board, and we would drop in. For example, he played melodica on 'Summer's Cauldron', and I had to tape-op that. And

when we got to San Francisco, there was a woman who came attached to the studio. Her name's on the sleeve—Kim Foscato. She would do tape-op stuff for Todd there. There was a fellow who he used to use at Utopia Sound, but he didn't actually do any engineering, because I think it was a case of saving money, you know? If he'd had to pay for an engineer, that would have blown a lot more of the budget. But, what other notes have I got here?

There are some different lyrics on the demo.
Ooh! I didn't remember that.

The lyrical structure is a little different, too.
Yeah, Todd did a great edit. We sent him demos on cassettes, and he dumped them on to some other tape, and edited them to what he thought was the right shape. Which I thought was pretty damned smart. I mean, initially, I thought, 'What? He's chopping our music up?' But, you know, when you get to play it in its edited form, it's much more concise, and I like that. It's something I've grown much more respectful of, as the years have gone on—chopping things down to size and getting rid of anything superfluous.

I didn't realise there are different lyrics on the demo. I'd forgotten that. I'll tell you what I do like: the answering vocals that I came up with—'hurt like Kryptonite' and all that. It goes up through that funny scale, creating a sort of tension, then release. You get that funny tense note, and *then* it releases on the top note.

Yeah, and it's also a good lead into [*sings*] 'Now that I found just what you're doing …'
Yeah, and then there's that big C—that *clang*. Which kind of comes out of nowhere, because we're in B-flat! Then that leads into the chorus. So this song is kind of in three keys simultaneously.

Right, and you've got to find the way to go from one section to another.
Yeah, let me grab the guitar again. It actually starts in that B-flat sixth [*plays a bit*].

It's interesting how you use the melody to 'walk' into the different chords.
I never thought about that, but I guess I do! There's that real vaudeville chord between the two verses, then at the end of the second verse, suddenly it jumps

to C. Then we're in another key again, which is A-flat. So, it's in B-flat and A-flat, with kind of a C joining section. I guess that breaks a few rules, but it seems to work.

Let's talk about the lyrics a bit more. There are a lot of little jokes in here, internal rhymes, and other things.
I can't even remember them right now!

'I can't hold you down / If you want to fly.'
That's the whole thing of, 'If you want to end the relationship, I can't hold you down.'

Right. And there's the pun with 'fly' there.
'You say you want to spread your wings and fly …' That's the sort of shit they tell you! 'Well, who the fuck do you think you are—*Supergirl?*'

'Can't you see I'm all broke up inside / Well, just you use your two X-ray eyes.'
Exactly. 'I'm really hurting in here—you've got X-ray vision, you can see that you've broken my heart!' It is really sarcastic.

'Hurt like Kryptonite / Put me on my knees.'
Of course. The one thing that can upset the super family is Kryptonite.

'Now that I've found out just what you're doing / With your secret identities.'
Yes. [*Laughs ruefully.*] Ooh, I'll tell you what, after my divorce, these words really hurt.

'That's really super Supergirl / How you saved yourself in seconds flat.'
Exactly—you didn't save me or the world! You saved yourself. And that's the sarcastic bit—'Oh, that's really super, that is.' That's that disgusted phrase that you use—'Oh, that's *great*, that's really super.'

'And your friends are going to say / That's really super Supergirl / How you're changing all the world's weather / But you couldn't put us back together.'
Yeah, 'you can do something as fantastic as spinning the world backwards, to

set time back to save someone, or change the weather, but you can't put us back together because of what you've done here.' Ooh, I'm such a sarcastic bitch!

[*Laughs.*] 'Now I feel like I'm tethered deep / Inside your Fortress of Solitude.'
Fortress of Solitude—had to get that in. And I managed to sneak the 'bottle city of Kandor' into 'Brainiac's Daughter' as well.

And there's that good internal rhyme there, where 'You couldn't put us back together / Now I feel like I'm tethered.'
Along with 'weather,' as well.

'Don't mean to be rude / But I don't feel super / Supergirl.'
Yep, the play on 'super' there.

'I won't call again / Even in a jam / Now I realise you could be on a mission / Saving some other man.' And that's the part that you edited, since this verse on the demo is twice as long.
Yeah, and I think that was a good move, that that got chopped out.

Then it goes on from there. Funny that you say, 'Well I might be an ape,' given the name of your record label!
There you go! And I'll tell you, when I heard that line on headphones yesterday, that hurt. 'I might be an ape / but I used to feel super.' Oooh …

That's one of the lines that gets me in this song, too, because you're saying, 'Dammit, I was *happy* before I met you.'
[*laughs.*] Kind of, yeah. Hindsight hurts. Hey, that can be a measurement of grief! The Hindsight Hertz scale.

Anything else you remember about the recording of the song?
Actually, now that you mention it—this just came flooding back to me. I've always associated smells and other stuff with music, as we've talked about earlier. For example, we talked about Steve and Eydie, and the sound of that single being, for me, the *Superman* eighty-page comic book. When I hear 'That's Really Super, Supergirl', I can smell something quite distinctively.

Which is … ?

Rotting rat! The previous band who were in the guesthouse*—I can't remember who they were—apparently had a rat problem. They put down rat poison, and the rat or rats died under the floorboards or between the walls, and the overpowering smell in the guesthouse was rotting rat. In fact, I can smell it now, because I've smelled it recently. I had a rat problem about five years ago, because some neighbours were doing some building, and they had a rat that ran from their house and hid in mine, so I had the rotting rat. And god, it brought back that whole album!

But the smell of that album, and specifically this song, is rotting rat mixed with lavender floor polish.

Why particularly this song?

I don't know! Maybe there's something in the chord shapes, or the sound of the chords or keyboards, that says 'rotting rat and lavender'. You know what lavender floor polish smells like?

Pretty sickly sweet, I'd imagine.

Oily, waxy, and a little sickly, because lavender also has that old-lady connotation. But mix that with essence of rotting rat, and that's my Proustian moment with this song.

And they had used the floor polish to try to clean up the house for you?

They tried to clean up the house, and I guess they were using this heavy, stinky floor polish to try to mask the smell. But there weren't only dead ones in there, because we were watching some TV one night, and a live one ran in front of the TV!

And it was a rat, not a mouse?

It was a rat, yeah. A big 'un. Well, you know, you're up in the woods there. I'll tell you, you step out of the accommodation at night, and there was the most phenomenal star stuff you could see, because there was no light.

You know, you're deep in the woods, in a clearing in these pine forests, and you look up, and there are just *billions* of stars. And the Milky Way is *so* distinctive!

---

* At Utopia Sound.

Yeah, when you actually get away from cities and light pollution, you can see what they mean by the name—it's stunning.

Yeah, you can't see that in many places in England.

Sure, there's enough light pollution in Swindon that I'm sure you never see the Milky Way at all. You'd have to go way up north, or out to Devon or Cornwall.

Yeah, you see those light-pollution photos from space, and the majority of England—apart from Devon and Cornwall, and parts of north Scotland—it's all light.

We're all light?

That's not what I wrote that song about! But in this sense—yeah, unfortunately we are.

Interview conducted March 15 2008.

CHAPTER 20

DEAR GOD

FROM *SKYLARKING*, OCTOBER 1986
RELEASED AS A SINGLE B-SIDE, AUGUST 1986
RELEASED AS A SINGLE A-SIDE, JUNE 1987

'Dear God' is probably your biggest hit, in terms of giving you notoriety and introducing you to the widest audience. Let's talk about God.
My goodness. Where should we start? Where should we kneel, to get this in the right perspective? [*Laughs.*] Get me a pint of that communion wine, and I'll tell you anything.

Mmmm … and some of those styrofoam wafers …
Yeah, some of those *yummy* styrofoam wafers. Yeah, if that's the body of Christ, what do you mean—was he actually *made* of styrofoam?

Well, maybe that's how he was able to ascend into heaven!
There you go! He was very light. He just blew up there.

So, tell me: why wasn't 'Dear God' on the original album?
It wasn't on the original album because I honestly thought that I'd failed. It's such a *vast* subject—human belief, the need for humans to believe the stuff they do, and the many strata involved, the many layers of religion and belief and whatnot. So I thought I'd failed to address this *massive* subject for all mankind—and also a big subject for me, because I think it'd been bugging me for many years. I'd struggled with the concept of God and Man and so on since I was a kid, even to the point where I got myself so worked up with worry about religion that—around about the age of seven or eight on a summer's day—I saw the clouds part and, you know, there was this sort of classic Renaissance picture of God surrounded by his angels looking at me scornfully.

Wait—what? Are you talking literally or figuratively?
Literally! I was so wound up about the existence of God, and all the questions

involved. 'Is there a heaven and angels there, and if they're there that means there must be a devil, and OH NO—what if all this shit is real?!?' My little kid brain was trying to grasp it.

I was out playing on this tiny little patch of land, all on my own, doing what a kid does on a hot afternoon. I looked up at the sky, and quite seriously, I hallucinated—the clouds parted, and there was God and the heavenly hosts—real Renaissance-painting shit, stuff I'd probably seen in encyclopaedias or something—looking at me, as if to say, 'C'mon—of *course* we exist! Here we *are*!'

I never told anybody at the time—who knows what would have happened if I had. I would have been St. Andrew of Penhill, or in a monastery getting buggered senseless. [*Laughs.*]

During the evenings, of course—you'd be put to work illuminating bibles during the day.
Yeah, exactly. [*Laughs.*]

Was it just visual, or did God speak to you?
I don't remember anybody saying anything—I just remember them staring from this vision-y vision, looking down at me stood on the grass there.

How long did this last?
I guess a few seconds. It was a genuine hallucination. I can't explain it, other that I was so wound up about whether or not all this religious shit was real.

Was your family religious?
My father insisted we say grace every mealtime, and I was encouraged to pray before I went to bed every night—just the standard stuff. But it used to wind me up terribly. 'Are they telling me the *truth*? Are there really gods and Jesuses in heaven, and devils and demons below?'

So, it lasted a couple of seconds, and then what? You were overwhelmed and averted your eyes and it was gone by the time you looked back? Did you run home screaming? [*Chuckles.*]
I felt really confused! I remember thinking, 'Was that *real*? What *was* that?' But it was a hallucination, I'm sure, brought on by extreme anxiety. I never told my parents or anyone else, until I told you.

Why didn't it make you then believe that it was real? Did you have a period of time where you were convinced it was?

Good question. Hmm. [*pauses*] I actually doubted it *more* after that.

Interesting. Why?

I don't know! It was as if it had appeared to say, 'No, we're not real.' Do you know what I mean? Anyone else might have said, 'Oh Lord!' and fallen on their knees, but I think, in the back of my mind—after this hallucination, this vision, whatever you want to call it—I thought [*sceptically*], 'No. None of this stuff is real.'

So, in a way, the absurdity of it became obvious to you because of the manifestation of this vision.

Yeah. For me, it seemed to tick a box in my head that said, 'You know—it's not real, any of this.' But I really did have this hallucination—unless they really *did* appear!

I guess you'll find out at some point!

Yeah, I'll find out. Ah, He knows I've been good. I'm not on the Naughty List.

Yeah. Santa God.

Or Satan Claws! To be truthful, do I really want to spend all eternity peering over the edge of a cloud, looking at people suffering torment in Hell? That's not my idea of a great evening out.

What do you want to do tonight, then?

'We could go watch the tormented souls …' 'Oh, not *again*!' [*Laughs.*]

Anyway, I guess the song 'Dear God' was me trying to come to terms with this thing. Though I thought those *Dear God* books—you know, kids' letters to God—were a pretty tacky concept, I liked the title. I liked the idea of writing to God to address the fact that I didn't believe he existed. I just wanted the thing to come back with an angelic stamp on it, saying 'Return to Sender.' Written in fiery letters!

'No such address.'

Yeah, 'No such address, redirect to Hell.' But I thought I kind of failed. I think it would have taken more than three-and-a-half minutes to do the subject justice. I'd also come up with a track, just before we started recording, called 'Another Satellite', which I thought was *much* more interesting. It was interesting because it was personal, and I tend to disguise or hide away a lot of my personal stuff, and it was interesting because of the arrangement. It was also fresher, you know.

And, I think Virgin were also a little—our contact there, Jeremy Lascelles, he's eleventh in line to the throne or something like that—I think he was a bit funny about 'Dear God'.* I went in to have a meeting at Virgin after the album had been recorded but not yet released, and he told me, 'The American market isn't going to like this song, and you're going to get a lot of hate mail. What would you say if I suggested taking it off the album?'

To me, that underscored or threw a spotlight on the fact that I thought I'd failed in my attempt to crystallise the subject matter in three minutes and a bit. I thought, 'Oh well, if he thinks it should come off the album, maybe it *is* a weak song, and it's also in kind of a weak spot in the album—three-quarters of the way through the album, where the weak kids get put.'

So, it wasn't the fear that some listener wouldn't like the song—I didn't care about that—but I thought that perhaps I really *hadn't* done the subject matter justice, so my already-low confidence in the song was further shaken.

So, he said [*in fast record-company exec voice*], 'Yeah yeah yeah, we should go with "Another Satellite", not "Dear God".' He had his own reasons. Maybe he thought that if he said yes to that track, it'd push him farther down the ascending-to-the-throne ladder!

Had your producer, Todd Rundgren, heard 'Another Satellite' and not included it in the original running order, or did you write after he had put the song order for the album together?
I'm pretty sure it was not included in the original order—I sent it in later. Side two was supposed to start with 'Let's Make A Den', but that got argued out of existence.

What do you mean?
He wanted to put into 4/4 time, but I wanted to keep it in 7, because that way it keeps tumbling forward, which I like. He said, 'C'mon, you've got too many

---

* Jeremy Lascelles, who rose to be head of A&R at Virgin and then CEO of Chrysalis Music, is second cousin to the Prince of Wales and in the line of succession to the British throne.

beats in there,' but I disagreed, and it got to the point where we just didn't finish it. There's a half-finished version somewhere on tape.

But 'Dear God' *was* originally in the running order, and it always *did* go into 'Dying'. People complain about that, and say they've gotten used to it, but it was *always* supposed to be in that position. The clock in 'Dying' is supposed to take over the rhythm from 'Dear God'.

Let's talk about the structure of the song.
It starts with a sinister change—A-minor with an F on the bottom. Cor, that's real antichrist stuff. When I found the pattern, I was probably messing around with 'Rocky Racoon', which, when I was sixteen, was the only song I could properly play on guitar. When I was in college, they'd ask me to get up on the desk and play, and that song is the only one I could do—it's that root note with the A-minor strum. 'Dear God' takes the same basic approach—it's an A-minor, and I move the root note around, to make a countermelody that is a little demonic.

That's the final form the song too, but if I remember correctly, this originally had quite a different feel.
Yeah—the initial music to this was much more skiffle-y. I knew I wanted to write on the subject, but hadn't figured out how to approach it so that it felt right. When I tried it in a faster, more upbeat fashion, it sounded too frivolous.

Had you written the lyrics already, and you were trying to write music to fit them? Many times, you talk about how you'll stumble across a chord, and it will evoke a feeling or image for you, and the lyrics flow out of that.
That is indeed the usual case, but with this one, I think I had the lyric of the subject matter and the sort of basic intention, but the music was not right. Once I found this 'gunfighter ballad' approach—which is a little more serious-sounding—I realised it was the right thing. I thought, 'Oh, that fits what I'm looking to say.'

And what I was looking to say, as you know, is this paradoxical thing where you're addressing somebody who you suspect doesn't exist. But rather than praying and asking for something for yourself, you're saying, 'You've caused so much shit down here—why?' You know—'If you're omnipotent, you *know* you're causing this shit.'

The demo for this song is one of the more 'produced' that I've heard from that era.

Because there were some songs that we hadn't properly demoed for Todd to hear, we got together one day down at Dave's and demoed it. I think we might have done 'Summer's Cauldron' as well.

That was the version I was thinking of. It's on *Coat Of Many Cupboards.* **I was surprised at how finished it sounds.**

It's just us playing into Dave's four-track tape machine in his living room. I did say to him, 'Look, I'd like some strings in there, and would like them to have sort of a Gershwin-y, bluesy, "Summertime" feel.' I always feel that strings, when they're full of blue notes and slides, have a slightly demonic cast to them. I wanted the song to get a little darker in the middle, so I thought that strings would be a great addition to it. I thought they would blend well with the acoustic guitar.

Right. That mix of musical styles adds, of course, to the inner paradox of the song, in the lyrics themselves.

Yeah, that paradox! People still say, 'Well, what's he doing addressing God if he doesn't believe he exists?' [*Fast*] But that's the paradox, arsehole! C'mon, get with it! Wake up, that's the whole idea—that you're talking to somebody you don't believe exists, and you're asking them why, if they do exist, they're causing all this trouble, but you're saying at the same time you know they don't exist! [*Sighs.*]

And, of course, I got all the hate mail and the booklets. It all came from America, by the way, all the hate mail. None of it came from England. Somebody sent me one of those books called—and I've still got it, because I thought the title of it was fantastic—*You Can Live Forever In Paradise On Earth.* And I thought, 'Wow!'

But all the hate mail, and the firebombing threats to the radio station in Florida, and all the rumpus caused by that—I found that so *medieval*. I really felt sorry for the people who [*pauses*] got so *upset* at someone expressing an opinion that might be contrary to their beliefs, or at who might have another take on their beliefs. How could that make them so violent, potentially?

All in a country where we supposedly have freedom of speech …

No, you don't have freedom of speech. That's just an advertising slogan, like

'I'm Lovin' It!' It's just another advertising jingle—'Come live in America, we've got [*sings syrupy melody*] Freedom of Speeeech!' I mean, let's face it—to a degree, white America was started by fundamentalist crazies who couldn't get on in England. So what happened? We threw 'em out, they turned up in America and began to pester the natives.

It's funny—we've always had this push and pull here in the US between reason and religion. We have the Enlightenment values of the Founding Fathers, who are totally revered, and then we have these people who say they revere them, but their actions show that they completely disregard what they were all about.
I was reading some of the comments on YouTube recently, and oh, man …

Don't read comments on YouTube, Andy. It's just one of those *rules*. I am 100 percent certain that I'm not missing anything of value when I skip the comments there. Intelligent discourse in the YouTube comments section is probably as existent as God.
[*Laughs.*] Yeah. 'This guy's a fat fag!' That's the sort of thing they say. Or, there's a lot of desperate ways of getting attention—someone on there was calling himself Satan, for example.

There's some irony involved in the fact that people who criticised you for this song, and your right to say what you had to say, are the same people who, for example, criticise extremist Muslims for their suppression of free speech.
That's true. But I didn't feel in danger of my life or anything. I actually thought that the letters ranged from bonkers to sort of sweet—there was an element of concern that some people showed, because they thought I was going to go to Hell for writing a song that questioned their particular deity. I'd read through some of them, and think, '*Aw*, they don't want me to go to Hell.' Of course, others would be much more aggressive—'You're going to burn in *Hell*, you piece of *shit*,' and all that sort of thing.

Even though I originally thought I'd failed with the song, I eventually felt sort of proud that I'd come up with something that stirred up the hornet's nest. Suddenly people are ringing into radio stations and saying, 'Play that again, because that's how I've always thought, and I couldn't express it,' or, 'Don't you *dare* play that song again!'

So, that was good—I felt as if I'd done good by igniting a debate. I couldn't really see what the fuss was about! If you believe in God A, why do you feel threatened by me saying that God A might not exist? How does that threaten the existence of your omnipotent being?

It might threaten their faith, because it calls it into question. It's like homophobia—you've got to wonder why homophobes are so bothered by other people being gay.
Yeah, it's true—the ones that are the worst are probably the self-hating ones who are really just in the closet. It obviously threatens a part of them that they're already unsure about. And it's true of religion, too—if their god is omnipotent, and they *truly* believe this, why on Earth are they so upset that *I* wouldn't believe in him? Because I say *I* don't believe in him, does that make *them* not believe in him? Do *they* feel duped? I could never figure out, logically, why they were so upset.

That's what happens when people follow 'user guides' that are hundreds or thousands of years old and were originally created to provide guidelines and laws for a much different people in a much different time and place. If you're outwardly thumbing your nose at the basis of that law by saying that the ostensible creator of those laws doesn't even exist, then you're a danger to society.
You're a danger to those who *control* society.

Exactly. It's the same reason Jesus was crucified, ironically enough. He threatened the power structure.
Exactly—that Jewish troublemaker! You tell a lot of white Christian fundamentalists that they're in love with an angry, radical, communist, and possibly Buddhist Jew, who comes back from the dead, zombie-like—they don't want to hear that! [*Laughs.*]

'What do you mean, I've got to feed the poor and give up all my possessions to follow him?'
Right. It's simple, really—God's inside you. We are all God. There's nothing outside. But that Old Testament fellow—what an arsehole. [*Chuckles.*] Here in England, Woolworth's, and a couple of other stores, banned the 'Dear God' single, with the sleeve that has a pen as a crucifixion nail going through a

hand. They didn't want to upset people, so they wouldn't stock the single. They were all sanctimonious about it.

Another irony of the song—which is perfectly fitting for a song that is full of paradoxes—is the fact that the song made you guys more famous than anything you had done up to that point.
Well, yeah. Of course, it started as a B-side, but later got added to the album. Which meant I had to sacrifice 'Mermaid Smiled'.

Which was too bad, because it's a beautiful song. But at the same time, I can see why you took one of your songs off, rather than asking Colin to— you guys were in a very delicate place then. The band had almost broken up during the sessions in San Francisco, right?
Oh yeah. There was such a bad atmosphere. Things were going pretty tough, working with Senor Rundgren. It was the first time we'd ever really fought in the studio. Over nothing in particular! So, getting through the album and still being a band at the end of it was quite a feat.

And it ended up being your salvation. 'Dear God' was your salvation.
Because it upset people! And radio stations—you know, they're kind of naughty, too. They figured this was going to piss off a certain part of the community if they played it, so they colluded in that. They began playing the B-side, and it took off, so yeah, it got added to the album, while 'Mermaid Smiled' fell on its own sword. [*Laughs.*] Fell on its own sharpened bucket and spade.

But managed to come back in the reissues, right?
Yeah. It would have been nice if we could have got everything on, but it would have made the vinyl a bit lopsided.

Let's talk about recording the album version—Colin's playing his fretless bass?
Yeah, I think he's on the Newport, which is the one that, if you put the damper on, it sounds like a cross between an upright acoustic bass and a fretless electric. There's a lot of buzz and *knurl* to the sound. It's fretted, though.

And Dave's playing electric? I assume you're playing mostly acoustic.
Dave's doing the classic Gregory arpeggio stuff. He's the King of Twinkle. He

can arpeggiate with the best of them. I can do some idiot finger picking, but he's great at that. I'm playing the acoustic, and Prairie's whacking away on the drums there.

Yeah, he has an interesting little thing he does on the snare, where he lets the stick bounce against the head when he hits every other 'three' during the verses. It almost has a slight military feel to it.
Yeah, it's like a continuous rolling sort of feel.

When you were talking to him about the song and telling him what feel you wanted, what kind of language did you use?
I think it was a case of—not jaunty, but the drums had to keep their head low, just roll on and roll on—nothing really strident. Usually, I like the drums to be in conversation with the rhythm guitar, and the bass in some way, or even the vocals, but in this one I wanted them just to sort of almost ignore the song and just patter along. Which he does nicely, you know. That was not necessarily the kind of drums we usually do—it was out of the ordinary for us, to have the drums play a very subordinate, 'don't bother me' kind of rhythm.

Finally, what role did Todd play on this song?
It was his suggestion for a kid to sing the first verse. I'd told him the title was inspired by these kids' letters to God, and he said, 'Well, why don't we have a kid sing the first verse?'

I thought, 'Hey, that's kind of interesting.' We might have talked about having the kid's voice cross-fade and become mine as the song went on, but in the end we decided she should sing the entire first verse.

The only person he knew who could do it was Jasmine Veillette, who was part of a musical family that played bars and things in the Woodstock area. He told us, 'Look, she's only nine,' or whatever age she was, 'and she knows me, but she may really clam up if she sees three strange English fellows staring at her, so could you just get lost for the afternoon while we do this?' So we did.

Oh, sure. You'd get a better performance from her that way.
I think we crept up and peeked in the window, where she couldn't see us, but we waited till she'd gone until we came in and heard it. I don't know how many takes it took to get it, but she did a great job. A lot of people think it's a

boy singing the part, because of the creepy-looking boy actor from the video, but it's not, it's a young girl.

Speaking of the video, what do you remember about it?
It's one of those we-had-absolutely-nothing-to-do-with-it videos again.

You had no input?
Not that I remember, no. But we didn't on most of our videos. You'd have a meeting with the director, and you'd say what you'd like to do, and they'd go, 'Oh yeah, great! Well, *here's* what we're doing!'

Did you have a vision for what you wanted with this one?
I don't remember having a vision for this video, because we originally thought it was off the album.

So, suddenly it gets big, it gets put back on the album, and what happened then?
Suddenly we start getting asked, 'Where's the video for it, chaps?' 'Wait, this was a B-side this morning!' I was so depressed about our videos—none of them looked very good to me. My concepts were always ignored. The woman at Virgin who was head of the video department was very outspoken and aggressive. Every time I took a video idea to her—I'd sketch it out and go and see her—she'd always ridicule it. 'What? A black-and-white film? Who's going to show that on colour-TV channels?' 'What, animation? Nobody wants to see a cartoon of a band!' 'What, you want to film this section underwater? You can't have electric guitars near water! No kids' show will play that! Plasticine? No! Silhouettes? No!'

She always had a fucking excuse, and it drove me insane. It was depressing.

And these are all ideas that have made it into music videos!
They were all ideas that other people eventually put in their videos, and won awards for! But in this case we were just told to turn up on a set day at a set place. They asked a couple of questions—'What size trousers are you, what size jacket are you, and do you have any objection to getting up in a tree?' [*Laughs.*] Which I didn't, but the other two did—if you look at them, they're consistently sat on the low branch. But even I didn't have to get up the tree much—I was mostly the slightly demonic 'son of a preacher man' at the bottom.

Did the director talk to you about the concept at all?
Nick Brand was his name, I think. I think we got his concepts, but I pretty much just went through the motions. I was so hurt that I used to have these video ideas, and every one of them was rejected for some spurious reason or another. That said, this one isn't too bad—I'll give you that. I got the notion of what he was going for—the Tree of Life, or the Tree of the Knowledge of Good and Evil, or whatever.

But I think anybody in England watching it would have giggled that the part of the old man in the tree was played by a fellow who was in a very famous ad in England for Yellow Pages—the telephone directory.* He plays an author who's looking for a book he's written—'*Fly Fishing*, by J.R. Hartley.' The ad was so well-known that everyone thinks of this old man as the character in the ad as J.R. Hartley. And because it's the same actor who's the old fellow in the tree, people would ask me, 'Why did you stick J.R. Hartley up there?' [*Laughs.*]

'Good question,' I'd say. 'One of God's mysteries.'

Interview conducted November 19 2006 and January 11 2015.

---

* The actor was Norman Lumsden. He died in 2001.

CHAPTER 21

MAYOR OF SIMPLETON

FROM *ORANGES & LEMONS*, FEBRUARY 1989
RELEASED AS A SINGLE, JANUARY 1989

So, after the worldwide-domination-type success of *Skylarking* …
Ahhh, don't say that, because that's the name of our first manager's company!
I jokingly said to him, 'You're going for world domination, are you? You're
going to call yourself Global Domination Ltd?' And he did! And he used to
send me memos on his letterheaded notepaper, with this name.

**Ah, yes, the man we all know and love. [*Laughs ruefully.*] Well, you
followed up *Skylarking* with the bright, shimmery *Oranges & Lemons*
album, with 'Mayor Of Simpleton' as the single. I suspect this was another
case, like 'Senses Working Overtime', where you were going for a single.
Is that true?**
It ended up sounding like a single, but it had a very confused birth, this song.
If you've heard 'REM Producer Enquiry' from the last of the *Fuzzy Warbles*,
that's how it started.* It was a half-speed, quasi-reggae, Quasimodo type of
thing! [*Sings initial version.*] It had a kind of jaunty vocal over this lumbering
quasi-reggae thing. I wasn't happy with the music at all. It didn't seem to suit
the intent of the lyric, which I thought should have something with more
propulsion behind it.

Then I found a little three-note pattern on the guitar—in ascending order,
it was C, E, and open G, and you move it up a tone and it becomes D, G-flat,
open G. I think I was kind of messing around with looking for the chords to
the Blue Öyster Cult's 'Don't Fear The Reaper', to be honest!

Seriously?
I'm not joking! I remember thinking, 'Wow, isn't that a bit like "Don't Fear

---

* Demo on *Fuzzy Warbles Volume 8*.

The Reaper"? How does that go? No, that's not it—but that's not bad! That's pretty good, in fact. It's got an essence of The Byrds about it—that big, ringing open-G thing—but it's nothing like Blue Öyster Cult, and I wonder if I could fit the lyrics to "Mayor Of Simpleton" over it?' So, I was kind of blundering around with someone else's song, and made the mistake of finding the 'Mayor' riff—it was not what I was looking for, but I found something all my own.

It's interesting to me that you have no problem with taking pieces of songs you've written—or half-written—before, and repurposing them. Other people might have felt protective, and said, 'No, those lyrics belong with that melody, and I'm not going to take them apart,' but you didn't mind lifting those lyrics and putting them to a new melody, to fit these new chords.
Sometimes you can make a great roof, but the building it's on top of is just not happening. You know—you've made the roof of the Louvre or something, and put it on top of a mud hut! So, you mess around a bit—and in my case, I blunder—and then suddenly you sometimes find the key to the rest of the building under it, and you keep at it until it looks in proportion.

It would seem to me to be a valuable lesson for songwriters.
Never throw anything away.

And be willing to cut things up and reassemble.
You can't be precious with your own material. You've got to get the knife into it, and cut it up and hack it about, and be very uncaring about it. Because if you don't, you'll never find the potential goodness in a lot of it. You've got to get in and hack away the dead wood that comes along with a lot of ideas.

But some people don't want to do that. [*Whines*] 'They're my words, I don't want to change them!' Sometimes I do co-writes with people—and I've got to vow to stop doing it, because sometimes I get sent people who *just can't write*. And I say to them, 'Look, this line is great, but those three lines are rubbish, so let's come up with …' [*Whines a response*] 'Oh no, it's my *poetry*, I can't change it!' And I'll say, 'Well, then you're not going to get a good song out of this, because the opening line's really good and the next three are just dogshit!' But they don't have the attitude of, you'd *better* be tough on your material, because the whole rest of the world is sure as hell going to be!

And you've got to be willing to sacrifice some of your children so that others may live.
Exactly! In a kind of Scientology way! [*Laughs.*] Is that the sort of thing they do? Don't they eat babies and stuff?

They do now! 'Andy Partridge Reveals The Truth About Scientologists!'
That's right. Scientologists eat babies—you heard it here first!

Back to the song—let's talk about the bass line.
Yeah! I'm going to be immodest, because this is part of my drive toward immodesty this year …

Well, the line is yours, after all! It's obvious—it's there on the demo.
[*Chuckles.*] People do these survey things, and say, 'Let's vote for Colin's best bass line' or something, and they don't realise that the two bass lines they vote for are ones I came up with—'Vanishing Girl' and 'Mayor Of Simpleton'. That's me playing bass on 'Vanishing Girl'.[*]

Oh, I didn't know that.
Yeah. And 'What In The World?', that's me playing bass as well.[†]

Get out of here!
That's me on bass—Colin's on rhythm guitar.

And you came up with that bass line?
Yeah.

That's funny—I've always thought that was him channelling McCartney.
No, we had to cut it live. He obviously couldn't play the bass and the rhythm guitar, and I didn't know how the chords went, so instead of him teaching me the chords, I said, 'Look, you play the chords, I'll play the bass, and we'll get this thing done before lunchtime!'

But the one they mention most frequently is 'Mayor', which I wrote. Colin had to work very hard to get that bass line—it's very precise. It took me

[*] From *Psonic Sunspot* by The Dukes Of Stratosphear.
[†] From *25 O'Clock* by The Dukes Of Stratosphear.

a long time to work it out, because I wanted to get into the J.S. Bach mode of each note being the perfect counterpoint to where the chords are and where the melody is. The bass is the third part in the puzzle.

You do that a lot in your songs.
Yeah, it's a compulsion. On many of the songs I didn't tell him which exact notes to play, but with this one, I said, 'You *have* to play this bass line, because it's taken me weeks to work it out.' I created it a note at a time, to go with where the vocal note was, where the implied guitar chords were, where the actual notes of the guitar being twanged to make that implied chord were. It was built scientifically—it was [*laughs*] precision-engineered so that every note is in the perfect place. And I think Colin liked the bass line, because we talked about it sounding like a collegiate peal of bells.

Why did you feel you needed that kind of driving bass line in there?
To keep the song moving, moving, moving. I wanted it to have a fleetness of foot, a joyousness to it. I used to love running as a kid—in fact, I still dream of running. If I ran now, I'd die of a heart attack in about thirty steps [*laughs*], but I used to love running, and got really high on it as a kid. I wanted this track to have a sense of fleet, forward movement, so the bass *had* to be very propulsive. The guitars are doing that kind of [*sings guitar pattern*]—they almost sound sequenced, but they're not. They're played. I wanted the bass to move against that continuous arpeggio. And of course the drums locked into that as well, with the bass drum really hammering along.

So, yeah, it was tough for Colin to get, but he did get it. We even ended up playing it live during the radio tour we did, and he would play that line on the acoustic guitar. He's on it! Normally I didn't dictate to Colin what to play, as he's brilliant enough on his own, but with 'Simpleton' it was a different case.

Let's talk about the lyrics a little bit. Where did you come up with the conceit of feeling inadequate? I know that it's kind of a theme with you, but it's usually centred around money, where you want to provide for somebody.
Oh yeah, there are lots of money worries in my songs. [*Sighs.*] I guess I'm being a little bit of a fibber in this song, because I'm not a stupid person. Instead, I suppose it's saying that emotion, and the warmth of emotional honesty, is better than some sort of stinging, cold, rather antiseptic brainpower. It's better to not be so intelligent and instead to be more loving—quite a simple

message, really. I think I've been criticised for rewriting—what's that old rock'n'roll song …?

'What A Wonderful World It Would Be', by Sam Cooke?
Was it? If I did, it was a subconscious lift. It's not the sort of music I heard as a kid, and when I was old enough to choose my own listening spectrum, I certainly didn't go for old rock'n'roll.

Well, I think it's a well-worn groove in terms of subject matter.
So, if people see it as a Sam Cooke lift, that wasn't intentional. But I can see that you could find similarities in the overall conceit of the lyrics.

Was there some instance that you can remember where it suddenly struck you that the word Simpleton could be the name of a town?
Oh, sure. That was why it was chosen.

Did the lyrics just kind of flow from there, or was that a joke or pun that occurred to you one day, and you decided you needed to do something with it at one point?
I remember thinking that the word 'simpleton' sounded like a place, like Wimbledon or something. [*Laughs.*] 'Mayor Of Wimbledon'. So I guess that, after I realised that, I filed it away for later use.

I guess there's also a little bit of autobiography in the lyrics. I recently found a load of my school reports—you look at them, and you can just see my interest in school going down through my teenage years. In my first school reports, I'm pretty good a lot of things—and then I really lose interest. You can see that I'm just not bothering by the time I'm fourteen or fifteen—I'm just not bothered with school at all.*

It was largely expected that I would fail at everything. But I knew it was not about being academically successful. I *knew* that that was not going to be important to me. I actually asked my parents if I could stay behind, rather than go on to grammar school and do another three or four years or whatever it was. I asked, 'Please, let me stay back just one more year, I'll do one more year with all the stupid kids, and then I can leave school.' Best thing my

---

* Andy attended Penhill Secondary School in Cricklade Road, Swindon. It is now St Luke's, a school for boys with educational and behavioural difficulties.

parents ever did for me, agreeing to that. In the end, I decided to leave school at fifteen, rather than go on to grammar school.*

Tell me again about the grammar school system?
It's like high school in the US, and you have to pass tests to get in. You can carry on until you're eighteen or nineteen, or whatever. Or you can be a dimwit and leave at fifteen, which I did.

Oh, you left that early?
Yeah. I couldn't wait to get out of school. I detested it. I detested the idiots—the idiot teachers, and the idiot pupils even worse. I was bullied a lot because I was sort of weak and thin and artistic, and I didn't like sport. So yeah, there's some autobiographical aspects to the song.

You did go on to art school, though.†
Yeah, at one time I thought I might want to be a graphic designer. Nowadays that surfaces in sleeve designs and other stuff, but I very soon found out—after a year and a half or so at college—that it was just school, too. And of course by then I was getting more and more interested in making music, and I had this *craaaazy* fantasy that I could have a career in music.

You'd be Big.
I'd be grotesquely large! [*Laughs.*] With my own gravity. My own rings.

So let's talk about the music a bit. Dave's doing the twelve-string in there.
Yeah, Dave's doing his usual stellar work. And Pat Mastelotto's doing a great job on the kit, powering along there.‡ It's actually a mixture of looped stuff and played stuff.

I had read in an interview with him that he recorded all the parts separately—so, he'd record just the hi-hat, then the snare …
I think what happened is, we did a pass where we kept a number of bars of

---

* Unlike Andy, Colin went to Headlands School, which had been a grammar school and had a Sixth Form designed to prepare pupils for university entrance.
† Andy went to Swindon College in 1969 to do a foundation course in art and design.
‡ Pat Mastelotto was with Mr. Mister before working with XTC on *Oranges & Lemons*. Aside from session work, he has toured and recorded with King Crimson since 1994.

bass drum that felt really good, and then we looped it, and he would then play in certain sections with hi-hat and snare to that. Or maybe he even played them separately! I can't remember.

If I remember the interview correctly, he said he did it because you guys were trying to get the clarity and separation of instruments—you know, no bleed-through in the mics.
Yeah, that sounds right. We *were* trying to get no bleed-through, and I wanted it to have—like 'Stupidly Happy'—an almost-mechanical sense of propulsion to it. I did not want it to slow down or speed up in any way. So I seem to remember that we started with a few bars of a take of his drum track, but we only kept the bass drum. And then I think we may have lined everything else on top, so many bars at a time.

Structurally there are a couple of cool things that you do in the song. The first is in the bridge, when you change the feel completely. I remember someone in an online fan forum commenting that you're the 'master of bridges'.
The Christopher Wren of bridges! Or, no—Brunel did the bridges.

Yeah, Wren did the churches.
The Isambard Kingdom Brunel of the pop world. That's me. [*Laughs.*]

The change of pace in the bridge is intentional, obviously. You probably like doing that in bridges—setting them apart, I mean.
I do, but I also like to try to involve them in some other way in the song. So, with 'The Disappointed', for instance, the bridge becomes the intro. That's a George Martin trick. But on this one, the change of pace in the bridge was just kind of like a breather—I wanted to take a breath. I kind of had to slap our producer's wrist. Paul Fox really wanted to drop in all these kind of dub echoes in the middle section.* I think there is one weak one, on the word 'act', but he was putting those all over, and I said, 'No no no no, you're spoiling the propulsion of it!' I felt a little sorry for him there, because he felt as if he couldn't put his fingerprints on that track—you know, his imprint.

---

* Paul Fox is an American producer and musician. *Oranges & Lemons* was his first major production. He has since produced Robyn Hitchcock, 10,000 Maniacs, The Sugarcubes, and many more.

The ending of the song is very distinctive, too. Having sung and played the song in a band myself, the timing's a little weird—but it's also very cool and original.

I was very proud of the outro, actually. What we're doing is, I got Colin to play the backing vocal, the 'please be upstanding for the Mayor of Simpleton' part—I said to him, play that part …

But with different phrasing, right?

Yeah. The backing vocal becomes the bass line, but slowed down, and that throws it into this realm where the 4/4 of the guitar and drums becomes dislocated from the implied different timing of the bass. It was a case of 'here, try this out'—and it just seemed to work beautifully.

And, like 'Thanks For Christmas', it's one of those plateau fade-outs.

Right, because it stays on the same chord.

It stays on the same chord, but you're into that suggested dislocated rhythm, because the bass is now playing the backing vocal.

And the backing vocals have a 'round' feel to them, where they repeat and intertwine.

Exactly. A slight tip of the hat there to something like 'Good Day Sunshine'. Just call us the Fab Three!

Interview conducted December 17 2006.

CHAPTER 22

CHALKHILLS AND CHILDREN

FROM *ORANGES & LEMONS*, FEBRUARY 1989

The next song I want to talk about is one that I've heard Dave say is one of his favourite songs by you.
[*Cod German voice*] Jah, the hills of chalk! Und der little children ... I know who else's favourite song it is, but I can't remember his name—synthesizer fellow from the 80s—Howard Jones.[*]

Really?
I think Dave was working with him on some project or other, and Howard Jones told him that.

Interesting. It's one of your favourites, too, right?
Yeah, I'm pretty proud of it, actually. Although I do make an ass of myself in it by showing that I didn't understand what the word 'nonsuch' meant. I thought it meant 'a non-existent thing'—a thing that was not there at all, and I liked the alliteration of 'nonsuch net'. But I got it wrong, because it doesn't mean 'no such net', it means 'incomparable net'.[†]

You mention alliteration—let's talk about that a little bit. Is it a device that you purposely use sometimes in your lyrics, or is it a happy accident when it happens?
No, I work at my lyrics until I'm sweating blood.

And alliteration is something that you like, that you'll strive for?
Oh, I *love* it. I really love it. I love that almost sort of Doctor Seuss tongue-

---

[*] Howard Jones had ten top 40 hits in the UK between 1983 and 1986.
[†] Andy didn't know this at the time, but 'nonsuch' is also eighteenth slang for 'vagina'.

tripping way it affects words. It just makes it more pungent if you have lots of *L*'s in a row, or lots of *S*'s, or sounds that sound similar between one word and the next, and the next, if possible. It becomes its own little internal kingdom—it's *lovely* to do.

Do you think you did more of that after you stopped touring? I could see how it could possibly get in the way sometimes, singing and projecting live.
Well, in the very early stuff, the lyrics were pretty shamefully rotten. They were probably chosen for the sound that cut through shit PAs—you know, *O* sounds cut through, while *E* sounds don't. But as far as actual words go, I guess I started to become a half-decent songwriter at some point, and you can sort of see that I start to use more word games and alliteration and the odd pun or two. But I love alliteration. It seems to shake hands with itself, and it seems to be like a little infinity loop, perfectly completed. I like that in other people's work, too.

What inspired you to write this song? It's very dreamlike, but did it actually come from a dream?
No, it didn't come from a dream, apart from the fact that occasionally I do dream that I can fly. I'm sure there's somebody out there who knows all about dreams, but it's usually a similar scenario—I'm out in the street, and I'm telling people, 'Look, I can actually will myself up into the air!' They're saying, 'No, you can't!' And I say, 'Yes, I can—watch.' And I sort of *strain*, and then, in a standing-up position, I levitate about three or four feet off the ground. And they go, 'Wow! You really can! Is that as high as you can go, or can you go any higher?' And I sort of *strain* a bit more—I can feel myself straining in the dream—and up I go, about twenty feet. And they ask again if that's as high as I can go, and I will myself up to fifty or a hundred feet or so, and then I wave to them—'Bye, I'll be back in a bit!'—and then I travel across the hills around here, in that standing position, about a hundred feet in the air.

I have flying dreams, too. A lot of psychologists apparently regard them as 'reward dreams'.
What do you mean?

In that, if you're feeling good about yourself, or you're feeling a sense of accomplishment about something that you've done, you'll have a flying

dream, because usually flying dreams are freeing, and liberating. It's interesting to hear about the way you fly in your dreams, because in my flying dreams, I have a feeling of swimming through the air.

So you're lying down and sort of swimming?

Yeah! And there's always a feeling of, 'Why didn't I realise before that I just had to move like *this* to be able to fly?' There's a certain feel to the stroke—it's almost like a breaststroke or something.

With me, it's not like doing a stroke—I'm standing, slightly leaning forward, and straining. But yeah, it's a dream I have every now and then.

I can actually tell you what inspired the song—I was sitting with my relatively new keyboard I had at the time, a Roland D-50, and I bought a little thing that you plumb into it via the MIDI, I think. It was a little box where you could move all these sliders and things, and build up tones. I noticed that I could tune a second note to go against the note I was playing.

So it was like a harmonizer?

Kind of. I had this organ tone, and I set this control so that each note had another note on top of it, a fifth higher. I came up with that funny little [*sings pattern from intro of song*]—but, because it was all fifths, it sounded really medieval. It sounded like the hills. Because, in Swindon, we're surrounded by these hills—the Marlborough Downs, these chalk hills.

I thought, 'Ooh, that's the countryside around here.' I guess I started to associate with the hills, and maybe I'd had a flying dream recently, and I just remember playing these long, languid, very simple chords, but because they had this automatic fifths tuned into them—I don't remember thinking, 'Wow, these are very musical, swish chords', but Dave said to me, 'God, this is so well-composed. These chords are fantastic! How did you find them?' I don't remember them being a strain—I just remember being guided by what sounded right, with this automatic fifth tuned in. I mean, they were probably three-note chords, but because there was a fifth dialled into each note, they were like six-note chords, you know?

I think I was still 'Mr Cardboard Hand' at the time—if I found a good shape on the keyboard, I would cut out a cardboard hand to remember it! Actually, come to think of it, I owned a sequencer by this point. But once I started playing this very dreamy thing, I started thinking, 'I'm floating over the hills. Why am I floating over the hills? I'm dreaming, and my whole career has been like some weird dream', and I just started to associate from there. The whole essence of the song is, I feel uncomfortable with the whole star thing.

And this was almost at the height of your fame, because by this time *Skylarking* had hit big.
And everyone was saying, 'Wow, what's the *next* one going to sound like?'

Yeah, a lot of notoriety with that album. You had seen both the light and dark side of fame, what with all the hate mail you got over 'Dear God'.*
Exactly. And there was that internal wrestling over that I *loved* making and recording music, but I was disgusted by the fame it seemed to bring. I wanted the music to be famous, but not *me* to be famous.

Yeah. The 'reluctant cannonball'.
I'm the reluctant cannonball, fired from some weird circus thing. With no safety net—or that's what I thought I was saying! So I do apologise for to anyone who was confused by me grabbing the wrong word for that.

Oh, they'll get over it.
Yeah. And they think that's why the *Nonsuch* album was named that, but it's not. [*Laughs.*] Pure coincidence.

Given that *Skylarking* was so successful, I assume you were given a fairly solid budget in advance to do *Oranges & Lemons*?
Oh, we went well over budget on this album. They said, 'Look, we're going to pull the plug fellows, we can't afford for you to finish it off.' I think we'd run up a bill of a quarter of a million pounds.

Is that because you decided to do so many songs?
No, a lot of it was just us living in LA, in this rather wretched apartment block. Everyone was living there with their families, and we were paying session musicians.

Of course, our engineer, Ed Thacker, and our producer, Paul Fox, weren't

---

* Originally released in August 1986 as the B-side to the UK single of 'Grass' and subsequently added to the US *Skylarking* album in place of 'Mermaid Smiled'.

cheap, and the studios weren't cheap—plus we spent a hell of a long time out there.*

Well, after the experience you had at Todd Rundgren's studio in Woodstock, you wanted your families with you, right?

Yes, but I was also really stressed at the end of this album, too, because we were fighting our original manager legally, and I was really coming unwound, and drinking far too much. I was drinking whisky, and if I'm drinking whisky, there's something very wrong. So, funnily enough, we end the album with a song I wrote in honour of being rather ordinary, and being glad, ultimately, to have my feet on the ground, on these hills around Swindon. And the flying over it—being up there in the sky like a marvellous thing—was, in fact, just a dream. As the majority of the career had just been a dream.

Tell me about the 'chalkhills and children' image.

Well, that's another bit of alliteration. What do I see when I look out my window? Chalk hills. What do I see when I look down in the kitchen, or look in the garden? I see children. They're real things. They're the real countryside around here, they're the reason you're 'responsible old dad'—it's the stuff that keeps your feet on the ground. It keeps you level—there's no fakery involved. You can't be fake for the kids—I mean, OK, you can dress up like a space monster from the Planet X and scare the shit out of them by chasing them around the garden, but that's not fake—it's not like show business. Show business is all fake. But being a father is not fake, and the hills around here are not fake.

So, why did you bring up Ermin Street? Because of the ancient quality?

It's the ancient quality, and the fact that it's only a few miles away. Ermin Street is an ancient trackway that Iron Age man would have trodden along with his horse or his cow, and it runs right past Swindon.† It just seems to have a feeling of real permanence. There it is, in the chalk, up on the hill, trodden for thousands of years.

---

* Ed Thacker's previous clients included Natalie Cole, Manhattan Transfer, Starship, and Tom Jones.

† Ermin Street (not to be confused with Ermine Street, further East) is a Roman road running from Silchester in Hampshire to Gloucester. It mostly lies beneath the A417, A419, and B4000 roads. It may well have been built over existing Iron Age tracks.

Whereas fame is transitory.

Fame will last you five minutes, and will *not* buy your groceries. I still wrestle with that now. I know that what I do makes fans, but I don't want them to be fans of *me*. If anything, I just want them to be fans of the music that I—that *we*—do.

Right. You're facing the quandary that a lot of artists face—the difference between themselves and their art is obvious to them, but some people don't see the difference—they think that the art is the artist. I've read interviews with Joni Mitchell where she talks about this. She says, 'No, this is me being an artist—I have personas, I'm telling stories about different people, but people assume they know who I am because they know my music so well.'

[*sighs.*] That's a tricky one. The music is one thing, and the person that's written the music, or made the music, is another thing. The music does exist outside of that person.

Though there is some of you in the music, obviously.

Yeah! There are big dollops of me. And there are not. I get to be very truthful, or I get to be a big fat liar. You get to do all those human things in your music. You get to pretend to be other people; you get to be yourself. You get to wear disguises, you get be stripped naked. But people shouldn't assume that they *know* you because they like a piece of music that you've done. That's a big mistake.

Back to the dreamlike quality of the song …

I associate the sound of dreams with an organ—if there's music in my dream, it's probably an organ. I remember when I was much younger, hearing about a record called *Escalator Over The Hill*, by Carla Bley.* I've never actually heard the music, and I sort of don't want to, because I remember, after I heard the title, that I went and fell asleep and dreamed what the music would be like. I know I would be incredibly disappointed if I ever heard the real music, because in the dream it was these multi-layered, multi-coloured organ pieces, probably more akin to some things that Philip Glass or Steve Reich or Terry Riley have done.

---

* Released in 1971.

As soon as I started to play this organ with the added fifths, I was in medieval time, on the land, and it was a dream, and it all tied together, you know? And, funny enough, this song about reality and having your feet on the ground was recorded in the very cardboard bowels of fakedom!

[*Laughs.*] Los Angeles.
Which, everyone knows, is Spanish for 'City of Lying Bastards'!

So that's how it translates! Interesting. Let's talk about the recording process. You have Pat Mastelotto on drums.
This is Pat, and the first thing we recorded for this track was the straight cymbal.

I was going to ask you about that, because I think I'd read in an interview with him that he couldn't play that straight eighth-note pattern on the ride cymbal while playing the kick-and-snare pattern that you hear on the album.
No, I *wanted* that—it's on the demo. I wanted the tension between the straight cymbal and then the swung-played kit, inherent with the jazz feel of the piece.

Had you ever intended him to play that part?
Not at once, because I know he's not an octopus! But the first thing we recorded was that straight cymbal.

And that's him playing? That's not a machine?
I think that's him. It could be a loop, but I think it's him. And then, in Ocean Way studio, where we did all the drums—beautiful-sounding room—we recorded him on the whole kit, playing along. But the kit is played in this very lazy, swung jazz feel.

I liked the tension of the swing jazz feel against the very straight ride cymbal—it's the same sort of tension that's in the music of 'Summertime Blues' by Eddie Cochran.* You get [*mimics beat and chord pattern*]—part of it's straight, and part of it's accented. It's the slightly dotted feel against the very straight feel. The tension between those two feels, against each other, is *marvellous*. And that's what I wanted with this. I wanted the tension of the straight cymbal against the dotted jazz-feel cymbal.

---

* A hit in 1958.

I love how he throws in the hi-hat crash on the 'and' after 'two'.
Yeah, he just lets it ring open and wobble.

Yeah, kind of using it as a crash almost, but the two cymbals continue—I would say beating off each other, but that doesn't sound right.
Well that's a different sort of instructional DVD, isn't it! [*Laughs.*] Anyway, I found out at one point—and I can't remember whether I found out when we were rehearsing, or when it was finished—that jazz drummer Tony Williams would have drummed on this track, which could have been very interesting. *

Meaning that he wanted to, or that if you'd asked him, he would have?
Well, you'd have to talk to Paul Fox to get the story dead straight, but from what I remember, Paul knew him and was going to be doing an album with him. They were talking, and when he found out Paul was working with us, Tony said, 'Man, I'm a fan of that band! You've got to let me drum on that album.' So, this could have been Tony Williams on here. Which means it would have sounded totally different, I think. But I seem to remember Paul telling me that he was not in the most reliable place at that time, so it was a case of, 'We really shouldn't use him—it may be too difficult.' But just as a fan thing—I'm a huge fan of his band Lifetime—it would have been good.

So, he would have played only on this song, or on other songs on the album as well?
I think he was offering to play [*laughs*] on the whole damn album, actually! You know, I think he could have been very interesting on 'Miniature Sun' and some others. But how he would have fared on things like 'Mayor Of Simpleton' or 'Garden Of Earthly Delights' is another matter. They would have gone in a very different direction.

Yeah, he wasn't the kind of guy who took direction easily, or so I've heard. He was used to being a bandleader.
Yeah, I think Paul thought that he'd be making a rod for his own back if he said, 'Come along.' But that could have been an interesting alternate route we could have taken.

---

* Tony Williams (1945–97) came to prominence after playing in Miles Davis's band. His own band, Lifetime, pioneered jazz fusion.

Did Pat know about that when he was doing his version?
Not that I know of. I don't know if Paul told him or not.

Because the way he stretches out at the end of the song makes me wonder if it's trying to emulate Williams …
I told Pat he could go wild, within the rhythmic feel of the rest of the playing. I wanted the end to really fall apart into this droning, dreamlike thing, where parts of the lyric come across, and there's lots of repetition. Everything's sort of smashing together, like you're trying to frantically grasp for bits of reality in the dream, you know?

It's very well recorded—great stereo separation as he goes around the kit.
Yeah. I mean, Ed Thacker—when he records tom-toms, they *stay* recorded!

What else can you tell me about the arrangement of the song?
Let's see—the wind chimes are Paul Fox's. You know, the part where it builds up to a title line that's not there [*at about 2:30 in the song*]? Where I sing, 'rolling up on three empty tyres, till the …'

Yeah, then it's just keyboards.
And Paul Fox's wind chimes. They were hung outside his apartment, and I thought we should put them on there as an homage to 'Wind Chimes' by The Beach Boys, which I'd only really heard two years earlier.*

This song does have a Beach Boys feel to it.
I felt a bit tricky about that, because they were a big influence on me, especially since I'd starting hearing their albums, from about '86 onward. I was only aware of their singles before then, but once I started hearing their albums, I realised they'd gone in deeper than I thought. I could see that this song was kind of coming out Beach Boys-like, and it was a case of, 'Well, just try to rein it in a bit, but if it wants to come out like that, don't be too ashamed of it.'

Sure. It's not like you were doing the 'ah-ooo' background vocals or anything.
No, there's no 'bap da-dooby-dooby' stuff in there. But I thought the wind

---

* Written and recorded for the abortive *Smile* album in 1966. Re-recorded for *Smiley Smile* in 1967.

chimes would be a great little texture, and a little nod from me toward 'Wind Chimes'.

So, what's up with the line about 'three empty tyres', anyway? I've always wondered about that.

Well, that's me, Dave, and Colin, you know? How the hell we got there, I don't know. We're just three empty tyres rolling along.

That's funny, I never even thought of it that way, but it's obvious once you say it. So, Dave's playing keyboards on this song?

Dave's playing keyboards—and there are a lot of them. There are a lot of different keyboard textures laid over each other. You can hear some that are a bit like voices, some that are kind of wheezy and reed-like, some that are more Hammond organ-like. The fact that there's a lot of them makes the patchwork of fields you're going over, if you know what I mean.

I do. Colin has a nice bass tone on this, too.

Yeah, very placid-sounding. It has to be, because you're floating over hills. He also plays a bass line that echoes the singing—echoing the 'Even I never know' part.

And what are you playing?

I'm not actually playing on this track at all, apart from singing.

So there's no guitar at all? I thought there might be some acoustic mixed in there.

Nope. There's nothing. Not that I can remember. I just get to be the sleepy nightclub singer on this.

How many different vocal lines do you have going on at the end there?

Oh, sheesh, there were all sorts, you know, that had to be faded up and faded back. It's just meant to be a real dreamlike mash. I mean, really—given what we did there, we just *had* to finish off the album with this song.

Interview conducted September 30 2007.

CHAPTER 23

THE DISAPPOINTED

FROM *NONSUCH*, APRIL 1992
RELEASED AS A SINGLE, MARCH 1992

'The Disappointed' seems to me to be another one of your prescient *Nonsuch* songs, given that your marriage would end after the album. Maybe we should start by talking about the lyrics.
It is pretty prescient! Actually, could I just derail you for a moment? Could I start with the video?

Sure!
Which I hate—hate, hate, hate! You think I'm *acting* disappointed in that video? [*Laughs ruefully.*] I'd had meetings with the video's director at Virgin, and I'd brought up books, and I'd done sketches, and we'd gone through what I wanted.

I turned up in the morning, and walked in at this big sound stage, and it was *nothing* like I'd asked for. And so, I started to say, 'Hang on, this looks nothing like what we'd agreed on,' when the producer wandered over to me, and said, 'Look—shut up, sonny, we're trying to make a video here.' And I just *knew* the day was not going to go my way! [*Chuckles.*] 'Be quiet'—I don't think it was 'shut up'—'Be quiet, sonny, we're trying to make a video here.'

Had you intended it to be more like a house of cards—kings and queens?
Actually, it would have been mostly computer-generated, but I wanted the perspective to be all wrong, as in medieval paintings. You know how we used the 'Siege of Jerusalem' picture on the twelve-inch of 'King For A Day'? I really liked that, and I wanted to go on from that and do a fully fledged, weird-looking medieval-perspective thing, where the towers of the castle are slightly smaller than the people in them—so, their heads are looking out the towers, but there's no way they could actually fit them in the towers! [*Chuckles.*] Or, an arm would come out of a doorway, and fill the doorway.

Or, there'd be somebody stood at one point that looked about three inches tall, and somebody next to them looked about ten inches tall.

It was that kind of medieval perspective, where they used to make the most important things larger—it didn't matter whether it worked perspective-wise or not. If the king's in the picture, he'd be a foot tall, and everyone else him would be six inches tall. He'd be sat in his castle, and the tower he'd be in would be drawn massively, and the rest of the castle would be tiny. So, it was all that weird, messed-up medieval logic of …

Hierarchy, rather than perspective.
Exactly, hierarchy—which is like a lower-archy, but it's the taller one. The one on the top shelf. Or, it's one where you can't afford your own archy, so you pay the rent on one. 'Is that a hire-archy?' 'Yeah, don't scratch it!'

Anyway, I'd had a meeting with this director, and had brought up these books of medieval art, and did drawings, and I said, 'I want this bit to look like this—I want the sky to have a kind of grid pattern, like you get on tapestries. I don't want it to look anything like real life, now or medieval—I just want it to be this totally insane perspective thing.'

But when I turned up on the day of filming, they'd gone and built this set and booked these actors that were all friends of theirs from some university thing. I felt like saying, 'No, I don't want these New Romantic-looking idiots in my film, please!' And then, when I saw the dwarfs wander on set—game over.

[*Laughs.*] I think it was all an elaborate ploy to make you genuinely disappointed.
Yeah—it was the big thing to get me in character! Of course, then they keep you waiting around all day till about 11:00 at night, from something like 6:00 in the morning, and they say, 'OK, we've got to wrap up now—ohhh, we haven't filmed the group!'

No!
Seriously! That was what they said. So, they crammed us all in, in about a half-hour at the end.

And it was the most we ever paid for a video. It was something like £45,000, which is the equivalent now of something like £100,000 or more.

And you certainly didn't get the return on your investment—that was *your*

money—that you'd hoped for. Did the £45,000 invested in that video earn back the equivalent amount in more copies of *Nonsuch*?

Oh, no no no—I think it was shown on TV a couple of times, and that was it. *Nonsuch* was a very poor seller in England.

It did all right around the rest of the world, didn't it?

Don't think so! It sold very poorly in the States as well. And, at the time, I thought it was our best album, by far. I don't think it is now—I think it's our second-best album. I think *Apple Venus* is our best.

How did the song come about?

I recently found my track sheet for this, and it shows that I started the demo on the 15th of April 1991. The song before it was 'Wonder Annual', and the song after it was one I worked on with Peter Blegvad called 'In Hell's Despite'.* That's where this fell out, historically.

I offered 'The Disappointed', in its unfinished state, to Terry Hall, who had been in The Specials and was now doing his solo career. He wanted to write with me, and I agreed. I offered him the song—gave him a really rough cassette version of me strumming through it, with unfinished lyrics—and for some reason he turned it down. He didn't like it. Which is a shame, because it might have been a hit for him, who knows? Though it wasn't a hit for us, so maybe it wouldn't have been a hit for him.

After he turned it down, I thought, 'Well, I'll just finish up and we'll use it, if the rest of the band think it's OK.' I did a new demo, later released on *Coat Of Many Cupboards*, that is possibly the most finished demo I've ever done of any song that the band went on to do. Consequently, it really shut them out—which I feel a little guilty about, but I guess if you know exactly how a song has got to go, that's how it's got to go.

I listened to the demo today, and I was going to ask you about your setup in the Shed at this time—had you gone digital by then, or were you still working with an eight-track cassette?

It was an eight-track cassette machine.

---

* 'Wonder Annual' was released as a demo on *Fuzzy Warbles Volume 1*. 'In Hell's Despite' was co-written with Peter Blegvad, an American cartoonist and singer-songwriter who has collaborated with Andy on several occasions. The song appeared on the Blegvad album *Just Woke Up*.

Because it *is* very fully realised, almost at the *Apple Venus* level. I don't know if I'd say it's your most finished demo, though, because some of the *AV* demos are at least as finished, if not more. But it's pretty much all there, except for the string parts and some of the backing tracks.

The string thing was more of an idea of a part, rather a finished product. I haven't heard the demo recently, but the string arrangement on the final product was one of those committee arrangements that we did with the Proteus, which for the time had great string samples in it.[*]

But you have string players listed on the liner notes.

We do, yeah.

You figured it out on the Proteus, then they played their parts?

We figured it out on the Proteus, and got the string players to play it, but they were so fucking out of tune that we put Proteus on and ended up using more of that in the mix than them.

Actually, they were good players, all apart from one. I think it was the cello player, who was appallingly out of tune. We asked violinist Stuart Gordon[†] to put the quartet together, and he rang up on the morning they were due there and said, 'Look, I'm really sorry chaps, I can't get this really great cello player—he's ill—so I've just grabbed the only one I can get,' and I don't think she'd ever been in a studio before. She just couldn't get in pitch. It was horrible, because it was spoiling the other three players, who were fine. Stuart Gordon is fantastic. But once she started rubbing the rosin across that enormous brown thing clamped between her legs, there was a horrible sound filled the room.

The same thing happened during the recording of 'Rook', yes?

Yep. We only had one day to do all the string parts for the album, and the quartet that showed up did not have the cello player Stuart wanted.

Still, they're not as bad as the quartet that turned up for the original *Apple Venus* recordings at Chris Difford's place.[‡] They were truly awful. We'll save

---

[*] The Proteus was a sample-based MIDI sound module system developed by E-mu.

[†] Stuart Gordon (1950–2014) had worked with The Korgis, Peter Hammill, The Beach Boys, Icehouse, and The Lilac Time.

[‡] The first sessions for *Apple Venus* took place at Helioscentric Studios, adjoining Chris Difford's farmhouse in Rye, East Sussex.

that one for another day. Anyway, we ended up doing it with the Proteus and I think mixing that quite a lot higher than the actual strings. Which is crazy—you pay all this money to hire these players, and if they don't play in tune or in time or whatever their fault is, you're lumbered. You've still got to pay them!

That's the nature of the game for the studio musician—they only get a paycheque for the time spent that day. They don't get equity in the album.
But there's not any comeback—if they're crap, you can't say, 'Well, I'm not paying you.' You've still got to pay them.

True enough. Now let's talk about the lyrics.
I guess they are prescient, yeah. I don't think it's all about affairs of the heart, although that's the framework it's hung around. I think it's about life in general. I think some of my take on the music business in general is in there as well.

I guess that's pretty much the lot of anyone who gets older—life is bound to have more disappointments by that time.
I guess so, but also if you feel that you've given your all, and it's not been welcomed, it's not been rewarded—and we really *did* give our all—then it's discouraging. But I've got to go careful, so I don't end up sounding like a bitter troll. [*Laughs.*]

It's interesting to hear you say that, because in terms of your career, you were in a relatively good place at this point—*Skylarking* and *Oranges & Lemons* both had sold pretty well. But at the same time, you'd been dealing with litigation with your ex-manager, and facing record-company troubles, and …
Yeah, we were only fresh out of that when we were writing this album. So, I think there are big dollops of different things. My marriage—my disappointment with that—is in there. I think the disappointment with the musical career, with not getting the recognition that I thought we were due—and *certainly* not getting the financial recompense that we were due—is in there. All that genuine disappointment filtered into this.

But I can tell you why I started writing this—it was from a totally different reason, which I abandoned, because I thought, 'Oh, you posey git, you can't possibly know that pain.' There was a story on TV about the mothers of 'The Disappeared' in Argentina.*

I often sit with the telly on and strum a guitar. I read that John Lennon used to do that, and I thought, 'How the hell could he do that?' But now I think about it, a lot of my best songs have come out while I'm sat watching the TV with a guitar on my lap! I'm sitting there watching this documentary, thinking, 'Oh, that is *awful*,' and I'm strumming away, and singing in my head, 'The Disappeared'.

I liked it, but as I worked on it more, I thought, 'No, I can't sing about this. It's not my experience. I haven't had sons and daughters taken, with a bullet put in the back of their heads and them thrown in a shallow grave by a dusty roadside somewhere. How can I write about that? It's not in my experience.'

You can imagine the horror of it, of course, but ...
Exactly! But I knew I couldn't write about it truthfully. But that is what started the whole song off.

You and I have talked in the past about how you like to offset the tone of the lyrics with the tone of the music—so, you sometimes put sad lyrics to happy music or vice-versa. But in this case, both strike me as fairly sombre.
I don't know—it's major key, isn't it? I guess it's major/minor-type mixes, so it's sweet-sour, sweet-sour.

And you're moving down the neck, taking people down with you as you talk about 'The Disappointed' and how they want you to do this and that.
[*Dramatically*] I'm descending lower than a Kinks bass line! Yeah, I'm going down—'Next floor, Disappointment!' You know, like in 'The 5,000 Fingers Of Dr T',† where they're going down into the dungeon, in the elevator: [*sings dolefully*] 'Third floor, Dungeon, and several assorted tortures.' [*Laughs.*]

I guess you're right—it's a sweet-sour mix of music. In fact, I remember

---

* The Disappeared (los Desaparecidos in Spanish) were the thousands of alleged political dissidents abducted or murdered during Argentina's internal 'dirty war' of the late 70s and early 80s.
† A 1953 musical fantasy written and directed by Theodor Seuss Geisel, better known as Dr Seuss.

I was appalled when one reviewer said, 'The intro and middle section sound like Fleetwood Mac.' I remember thinking, 'I'm not supposed to like the West Coast Fleetwood Mac, but maybe they're quite good if someone thinks we sound like them!' But seriously, that was very far from my mind when we put this song together.

Of course! The thing I was going to ask about that part is, I realize that you start the song instrumentally with the bridge, and then you go into …
This song is kind of a 'vhorus'!

Exactly! This is a vhorus song—where, after the intro, you start with the chorus, instead of a verse.
It's the title line—it's that Burt Bacharach/Hal David structure: title line / some response to that / back to title line again / another rhyme-y response to that. So, yeah, it's well in vhorus land.

Is the bridge, or middle part, of this song one of your shortest? Lyrically, it's only two lines.
[*Sings it to himself.*] Is that eight bars? I think it is.

So it really is a middle-eight.
An old-fashioned, Tin Pan Alley middle-eight. A Tin Ear Alley middle-eight! [*Chuckles.*]

You've said before how you like to start songs with the bridge.
It's just one of those little songwriter tricks. You think, 'Fuck, where do I go now? I've got myself to this point in the song, and I don't know what to do. Wait! The intro can come back!' Why waste a good intro?

Speaking of intros, where did you guys come up with starting it with the drums like that?
I *love* that spastic roll Dave Mattacks does there. I said to him, I want a *really* distinctive roll into this.

And he moves up through the drums, from the lowest to the highest tom, then the snare.
I said to him, 'Look, the playing in this has got to be really solid, really regular.

There are not going to be many rolls in the song, because it's just got to keep going, so I want a very distinctive one to get in.' He really done me proud— and as you say, he's playing it backwards, starting it from the lowest tom up to the snare, playing all flams, and playing it on the 'ands'.

In rehearsals, when we started on the album, he said, 'I'm looking forward to doing this, as long as you haven't got any shuffles for me to play, since I can't play a shuffle.' And not only is this song a shuffle, but it's a shuffle with an offbeat hi-hat. It's an offbeat, triplet hi-hat.

I was just going to say, in Dave's defence, this is a hard pattern to play. The hi-hat part is what makes it hard. If he was just doing your standard, dotted-eighth hi-hat pattern you find in a shuffle …
Well, that's what he can't do! He said he can't do your average shuffle.

At least he knows his own blind spot, right?
Sure! So we ended up doing quite a lot of editing with the drum performance on this, because I wanted it *really* solid. I don't know how many takes we did of him, but this is not one drum take all the way through. It's best bits, you know? But the poor sod had to play these off-beat triplet hi-hats, because Gus Dudgeon, our producer, loved that on the demo.* It was easy for me, because I could just program a drum machine. But Gus said [*mimics him*], 'Ohh, yes, I *love* those offbeat triplet hi-hats—we've got to keep that in! That's such a hook!' And poor Dave had to play these triplets cutting across the rhythm that hit on the offbeat.

It's very, very hard to play well, and consistently, for a long time.
And, after that roll! I mean, the man's a giant, really.

Let's talk about the rest of the song—who is in which channel? Are you in the left channel on this one?
Dave [Gregory]'s playing the sort of choppy guitar. He's also playing the arpeggios—that's his forte. I'm doing the chug-y guitar, which I think is over on the left. What else do my notes say? 'Good use of echoes in the mix to double up all the rhythms.'

---

* Gus Dudgeon (1942–2002) was most celebrated at that time for his work with Elton John, but he had also produced albums by Elkie Brooks and the Bonzo Dog Band, and David Bowie's single 'Space Oddity'.

Yeah, the guitars sound very big on this song.

That's all those rhythmic echoes, picking up all the parts. That's the trick.

Dave is credited with keyboard on 'The Disappointed'—does that have to do with the Proteus strings?

I think so, yeah. There's also this bendy, echo-y, reverb-y thing at the end that I think is keyboards.

This was one of the singles from the album, yes?

It was, yes. There's this notorious old-women's show that used to be on called *Pebble Mill At One*. Pebble Mill was the name of the BBC's Birmingham studio, and they did this kind of 'glad to be grey' chat-show thing at lunchtime. [*Mimics old woman*] 'Ooh, and we'll have a pop act on as well!' We went on there to mime the song, and I think that was our only shot at fame with it in England. [*Chuckles.*]

Who played drums? Ian Gregory?

It's Ian, yeah. He always used to do our last-minute mimes. He'd do it for the drink alone, I think! And I do remember we got rather drunk on the way back from doing this.

We decided we were going to hire a chauffeur-driven car—we thought, 'Fuck it, if we've got to go and play to a load of old women up in Birmingham at a lunchtime show, and do a mime, we're going to get some booze on the way back and have a party.'

Like proper rock stars!

[*Chuckles.*] Like proper rocks stars, yes. So we did. We got some bottles and had some fun on the way back.

Did Virgin tag this as a single, or did you push it as such?

I sensed that they were going to go for this as a single, as it was being written, because it was so sort of solid and, face it, old-fashioned. So, I thought, 'Yeah, they're gonna home in on this.'

But it came second, after 'Peter Pumpkinhead'.

Yeah. But I knew they were going to go for it, as a single. But, again, I don't think it got very high in the English charts—probably somewhere in the lower

20s or 30s—because nobody played it. We hadn't bribed the right people. We hadn't even bribed the *wrong* people! [*Laughs.*]

So, after this, 'Wrapped In Grey' was the next—and last—single?
Yeah, that was it. That was the end of *Nonsuch*.

And we all know what happened after that—the Great Strike.*
Then Dave had the idea to go on strike. Which I think he said facetiously, but I thought, '*Great* idea!'

Well, it worked, right? Took a while, but it worked. Let's talk about the end of the song—how it fades into 'Holly Up On Poppy'.
Yeah, what a lovely cross-fade that is! That worked out really well.

It does, and I guess what I wanted to ask about involves a larger question—you guys love to do cross-fades.
I know. I love them, but some people don't, I suppose. There's someone who gets on the various fan and review websites who these cross-fades have mentally unhinged—he continually rants about how much better it would be if there were no cross-fades.

So, let's talk about that—'In defence of cross-fades, by Andy Partridge.'
For me, listening to an album is an event. It's a film. It's a play. It's reading a book. You wouldn't read chapter nine first, then jump to chapter two—you read the book the way the author intended you to read it, from page one to page last. You watch a film from scene one to scene end. You hear a collection of music on an album from track one to the last track.

It's like saying that there should be one or two seconds of blank screen in between every major scene in a film. No! Some scenes cross-fade. Some scenes are blank. Some scenes dissolve. It's how you're pulled through the experience. It's the order in which we want you to hear it, the way we'd *like* you to hear it. The fact that one blurs into another—that's *intended*! That's not some weird accident that happens at the pressing plant! He must think that it's some terrible disease that has infested all of our records, that

---

* The band refused to work for Virgin after 1992 and were released from their contract in 1998.

we have no control over the cross-fading. No, you fucker! I *want* it to happen that way!

You can tell—it's absolutely intentional, because you do so much of it.
With so many of my favourite albums, I am led by the hand from song one right through to the spindle. And that's how I like it. As I say, you wouldn't watch a film watching scene nine before scene five—you go through in the way that the director and editor and writer *want* you to see that film. It's the same with an album of music.

I had some friends over the other night, and by the end of the evening, we were sitting there drinking and bemoaning the Death of the Album.
That's what all this separate stuff in the digital domain has done. It's turned the film into a bunch of scenes—it's turned the book into a bunch of chapters.

One of the examples I used was XTC—I wouldn't love some of the deeper cuts on your albums as much as I do if I hadn't been able to listen to them multiple times, in the context of the other songs on the album. They're not all sugary-sweet singles. Instead, they reveal themselves to you over time, and if I didn't have a commitment to listening to an album—of being led through the album as you'd intended, as you were just talking about—I don't know if I necessarily would have discovered those songs to the same degree that I have. It's a sad thing—to know that future generations might not have the joy of having an album reveal itself to them over time.
Well, the album is an art form, as much as the single is an art form. The threads that carry through are what pull you through the whole experience. Nothing in life is ever unseparated, so why should this one art form be totally separated? There are not many art forms you can think of where it's not an interactive thing, or there isn't some kind of journey involved.

Anything else you remember about this song in particular?
I do remember being shocked that this song was put up for the Ivor Novello Award. It's for songwriting excellence, supposedly. Ivor Novello was a rather handsome heartthrob songwriter and actor from waaaay back when.

I was told that, 'Andy, you're up for it, with "The Disappointed", and you're in competition with a Madonna song—can't remember which one it was—and with Eric Clapton for "Tears In Heaven".'

Oh. Jesus.

Yeah. I thought, 'Oh, fuck it. I've lost that one straight away.' And 'Tears In Heaven' did in fact win it. I knew I hadn't won it, because I didn't get invited to the ceremony. That's just nature's way of telling you you're shit, because you don't get the tickets to the ceremony. [*Laughs.*]

But I think this song is one of the only two things we've ever been nominated for. The other thing is the album it was on, *Nonsuch*, which was nominated for 'Best Alternative Music Album' in '92. My Grammy nominee medal is on the sideboard over here. But I knew we weren't going to get that, either, because [*sing-songy voice*] we didn't get the tiiickets!

Oh well. One more reason I'm the 'king of broken hearts'. [*Laughs*]

Interview conducted August 15 2009.

CHAPTER 24

ROOK

Let's talk about 'Rook', the 'first song from *Apple Venus Volume 1*', as you've sometimes called it—that, and 'Wrapped In Grey'. In terms of the songwriting cycle, when you were writing songs for *Nonsuch*, where did 'Rook' fall? Was it one of the later ones?

It was about in the middle. I looked at the track sheets this afternoon—I've still got the track sheets from my home demos—and I saw that there was a three-month gap where I didn't write anything. I was recording some bits and pieces with Peter Blegvad, making this thing for him to sell his album, *King Strut and Other Stories*, called 'Peter Who?', but otherwise I wasn't doing any stuff for myself. I think the only thing I did was 'It's Snowing Angels', which was for the *Strange Things Are Happening* magazine.*

I couldn't find a song—I'd sort of dried up, you know? I was getting really worried, because it was three months, and I was rather concerned that I couldn't find anything.

Was the album scheduled and looming on the horizon?

Well, people were saying, 'When are you going to go in? When are you going to be doing this album?' And I seemed to have ground to a halt in the songwriting. I wondered, 'Whoa! Have I written my last song?'

It wasn't like today, where I'm writing lots and lots of little bits, but I'm just in a funny state of mind where I don't want to finish any of them off. It's about 350 at the last count.

---

* Andy recorded 'It's Snowing Angels' with The Dukes Of Stratosphear, claiming it was by a little-known 60s group called Choc Cigar Chief Champion, and sent it to the UK magazine *Strange Things Are Happening*. The editor was in on the joke and it was to have been issued on a flexidisc, but the magazine folded. The song can be heard on *Fuzzy Warbles Volume 2*.

Back then, I was in the state of mind where I was desperate to write songs, but couldn't. Then, one day, I found this chord change on the guitar—I don't know where it came from—and I thought, 'Oh, that's *really* nice. That almost sounds like a piano. *Hey*, let me work out what the notes would be on the piano!'

I didn't realise it had started on guitar.
It started there, yeah. I don't know where the words came from, but I started to sing 'Rook'. And suddenly I was in floods of tears! In fact, I got really quite moist under the peepers when I was listening to it on headphones today—sort of tapping into that emotion again, you know?

Well, I think you're not the only one. It's one of the reasons people respond so well to this song. The emotion really comes through.
I also think I got emotional because the dam broke—I had thought, 'Oh, well, I've written my last song, then. This is what happens—you just run out of songs.' Then, after three months, out fell 'Rook'. And not only did it fall out unexpectedly, like rain from heaven when you're in the desert, but it also scared the living daylights out of me! There's something about the chords and the melody—that rather doomy folksong melody, over these bell-like, summoning chords. It really gives me the shivers now, even talking about it.

It did at the time, too. I remember thinking, 'Where did *this* come from?' It was like *I* hadn't thought of it. It was like I'd been delivered it by some suggestion of a genie or an angel watching me. I don't believe in all that shit, but it kind of felt like that.

There are lots of musicians who've talked about how sometimes it seems as if you tap into a great channel where Music is. You become the means of conveying it, rather than the creator.
Yeah, you're just digging away, and you go through the last few inches of soil, and suddenly, *bwooof!*, you're covered in the most sparkling, clear water. And you think, 'Wow, was that there all the time?' I don't feel like I wrote this. I'm not saying that I *stole* it, but I'm saying that it feels as if it was written for me, and dictated quietly into my ear or something.

Tapping into the collective unconscious.
Yeah, I had my head switched inadvertently to Radio Wonderful or something.

So, how fast did the song write itself?
Pretty quickly, I think.

Over the course of an afternoon, or several days, or what?
Oh, it would have been several days. But certainly the idea of the rook, and those chords, came quickly.

When you talk about the chords, you're talking about that beginning pattern?
Yep. The next section, the faster part, I wrote on piano. [*Laughs.*] I couldn't have found that on acoustic!

I really like that second section as well. To me, that says moderne—with an *e*—composer, the sort of thing you would hear on the soundtrack of black-and-white films in the 50s. You know, a couple would be up on the moors somewhere—in fact, there's the instrumental version of 'Rook' that we've got somewhere, and it just sounds like Basil Kirchin or somebody, or something like you'd hear in a movie like *A Taste Of Honey.**

So, yeah, it really frightened me, and I don't know why I was so frightened. I sort of feel like I had a weird glimpse into mortality or something.

That comes through in the lyrics, certainly. Did you write the lyrics and piano parts together?
Certainly, the 'rook, rook' part came with the chords. Those chords made me think of the moors, and it was a matter of, 'Oh, what's up there? There are birds, there are crows, there are *rooks*—that's even better.' Then the rhymes started to fall out from there, rather quickly. But it was the scenarios from the second section that took a bit longer. I think that comes from my desire to fly—I do have that desire, which comes in out in a few songs.

Sure, like 'Chalkhills And Children'.
Exactly. There's this thing about 'Take me up there, but I want to see down on the rooftops, I want to see those chimney pots and washing lines all flapping away.' I'm garbling a bit here, because this is tricky to talk about. It

---

* Basil Kirchin (1927–2005) was an English composer of film music, known for the manipulation of environmental sounds. *A Taste Of Honey* was a 1961 film adaptation of a play by Shelagh Delaney, and is one of the first examples of so-called 'kitchen sink realism'.

does tap into some funny, dreamlike, glimpse-of-your-own-mortality stuff for me.

Was there something specific going on in your life that might have even caused the block, and then allowed the floodgates to open? Is there some reason you were storing up this psychic energy?
That's a bloody good question—I don't think I have an answer!

Maybe with hindsight, you can look back and see something. I mean, we've talked before about how Nonsuch contains a lot of foreshadowing of the demise of your marriage.
Yeah, sure, I'm predicting it's all going to crap. With this song, I think it was my age, and it was a matter of realising, 'Hey, I'm going to die.' [*Laughs ruefully.*] There's no limit on how late you can realise this, but I think I was realising it then. And thinking, 'Well, hell—and I've never even flown! I've flapped my wings and flown in my dreams, but perhaps when I die I'll get to fly somewhere. Perhaps this nice little bird here will take me up—my little soul will be on his back, and I'll get to see the tops of the roofs and such.' Nearest I can get there now is Google Earth!

When I first heard the song, the first thing I thought of was John Donne. Are you familiar with his poetry at all?
Not very, no. I think we have some in the house here, but it's not a matter of [*chuckles*], 'It's Friday night—crack the beers open and get the John Donne out!'

'Crack open the mead!' But, you were familiar with the phrase 'for whom the bell tolls'?*
Oh, sure.

Was that kind of concept consciously going through your head as you were writing this, when you were saying, 'Is that my name on the bell?' Or was it something else?
I'm not sure about the concept about having the name on the bell. I think I

* Not from a John Donne poem but from 'Meditation 17' in *Devotions Upon Emergent Occasions*, a work of religious prose published in 1624.

must have made that up, since it's not in Donne. I like the scary proposition of the bell ringing, and it's got your name engraved on it. That's like *more* than permanent—there's no doubt then. That's you. It's *your* funeral, buddy.

I don't know if you've read any Carlos Castaneda, but the other thing that struck me was the imagery you used of the bird as the carrier of your soul.
Yeah, I think somebody gave me one of his books when I was at college or something.

He talks about the idea of reaching a mystic state where you can become the crow, or hawk, or whatever your spirit animal is.
Oh sure, that's very common among those who worship nature.

Suddenly the secrets are revealed to you, and here you are, in this song, saying, 'Rook, show me the secrets. I know you know.'
Well, I mean, rooks do have a reputation, and I'll tell you what—if I wander over here to my bookshelf—I'll start with Barbara G. Walker, my favourite, and see if she's got anything on rooks in *The Woman's Encyclopedia Of Myths And Secrets** [*leafs through book*]—no, she doesn't! Bugger. Stay with me. [*Looks for another book.*] It's a wonderful book, that—you should read it, if you haven't already. Let's see, maybe it's in *Hall's Dictionary Of Subjects And Symbols in Art*†—I wonder if there are any rooks in here. Nope! Don't go away, give me one more month … here we go, *An Illustrated Encyclopedia Of Traditional Symbols*‡—do you know, after all this waiting, I probably won't be able to find anything on rooks. No, nothing on rooks in there! Dammit.

But you had this idea about them as mystical creatures, or connections to the underworld.
Yeah, I like the idea that animals have secrets and they know things that we don't. That's not really a new idea. That's Cro-Magnon or earlier!

Back when we were more in touch with nature.
With flint! *Our Man Flint* meant something totally different!§ [*Chuckles.*]

---

* Published 1983.
† Published 1974.
‡ By J.C. Cooper, published 1978.
§ A 1966 spoof action movie.

Let's talk about the recording of the song a little bit. Dave plays beautiful piano on this.

Beautiful—that's the piano in the Chipping Norton studios.* He does a very nice job on this. And how he handles those B sections with the faster playing is beyond me. That's tricky stuff.

I do remember that the song began by not coming out well. At the time, while we were making the album, this was my favourite of the songs. It wasn't going right for some reason, and our producer, Gus Dudgeon, made the glib remark of, 'Oh, just bin it, then.' I was furious. It wasn't like, 'Well, let's see what it is that we need to get right, to make this work for you, because I know this is your favourite.' All he said was, 'Oh, let's bin it.'

He knew it was your favourite of the songs?

Well, I *think* I made that quite clear to him! But this flippant remark was just one more reminder that he was just not quite the right producer for that record. I was *so* upset. That was quite a slap in the face for me.

What did you do to save the song?

For some reason it wasn't working, and I can't remember the exact reason why.

It was during rehearsals?

No, it was during the recording process.

So, you guys pretty much knew what you were doing—it was just a matter of execution.

I think it was just getting the right feel. I can't remember whether if the vocal was not quite right, or the piano was not quite right, but I guess Gus felt, 'Oh, they've got loads of songs, we'll just not bother recording this one.'

Do you remember the order in which the instruments were put down? I'm assuming piano was first.

It would have been piano to a click track.

Then strings next?

Well, we had a small string quartet, because that's all the budget would stretch

---

* The renowned Chipping Norton Studios, in Oxfordshire, closed in 1999.

to. So we got in contact with Stuart Gordon, the fellow who did the violin on *The Big Express*, and said, 'Can you get together three other players'—you know, two violins, viola and cello—'and we'll track you up and put you on this album.' He came down and took me to one side [*chuckles*], and said, 'Look, I couldn't get the cello player I wanted.' We tracked them up a few times, but it was a little sour-sounding, and I think Stuart felt a bit difficult about this. So we ended up putting fake strings under them, to bolster them up. I'm not sure what percentage the fake strings are used in the mix—was it 50/50 fake ones and real ones, or the fake ones a little bit more dominant?

Come to think of it, maybe it was the strings going wrong that put Gus off. Stuart's a fantastic player, but when you just get people out of the book and put them together, you don't know who you're going to get.

And then you had Guy Barker playing flugelhorn on this, too.* **He shows up later on *Apple Venus*.**
That's right. We probably recorded his part for 'Omnibus' the same day. Any flugelhorn or trumpet you hear on *Nonsuch* would have been done by Guy during that mad rush. All in one day, I think. On *Apple Venus*, he does that lovely solo on 'The Last Balloon'.

You and Gus are both credited with tambourine, and you play shaker too?
Usually I get the percussion jobs, because I've got a pretty good sense of rhythm.

Can you tell me a bit more about the lyrics?
I'm very proud of the lyrics on this, actually. The B sections are about the everyday. I'm talking about all the stuff that made a big impression on me as a kid, like, is the washing on a line, or the puffs of smoke coming out of chimneys, a signal or code or something?

It's funny—you get glimpses of this song on 'Chalkhills And Children' and even songs like 'Red Brick Dream', but I think you do it particularly well here. You're talking about the everyday, but in such a spiritual context. Even as you're soaring above the earth, you are talking about very down-to-earth things.
Sure. You get a new take on it, because you're seeing it from another angle.

---

* Guy Barker is a British trumpeter, composer, bandleader, and prolific session musician.

The line where you say, 'My head bursting with knowledge till I wake from the dream'—you're *there*, you have it. Everyone gets that feeling in a dream where they're omnipotent, or it all gets revealed to them, and then they wake up and feel it slipping away.

See, I'm being a real doofus here—you're talking to me about these lyrics, and I'm getting emotional! How stupid is that? This song pushed so many buttons for me.

It's understandable, and it comes through—again, I think that's why so many people connect with this song. I know the first time I heard it, I thought it was something really special.

Have you heard the a capella version? There's a group called +4db who've done a version of the song.*

Let me find it. [*Both listen a bit to the a capella version.*] Now, how can you not get emotional when you realise you've created a song like this? It's beautiful.

Well, as I said, I don't feel I wrote it. I feel like somebody whispered it all in my ear, and I just had to write it down.

Even there, I would give you credit for feeling emotional about this, because if I were you I'd feel privileged to have been the conduit.

The sewage pipe of such beautiful waste!

Oh, c'mon now, take credit where credit's due!

Yeah, all right. You're right. I'm very proud of it. Like I say, I was very excited to think that this was my favourite track off of *Nonsuch*. And it still might be my favourite track off the album! I do think it's the first track off of *Apple Venus*, as we said.

Because it set you off in that direction. Now, Colin plays nothing on this?

I think he might be doing background vocals.

He's not on the credits. Was that an oversight?

Oh, I guess he wasn't on it, then! It must be me doing the high background

---

* You can hear it on their album *plusfourdb*.

vocals. Which, I have to say, is something that affected me as a kid. On the record 'I Can't Let Maggie Go', by Honeybus—wonderful record, a real piece of 'chamber pop music'—they actually do this nice little section in there, with this high, semitone harmony.* I gently borrowed it. That's a wonderful song—if you don't know it, you should find it. It's *really* warming. I hope they can forgive me for stealing two notes.

Imitation being the sincerest form of flattery.
But, like I say, this song almost didn't get recorded. Gus was OK, he was good fun in a 'one of the boys' kind of way—he was great with fart gags, and lots of interesting tales of rock'n'roll madness. But he did have this strange, headmaster kind of mode he could click into, where you felt like if you sang a bum note, it'd be, [stiff-upper-lipped voice] 'No! Come to my study. Receive six of the best across your taut buttocks!'

He did tell me, when I did this high harmony vocal in 'The Ugly Underneath', that [*posh voice*], 'That is the most *ludicrous* harmony I've ever heard! *Elton* wouldn't have done a harmony like that!'

To which you said, 'Precisely!'
Exactly. [*Laughs.*] But what else about this? I don't know—like I say, it's a tough one, this. It's tricky for me to talk about, because I don't feel that I wrote it. I feel that it wrote itself, and gave itself to me in some way.

And you gave it to us.
I guess so. Don't shoot me, I'm just the massager!

Interview conducted April 20 2008.

---

* 'I Can't Let Maggie Go' was a UK hit in April 1968.

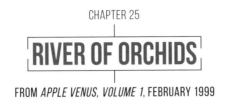

CHAPTER 25

RIVER OF ORCHIDS

FROM *APPLE VENUS, VOLUME 1*, FEBRUARY 1999

Let's talk about the opener for *Apple Venus, Volume 1*. When exactly did you write this song? According to the notes for Homespun, while writing *Nonsuch* you had a Proteus sound module.*
That's right, yep. It was a Proteus One, I think. An emulator.

But the liner notes don't give an actual date of when you wrote it.
It was very early on in what would be the material *for* the next album—about 1990, I think. I was going toward the whole orchestral thing because I got very excited by 'Rook' and 'Wrapped In Grey' on *Nonsuch*. To me, those two songs are the first two *Apple Venus* tracks.

I can see that.
You know, just like 'Funk Pop A Roll' is the first *Big Express* track. There's never a dividing line, you know? Bands just write stuff and work on stuff and record stuff, and you find that there's never a clear demarcation on how it gets apportioned into being on this or that album.

Was it the pizzicato string sound that first got you going on this?
Some days you just sit there and noodle on the guitar, which I do constantly, or you noodle on the keyboard, which I do less, because I'm not such a good keyboard player. Any keyboard noodling from me is naïve and primitive, to say the least. But with a sequencer, which was a relatively new addition to the arsenal, it was great.

Previous to then, I had to drop in everything one chord at a time, or just not play keyboards very much. With a sequencer you can run around and

---

* *Homespun*, released in 1999, is an album made up of the demos for *Apple Venus Volume 1*.

around, and build up the layers that you want until it almost sounds like you can play!

It was those beautifully recorded pizzicato sounds in this emulator—I just had a little two-bar pattern going around, with a pushed double-bass line. That's the thrower. That's the thing where people think, 'Wow! What weird time signature is this in?' Well, it's 4/4, but the bass plucks are all on 'a-one'. They're all pushed. People tend to think of the bass line as being on the 'one', but it's not.

I built up this little two-bar pattern of plucked bass, plucked violins, plucked violas, plucked cellos—plucked chicken!—and some little trumpet 'parps'—little balloons of sound. Rhythmic balloons. It's the close clusters of the trumpet that I thought were sort of exciting. You know, they're seconds and close intervals like that. They really grate in a nice way.

I just let this two-bar loop go around and around. I was really excited, and thought, 'God, this is so rhythmic.' I actually remember dancing to it for quite a while. I started to improvise vocals, thinking, 'I wonder if I've got a lyric that would somehow fit this.' I went back through my notebooks, and there was something I'd written in my notebook while we working on recording *Nonsuch*—it was the phrase, 'A dandelion roared in Piccadilly Circus.'

I like the silly juxtaposition of 'a dandelion roared'—a dandelion isn't an animal, it's a flower, a weed. And it can't roar. And where do lions roar? In a circus, but Piccadilly Circus is not a circus! And there are no weeds in Piccadilly Circus! So, it was a circular chain of events contradicting themselves into a perfect circle. I remember thinking at the time, 'That's a nice phrase— I'll write that down, I might be able to use that at some point.'

I started to scat this out over what I thought was an intensely dance-y kind of rhythmic thing. But it wasn't the usual thing you'd think of as a groove— like a beefy drum groove with a funky bass and a choppy rhythm guitar—it was plucked strings, and little offbeat parp-y trumpets. It's all very percussive in its way, but it's not standard instrumentation.

I took my shoes and socks off and was jumping around my shed—as you can, that is. There's not much room to jump—you've seen it. No room to swing a Strat! Anyway, this phrase just seemed to fit perfectly, and that was it. That opened the floodgates—I started thinking about London, and traffic, because of those little parping horns suggest cars. Like irate people stuck in a traffic jam or something.

Plus, there's something about pizzicato strings—the shorthand for them in my head is raindrops, or water drops. So it was [*fast*], 'London, water, the Thames, river—river of what? River of traffic! Oh no, that's awful! Wouldn't it be nice if it were a river of … orchids!' That's the sort of sound and word association that led to that conclusion.

With the thrust of the song being to replace the river of traffic with something natural.
With a river of flowers, yeah. Either going through London floating on the Thames, orchids and pond lilies and lotus and all that around you, or—quite literally—stopping the traffic on all the roads and motorways, and planting them out with flowers. So, that was the rather convoluted way that I got there.

Where did the line about wanting to walk into London on your hands one day come from?
I've no idea! I guess it's because you wouldn't want to put your hands on the ground in London as it is. But you might want to if it were soil with flowers. Plus, you wouldn't get knocked over, you could appreciate the smell of the flowers—it's like a free-spirited, acrobatic gesture, where you're freer—you can walk on your hands through London. It's going to smell nice, it's going to feel nice, and hey, you don't have to worry. But I *can* tell you were the line 'a Peckham Rose' came from.

It's from the Jan Svankmajer short, right?
It's the Svankmajer shorts, yeah! Mmmm … lovely! 'Eat my Svankmajer shorts.' How's that for a Czech surrealist Simpsons line? Bart's writing it on the blackboard. And then, when they rush to the sofa, they're all pieces of meat! One's a severed tongue, one's a steak, one's an eyeball—oh, c'mon, how did they miss that? [*Laughs.*] So yeah, I was watching Jan Svankmajer's short, 'Punch And Judy', and when they're lighting the candles because the Judy character—or, it's more of a harlequin character; I think the English translation of Punch and Judy is not quite right—has gotten killed, Punch lights some candles with Peckham Rose matches.

When I saw that, I remember thinking, 'Oh my god, there they are!'
That's where it came from, yeah! I thought, 'Wow! That's lovely. A Czech has used an area of London, and the name of a flower, in this little film.' Then I thought, 'Ooh, but wait—we have matches in a few of our other things.'

We have 'England's Glory—a striking beauty' in 'Senses Working Overtime', and we have the front of the Ship matches box on 'Wait Till Your Boat Goes Down'. So I thought, 'Yeah, we have to have Peckham Rose to complete the trio of match references.' Wait! There're also matches in 'I'll Set Myself On Fire'!

There you go. So, it's a quartet.
It's a quartet of match references. Now you've got me thinking—are there more?

There probably are. We'll have to get the fans enlisted in this quest.
So, are there more than four match references? Let us know!

Plus, the match reference is a joke—it's the same thing as a dandelion roaring in Piccadilly Circus, right? Because you're pretending it's an actual flower …
Yeah. Do you know, it might be! Google it—is there a Peckham Rose? I just associated it with matches, and I thought, 'Well, that's a great metaphor for London—a sulphurous-smelling match.'

Let's see [*checking Google*]—you come up number one! … Oh, that's funny—there's a woman named Rose Peckham, who was born in 1930!
Is she a striking beauty? [*Laughs.*]

Well, she's sloughed off this mortal coil, so not anymore! There's a bed-and-breakfast in Peckham, there's a pub with the name, but most of the references come from your lyrics.
I feel bad about that, because they obviously are a match company or brand. *

Maybe not anymore.
That's a shame! You know, I *love* matchbox art. I've been trying to get that sort of tidy graphics approach into our stuff for a long time.

Which you were able to do, with stamps, with *Fuzzy Warbles*.
I did stamps instead, but do you know, I *still* fantasise about match-cover art.

---

* 'Rose Of Peckham' matches were imported by D. Rose Ltd of Peckham, south-east London.

Well, that's the next CD cover then, right?

Oh yeah—with free matches, to encourage pyromania!

The demo for this song is quite detailed.

The demo—it's all there, really, apart from the fact that it's not a real orchestra.

So, as you were building it out, you came up with different counter-lines and things.

I was thrilled by the fact that it never changed. I do like repetition. For me, repetition is immensely inspirational. It's been a theme running through our work right from day one.

But I felt like a modern composer for the first time with this song. When I finished it, I was so thrilled to have done something that was unlike any structure we had ever done, unlike any instrumentation we'd ever done, unlike *anything* we'd ever done—I just wanted to do it again. I guess it's tapping into the spirit of yourself at that time, and for me, I'd hit—well, I can hardly say pay-dirt, because it didn't make a lot of money.

Artistic pay-dirt.

Yeah. I'd found my little soul perfectly, at that time. I was so thrilled that I wanted to go further into that. I don't know if I did. I mean, some things on that album got near it—things like 'The Last Balloon', or some bits of 'Easter Theatre'—but there's something about the purity of that repetitive pattern. I mean, there's less movement in that then there is in a Philip Glass thing. Because in one of his songs, you at least get things mutating or changing or a sudden switch of gears.

But I think you do that, with the vocals.

I do it with the vocals, but the *music* is unchanging.

But don't you actually grow the music throughout the piece? You do build it up in complexity and layers.

At the beginning, you get the surrogate river being built from drips of water. Which is not on the demo, but after I'd finished the demo, I thought, 'Ah, damn, it would have been *great* to have had that build.' So I sat with our producer, Haydn Bendall, who came down to my shed, and we mapped out how the track would build from one pluck and one drip to be that cyclical riff.

We decided the best way to do it was to have it all in time—all the plucks and ploops and stuff—but have them appear in a seemingly random way. They're all in exactly the right place, but it's only pieces of them at first.

Right. It's just as if you have a piano roll, but the holes are not all punched in yet.
Exactly! You know where they're going to be, because you marked them out with pencil, but you haven't actually punched them out. So, I don't know if people have figured this out yet—I'm sure some have—but all the plucks and ploops you hear are exactly where they're going to be by the time the whole orchestra doing its bit.

That's one of the really fascinating things about the way it builds there—you can actually hear the way that the song is constructed.
It's starting to become rhythmic from the first drop.

And you also put the listener on notice about the production quality—I remember listening to the demo and loving it, but when I heard Apple Venus the first time, and that double bass comes in at the beginning of the song—it knocked me out. It's big.
Well, that big plucked bass—I mean, you get a plucked bass in Abbey Road Studio 1, in England's most beautiful orchestral room—you just get *BOOM*. All the natural ambiance around that hall is—oh, it's *sexual*.

I remember when Colin and I went to New York to do some press stuff for this—we were asked by a magazine to review some top-end stereo systems. They wanted us to hear some tracks from our album on these two or three swish systems—you know, more expensive than my house! We sat in this room, and just to hear 'River Of Orchids' with the depth and clarity on these top-end stereo systems was really exciting. It was almost as good as being in the room while the orchestra were playing it.

Speaking of which, let's talk about recording the orchestra.
It was a hell of a lot to expect this forty-piece orchestra to stay in a perfect, mechanical groove for the whole of the song, so we cut out the best sections, and reproduced them—if they lost the groove at all, it'd be, 'OK, cut that bar out,' or, 'Those few bars are brilliant—can we have a few more of those?' We pieced it together from the best bits. But hey, that's the nature of orchestral

performances. They do that with the great classical recordings—they take the best bars from here, there and everywhere. It's always a Frankenstein. Then, to give it a little more mechanical spine, we took the original demo sequence, which was the template, and said, 'Hey, what's it like if we feed the "fake" stuff in under the live stuff?' It did make it sound stronger and more robust.

So, the demo's on the album?
Yep. The demo is underneath the orchestra really playing it. And that goes for the plips and plups that make up the intro, too. That all had to be written out on sheet music for this forty-piece orchestra, and they had to play that intro in real time.

Who did that transcription?
Well, because Dave was not in the band at that point …

I thought maybe he still was.
No, one of the big bones of contention for him was that he saw the orchestra as a waste of money. He wanted to do it with samples, and I was convinced it wasn't going to sound quite right with samples. It seemed like getting in touch with my orchestral soul was being somewhat thwarted by Dave stamping his foot, saying, 'I don't want to spend all that money on an orchestra!' And it *was* ludicrously expensive. He wanted to do it all with samples, and Haydn said, 'It's not going to sound any good,' and I knew it was not going to sound *as* good.

In your head, you knew what it could sound like, I guess?
Yes. I thought, 'God, this is going to be great with a real orchestra doing "Easter Theatre" and "Last Balloon" and "Harvest Festival" and "I Can't Own Her"'—all that stuff. But it was the catalyst for Dave leaving the band—the last straw for him. I wasn't listening to his wishes. But his wishes were pretty much in direct conflict with what I totally and utterly felt was the direction we needed to go in at that time. So, unfortunately, it was splitsville. That was the big boil that brought it to a head—the expense of the orchestra. What a shame.

Let's talk about the vocals a little bit, because—as we were saying—this is where you do build complexity, and you have variety. I know one of

the things that really impresses me about this song is how layered and dissonant you get, especially toward the end.

It's that sexy thing of, 'It *all* works.' That's the sexy bit—you can stack up this many oiled asses. Some of the best porn I've ever seen is where they get two or three women to lay on top of each other, and you can just select from one to the other. [*Laughs.*] I mean, is that every man's fantasy or what?

When all these pieces lay over each other, it's *so* thrilling. J.S. Bach knew that, and a lot of other great composers knew that. I was just late stumbling into this thing and finding out the joy of getting a piece that works when you lay it over another section.

With this whole song, because it's just built on two bars, you're sort of governed by what you can use. If you've done it well, it's all going to fit! And, in this case, it does. Because the actual melody is sort of a jazz nursery rhyme, if such a genre could exist. Oh, I've said the word 'genre'—I'm so sorry! [*laughs*] I'll rewind and de-Frenchify myself there. 'Type'—this *type* of music. There you go. God, I *hate* myself when I say the word 'genre'.

'Type' is much more Saxon of you.[*]

Exactly. 'Genre' is *so* effete! It's so pretentious!

At least you didn't say 'oeuvre'!

Ohhhh. I always think of 'egg' when I hear that! 'That's my egg. That's the type of egg he does.' [*Laughs.*] Where were we? It's a nursery rhyme, and the vast majority of it is in that jazzy triplet feel—which I can't leave alone.

Well, as you say—it works.

And it especially works over that pushed bass line and the offbeat string plucks.

The vocals on the studio version are much more complex than on the demo.

They're also split in stereo. If you listen, a vocal will be on one side, and a distorted reproduction of it will be on the other side.

A distorted reproduction of the original vocal, or did you sing it again?

It's the same vocal, but reproduced and distorted so that it comes seemingly from two tonal places at the same time. One's sharper and more distorted, and

---

* 'Type' is not a Saxon word either. It's French.

one's more natural. On headphones, you can hear that easily. You hear one vocal, but it's been split and processed in two, totally different ways, to give it this unusual, faux-stereo thing.

Then, you get all those different, crossing patterns as well. And there's the rather placid and Thames-like part in what I guess you would call the chorus section—there are no choruses, because it's not a conventional song structure by any means—but there's that section of [*sings*], 'River of Orchids, winding my way.' That's very placid, and it does actually make me think of the Thames. There's something big and flat about it, with a slow, placid pace leading up to the faster triplet part—which is more scurrying feet and scurrying traffic.

Sure. If you think about the subject matter for each of those parts, your approach there is perfectly appropriate. When you're talking about the River of Orchids, the place you want to get, you are more placid. And when you're 'complaining' …
Having a good jazz moan!

That's when it's more staccato, and you're doing the triplet thing.
Sure. And I'm pushing the undesired car off of the road.

When you were adding these additional intervals in the vocals, did you chart it out, or was it a matter of going through and saying, 'Oh, if I add a second or a seventh here, it'll sound good'?
I might not be—how shall I say it—as smart as that, actually. I just feel things instinctively.

Well, then, you *are* as smart as that. You're just doing it without writing it down.
It's just animal, as opposed to mathematical. I mean—I knew that, to make the 'chorus' section more placid, I should split it into two octaves, so it's got a thickness to it. The Thames has a depth.

Right. That's the sonic metaphor there. And again, when you go back into the other part, not only are you more frantic rhythmically, but you have the dissonance in there, with notes rubbing against each other, and there's the tension that you create that way as well.
Mmm.

How about Colin? Was he involved in the vocals on this song, or was this all you?
He's on those chorus sections, because it's a whole crowd of us singing sedately.

I was going to ask, is there a bass part that he plays?
Because it's a double bass in the studio, being plucked, the poor devil was somewhat locked out of this. He does play on some of the other songs on the album where there is double bass—he plays either a counter line, or a higher, sort of more tenor line on the bass. But on this one, I think he had to go get a few cups of tea in the Abbey Road canteen.

It's a bit of a difficult situation—you're sort of juggling egos, but you're also thinking, 'The song is greater than me, and it's greater than him, so what does the song want? The song wants to be like that, and there's just no room for an electric bass guitar in this one.'

It's very difficult for me to put into words the excitement I felt on finding this song, because I guess I needed to go in a different way, and the signposts were all there on *Nonsuch*. It was as I finally discovered 'the turning'. You know, your SatNav is saying, 'You need to turn left soon!' and I couldn't find that left turning, and then suddenly 'River Of Orchids' fell out, and it was a matter of 'Turn *now*.' I felt I was on the right road, finally. And that's very difficult to put into words.

Didn't Harold Budd use 'River Of Orchids' as an example in his composition classes?*
Do you know, I'd forgotten all about that! Yes, he was lecturing about modern composition. I'm not sure where he was—somewhere in California, I think. And he was using this as an example of good modern composition using traditional instruments. Which is [*laughs*] very nice of him! It's great. Very flattering.

And well-deserved, I think.
[*Fluttering voice*] Oh! Oh, headmaster! Oh vicar, that's so [*laughs*] … I knew that people were going to be a little thrown by this, and I remember when Martin Goldschmidt from Cooking Vinyl Records—one of the labels

* Harold Budd is an American composer who has worked extensively with Bill Nelson and Brian Eno as well as Andy.

we signed to after we finally got out of our Virgin contract—came down to Rockfield Studios in Wales. We had sort of a grand playback for him. I remember we played him 'River Of Orchids' and said, 'This is the opening track, Martin!'

There was this *real* pregnant silence after the last water drip had wiped it out, and it was like, 'Ohh, is somebody going to say something?' He obviously didn't know what the fuck to say.

I was going to ask about it being the album opener—that was pretty ballsy of you.
He just sort of smirked, in a kind of 'Oh my god, this is embarrassing' way, and said, 'Wicked!' 'For fuck's sake, Martin! It's not some skateboard nu-metal! We're hardly fucking Korn! *Wicked*? Is that all you've got to say about it?' [*Laughs.*]

'Bitchin'!'
He obviously didn't know what the hell to say, so he thought he'd say something 'young', I suppose. But it was so beautifully inappropriate.

So, what do you think this song bodes for your future compositional career? You've talked before about how writing is getting increasingly difficult for you, so I was thinking that perhaps instrumental works are the way to go—you seem to almost torture yourself over lyrics at times, and I wonder if you did an instrumental album it would open the floodgates again, because you wouldn't feel the weight of having to write lyrics.
Well, lyrics are tortuous! You really do lock yourself in the iron lady there, and you're putting those spikes in your own head and your own heart, thinking, 'Oh, can I say this, or should I say that, or have I said that better before?' That's a lot of it—'Have I said this better before?'

Or has someone else said it better before?
Exactly, which is even more hurtful. What was that line in that old Talking Heads song? [*Imitates David Byrne*] 'Say it once, why say it again?' I know that's a kind of extreme, nutcase view of things, but he's got a point there.

But I guess that's the 'editor' taking control, and I'm a bit scared that my 'editor' has now taken so much control that it's stopping me.

You and I have talked before about how to trick the 'editor', and I'm wondering if something like this—where you just say, 'Fuck it, I'm not even going to worry about lyrics. I'm just going to write music'—could be the way of doing that.

I guess so! Because some of the little things I've done …

Monstrance is an example of that, right?

That's an example of improvised instrumentals, but I've even done a bit of work on themes for things. A good example—I caught myself humming it the other day—is a track that got used on *Fuzzy Warbles* called 'Ice Jet Kiss'.* That was one of the ideas for the *Wonderfalls* TV series—they said, 'Oh yeah, we want it to be instrumental.† We don't want any singing, and we want it to sound cool and modern.'

So I came up with this thing that sounds like a cross between The Swingle Singers‡ and a little bossanova/metal thing. [*Laughs.*] But I really like the melody of it—and that was a case of creating a composition that was very structured but purely instrumental, and it's one of my favourite little pieces of music I've written. And—as you say—there was no pressure of words, because they specifically asked for no vocal.

Little did I know they were going to pick the first idea I had, which was the 'Wonderfalls' song! [*Sighs.*]

Given the capabilities you have at your fingertips now—all the samples and good equipment you have in the Shed—perhaps an instrumental album is in your future?

I wouldn't rule it out. I quite like the idea of having a part-instrumental, part-lyrical album, where maybe the lyrics are in smaller pockets, and they're possibly more pungent because of their scarcity on the record.

Kind of like *Through The Hill*?§

I guess so! [*Sighs.*] I guess that almost got near it. But, do you know, I can't listen to that album anymore.

---

* On *Fuzzy Warbles Volume 6*.

† *Wonderfalls* was a comedy-drama series on the Fox network. It was cancelled after four episodes, although thirteen were made and are available on DVD.

‡ An a cappella group formed in 1962 in France.

§ Andy's album with Harold Budd, released in 1994.

Why not?
Because it was a really, really tough time for me, mentally. You know, I was getting divorced, and when I hear those themes and stuff, I just think, 'Oh my god, I never felt so unwanted in my life.' Divorce will do that to you—when somebody says, 'I'm going to divorce you, and I don't love you, and I prefer him'—my god, you feel like dog shit! So, to be creating a work of something while you're feeling like dog shit—all those feeling-like-dog-shit vibes went into that record.

I hope I'm not spoiling it for anyone now! [*Laughs.*] You know, people who might quite like it. I don't want them to feel like dog shit when they play it!

Or, for the sadists in the audience, you can use that as a marketing line—'Buy this album to find out what Andy Partridge sounds like when he's really suffering.'
You're a twisted man, Mr Bernhardt. I like that in a person. [*Laughs.*]

Interview conducted February 24 2008.

CHAPTER 26

I CAN'T OWN HER

FROM *APPLE VENUS, VOLUME 1*, FEBRUARY 1999

I was reading the liner notes about this song, and you said that you didn't originally think this was going to make the album.
No. I thought it was a little square, and a little wet.

Meaning?
I don't know, it's little bit, 'Oh, listen to him whining there and being a bit too loungey.' [*Imitates lounge singer*] 'Ayyyye own this ri-ver—thankyouverymuch ladies and gentlemen.' Polite ripple of applause after the first line, you know. [*Laughs.*]

Viv Stanshall would have done a great job with it!*
Exactly! So, I thought, 'Is this just too fucking lounge-y?' If it wasn't for our producer, Haydn Bendall, pushing pushing pushing to record this, I think I would quite easily have dropped it.

How did Dave and Colin feel about it?
I think they were OK about it. I don't remember getting a huge rush of, 'Wow, yeah, we've got to do this one.' So, maybe they weren't so keen on it. But certainly Haydn said it was his favourite thing on the record, potentially. 'We *must* do this song.'

Interesting. I didn't know he was that passionate about it.
He loved it. And, hearing it again yesterday, first time in ages, I give all the credit to Mike Batt, the part-time Womble and arranger.[†]

---

* Vivian Stanshall (1943–95) was the singer with The Bonzo Dog Doo-Dah Band.
† Mike Batt (born 1949) is a prolific British songwriter, arranger, and producer, known for creating The Wombles and discovering Katie Melua.

This wouldn't have happened if Dave had been in the band. I wanted Dave to do the orchestral arrangements for this record—to take what I'd sketched out in the demos, and go forward with that.

I wanted *Apple Venus* to be two discs, where one disc was orchestral-based, and one disc was electric-based, but he said, 'Why don't we just take the best songs'—in other words, the songs that *he* thought were the best ones—'and put them all one record?'

I said, 'That's just going to make another rather schizophrenic record, and I don't want to do *Nonsuch 2*. I want to do a two-disc set, with two definitive faces to the coin—one side of the coin looks like this, the other side looks very different, like this.'

He didn't want to do that, and he did *not* want to spend the budget on an orchestra. So, unfortunately we had a lot of horrible, running-round-the-houses bad vibes about this, and Dave was putting off working up the orchestral arrangements. Sometimes I wonder if that was his way of saying, 'I'm going to make it so that you can't do this with an orchestra.'

Because he wanted to use samples?
Yes, he wanted to do them with samples, but I just knew that wasn't going to sound very good. In my opinion, you can only do it if it's going to be buried under guitars or piano or whatever—not if it's going to be the detailed, foreground stuff.

So, Dave never did the arrangements; after one argument too many about this, he said, 'Well, I'm off. I'm going.' He just left us down in Haydn's place, in East Sussex. Then it was a case of Colin and me just looking at each other, then looking at Haydn, and saying, 'Well, what the fuck are we going to do now? We're supposed to be doing the orchestral volume of this record, and we don't have the arrangements.' You know, we only had my sketched-out stuff from the demos.

Haydn kicked in and said, 'Look, I know a great arranger, and he owes me some favours, because I've done a lot of bits and pieces for him over the last few years. It's Mike Batt.'

Had you been aware of him anyway?
Sure. He kept cropping up on various projects—The Wombles was only one of them. So, he called Mike, and said, 'Look, we've got Abbey Road and an orchestra booked, and we haven't got the arrangements for these few songs.

Can you do something?' And [*chuckling*] Mike obviously knew he owned Haydn some favours, so he said, 'Sure! I'll do them.'

I spoke to Mike a couple of times on the phone, and sent him the demos, and he worked a little bit on them. He'd call me up, and I would sit with a guitar on my lap and the phone under my chin, while he was sat at the piano at his end with the phone, and he'd play me what he had.

With this one, I knew that I wanted the 'swirling sky' to be very passionate—I wanted it to sound like a sped-up film of boiling clouds, and at the same time I wanted it to be like hair in water, swirling and dancing around. He'd be playing me some things, and I'd be saying, 'OK, when you do that run-up, can you make that bit more whatever', and he'd say, 'OK, how about this?' And I'd say, 'Good, now try that.' And together, we worked on these things on the phone for an hour or two.

And then he'd call me back and say, 'OK, is this more like it?' And I'd say, 'Yeah, that's good', and he'd say, 'Well, imagine this hand here is what the woodwind is doing, and this line here is what the cello is doing, and this line is the violins', and all that. So I had to imagine it from him playing it on the piano down the phone. It wasn't until we got to the one mad day at Abbey Road, to do all the orchestral stuff for the whole album, that I actually got to hear the arrangement. And I can say that my socks were well and truly blown off!

Of all the arrangements, I think he really put his mark on this one.
He really did. This is a master arranger at work here, taking your chords and your pictorial sentiment—'I want it to be all grey there, and that's got to swirl, and then there's got to be a release at that point, and I still want a heavy suggestion of this hanging note here.' He did a phenomenal job—I was almost in tears, listening to this orchestra playing this stuff. I was just so thrilled.

I can imagine. Even now, as many times as I've heard the album, I still get a thrill at the base of my spine when they do that 'swirling sky' swell.
Oh, it's phenomenal stuff! And I really felt unworthy. I thought, 'This is my wretched body, dressed in the nicest material, the best cut of cloth'—do you know what I mean? It's velvet and ermine and jewels, and it's just on my stinking carcass.

Oh, c'mon—despite what they say, clothes don't make the man. You still need a solid person underneath.

I just felt so humbled, that my basic little idea of a song had this phenomenally pictorial arrangement, which I'd only heard little sonic glimpses of down a telephone. To me, he made this track happen. And he didn't even hang around so we could thank him! After we did the largest orchestrations, which he conducted, he then ran off, because he had to catch a plane to Germany. So, he just came in, waved his baton around a few times, and ran out! [*Laughs.*]

Who was that masked conductor?

And *why* was he waving his baton at me? [*Laughs.*]

Yeah, totally and utterly fantastic job he did. And if ever he needs a favour out of me, he should call me, because—damn. I owe him one for that.

Let's talk about some of the instrumentation, and the changes and choices between the demo and the recorded version.

The demo is so lumpen, I think. I found a patch on the keyboard that is a piano mixed with some strings, so when you hold a note down, the piano dies, and the strings kind of swell. And, of course, every note you play is exactly the same on the piano and strings. So, it has this rather stodgy, porridgy kind of quality—like a big wedge of plasticine or something.* The arrangement ideas are not fully fleshed at all on the demo.

I don't know if I'd totally agree with you on that. Like I said, the body of the song is there, and that was what everything else was built on. The melody and the sentiment behind it are more or less unchanged.

Yeah, I guess so, but I didn't feel worthy of that arrangement, really. But also, Haydn kicked in with some great suggestions. We were talking, while we were putting this track together, arrangement-wise, and when we got to the title line, I said, 'Isn't it great the way that Brian Wilson would do things like using different-range harmonicas, specifically bass ones—isn't that a lovely texture?'

Haydn had some beautiful samples that he'd probably made of bass harmonicas, and said, 'Well, you know, I've got some, so let's try it!'

---

* A brand of modelling clay.

I'd wanted to ask what instrument is in the left channel during the chorus—I thought it was some kind of a horn or keyboard, but you're saying those are harmonica samples?

Yeah, there are bass harmonicas vamping on that part. They've all got that very dark, huffy timbre. 'Fool On The Hill' has got the same sound, as well as some Brian Wilson things.

Just talking about how some other people approached similar things really prompted some good ideas, and he had the tools to back it up. Like, 'If this was a big show tune, wouldn't it be nice if that little counter-melody that I've done with some twinkly sound on the demo, wouldn't that be lovely if that was a harp?' Well, Haydn had a *beautiful* Celtic harp, which he'd made recordings of, into his own sample set, and they were just stunningly gorgeous. It was like, 'Oh, that is so sensual, and so beautiful—please, let's have that.'

Actually, now that I think of it, the harp may belong to quite a famous player, but I can't think of his name. It's somebody with a French name. Haydn recorded him, and got him to make this beautiful set of samples with him. As soon as he played these things, it was a matter of feeling like you're *inside* that sound. It's all around your head, beautifully recorded.

Do you remember some of the other instruments that make up the orchestration? I know I hear flute and woodwinds. There's an oboe, certainly.

There are some beautiful woodwinds. In fact, there's a lovely section at the end that we refer to as the 'ducks' section. We'd always be saying to Haydn, 'A little more—can you turn the mics up over on the woodwinds stuff? A little more of those ducks, please.' Those quacking woodwinds are over that suspended-moon section—the F-sharp over the C at the end.

But otherwise it was something like a forty- to fifty-piece orchestra. It was the kind of thing where you do the full arrangements earlier in the day, then the people you don't need anymore go home. You know—'OK, all the woodwinds can go home.' And, 'OK, now the strings can go home, and we'll just keep the brass and the double-bass, or the cellos.' Then, 'OK, now we'll just keep the brass,' and, 'OK, all the brass can go except for you, Mr Flugelhorn Player—you're still playing on "Last Balloon".' See what I mean?

Because Haydn was a master at recording orchestras, he knew these wrinkles that I wouldn't have thought of.

Right. The most efficient way to do it.
Yes. Don't pay for the whole orchestra all day. You use the whole orchestra, then a lesser part, lesser part, right down to one person. That one person's got to be here all day, because he's part of the brass section, but you don't keep the strings and woodwinds hanging around while he does his solo bit.

Another reason we worked with Haydn is because he had this reputation for making orchestras sound beautiful.

And he did. It's a beautiful-sounding album.
It's stunningly recorded. But it was not what Dave wanted to do, and he wasn't going to hang around while we spent the budget on an orchestra.

It must have cost a pretty penny to get all those people in Abbey Road.
Oh, yeah. Jesus. It was £20,000, just for one day, with the orchestra and Abbey Road. Might have been more than that, but that figure seems to be hovering in my head.

One of the biggest differences between the demo and the recorded version is that there are drums on the latter. Let's talk about that. Prairie Prince must have recorded all of his drum parts at Chipping Norton in the absence of any of the orchestra, correct?
He did the drums just to the piano and guide vocal. It was a case of, 'Well, the drums don't need to be all the way through—that'll just be too ponderous. But I would like this kind of tribal throb at certain points.' And he did great. He just clicked into this groove, and it was a case of, 'Stay away from those cymbals. Let's just use that tom and that tom, and use felt beaters instead of sticks.'

He did just what was required. I think anything bigger would have been obtrusive to the sentiment.

I agree—the drums are basically on the chorus, and on the end part. I love the end part, too, where he's doing those melodic runs down the toms. You guys must have worked together on the tuning of the toms, to make sure that they fit right in with the rest of the music.
That was the sort of thing that I was keen on, at that time and on the previous couple of albums—getting the drums tuned to the track. I think that that pretty much started around the time of *Skylarking*, when I was awakening

to the fact that drums could be very musical, as opposed to just going bonk-bonk-bonk.

Of course, this was being done even before I was even aware of it, by people like Steve Nye, our producer on *Mummer*, working with Pete Phipps on things like 'Me And The Wind'. You know, getting the drums musically tuned to be in with the track. *Nonsuch* was probably the apogee of that for me. There's Dave Mattacks drumming, and us saying, 'Can you tune the snare so it's a seventh of the scale,' or, 'We're going to add this sample with the snare, so it'll be a third,' or something that's in musical relation to the music going on.

And I'm sure Dave Mattacks was into that, given how musical his drumming is.
Very much so. Because if the drums are musically conversing with the other instruments, as opposed to just making knocking noises, it makes the drums much more part of the track.

Well then, I think what's left to talk about are the lyrics.
Ooh, I knew you'd say that! You're going to put a little pin into my coiled winkle of man-ness.

[*Laughing*] I think the message of these lyrics is an important thing for any man—or any person, for that matter—to understand. You can only be with another person. You cannot possess them.
Yeah. No matter how emotionally attached you are, they're not a chair. They're not a book. You can't say, 'Yep. That's mine. I own that. I bought it, that's mine. I can sit on this chair, I can take this book anywhere I want.' You can't do that with people—it doesn't matter how fucking attached you get to them!

And that realisation ultimately makes relationships stronger, because you realise you can't take people for granted—you have to constantly work at it, because it's always a mutual agreement.
But when they pull that stool from under you, when they pull that carpet from under you and say, 'I'm off'—whoa! It's the fact that one person who you thought was with you for life is going, and you're left with that realisation of, 'Oh my god, I didn't *own* them! I couldn't possess them, I couldn't keep them for evermore, despite the whole [*adopts over-important voice*] Judaeo-Christian

marriage thing.' And here comes a new person into my life, and I realise I will not be able to own them, either! You know, my third eye has been opened here, and I've now been rudely awakened.

Which, again, only makes that relationship stronger—it's both edges of the sword.
I guess so. You realise that all the shit like wedding rings and vows and all that kind of stuff don't mean anything.

It's all a choice.
It's down to human foibles. A kick in the foibles!

And a sense of commitment and dedication and work …
Yeah. Making it work.

Too many people, I think, get caught up in the whole fairy-tale aspect of 'Till death do us part,' and 'They lived happily ever after.'
I think I was, until this kick in the foibles that I got. And suddenly I realised that you do *not* own people, despite whatever ceremony you did. That's a tough feeling! That's a painful awakening.

When we discussed 'The Man Who Sailed Around His Soul', you were talking about existentialism, and this is kind of a flavour of that, isn't it?
Yeah! I can't remember the brand of cigarettes,* but in the 50s there was an ad where there's a fellow wandering by the Thames in his mac—you know, lonely man with his cigarette, being all very French and Left Bank, looking at the river—and I sort of imagined myself as this existential actor caught between two scene changes. Here I am—I can look at the river and say, 'Yeah, that's my river. I live in this country, that's my river, I can own that if I want. But I can't own that person. This is my town, but I can't own that person!' The closest people to your heart—they're going to run off, or they're going to die.

Exactly. You can fool yourself—you can say that there is a god, you can

---

* Strand cigarettes were launched by W.D. & H.O. Wills in 1959 and withdrawn after disastrous sales, widely blamed on their advertising campaign.

say there is an afterlife, or that there is an enduring love, such a thing as 'happily ever after,' but in fact there's not.

There's not. And that was a real slap in the face for me.

Do you remember sitting and writing this? Did the music and lyrics come to you together? Or were the lyrics prompted by chords you'd discovered, or by that keyboard patch you mentioned?

I think I was messing around with it on guitar first of all, and found this interval [*picks up guitar, plays interval*]—it's a C with a F-sharp. To me— because chords do this to my mind—that's sort of a moon hanging on a string, and you can reach and reach and reach for it, and you can see it, and it's lighting you up, but you *can't get it*. You can't own it.

You're the moth that's always flying toward it and never getting there.

Yeah. So, it was that interval—which I'd been trying to put that into a song for a while—and then finding that rising figure [*sings melodic intro to verse vocal*], just sitting at a keyboard, with this piano-strings patch, that got me going. And then I fell into being Left Bank cigarette man.

Did the song come quickly, or did you build it over time?

I think it came reasonably quickly. I'm not sure, though. The process of writing this is a little unclear in my memory—as in, maybe I was trying to detach myself from this awkward emotional feeling whilst it was being written. I know that sounds contradictory. I was sort of proud of it, but I didn't want to be proud of it.

One of the distinguishing characteristics about this song, as well as 'Your Dictionary', is that you don't hide behind another persona.

Yeah. See, I felt difficult about doing that one, as well. I felt that was just sort of a musical tantrum. After I'd gotten it down in demo form, it was a matter of, 'Now that I've had that tantrum, it doesn't need to be permanentised.'

That's one of the reasons I was asking about Dave and Colin's opinion of 'I Can't Own Her'. If I remember correctly, the reason 'Your Dictionary' made it on to the album is because the two of them advocated for it very strongly. Is that correct?

They did. I think also that the record companies also liked 'Your Dictionary'.

I remember talking to you when the album first came out, and saying that the song should have been a single, since there was potential in it to be controversial, with you spelling out the words 'shit' and 'fuck'.
Yeah, I remember that. I know they liked that song, but I can't remember their reaction to 'I Can't Own Her', for some reason. I don't know why it seems I've got this screen in the way of remembering—some sort of embarrassment about my 'weakness' in the lyric, because I'm showing vulnerability. I've still got some sort of wall up about it. But hearing it yesterday, in headphones, through three or four times, I thought, 'Wow, this is very beautifully arranged!'

Colin's bass playing is great on this.
Oh, yes. Totally sympathetic to what's required. He does that beautiful, kind of bubbling counter-melody. Plus, he and I did things like sitting and listening, and I'd say, 'You know, when it says 'Winos sliding down,' can you turn the tuning peg of the bass to wind the note down?' He did that, and you end up with that great aural metaphor.

I think we were quite sensitive to the arrangements of the counter vocals as well, in the middle section—which I'd forgotten all about until I played them yesterday, and it was like, 'Oh, that's not half bad!'

I like the holes in this track. And the exchange of sounds—you know, one sound ends, another sound takes over. What else about the arrangement? Oh, there's a hammered dulcimer as well—that's the thing that plays the marimba-like part.

And the swirling sky bit—it had to swirl like hair in a bath, or in a washbasin, because before I got together with Erica, I would fantasise about washing her hair. It makes me weirdly emotional to say that. It struck me as the ultimate intimate act, so I wanted the strings to do that. It's that dark-haired thing, and I used to think how gorgeous it'd look in the bath.

If I remember correctly, several other musicians have mentioned this album and song as favourites.
Harry Shearer likes this song[*]—he did an interview where he was asked, 'If push comes to shove, what's your all-time favourite album?' And he said, 'It'd be *Apple Venus* by XTC. Every fucking song on the record is a killer, and I

---

[*] Harry Shearer (born 1943) is an American actor and comedian who plays numerous parts in *The Simpsons*, including Mr Burns, Ned Flanders, Kent Brockman, and Principal Skinner.

just think it's Beatle-esque in the best sense of the term. We'll never see it live, which I both treasure and bemoan.' That's a nice thing to say.

Do you realise what you're saying? One of the members of Spinal Tap thinks this is the best album ever. That's high praise. You can't do any better than that!
There's none more better! But isn't that nice? Isn't it nice that Mr Burns likes our album?

Louis Philippe did a cover of this song, correct?*
He did a cover version before we did! He got the demos and called me up and asked if I minded if he recorded it. I think he did a lovely version. But it's a funny old song for me, because I did feel that, unintentionally, I gave too much of myself away. And it's still a little bit raw because of that. There's a lot to this songwriting shit! [*Laughs.*]

You didn't know you were working so hard, did you?
No! Almost broke into an anal-cleft sweat!

I thought there was just a treble and bass cleft! I didn't realise there was that one, too.
The anal cleft! That's the one that does all the clenching when you realise you're playing wrong.

Interview conducted January 5 2010.

---

* Louis Philippe is a London-based French singer-songwriter.

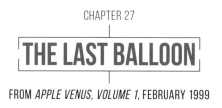

CHAPTER 27

THE LAST BALLOON

FROM *APPLE VENUS, VOLUME 1,* FEBRUARY 1999

So, let's start this one talking about the demo. If you listen to the demo and the studio version, some of the instrumentation that you chose is pretty different. For example, in the demo, the harpsichord is more prevalent.
Well, on the demo, it's actually a sample of a nylon guitar. The sampled sound of a harpsichord just didn't sound right to me.

Interesting, because on the studio version it sounds more guitar-based to me.
No, the keyboard on the demo is a sample of a nylon-strung guitar, and the studio version features Chris Difford's Baldwin electric harpsichord, which has a pickup. We recorded it through that, but it was so muddy and fluffy that our producer, Haydn Bendall, said, 'You know what, I'm going to put a plate mic on the plastic top—the Perspex lid—and pick up the vibrations coming from the plucked strings.' When he did that, the blend of the two of those sounded fantastic! Sounded like a real, 3-D, world's-biggest harpsichord. It was gorgeous.

Did Dave play the harpsichord part?
It's Haydn Bendall. Dave had originally done it, and I can't remember for what reason we didn't use Dave's playing, but on the finished recording, it's actually Haydn Bendall playing the harpsichord.

I'm not sure whether it's Dave playing the Mellotron bit. I've got feeling that it's part Mellotron, which would have been Dave, and part Proteus strings, which would have been either me and/or Nick Davis who would have played that on the finished recording.

The song was written on a nylon-string guitar, but balloons to me mean harpsichords, which is why, when I did *Orpheus: The Lowdown* with Peter

Blegvad—what's the track where the lyric is 'Blow him up like a balloon'? 'The Blimp Poet'? That's a harpsichord sample, but it's actually a harpsichord playing the sequenced backing track to 'Omnibus'.

So, you wrote this on your daughter Holly's guitar?
Yeah. An Italian musician—I can't remember his name now—came to see me and asked if I'd play on a track of his. I said, 'OK, fair enough, very flattering. Get me the track.' So, he got me this track, and it was just a bunch of chords. He said, 'I want you to come up with a melody.' So, I came up with this melody [*sings the vocal melody*] over the top of these chords, and I thought, 'Do you know, that's a really good melody!'

Then he started asking me to introduce him to Peter Gabriel, and asking if I'd come to Italy and play all over this record he had, and I thought, 'Hang on a minute, he's really using me here. He wants me to come up with the melodies over these chord patterns that he's come up with, and I suspect that's what he wants me to do over the whole of the album.' So I decided to drop out of the project, but I had come up with a really good melody that I liked. I changed the chords under the melody, so that it was me coming up with the chord pattern *and* the melody. That's the genesis of the song—the melody came first. It sounded like some sort of placid balloon ride to me.

The working title for the *Nonsuch* album was *The Last Balloon Home*. Originally, it was just going to be called *Balloon*, but then it became the longer name. I talked to Dave and Colin, and said, 'Look, it'd be great to do a sleeve around the concept—we can make it like a 50s musical. Like, you know, the sleeve for *South Pacific*—one of those big, over-blasted colour photos. What we do is, in the photo studio, we mock up a hanging basket from a hot-air balloon, and we're in Victorian gear, but really bright-coloured—sort of pastel colours, like lilacs and pinks—with top hats and frock coats and stuff. We're climbing in the basket of this balloon, and there are ladies in parasols around, so it looks like an outtake fantasy sequence from *My Fair Lady* or something.'

I said, 'We'll give it all the trappings of a musical on the cover, and maybe even put a fake synopsis on the back, and a dozen or so large-format photographs inside 'from the film', so to speak, done in this over-blasted colour effect, so it really looks like a sleeve from a musical film that never was.' And then Dave said, 'I'm not putting on stupid clothes and climbing in a basket!'

'You've already had me in a schoolboy's outfit, in train worker's gear, and wrapped in newspapers …'
Exactly! Or 'a diving outfit!' And then they came up with the idea that I was the organ grinder and they were just monkeys, and they weren't going to get into any stupid outfits. Although, I must say, Colin initially was really into it, because he has a love for musicals as well, so he was into the concept of the album being a fake musical. So, unfortunately, the title *The Last Balloon Home* kind of fell by the wayside, because Dave wouldn't do the concept—he wouldn't put on the lilac-y frock coat with a pink top hat on, and climb in a basket. I can't blame him.

He didn't want to be Phileas Fogg, eh?
No. I thought certain songs could fit the concept—'Omnibus' would have fit the concept really well.

Sure. 'Bungalow.'
'Bungalow' would have fit the concept well, yeah. It'd be sort of a concept album without really being one. But it was not to be, and that's when the *Nonsuch* thing came up. I found a drawing of Nonsuch Palace, and I thought, 'Wow, that's great." I read about it, and thought, 'OK, we'll call the album *Nonsuch*. I've got to get out of this whole balloon thing.'

That said, when I found myself with an orphaned melody and some orphaned chords from this aborted Italian project, I thought, 'Well, what does this sound like? It's sounds like a balloon—ooh, "The Last Balloon"!' And that's really what triggered the whole thing—and that's my rambling explanation of it. [*Laughs.*]

When in the cycle of songwriting for the *Apple Venus* and *Wasp Star* albums did you write this? When I was getting the demos from various sources for these albums, I'm pretty sure it was one of the later discoveries for me. Does that reflect when you actually wrote and demoed it?
I'm trying to remember—if I went to the Shed and dug out the digital audio tape with all the original mixes on it, or got the track sheets, I could show in what order it came out.

---

* Nonsuch Palace was built by Henry VIII in Surrey in 1538. A mistress of Charles II was given it, then had it pulled down in 1682, selling the materials to pay off her gambling debts.

I seem to remember that it came out reasonably early. I think the earliest stuff was, oddly, some things that ended up on *Wasp Star*. But when I got into 'River of Orchids', 'Easter Theatre', and things like that, 'The Last Balloon' seemed to hang in with all that.

Another big difference for me between the demo and studio version is the trumpet patch you use on the demo—you're being Miles Davis, as opposed to Guy Barker.
I didn't have a nice flugelhorn patch!

If you had had one, would you have demoed that?
I actually prefer flugelhorns to trumpets. Trumpets are yellow, and flugelhorns are a slightly brown-y/orange.

And on the demo, you made the trumpet even yellower by putting a mute on it.
Yeah. It was kind of a case of, 'Let's just make the demo work as a demo. I know what I'll ultimately want.' But, god, didn't Guy Barker play a beautiful solo?

It's gorgeous.
That's the best of two-and-a-half solos, which were done at about two in the morning. It was at the end of the orchestral day at Abbey Road, where we did the strings and brass for all the other songs. We started with a full orchestra, then kept sending sections home as we finished with them until only Guy Barker was left. By that time it was two in the morning. So, we knew we wanted a flugelhorn solo, but were all falling asleep, with the faders pressing in our foreheads on the mixing desk!

That's actually kind of the perfect situation, because it's got this great, late-night jazz-club feel. You can see the smoke hanging in the air, almost, as he's playing this solo.
It's perfect, yeah. You know, we're trying to throw Phileas Fogg out of the bar! [*Chuckles.*] It's a beautiful solo. I think it's mostly from one take, with a few phrases from another take dropped in.
    The way he got the transition between the voice and his solo is wonderful. Lovely.

And because of the different timbre of the horn, and the fact that it's lower than the trumpet you'd originally had there, that gives the studio version a lusher and denser feel.
It's a little more melancholy, and I think better conveys the atmosphere that was required.

On the studio version, it sounds like Colin's playing two basses. One bass that sounds like a double bass …
That's his Newport, with the mute on. Yeah, he is playing two basses, which we give two different reverb treatments, so that one is much farther away. He plays the root stuff on a drier, closer-sounding bass, while the more melodic stuff sings off with the reverb, into the distance more. The two basses kind of weave through each other. And, you know, this is some of his best playing, I think, on that album.

He played the Newport for both tracks?
Yes, I think so. The trusty Epiphone Newport with the faulty felt mute!

And is there a keyboard bass in there as well?
I don't think so. I think it's the two tracks of real bass, and the keyboard would have been the electric harpsichord, the Baldwin—which goes down pretty deep—and the string things from the Mellotron and the Proteus. They would have been that more deep, brown, mid-sounding stuff. So, I think you're hearing some lower stuff from the electric harpsichord.

On both versions, you have a ride cymbal going throughout.
Yeah, that's me playing the ride cymbal. Prairie had an endorsement deal—I can't remember the cymbal maker—where, when he was recording with us, he rang up his cymbal sponsor and said, 'Get me a bunch of stuff—what have you got that's good?'

They trucked up a load of free cymbals for him, and at the end of the session, they never bothered asking anyone to get them back to them. Prairie didn't want to have to ship them back to the States, so we took them with us. We had all these beautiful cymbals hanging around in the corner of the studio, so it was a case of, 'Well, let's get the cymbal up on the stand there,' and I just stood with a stick and tapped that out. Wait—come to think of it, I actually used a biro to hit it with.

What starts the song out? There's a little ding-ding-ding-ding—it sounds like something electronic to me, or maybe a triangle.
It is a triangle.

Ah, OK. And then, later on, the third time you go into singing the verse …
Yeah, I know what you're going to ask—I tried to make a wristwatch.

***That's* what it is!**
What it is, it's two different-pitched stick sounds …

With a triplet feel …
Exactly. I wanted it to sound like a wristwatch, as in, 'time's running out'.

'You'd better get on board.'
I'd forgotten all about that, but when you play it on headphones, all this stuff is revealed! That was just two little samples of sticks tuned and tweaked to sound like a wristwatch ticking on.

How did you get that 'boom' after the 'Drop us off' line?
That's just a white-noise sample, shaped with filters.

There's a lot of low end to it.
Yes, there is—we played it way down on the keyboard, plus there's reverb. So it sounds like you're throwing something big and heavy overboard [*chuckles*] and it's hitting the ground. It just happens to be in rhythm. Sandbags—or people! You know, older people—it's us being thrown off the balloon. When I think about it, I see this as being like a Montgolfier brothers balloon—you know, it can't be just any old kind of balloon. It's not one of those comedy-type of balloons that look like a bottle of beer or something! It should be very elaborate and baroque.

Let's talk about the lyrics a bit. You had this melody, you had these chords, and the lyrics kind of fell out from there?
Yeah, they came pretty easily. It was funny—the more I changed the chords to make them my own, the more oblique the melody got, and the sadder-sounding it got. It was actually more pleasing to me. It was a very convoluted way of arriving at a song, but it did seem to pay off.

Did something prompt you into the melancholy feel of the song?
Well, kids'll do that to you. It's just that hope for the future, for your children—
for them not to make the same fucking mistakes as you! You know, surely your
kids aren't going to mess things up worse than *you* did, and *your* parents did.
You look back through history, and you think, 'Wow, we *can't* have World
War I again!', and there it is—World War II! You know—the sequel! [*Laughs,
adopts cod German voice*] *Adolph Strikes Back.* [*Cod German Darth Vader voice*]
'Jah! Ich bin your father!' [*As Luke*] 'Neiiiin!!'

So then we had World War II, and you think it can't get any worse, but
then we have this nuclear standoff, and then 9/11, then Iraq and Afghanistan,
and—*come on*! Do you know what pissed me off about 9/11?

What's that?
The phrase '9/11'. It sounds like 7-Eleven or something. It sounds like a
commercial product. They gave it a snappy name, like a commercial project.

It's become a 'brand', yeah. Have you guys done the same thing with 7/7?
We resist that, I think. If people talk about it, they say, 'the seventh of July'.
They refuse to brand it, like Pepsi Max or something—which robs it of any
nobility. 'The eleventh of September' has a nobility to it. But '9/11'—that's
just Pepsi Max. 'Open twenty-four hours!'

**I admire your optimism in this song, because I understand what you're
talking about when you say having kids does this to you. During the
darkest hours of the night, especially with what's been going on with
the economy and the environment lately, I sometimes have real despair,
wondering whether things are going to be better for my kids. But you
seem to manage to hold on to a certain amount of optimism here.**
But it's an optimism that says, 'You have to throw us off if you're going to
learn. Don't make the same mistakes as us—don't listen to us. Because if you
do, you're going to make the same mistakes.'

**You and I have talked about how you, as a young man, actively pushed
away the past.**
Oh, yeah. I think everybody does. You know, if you don't hate your parents
at some point, you're not normal! These families that say, 'Ooh, I *love* my
parents'—I didn't! I wanted to murder my mother with an axe! And I was

afraid of my father—he was competition! I think that's a healthy way of being. *Now* I'm different, of course—you move beyond that, beyond the anger and frustration and resentment that they said 'no no no' to things. You move beyond that teenaged or young-man thing, and you can say, 'Yeah, I can see why they were like that.'

I don't want my kids to make the same mistakes that I made. I think of my daughter, getting into the pop music industry, and I think, 'Oh no, she's going to have to sign this, that, and the other, and it's going to turn her inside-out, and I don't want her to have to go through what I did.' And I don't want Harry, who's really getting into animation in a heavy-duty way now, to sign rights away to stuff and make the same mistakes as me. I want them to make a better world for themselves and for others.

I sound like I've just won 'Miss Nebraska'! [*Chuckles.*] I actually think that, given the competition, I'd probably stand a good chance!

We've got to get you in that swimsuit, though.
[*laughs.*] Yeah, a swimsuit with a nice pair of Y-fronts over the top, so there's nothing hanging out.

You recorded some of this at Colin's house, correct?
Right. We did the vocals, and the bass, and some of the other keyboards at Colin's house, in what would have been his front room on the left, as you look at it. The harpsichord was done at the studio that Haydn was renting, but the Proteus, and triangle, and vocals and the basses were done at Colin's house. If you have a nice enough desk, and a nice microphone, and a nice compressor and stuff, you can record anywhere.

I knew that you had done the acoustic guitar for 'I'd Like That' there ...
We did a hell of a lot of that album in Colin's front room! He did save our bacon, offering up his two front rooms—they were being decorated, so it was a case of, we've run out of money to afford studios, and seeing how the two front rooms of his house were a mess in any case, it was like, 'Well, we might as well do it in here, because they can't get any messier at the moment.'

The ending of this song is particularly beautiful, with the solo and the slow fade-out.
'Morse-code flugelhorn'—that's one of my notes here. You know, [*mimics horn*

pattern played before and throughout the verse]. That's great—Morse code and balloons. It's real 'Siege Of Paris'*, isn't it?

Bismarck at the door ...[†]
Bis-Marc Almond! [*Laughs.*] 'Jah, "Tainted Love"!'

Yes, I wanted a really slow fade, because it's got to be that the balloon is flying slowly away. And I wanted it mixed with that picture in mind—I said, 'It won't be right if the balloon flies away straight—the wind's going to take it.' So if you listen in headphones, the fade goes off to the right, as if the wind is taking the balloon. I thought, 'Yeah, that's really pictorial.' The balloon is drifting off to the right there.

I do like the pictorial imagery of that—doing this is really big for me, really important. You have to have the 'picture in the sound'. The stage setting has got to be right. The lyrics are what the actors are saying, and the scenery also has got to be just right, to give you the right feel.

Interview conducted October 25 2008.

---

* In 1870–71, during the Franco-Prussian War, Paris was besieged and mail was sent by balloon.
† Otto von Bismarck was Minister President of Prussia at the time of the war.

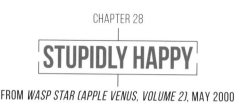

CHAPTER 28

STUPIDLY HAPPY

FROM *WASP STAR (APPLE VENUS, VOLUME 2)*, MAY 2000

People I play this song for seem to like it right away—maybe that's because it's just a happy, straightforward love song. So—why would you write such a happy, straightforward love song?
Certainly, musically it's very straight.

Except that you build and layer things throughout the song to create complexity.
Yeah, it builds and builds. It's like Sting making love! [Laughs.] It lasts a month.

It's your Tantric love song!
It's a Tan-tric of the tale! Yeah, it's a very, very simple construction, because it's that same guitar figure without interruption.

So, why did you eschew—if I may use that word …
Good word!

… a chorus and a bridge on this? I know that you create these parts melodically and lyrically, but what is it that made you decide, 'No, I'm going to drive this guitar pattern throughout the entire song'?
It was just *so* pleasing! When I blundered on to that pattern, I was just messing around, trying to work out something like 'Miss Amanda Jones', the old Rolling Stones number.* [*Sings*] 'Round and round she goes, Miss Amanda Jones' [*sings guitar pattern*]. I played something wrong and thought, 'Whoo! That's nice.'

I'd already thought, 'I'm not going to write a song this afternoon, I'm not in the mood,' so I'd managed to program a really nice Charlie Watts sort of

---

* From the 1967 album *Between The Buttons*.

lollopy rhythm—a-*one* te *tah*, a-*one* te *tah*, on the bass drum there—that I was playing along with. It's the kind of thing he does in 'Jumping Jack Flash' and a whole load of others. In fact, believe it or not, this song owes a little to 'Jumping Jack Flash', but we'll get on to that in a second.*

I'd blundered on this little guitar figure that just sounded like blocks of noise, and it fell into the hands nice to play. It sounded lovely—these big, square, fuzzy chunks. I just couldn't stop playing it! I thought, 'This is *great*, I just love this pattern, and the way it goes with those drums.'

So I just put down a load of it on to a cassette, thinking, 'There's something in this, it's so attractive.' Then it was a case of just improvising vocals, just one of those things where you let your mind go. And I must have been feeling happy, because this *thing* made me feel happy, this repeat rhythm.

I *love* repeat rhythms. I could name you dozens and dozens of songs, from 'Battery Brides' to 'Travels In Nihilon' right up to 'River Of Orchids', that are built on repetition. And this is another one. Repetition is incredibly inspirational to me, and I don't know why this is. It puts you in that *state*, you know?

When you think about religious or tribal ceremonies, or meditation— when you're trying to get 'outside of yourself'—a lot of that is built on repetition, and on using whatever you're repeating as the basis of distracting your consciousness, so that you can then get beyond it.
Exactly. You click into another place. So, I was just blah-blah-ing some lyrics—I was actually dancing around in the Shed, probably doing my best Jagger impression! And I thought, 'Wow! This is great. This is making me really happy.' And I just started la-la-ing [*sings rather tunelessly*], 'I'm really happy, I'm *stupidly* happy, because this is a stupid riff going round and round with no end', and it just fell out instantaneously.

The only real piece of arch thought that went into it, I guess, was that once I had the first melody—[*sings*] 'I'm stupidly happy'—I thought, as I do with these repetitive patterns, 'Let me find another pattern vocally that could go over that, so that if the two ever get to meet, it'll be fine—they can marry, almost like a round or something.'

You tend to do that a lot.
Oh yeah, I *love* that, too.

---

* Released as a single in 1968.

Is that always a conscious choice?

Usually. I must have been scared as a child by some old folk song in infant school or something—[*laughs*] My mother was scared by The Swingle Singers when I was in the womb!—because I just love those overlapping songs. You know, the Frère Jacques thing, where one line will lay over another and so on.

It's a convenient way of bringing closure to a song, too—you bring back all the players in the play, and let them take a bow.

Yeah, it's great, when you bring back the parts and they talk to each other. First they talk to each other separately, and then, when you lay them on top of each other, it makes some new pattern, like a moiré pattern.

So, I found the 'I'm stupidly happy' melody first. And then it was the cascading, 'All the birds of the air' piece. Then I came up with the chiming guitar solo piece. I'm really proud of that, actually—I think it's one of the most melodic guitar things I've ever come up with.

At the end, on the sort of plateau—well, the song's one giant plateau, really—at the end plateau of this, you get all those things going over each other. You get that chiming guitar solo piece; you get the cascading-down vocal line—that works with the guitar; and then you get the actual 'stupidly happy' melody. They all work together, and when all of it comes together at the end, whoa! That thrill goes up the back of my incontinence pad, and it feels just *wonderful*.

And I said we were going to come back to 'Jumping Jack Flash'. What makes that song really tense is the fact that he just plays one note on the bass. I think it's a B. You know, the chords are changing around that, but he's pumping away on that B, and it *really* keeps the tension in what would be what you would call the verses of 'Jumping Jack Flash'.

And of course 'Stupidly Happy' does the same thing.

Right! I couldn't figure out what key 'Stupidly Happy' is in—it's kind of in E and B at the same time—so I thought, 'Well, I'll try that trick of the tension.' And it really, really worked.

Although in the studio version you double-track the bass, right?

We do. Colin's playing a higher B until about two-thirds of the way through, where I sing, 'All the lights of the cars in the town form the strings of a big guitar.' And then you hear the other electric guitar come in, and that's where we add a second bass part, an octave under his other part. Suddenly everyone seems to like it from there on. It's like it goes widescreen, like *The Girl Can't Help It*'s widescreen moment, you know.* [*Laughs, does announcer's voice*] 'Now let's hear this song in *Partridge Vision!*' You push it out there, and it suddenly gets really 3-D. Plus, the rhythm guitar that joins in at that point—I wanted it to kind of sound like the original fuzzy block guitar, but not be playing the same thing, so I tuned it to the chord of E, and actually played parts of chords. But the open-E tuning makes them sound very pure.

Did that enable you to focus it and only play two or three notes at a time, or did you have more open strings ringing out?
It was just because it was tuned to the chord of E; when you play these little passages it just sounds cleaner and stronger. Again, it's a Stones trick. Keith Richards, after about 1969, played pretty much everything on a tuning. It keeps it sounding purer, because you're not having to hold the notes down, they're already tuned.

I guess that's what I meant—you don't have to actually fret all the notes; more strings are just ringing out open.
Kind of, yeah. It's just a purer-sounding things. So I played a little pattern that was imitative of the original fuzzy chunk guitar.

And during this part you can have your bass and eat it too, because the low bass keeps the constant note, while he starts playing around a little bit on the higher bass.
With the 'Devil drove up' pieces—which, I think, on the demo, I sang while holding my nose. I've got a funny feeling that we might have done that on the album as well. We screwed it up with telephonic EQ, but I still think I sang pinching my nose. Because I like the idea of this part of the song being phoned-in, like advice to you.

Right, while Colin is doing the slides up and down the neck there. But even during the 'stupidly happy' part, there are places where the higher place goes off the B.
I think just once or twice he drops in a little riff, during the line, 'I roll like a

---

* A movie of 1956, starring Jayne Mansfield.

train.' I like what Colin does with the 'Devil drove up' pieces, where he copies the whooping bass off the demo, but because he thinks more like a bass player, he anchors it on the four, which I didn't think of, not being a bass player. There's a cymbal splash when he does it—there are only a couple cymbal splashes in this track, and that's one of them. They're important, though.

You can tell they're very considered and placed. The drum part is a loop, correct?
That's a two-bar loop, I think, of drums. It's Chuck Sabo playing, but I wanted it to sound really robot, so we kept only two bars of his playing.

You have some sort of effect on the kick drum, where it kind of 'swallows itself'.
Yeah. We used the real kick drum, but we also fed in an electronic, gulping kick drum and mixed them together.

Tell me more about the chiming guitar part, which you've said you're proud of. It's got a keyboard part layered over it, right?
Before Dave left, we'd planned to have him play that on a twelve-string. But because I didn't have a twelve-string guitar, we did it by playing octaves on the guitar, and we added in a really sparkly keyboard, a ring-y kind of chorus-y keyboard, to make it sound like an ultra-twelve-string or something.

The vocals are layered, too. You sing lots of parts above and below the main melody.
I think the harmony under the lead vocal is really important.

Let's talk about that a little bit, because I know it's something you guys have focused more and more on through the years.
Years ago, I read an interview with George Martin, where he said that when he talked to The Beatles about doing harmonies, he would try to get them to pitch the harmony underneath the lead line. Because your ear is usually drawn to the highest singer, if you pitch the harmony *underneath* while the actual lead melody of the song is still the highest-pitched thing, your ear stays on the main melody. After reading that, I thought, 'Jesus, maybe that's why a lot of those records still sound very strong.' So it was something, I guess I *caught* years ago, and it's something that we've done a lot of since.

I think it increases the lushness of the harmony, too.
Sure! And, if you want to make the lead vocal line sound higher and wider, you can pitch an octave above it, if you can do it, or an octave below it, or both. In that way, you can still slot an apparently higher harmony, but then if you add an octave above the lead line, your ear is still drawn to the lead line.

As a prog rock fan, listening to the 'dood-n-doo' backing vocals, I'd be tempted to say that you were tipping your hat to Yes there.
You know, it hadn't crossed my mind, but I guess an argument could be made that, with my balls in a vice, I *am* Jon Anderson! [*Laughs.*]

You know what I'm talking about there, right? The way that the vocals layer on each other at the end of the song, and even Colin's approach to the bass there …
Yeah, I can kind of see that. I mean, I always thought Yes were a great pop band that just went flaccid. If you take any Yes track and edit it down to two minutes thirrty seconds, they would have been great pop singles.

Sure, and this reminds me of when they were still doing that, back in the early 70s.
I guess, when I write a song, that I sometimes have other bands in mind as a template. Not as a stealing thing, but you're doing your own little Sistine Chapel, and you use bits of songs by other bands as some sort of scaffolding to help you up there while you're doing your own thing.

As I said, there's a nod to Charlie Watts in the drumming, there's a nod to Bill Wyman's 'Jumping Jack Flash' bass line in the constant-B bass, there's a nod to Keith Richards and 'Miss Amanda Jones' in the crunchy guitar thing, and there's even a little tip of the hat to the Byrds with the voices cascading off of each other.

As you say, with the intended twelve-string.
Sure, yeah. In fact, before he left, Dave was going to learn that whole cascading-guitar thing in two sections. He was going to learn every alternate line.

Really?
Yeah, so it was going to be [*sings first three notes*] in one speaker, then [*sings next three notes*] in the other speaker, and so on, in chunks of three notes at a

time. Which is very difficult to do! And then we were going to have slightly different sounds, so it would seem to sway backwards and forwards across the speakers.

For a call-and-response thing.
Two different chiming sounds. But Dave left before we got to recording this, and it was up to Muggins here [*laughs*] to do the electric guitar, and I thought, 'No, I just can't learn it, I'm not a learner like Dave is.' Dave can write it down on sheet music and sit down and practise it, but I can't do that. I just have to shoot from the hip. I just have to sort of pull it out of the bag as one thing. So, as I said, we tarted it up with different octaves of the same thing, and some keyboard as well.

Is there anything else about the recording of this song that you particularly remember? You did this at Idea Studios?*
We did this at Idea, yep. It's Chuck drumming away there. He said that the Idea room—[*clears throat*] which sadly no longer exists, I don't know what the hell it is now—was the nicest acoustic room he'd ever been in for his drums. It really flattered his drums.

Yeah, I remember him telling me that. He really liked recording there.
In fact, he went around the room until he settled on playing in one corner, because he said he liked the way it threw the sound of the drums out of that corner. That's an old trick they used to do on blues recordings—they would put the singer in the corner, sometimes facing the corner, because then the voice would bounce off the two corner walls, into the microphone, and you'd get a brighter, harder sound.

So, he did that—he took his bass drums around, and he played in the middle of the room, then he tried one side and the other, and he tried every corner, and he settled on one corner specifically, and said, 'This is where it sounds the best.'

Facing out into the room?
Yes, facing out, with his back toward the corner. We close-miked his kit. In fact, the drums were all engineered by the engineer who did *White Music,* a

---

* Converted from the garage and stable block at Colin Moulding's then home near Swindon.

fellow called Alan Douglas.* Our producer, Nick Davis, said, 'Let's get Alan in—he just makes drums sound so good.'† Alan came in for a week or ten days, and brought a selection of great microphones of his own, and great little pre-amps and stuff, and what with Chuck's drums, which sounded very musical in any case, and the flattering sound of this double garage, the drums zinged! They zanged! 'Zangeth they, the drums?' 'Aye, lord, they zangeth.' It was a great-sounding kit.

How about recording the guitars and bass?
Well, we'd discovered the Pod, the guitar-amp modeller.‡ In fact, it was Nick who turned us on to the Pod. He brought one along, and said, 'Have you ever seen this thing before?' And he pulled out this red kidney-bowl-looking thing. We tried it, and thought, 'Ooh, wow, this is good.'

What we did on that whole album, we tended to play the guitar through the Pod, and then we'd send that to my Sessionette amp. [*Announcer's voice*] 'The Sessionette 70!' That sounds like a really cheesy kitchen appliance, doesn't it? [*Same voice*] 'Are you mixing your bread with the Sessionette 70?' [*Syrupy jingle*] 'Sessionettttte, seventeeee!' You know—'Can you imagine the future in *1970*, when everything is an atomic wasteland, but the Sessionette will still be working?'

So yeah, I remember on this in particular, I played though the Pod, and I got a sound that I liked, which we then shot through the Sessionette, and miked that up for punch.

So, you double-tracked? You'd have your performance already tracked going through the Pod, and then you'd run that back through the amp?
No, we'd probably do it live, so I was playing live through the Pod, and that would come up on one channel, and then we'd put a mic or two on the Sessionette at different distances, and then would blend that together. Because though the Pod is good for modelling the appearance of a sound, it doesn't have any real speaker punch.

---

* Alan Douglas started his career as an engineer at the Manor, Virgin's studio in Oxfordshire. He went on to work with The Jam, Queen, Squeeze, Eric Clapton, and many more.
† Nick Davis had previously worked with Genesis, Marillion, Tony Banks and Mike + The Mechanics.
‡ The Pod, designed to digitally simulate the sound of various amplifiers, is made by Line 6.

Right. There's no ambience.

So, what you do is put it through an amp, and you get real speaker punch. The Sessionette is kind of good for that, because it's rather flat and bland-sounding, so you can push a shaped guitar sound into it, and it won't colour it too much. We tended to do that a lot on that album. I think Colin's going out through—oh, did he have a Gallien Krueger amp?

That's a well-known bass rig.

His GK. Or his 'G.K. Chesterton', as he called it. [*Laughs.*]

Was he also going through the Pod and then through the Gallien Krueger?

Sometimes. But usually he'd play in the control room, and we'd route it so it was going out through the amp.

I know one of the things he told me about this album is that he loved that you guys were completely digital by this time, so he was able to do multiple takes, enabling you to take the best bits of each one. It took a lot of the pressure off to get a good, complete performance, he said. Was that true for you as well?

Yeah, but I don't remember feeling that it was because of any gear reason, or whatever. I know we recorded this on an Otari RADAR recorder. I get the feeling that was more to do with Colin's *awareness* of the recording process, not so much that we were doing things particularly any differently. Because normally an engineer would just punch you in if you made a mistake, or you'd do another track, and you'd go and have a break, and the engineer would comp all the best bits that you'd done. That said, I guess with computer recording, it's a hell of a lot easier to make composites up. Colin was probably more aware of the ease of doing it this way because he was getting more involved in the recording process, as opposed to just performing and then going to get a cup of tea, and throwing it at the poor engineer, saying, 'Here, you fix it.'

How about vocals?

The room was very live and very flattering for drums and percussion and anything like that, but not so flattering to voices. It was *too* live. So we went out one day and bought some velvet curtains, and put them on a track that stretched across the middle of the room. That cut the room in half, sonically. And then, Colin knew somebody who was clearing out some screens from an office—you know, partition screens—so we bought a couple of these screens for a couple of pounds or something. They formed great gobos—you know, baffles.

So, in the half of the room near the control window, we built a little kind of booth with these kind of Dilbert office-partition screens—making a kind of V shape, and then hanging some cloth and padding over the top. Most of the vocals for that album were done in this little makeshift kind of geometric tent.

We just laid a quilt or something over the top of the booth, so sound didn't just shoot up and out of the booth. The overall room was an A-frame building, which is great for drums and percussion and stuff, but you want it a little deader when you're trying to control the voice.

Let's talk about the lyrics.
The lyric is very, very simple. It's almost like an old-fashioned folk song love song. You know [*sings very dramatically*], 'The fish of the air do tell me your name!' [*Laughs at his mistake.*] Fish of the *air*? You know what I mean.

Well, the Dukes would say that, right?
Yeah, they'd say that! Or, 'The shiny flying purple wolfhounds would show me where your kitchen roof needed repairing.'

It's a very exuberant lyric.
Not many people picked up on the 'I'm coming unscrewed' part. Which I thought was great, you know—get a bit of filth in there. I'm coming, but I'm not screwing! I'm coming, unscrewed! To me that's like the essence of the song, you know? You're so happy you're having an orgasm, but you're not having sex! But it also means you're going a bit crazy, you know? But absolutely nobody picked up on that.

And then you play all these natural, exuberant images against [*dramatic voice*] Satan.
Or, 'Natas'!

Was that just a natural thing, because you were thinking 'What's the opposite of happiness?', or what?
It was a case of, 'I'm so happy that even the appearance of Satan wouldn't get me down,' you know. You'd just easily defeat him, because you're so happy, so it's just [*German accent*] 'Strength Through Joy! Jah!!' Also, people have

said they really like the line of 'All the lights of the cars in the town/Form the strings of a big guitar.'

It's a great image.
It's kind of what it looks like, if you watch a long, straight highway from a long way away, it kind of looks like a lit-up fretboard. I quite like the idea of picking it up and being gigantic and playing any tune you fancy, you know?

So, how did Erica react the first time you played this song for her?
Oh, she loves it! In fact, she was very upset neither Cooking Vinyl nor TVT nor Pony Canyon chose to release it as a single. I was very frustrated, because I was convinced [*dramatic voice*] I'd written no. 1, in the world, forever! I'd come up with our 'Let's Dance' or something!

Was this one of those songs where you were thinking it was a single as you were writing it?
Because it was so 'idiot,' and so 'instant', it almost couldn't be anything but a single. But the only time I ever saw it used for anything was, there was a football tournament over here, it was one of those Euro tournaments, and they edited together a load of shots of goals and ecstatically happy players, and they had about a minute of this collage playing with 'Stupidly Happy'.

Well, that doesn't mean you still can't be out there hawking it, right?
It would be nice if someone were to pick it up, because I think it's like the ultimate product song. You know, 'Use our product, and it'll make you stupidly happy!' Which is not why I wrote the song, but you can see how it would be easily done. Actually, the mastering of the song—of the album, for that matter—was very important. It was, what's his name …

Bob Ludwig?*
Yeah, I think so.

He's 'Mr Master'.
Yeah. I think he mastered it about three times. He used different compressors,

---

* Bob Ludwig (born 1945) is the leading American mastering engineer, responsible for some 3,000 records.

and different heads—because we mastered it to tape, which flatters it. He'd send over a version, and I'd say, 'Oh, it's too flat here,' or 'It's too rumbly,' or whatever. But he did three cuts, and the third one, whatever combination of equipment he used, really sounded very chunky and lovely. Especially the drum kit—the snare drum's got all that great snap on it, and the bass drum, the blend of acoustic and electric bass drum, is lovely.

The whole album is great-sounding. It's very bright and shiny piece of work. Perfect for a commercial campaign!
Well, it would be nice to make the money! I mean, if an ad company picked up on it, it would be perfect—who doesn't want their product to be associated with being stupidly happy? In fact, something has just popped into my brain—*Jesus Christ*, I'd forgotten this! McDonald's wanted to use it!

Really?
Yes. In fact, they sent me a written-up storyboard. They wanted to use it for an ad campaign in Australia. It was not too long after it came out. They sent a storyboard—not a picture storyboard, but a descriptive version—for me to see, and said, 'This would be the scenario in the ad, could we use your song?' And before I'd had time to mull it over, and think, 'Oh god, is this good or bad? What a terrible thing, here I am, some big company wants to use my song, and it just happens to be fucking McDonald's,' I never heard another thing about it. So I guess that McDonald's or the ad company changed their mind, or whatever. Jesus, it's funny you picked that up. I'd forgotten all about the McDonald's thing!

See? And you thought you'd said all you could about this song.
And now you're going to say, 'Would you have done it?' And I'm not going to tell you.

Would you have done it?
The answer is … [*inhales sharply*] … and that's where the tape runs out!

Interview conducted February 3 2007.

CHAPTER 29

CHURCH OF WOMEN

Let's go to church, shall we?
Let's go [*adopts gangsta voice*] to the Church of Bitches! [*Laughs.*] Just think, how the choice of one wrong word could have totally upended the whole concept of the song!

'Yo, let me worship at the church of bitches.' [*Laughs.*]
'Let him worship, let him worship, uh-huh.' [*Laughs.*] You've always got to have, like, a professional interrupter in rap songs. I read a good thing in *Viz* a couple of issues back that said [*affects posh voice*], 'Advice to rappers: Instead of saying "You know what I'm saying," and "You know what I mean" all the time, why don't you just enunciate more clearly?'* [*Laughs.*]

I know what you're saying! [*Laughs.*] We were talking earlier about demos versus produced versions, and this is a song that I heard in demo form way before I heard the finished version.
I know. Unfortunately, so did most of the planet, and that really pissed me off.

I remember you not being happy about that, but at the same time, it's always interesting to get a glimpse into your creative process, hear how a 'rough draft' turns into a finished version and think about the choices you make. So, for example, I remember telling you back then how much I liked the guitar solo on the demo, which is now on Homegrown, and you poo-poo'd that.†
Oh, it's just silly! It's just this Eddie Van Halen-type of thing … [*Laughs.*]

---

* Viz is a British comic magazine for adults.
† *Homegrown*, released in 2001, is an album made up of the demos for *Wasp Star*.

I thought it was very angular and well-played! I saw it almost as a return to the type of approach you had to the guitar on the early albums.
Maybe—but I'll tell you what, I actually am immensely proud of the guitar solo on the album version, on *Wasp Star*.

Why do you like that one so much more than the other?
[*Pauses to think, sighs.*] Because it's more feminine—there's more thought going into it. It is more the nature of femininity. And also because I think I passed my audition for Steely Dan with that solo.

I'm going to say it now—I'm not usually boastful—but the guitar solo on 'Church Of Women', the album version, is as good as any Steely Dan guitar solo. There! I've said it now. Whoops, that's torn it! [*Laughs.*]

I guess I can say shit like that now, at my advanced age. But yes, I'm immensely proud of that solo. I don't know how many takes it took me to get it.

So you really tried it again and again?
What usually happens is, I either get a solo in the first couple of takes—say one or two—or then I go really off the boil and get *really angry* with myself for a dozen takes, in which I'm just playing crap, and then I go through the angry zone, and blunder in to something quite nice again. Most of my solos go like that. I can't work anything out. Dave's the worker-outer. I just fire from the unhip, and see what I've got.

Let's say you're doing that, and you're on the tenth take, or whatever—are you building on things that you're discovering during the previous nine takes, or are you doing something different each time?
I try to do something different each time, just to keep the brain agile and find accidents. Because the accidents are the creative stuff. So, I'm throwing myself into the wall, to try to find more accidents on each take. But I can't remember if this was one that I got in a couple of takes, or if it took a lot more.

I remember when I·first got some pressings of the album, Mike Keneally called me up, and just because he's a ludicrously good guitar player, I played that solo to him down the phone, and *made* him listen to it.*

---

* Mike Keneally made his name as a guitarist with Frank Zappa's band. He would go on to co-write his *Wing Beat Fantastic* album with Andy.

And?

Oh, he could probably play it with his toes, you know. He was probably snickering to himself, thinking, 'Is that all?'

One of the things that first struck me about the solo when I first heard Wasp Star was the big pause you put in there—that you had the courage to know you didn't need to fill up all the spaces.

That's what makes it more feminine. It's more curvaceous—it has a subcutaneous layer of fat, if you see what I mean. Whereas the demo one is masculine, and flashy, and 'Hey, look at my willy!' Waggle-wiggle-waggle. The album one is lither and smoother-skinned.

What guitar are you playing on this song?

Oh, it's the Ibanez. It's my favourite guitar. It's my baby.

I thought maybe you were playing that custom Fano that you'd gotten from Dennis Fano.*

Ah, you're joking! I've only had that Fano in my possession for a couple of months. It's been many years back in his workshop, and only a couple of months in my hands.

That's too bad—you obviously had it when you recorded 'I'm Playing My Fano'.

Yeah. He sent it over, and I thought, 'Wow, I'm overjoyed to get a guitar that I helped to design,' and then he asked if he could have it back, because he was sure he could make it better. He picked it up when he was in England, and took it back, and I've never seen it or its replacement or anything else since. [*Laughs.*] It wasn't perfect, but it was a nice guitar. But he felt bad, and he said, 'Look let me adjust it, or build you one that is perfect,' and I never ever got it back. We've spoken recently though, and we are OK about it.

Wow. The reason I asked that is, in the song 'I'm Playing My Fano', there's a tone that you use that's very much like the tone that you have in 'Church Of Women'.

Yeah, it's probably the Pod cranking its stuff into my little Sessionette amp.

---

* Dennis Fano is the proprietor of Fano Guitars of Fleetwood, Pennsylvania.

Another guitar that you have in common between the demo and album versions is Holly's nylon-string guitar.
Oh, yeah, which Mr Blushift, from the Idea Records online forum, is the proud owner of at the moment—he offered the most money in the charity auction we had for it. And the Swindon MS Centre is the proud owner of the money he donated for that. They're looking for new premises, because the premises they're in at the moment are not in good shape. That's where I've been doing the oxygen pressure therapy for my tinnitus.

Let's talk a little bit about how you stumbled upon the guitar pattern that is the foundation of the song.
I was actually stood up, in my socks, holding this guitar …

***Just* in your socks?**
Well, armour, and socks! No, I was just stood there in front of the TV, holding Holly's guitar, I think the sound on the TV was either off or really low, and I just found a couple of lovely chords that fell under my hand. Top three strings, in descending order, the notes are G, D, B, and I think the D string is ringing open. And then you play a D6, which in descending order is G-flat, B, A, and I think the open D string.

So, these two chords fell under my hand—I was probably looking at the TV, and not looking at what my hands were doing—and I thought, 'Ooh, that's nice. That's *really* a good bed to skate over.' I was strumming it really languidly, a bit like that girl in Strawberry Switchblade used to strum the guitar—just *gling-gling-gling-gling, gling-gling-gling-gling.** Like kind of campfire starters guitar.

It made me want to sing in that triplet feel over the top, because the rhythm is so languid but straight. It's every beat. And I *love* singing in triplets.

So, it gave you an idea for the feel of the vocal line?
I had the idea for the feel of it first. I knew I wanted to write a song about women, and I knew I wanted to write a song about 'church of something'. I actually had a couple of songs that I'd written and rejected—I can't remember the name of one of them, but the other one, the more finished one, was called 'Church Of Your Own Design'. [*Sings*] 'And now you're on

---

* Strawberry Switchblade were a Scottish all-female band of the early 80s.

your knees / You're saying / This is not quite what you had in mind / Now you're on your knees / Start praying / You're in the Church Of Your Own Design.' It's about how things are shitty because we *make* them shitty.

And so, I think I had that in mind, and I wanted to write a song praising women, and after finding these two languid chords—this G to D6—I think it fell out quite quickly after that. The pressure's building up and you've just got to kick a straw away, and down comes a whole mess of stuff that you've been building up, you know?

What was inspiring you? Why did you want to write a song about women at this point?
Because I *really* like women. I feel bad that they've had a bad deal, and that they still get a bad deal. You know, they still get less wages than men for doing the same job. So I wanted to protest about that, for all that it's worth. I wanted to tell women that I like them.

Was there any particular event in your life that was inspiring you to do that at that time?
No, not really. I'd had a long-term relationship with a girl called Linda, who was very strong, and really knew what she was trying to do.* She would promote her own rock'n'roll gigs, and stuff. She wanted to start her own fashion chain. I admired her drive, and I think she opened my eyes up years earlier to how strong women could be. I admire women. There's absolutely nothing wrong with them. I would never call myself a woman hater, or even a woman user, particularly. I've always been pretty damned respectful of women.

The lyrics themselves came out pretty quickly?
Yeah, although I did go back and make quite a few tweaks to them. What comes out quickly is your intention, if you see what I mean, and then you go back and you make all the screws, nuts, and bolts fit, and all the cogs work— that kind of thing.

Was this one of those songs where you were developing music and lyrics at the same time?
The majority of songs do certainly come out with an idea, a phrase, or a couple

---

* Linda Godwin was Andy's girlfriend in the early 70s.

of lines simultaneously with chords. Because, you know, the chords make the suggestion, or the words suggest what the chords are going to be. You usually don't come up with a whole lyric first—you come up with a phrase, or a couple of lines.

What about the bridge—the 'lie for a lie, and a truth for the truth'?
Well, that was all nabbed from another song, you see. On *Homegrown*, there's a little bit of the demo of the 'lie for a lie' song.

Why did you decide to plug that in there?
Because I needed an intro. I didn't want to just amble in.

So it wasn't just a matter of saying, 'I'm going to use this for the bridge,' and then saying later, 'Oh, I can also use it as the intro'?
I think I wanted it for the intro first. I really like those old Hollywood things, where they have a totally separate intro—you know [*sings intro to 'I Left My Heart In San Francisco' in lounge-singer voice, speeding up as he goes along*], 'The loveliness of Paris / Seems somehow sadly gay / The glory that was Rome / Is of another day / I've been terribly alone / And forgotten in Manhattan / I'm going home to my city by the bay'—*totally* different to the rest of the song. I kind of like that, so I wanted to some extent to have an old-fashioned, different intro. If you do that, it's kind of nice to bring it back later. I've done that on a lot of songs. 'The Disappointed' has an intro that comes back later. 'Respectable Street' also has an intro that comes back later on. So, I quite fancied doing it with this.

I liked the phrase 'a lie for a lie'. It's not totally relevant to the 'Church Of Women' idea, but I did like the phrase, so it was a case of getting the art hammer and banging that square peg into that somewhat elliptical hole, and just making the bloody thing fit. So, later on, when the phrase comes back, you can then append to it, 'Give 'em back their house / The walls, the doors / The floors and roof.' You know, let women have more a say in the world and in their life.

Yeah. Don't fight it.
Exactly! And stop trying to feed them on, what is it, 'wafers and wine'? And

---

* Made famous by Tony Bennett.

'some myth we're in control.' And then there's that little *hanging* piece coming after that, with Colin going, 'oofa-ah, oofa-ah'—doing a slightly Beach Boys-esque thing. You know, the kind of fake American Indian stuff that was lopped off of 'Heroes And Villains'.* It's like vocal percussion.

Was that your idea?

It's mostly Colin—it was like, 'Ooh, I've got an idea, let me do it.' And I thought, 'Yeah, that's pretty good. Let's track that up and make it really work.'

Speaking of Colin, one of the things that strikes me about this song is the bass line.

It took me a long time to find that for the demo. Because I wanted a bass line that was distinctive, and work in a way that spoke to the drums and the melody.

So you kind of had the drum pattern in mind before you created the bass part?

Yeah, there's a not-very-good take on it on the demo. But when we had our drummer, Chuck Sabo, there, and we had Matt Vaughan doing some programming bits and pieces for us,† I'd sit with him and say, 'Show me some crunchy-sounding bass drums. Show me a distort-y snare. Show me a little high-pitched snare. Now tune it up even higher.'

I got him to layer up a kind of groove [*imitates rhythm of song*], and then Chuck played with that live. We even screwed up Chuck's drums so they sounded more like these processed looped sounds. So, you know, that lovely fuzzy kind of roll that Chuck does when he comes in—we put that through the Pod.

So it sounds like a timbale or something.

Or it sounds like cheap samples, which is a nice way of taking something real and screwing it up, you know? I think he's drumming with brushes, and we distorted it. He's drumming with a loop of screwed-up samples as well, and further layers of samples come in during each section, if you see what I

---

* Originally part of The Beach Boys' abandoned *Smile* album of 1966, issued in truncated form on *Smiley Smile* (1967).
† Matt Vaughan had programmed for Pulp, Orchestral Manoeuvres In The Dark, and Depeche Mode before working with XTC.

mean. The whole album is Pod madness. There's so much on this track, getting screwed up with the Pod—the drums, different percussion bits, guitars, keyboards—we were like, 'Wow, we can distort that *just right*,' you know?

Was Colin putting his bass through your Pod as well?
I think he was. I'm not sure whether there was such a thing as a Bass Pod at the time. Certainly there was a guitar Pod, and we would be putting it through that, and then out through a bass amp—his Gallien Krueger.

What else do you remember about the music?
Well, the trumpet line *is* from 'No Woman, No Cry'—which I didn't realise for a couple of months after coming up with it. I thought, 'Where have I heard that nice little countermelody before?' Obviously, I must have had 'woman-ness' on my brain for that to go in there. It's one of those subconscious connections you make.

That's on the demo as well, right?
Yeah, I think it's played on the guitar. It just came into my head, and I thought, 'Oh yeah, that's a good little countermelody.' But it's the countermelody from 'No Woman, No Cry', so—sorry, Bob!

Any other parts that stick out for you?
I *really* like the lift that happens before the chorus, when it goes [*sings*], 'I'm on my knees but dancing.' It sort of sets up like it's going to go to the chord of E—it goes from B, because B is the setup for E—but instead it jumps to D-flat. And so you think the chorus is obviously going to be set up by this D-flat, and be in G-flat, but it's not. It drops back down again to the initial key, to E.

So there's kind of an artificial lift in there, where you think the chorus is coming, then there are a couple more bars where it raises up a tone, and therefore your expectations get raised more, and then it [*laughs*] dashes them cruelly back to the original key. But I think that's kind of a nice bit, actually. I was listening to the song today and thought, 'I wonder what made me do that?'

What *did* make you do it?
I don't know! Obviously I felt the song needed more of a lift there, but instead

of being corny, and doing the lift up and then resolving to the key you think the lift has taken you to, I resolved it back to the original key.

Another big difference between the demo and the album version is the ending.
Well, on the album we have all those cross harmonies at the end. That just fills me with ecstasy, the thought of crossing those vocal lines. It all the fault of old J.S. Bach. Then everything gets stripped down, where the track disappears, leaving our producer, Nick Davis, on the harmonium—Colin and I weren't quick enough to play the changes—plus our handclaps and the vocals. The very reverential congregation there.

How did you come up with the idea for the swelling, church-like ending?
I didn't know how the hell we were going to get out of this, and the idea to do that just came up in the studio. It was a matter of, 'Let's take the track down but leave the vocals up. Ooh, that's nice. Leave the claps up, so the congregation is clapping.'
So, it was built in the mix, in the studio.

So you guys originally did play instruments for the whole song? You just thought you'd fade the song out?
Yeah, I didn't know exactly how we were going to end it.

Speaking of vocals, I really like the vocal line on this song. You really show off your range—there's a big jump between the low notes in 'butter' and the high notes in 'like us men'.
Yeah. Well, that's because I'm a god this evening. [*Laughs.*] I'm a singer because, you know, I inherited the job. I never knew any other singers, so it was a matter of, 'God, I'll have do this myself.'

Yeah, but that's not why you're a singer. You are a singer because you're good at it, and you obviously love to sing, because you wouldn't write yourself melody lines like this if you didn't.
I *do* like to sing. The more I did actually do the singing, and the more songs I wrote that I had to sing, the more I kind of got into it, you know?
    And then there's that long process of finding your voice, and I obviously found it. I've probably lost it by now, and come through the other side! But

I'd certainly found it by *Wasp Star*. I think I probably found it by some stuff on *Drums And Wires*.

Was there any particular point that you remember saying to yourself, 'Yeah, I am a singer, and I like doing this, so I'm going to write myself some good melody lines to sing'?
Ummm … no, I never set out to specifically write some really good melodies. They're just what fall out because it's what seems right at the time, and it's pleasing. It gives you little goosey thrills as some of these lines come out, and you think, 'Ooh, wouldn't it be good to take the melody there, so it rubs against the chord?' Or, 'Wouldn't it be good to sing *those* notes, because they're not in the chord that I'm playing, and it sounds somewhat momentarily dislocated but achieves a certain effect?'

I mean, good vocalists are nice to hear, especially people with really attractive timbres. But no, I don't think of myself as a singer, and I do know a lot of people who do say, 'Well, he's not really a very good singer.'

People might be thinking of the old 'seal bark' of the early albums, but even then—these people have not tried to sing along with your parts, if they think you're not a good singer. I have covered your songs in a variety of situations, and they're not easy. You've always had a good range, both dynamically as well as melodically. That involves a lot of control, too—to be able to sing softly and then really project or bark something out.
I guess it's finding your voice. You feel confident once you've found your voice, but there was quite a few years where I didn't find my voice—I still had this cartoon thing going—a seal had eaten Buddy Holly, and was given helium to make him throw it up, and the end product was my voice!

But you were doing that for a certain effect—you wanted to get people's attention, and you were trying to cut through bad PAs and things like that.
That's true.

Let's get back to the lyrics. You've got lots of little jokes and double entendres in here.
Oh yeah, it's peppered with little things. They 'have you give praise with a laugh, bark, and stutter'—that's what women do to me. They make me nervous.

Then, 'Like us men, like us men / They are nothing like us men.'
Yeah! It's sort of like a plea—please like us!—but then you turn it on its head by saying they are nothing like us. A bit naughty that, but it seems to work.

'Men have gargoyles round their hearts.'
Yeah, they do! They like the ugly, hard side of things. And women are the complete opposite of that. They're the anti-gargoyle.

Men do that as a way of protecting themselves—in a way, you're saying, 'You don't need to.'
Not in this day and age so much. But, you know, I can understand why we're like that. You can't be a softie if you've got to go and bring down a mammoth, you know?

Or if you're going to survive on the playground!
Yeah!

I don't know if you intended it, but the image of 'I'm on my knees but dancing' has always struck me as a great sexual metaphor.
Oh, it's filth. Unmitigated filth.

[*Laughs.*] So you intended it?
[*Sheepishly*] Yeah.

'Want to worship / At the church of women / Breathe 'em in / Until my head goes spinning round.'
Yeah, I love the smell of women. Actually, the best woman I ever smelled was when I worked as a producer for Saeko Suzuki.* She smelled wonderful. I don't think it was any perfume, it was just her. She was just a very fragrant woman.

In the second verse, there's the whole joke about 'Church of women / Is making donations / Of loving and giving,' and then 'Performing that miracle / Raising the living.'
Yes. I think people get [*laughing*] several ideas about what that line means—

---

* Andy produced her album *Studio Romantic* in 1987.

and they'd be right! You know, they're giving you a hard-on—that's raising the living. Or they're bringing up the kids. So, they both work.

Then we were talking about the bridge before …
'Let's put things right'—that's a pivotal line. That's what the song is all about. Let's be good to women and put all the injustices right, finally. But, you know, that's going to overturn all of the world's major religions, for a start. They certainly don't like women being in control, because they're all male-centred.

There are a few out there that aren't, but they're certainly not in the majority.
No, they're really on the sidelines.

And then there's the joke in here about the 'loaves and kisses' rather than loaves and fishes.
Yeah, that's a bit crass, but it sort of works.

It's a good set-up for the next line, where you say, 'Till we have enough to love and eat for ever.'
Yeah. Not 'live'. Sometimes I wonder if I've tripped myself up with a lyric—is it too tangled?—but the thing is, you can go back to the songs, and pick them apart, and follow the different strands, and think, 'Oh, I'm going to go with that strand today,' and you can find it goes in a different place. So, I suppose that's the joy of slightly tangled-up lyrics.

And I wouldn't even necessarily call them tangled up—I'd say they're multi-layered. You've obviously worked these, because you want them to be interpreted in more than one way.
I've worked those babies with an uplift pen! [*Laughs*.]

Speaking of which, now that you're more computer-literate, do you ever write on a keyboard?
No, I hate that. I like to write in a book with a pencil, and then I can carry the book around, I can take it to bed—whatever. And I'm not a fast typist—I'm a couple-of-words-a-minute typist. Plus, I like the smell and feel of paper, and I like pencils.
    I used to *love* the smell of pencils at school. The teacher had on their desk a big pencil sharpener, and just the smell of going up to that desk, and smelling

all that shaved-up pencil—fantastic. Pencils are very sexy. I just love pencils. Pencils and hard-backed books of plain paper.

So, if any woman out there really wants to attract you, she just needs to get some pencil shavings …
Shave off her underarm hair and stick on pencil shavings instead!

Dress like a teacher—with her hair up, and glasses …
Yeah, totally. And have a pencil sharpener. A large one.

But no, I can't write on computers. The last lyric I tried to write on a computer was relatively successful. It was a lyric, potentially, for Jamie Cullum—he e-mailed me and asked if I had any lyrics, because he was writing some new material, and he liked using already-existing lyrics.[*]

So I wrote a song there and then, and sent it to him. I think it was called, 'I'm Raining Here Inside'—'I've got to go out to get dry, because I'm raining here inside.' I typed up the whole thing on computer and zapped it over to him. I'd tried it a couple of times before, but that's the first time that I'd done that to order, you know?

Did it ever see the light of day?
No, not unless he's going to do something with it, and he hasn't told me yet.[†] But I don't think it'll ever be a trend. I love the pencil and the book too much.

Interview conducted October 28 2007.

---

[*] Jamie Cullum is a British jazz/pop singer and musician.
[†] The lyric eventually ended up on the Mike Keneally/Andy Partridge collaboration *Wing Beat Fantastic*.

CHAPTER 30

2 RAINBEAU MELT

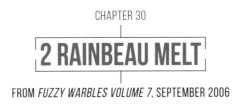

FROM *FUZZY WARBLES VOLUME 7*, SEPTEMBER 2006

Let's start with the title on this one. Why did you spell it this way?
I think I wanted to just have some mischief with it, and I like the idea of a rain-*beau*—a handsome thing caused by the rain. If a rainbow could spell its own name, I don't think it would just spell it b-o-w. I think it'd spell it b-e-a-u. It's more French and fancy, and sort of covered in ribbons and stuff. So, I think I was just being mischievous.

Same thing with using the number two there, rather than spelling it out?
Yeah. T-w-o just doesn't look right. It doesn't look like the rainbow would design it. But '2'—probably because it's got a *Sesame Street* connotation or something. [*Chuckles, falls into crazy kids' show voice*] 'Today's number is two! The rainbow is melting!'

Were you also punning on the fact that it could be 'to'?
No! I was thinking of the fact that the most spectacular rainbows you can see are double rainbows. And the idea of them melting is about as psychedelic as you can get, I think. All the colours kind of running, or the rain is getting them to melt, you know.

'Ballet For A Rainy Day'.
There you go—it all ties in, you see. Do you know, this started as a poem that was inspired by when Erica came to see me down at Rockfield Studios, where we were mixing *Wasp Star*. We had an *enormous* argument, and went out for a walk to get over it, still really boiling with each other. We wandered off, up some track, some hill, on someone's farmland, where I'm sure we probably shouldn't have gone—probably private property or something.

It'd been raining, and we got to the top of this hill, really in a bad mood with each other. Just as we came over the prow of the hill, we had the most *spectacular* view before us—this kind of hollowed out bowl in the land. The sky was a kind of steely RAF-uniform colour—a kind of blue-grey, with the most *phenomenally* bright, solid-looking double rainbow symmetrically poised above the valley.

It was *so* spectacular—I've never seen a rainbow that strong, that bright, so obviously doubled, so perfectly placed on the landscape and against that colour sky—that it brought the pair of us to being friends again immediately.

Sharing in a special moment together.
Yes. It was jaw-dropping. And the fact that we were *both* looking at it, together—that was it! The argument was all over, and we were great friends again from that very moment onward. So, I think I just probably had to say 'thank you' to this phenomenally beautiful double rainbow, and the thank-you came out as a poem. I had no intention of putting music to it, but I'm really, really glad I did.

What prompted you to set it to music?
I think I was just afraid it was going to go to waste if I didn't! That it was just going to lay in an exercise book, or lay dormant on a shelf forever, and nobody was going to get to hear it. I was very proud of it—I thought, 'I've really got the essence of this double rainbow.' To me, it's probably up there with 'The Man Who Sailed Around His Soul' for my favourite of all my lyrics. I'm just very [*chuckles*] smugly chuffed at some of the metaphors and things.

Let's talk about some of those. It says, '2 rainbeau melt in enormous colours. / Hot balloons swoon from an RAF sky.' By 'RAF sky,' I'm assuming you mean …
That's that steely grey colour, this dark—I always thought weirdly claustrophobic—grey. That seemed to be the colour of the sky, with this receding storm that had just dropped so much rain over that part of Wales. It was not cold, so I had the notion there could be 'hot balloons swooning'—it's an idea that hot-air balloons, which are already usually colourful, would be enamoured of the beautiful rainbows; that these stripy balloons are swooning with romance at falling in love with this rainbow. The balloons

are not quite gorgeous enough, and they've just been blown away by the beauty of this rainbow.

I'm glad I asked you about that, because I thought what you meant by 'RAF sky' you meant a sky that had lots of little white clouds, like flak explosions or something.
No, it's purely the colour of the RAF uniform, this blue-y, green-y, *claustrophobic* grey. That was exactly the colour of the sky, projecting this phenomenally bright double rainbow at us.

The next line is, 'Bloom fold and billow with sherbet fantastic.'
Yeah! That's a rainbow, isn't it? You know, you used to be able to get those kids' sweets, like straws, with loads of different colours of sherbet in them. They may have even called them rainbow straws, I think.*

Then, 'Wash brush in jam jar, leviathan's eye.'
Yes. Isn't it great, when you've been doing a painting with poster paint or water paint, and you've just put the brush in the jam jar? You make this coloured cloud.

Exactly. And you're swirling the brush in there to clean it …
Yeah, you look down, and there it is, turning round, and it could be a giant round cloud eye in the sky, you know? Or, that's what the rainbow could be—it could be part of some leviathan's eye, with an eyebrow there or something.

Right. Then, '2 rainbeau melt in sneezes of flour.'
Oh, yeah. [*Laughs.*] It's the idea of something that makes you sneeze, and you're out of control, and it's kind of gone *ka-POW* with fantastic-ness, you know?

'Slo-mo explosion from circus paint store.'
If you were going to have an explosion, where would be the most colourful place you could have it? In a paint store, that belonged to a circus! So, you'd have all these striped kinds of awnings and striped cloth and canvas and stuff, and then there's an explosion, so there are all these colours flying in all

---

* They are still available and are known as Rainbow Dust Straws.

directions *against* the bright-coloured canvases of a circus! Just about the most colourful thing I could think of.

And of course the paint from a circus paint store would be very brightly coloured anyway ...
Exactly. And the explosion would have to be in slow motion, so you could see all of this paint just sort of *reaching out* for these incredibly coloured canvases.

And then you get a little playful here—'Toucan spill four can on cloud turning Kodak.'
Is there anything more colourful than a toucan beak? Plus, the thing about paint is, it comes in cans, right? So it's 'toucan spill four can'—so we're talking about *lots* of paint in this explosion—'on cloud turning Kodak.' [*Stoned hippie voice*] 'How colourful can you get, man?' [*Laughs.*] That's about as colourful as you can imagine.

And of course there are so many puns embedded there—there's 'toucan' the bird, or 'two can,' where 'can' can be a noun or a verb ...
Exactly, because people *can* spill *cans*! But ultimately, it's me and Erica looking at this rainbow.

And finally, 'Rain falls applauding and whispers for more.'
Yeah, which it does—you know, you see something that spectacular, and you listen to the rain, and it's kind of [*imitates white noise*]—it's like an audience, isn't it?

Yeah, both sounds are contained in there—it could sound like waves of applause depending on the strength of the rain, and it could sound like a whisper as well.
Exactly. But, as you can see, it's only a short little poem, but perfectly formed, and I was really chuffed with it. I'd say it's head and shoulders above a lot of other things I've written lyrically. But it never intended to be a song.

Although you have rhymes in there, which helps them along as lyrics— typically, when you're writing pure poetry, is that something you try to do? Do you think maybe subconsciously you wanted to turn this into a song?
Do you know, I hadn't thought about that!

There is a definite rhythm to these lyrics, and they do kind of wrap in themselves that way.
[*Sighs.*] Maybe! But, do you know, when I write just poetry, it has to be rhythm-based, and I usually find after a while that it starts to fold in on itself with rhymes. So, I guess it's just my desire for boundaries.

Which I understand. I do that too when I write. I find that setting up some boundaries helps you focus more, and be a more disciplined lyricist. So, tell me how the song was built. How long did the lyrics sit dormant before you started to put music to them?
Oh, some months. I think I was starting to fret that, 'I've inadvertently written my favourite lyric—although it's not a lyric, it could become my favourite lyric—and I don't have any ideas for any music. So I'm going to let the music happen accidentally. I'm going to grab the first things that come to mind.' And I literally did. I started it not knowing what key it was going to be in. I just grabbed the first chords that fell under my hand on the guitar. And to do it quickly, I just grabbed a load of drum loops.

What was the order in which you laid the tracks down?
I started by grabbing a bunch of loops in a certain tempo …

Was this from *Beats Working?* *
It's Ralph Salmins again, yeah. And they're great. He just plays so well, you know? I just grabbed them at random—if you listen to them, there are no reasons for the patterns. What he's doing on the hi-hat is not related to what's happening at any given point in the track—they're completely random.

Because of the two chunks of the poems, I thought, 'I'm not going to go for conventional song structure here. I want it to have a long run-up'—not even an intro, because it's beyond an intro. It's almost like a long piece of improvised music. It's pre-*Monstrance Monstrance*!

Then, after I did the first part of the poem, I wanted the rhythm to go away, so I didn't put any in during the centre section. Then I wanted the drums to come back in for the last part of the poem. That's why you have this long section of melting guitars and keyboards, then the drums kick in, and

---

* A library of drum patterns played by Ralph Salmins and recorded at Abbey Road by Haydn Bendall.

you have this long passage of rather pictorial music, with lots of synthesized bird noises and things in the background.

There's a lot of dissonance in the organ you start the song with. The notes are really rubbing hard against each other.
Yeah, and I've got a lot of delay on the organ, which is being bent very deeply. So it sounds like the keyboards are melting. Imagine the keys of the keyboard being the lines of the colours of the rainbow, and then, as you're playing them, they just melt down.

Kind of a sonic metaphor.
Yeah. It's tough to call it a song, actually! I guess the end product of it is a song, but it's conceived more as a poem with musical pictures around it. So everything had to be extremely colourful, but melting as well.

In other words, what you've done is create a musical Dali or something.
A Salvador Dali Parton!

You're having a musical Daliance!
Salvador Dali Lama! The Dalai Parton! [*Laughs.*] There you go. Two enormous bald heads, contemplating the universe. With the Dalaiwood theme park!

You could just go and go with this one … !
You could really go with that! You're on a roller coaster, but you're not screaming—you're calmly sat there, cross-legged.

And the roller coaster is not really going anywhere.
You don't need it to! And as you get off, they give *you* money, in your begging bowl. That's Dalaiwood. [*Laughs.*]

Sorry, we kind of got off the subject there! What else do I remember? When I'd got to the second part, after the piece where it all breaks down and you get the sense that it really is melting—because of the very distorted guitar, I'm just wiping my hands up and down the thing—I stumbled upon a linnet.

In the Shed? [*Laughs.*]
Yeah, he followed me in. [*Laughs.*] No, I'd bought myself a library of sounds

that were all recordings of Mellotrons, and under one of the sound effects banks, I just put my hand on the keyboard, and there was this linnet tweeting away, and I thought, 'Jesus! That's perfect.' I mean, all of the things that I did, I sort of grabbed them whether they were right or not. For example, I dialled up a patch on the keyboard, and got something like 127 different cowbells, so I just ran my hand all over them at one point. And you can hear all these cowbells going—there's a storm of cowbells.

Ah, I'd heard that and wondered what it was.
It's just dozens and dozens of different cowbells being played really rapidly on the keyboard. It was one of those things where, 'Whatever sound comes up, I'm going to use it.' In this case, it was cowbells, and I thought, 'God, if I do that, it's almost like super-descriptive rain or something.' So, I was very lucky with the sounds that came up. This little thing of a linnet coming up was perfection itself—just a great piece of happenstance, you know?

I didn't want it to be a 'song' song. I didn't want it to have verse-chorus structure-y bits, so I just *grabbed* the first things that came to hand, quite literally. I just grabbed *a* key; and once I'd laid down what you'd call a rhythm guitar with the drums, it was a case of, 'Well, how am I going to do these words?' I just grabbed the first melody that came into my head that sort of fitted that key. It was all pretty instant.

And, once again, you're singing triplets across the rhythm.
I'm doing the triplets! [*Imitates smacking sound.*] Naughty boy! Smack smack. Yep, can't stop them old triplets.

Hey, whatever works. Let's talk about your vocals and how they were recorded.
On a lot of the later records, it's what I've called the 'honey effect'. Usually, you get your one performance that you're happy with, and then you do a half-dozen to a dozen other performances, which don't have to be tight at all. They can be a bit out of tune, a bit out of time—it doesn't matter. And then you have those bunches of up to a dozen of you 'surrounding' your main take, and then you blend them in under, not very loud, to make this sort of a honey glow around the vocal.

Now, because I did this in the Shed, I don't think I had the patience to do that.

But the vocals are at least doubled—it sounds like more.
Oh, it's probably, say, three or four of each part. I would have had one in predominance, with the others in support, so it's a sort of a semi-honey glow. [*Chuckles.*] But I'm also singing it very lightly, and sort of 'choir boy'. You know—[*sings '2 rainbeau melt,' overemphasising the slow attack of each word, almost Gregorian chant-like in nature*]. It's almost singing it like you're fourteen years old, and you've got your cassock on.

Because you're sitting there in the Church of Nature in awe of what you've just seen?
Actually, I was standing, because it was wet. [*Laughs.*] I was hovering, like a Dalai Lama. Dalai Llama Farms—what kind of wool do you think they'd give off? [*Laughs.*] Sorry, I can't stop myself.

I was trying to sing it, I think, almost like a piece of church music. And I don't know why. Maybe I was that in awe of the subject and the vastness of the vision, that I felt it should be somehow quasi-religious.

Let's talk about the bass part—did you do that at the end?
Yeah, I think it was the last thing that went on. I did it in two takes, I remember that. I *love* playing bass.

I guess the reason you wanted to wait until the end was because you wanted to use that as the glue to hold everything together?
Yeah, always. When you leave it until last, you know what you've got to do in terms of tying the rhythm down, *and* what melodic room you've got. If you don't have much room, or you want to go for a very minimal approach, you just hit those root notes, on that bass drum, and that's it.

At the same time, you must certainly write songs with bass lines in mind from the beginning.
Oh yeah! Yeah, a lot of them, the bass and drums are completely integral right from the start.

Sure. Even if you're going to lay down the bass last, you have it in mind.
You have it in mind, because you're weaving it around what you're playing on the guitar, and what you're singing. I mean, the best example of that is 'Mayor Of Simpleton'. That was very integral right from the off.

On this one, you're sliding down the neck, for that melting sound, but you're also punctuating what the drums are doing too. You're holding it down, but doing a couple of pops to keep it interesting.

I remember not wanting the bass to be particularly important in this. For me, on this song, the most important thing—other than the words—was getting the 'scenery' right. I wanted to put into music the visual idea of these rainbows getting somehow washed away by the rain—they're so transient that you can't take your eyes off them for the few seconds that they're up there, because they're going to melt away, you know? Hopefully I accomplished that.

The other part that really stands out to me in this song, reminding me a bit of Robert Fripp, is the guitar pattern that slides up the neck.

Oh yeah, that guitar. It reminds you of Fripp?

Absolutely!

Do you know, I don't think I own any records with Fripp on them.

Which is funny, because I hear a lot of similarities in your playing. You and he seem to me to be cut from the same cloth in your approach to dissonance in your lead-guitar playing. It's funny to hear you say that, too, because listening to *Monstrance* there are several songs where your tone, and the way you use sustain, reminds me of a tone that he'll use. I know that you've heard this, because he's been using this for a long time.

Well, '21st Century Schizoid Man' is one of my favourite guitar solos by anyone.* And it was the tone, and some of the unexpected notes he played. But I have to say that I don't think I've heard more than a half a dozen things with Robert Fripp on them.

I know you're a fan of David Bowie, so I know you've stuff from his Berlin era. Or 'Fashion', off *Scary Monsters*. Fripp is all over that.

Is it? I never knew that. I've heard *No Pussyfooting*.†

So you're aware of some of his more ambient stuff, then.

I suppose, with this song, I was kind of thinking, 'Is this where I want to go?

---

* '21st Century Schizoid Man' is a song from King Crimson's 1969 album *In The Court Of The Crimson King*.
† A 1973 album credited to Fripp & Eno (Robert Fripp and Brian Eno).

Do I want to start blowing songs apart, and having less structure to them?' And then, glory be, look what should happen. I went and did *Monstrance*.

Let's talk about that—do you think this is the direction you're going to be headed?
Maybe! I've been thinking, because I've been working on some of the other improvs that we recorded during the *Monstrance* sessions, and beginning to think, 'Maybe we should improvise songs, and try improvising lyrics at the same time.' You know, bring some prepared things that you like, as a springboard, and see what happens. I kind of did that on some of the *Take Away* stuff, but I was wondering what would happen if all of the music was being made absolutely improvised simultaneously as the song was being improvised at the same time.

I think you'd probably end up with the same success rate as you had before. Some of it could be exciting, but you've got to be prepared for some of it to fall on its face, you know?
That's what you get when you're willing to take those kinds of risks—great results, along with great failure. But at least you get something great!

Interview conducted December 16 2007.

EPILOGUE

SONGWRITING 101

As Andy and I were compiling and updating the song-specific interviews for this book, he came to the realisation that it would benefit from an overarching examination of the art of songwriting—from his perspective, anyway. Though the interviews about each song contain insights about Andy's creative process and how he approaches songwriting, this was an opportunity take a step back and discuss the subject as a separate topic. So here you go—Songwriting 101 with Andy Partridge.

What prompted you to finally take the leap and write your first song? Bridging the chasm between being a listener and a writer can be scary, and a lot of people never work up the nerve to do it.
I guess I thought it was *easy*—which it really is, but first you have to walk through a few thousand miles of Easy, which is usually in the County of Bad, until you finally cross the border and start writing good things. [*Laughs.*] And I also think the 'crap gene' played a role—I was crap at learning other people's material. I figured if I made my own songs up, they would be easier to play. It was a real 'necessity is the mother of invention' thing.

So, you just begin. And as the years go on, you start to think about things like, 'Perhaps I should keep that shorter,' and 'Perhaps I should make it so the title line is near the front of the song,' and 'Let me see—how do these other people do it? How do those Beatle fellas do it?'

As people say, it's not rocket science—but even rocket science is easy if you practise it enough! It's the 10,000 hours thing—who said that, Malcolm Gladwell?* 'You're never going to really be a master at anything until you've spent at least 10,000 hours doing it.'

---

* Discussed in Malcolm Gladwell's book *Outliers*.

At the same time, you must have felt you had something unique to say.
Initially, no—not for many years. I just thought that you could say any gibberish, and as long as it rhymed you could get away with it. All my early stuff is centred around words that I thought could be stimulating and *fun,* and set up a kind of futuristic space sci-fi monster ambiance in a song. I know this sounds a stupid reason for doing it! [*Laughs.*]

When I started writing songs, around the age of fifteen, I figured that as long as I could play a couple of notes on the guitar in sequence, I could make up a song to go with it. Really, from that age up until a few albums into our career, that's how I did it. I now look back on all those years of songs— hundreds of songs—and I realise they were not very good. Because I wasn't talking about *me,* and I wasn't saying things from my heart and soul—*that* takes a lot of digging. I don't think you can get to that stuff until you've done an awful lot of tunnelling.

Instead, I was writing by using words and phrases that, at the time, I thought *I* would like to hear in songs. *I'd* like to hear songs about rockets and the future and fastness and space and comics. I was a big US comics fan, as you know.

So, in a way, I suppose I *was* writing about me—by putting what I wanted to hear in songs—but in another way I wasn't digging any deeper than just below the surface. Really, you have to write so much rubbish—you have to dig so much dirt—before you can find one diamond or one vein of gold.

Another way you *were* writing about yourself was because you were presenting your own worldview to the world—you were saying, 'Here are the things that *I* think are cool.'
That's true, I suppose.

'And *you* should, too!' Isn't that the point of the kind of aggressive communication that's involved in being in a rock band, and being onstage and playing for other people?
There *is* a lot of the show-off gene involved at that young age. The show-off gene gets to have its moment in the sun. But I don't really *value* any of the early songs I wrote. I mean, there were hundreds of Helium Kidz songs: things like, 'My Baby Was A Reptile From A Horror Movie On TV'. I probably turned on things like *The Rocky Horror Show* soundtrack, and thought, 'Yeah, I can write stuff like that!' So, yes—it *was* about me, but I was mining only the

very thinnest skin on the surface. I hadn't gotten to sticking the shovel down my throat at that point. [*Laughs.*]

What do you think it is about you—and about you *then*—that enabled you to not be precious and hold on to these first creations? Instead, you threw them away and kept digging.
Because it was so *easy*. It was easy come, easy go—you know, you can think up this stuff in five minutes. I remember writing a song called 'Phaser Falls'—ostensibly about buying a phase pedal, but also a sort of song story about a future spaceman and his bride going somewhere on a distant planet called Phaser Falls on their honeymoon. It's just nonsense! But it's the sort of shit I'd be reading about in comics, and I'd think, 'Well, how hard is it to write this stuff?'

It was also because I liked the word 'phaser'—I thought [*speaks rapidly*], 'Phaser pedals and phaser ray guns and YEAH, I've got to get THAT in a song! What word can I pair with phaser? Phaser fries? No. Phaser ... Falls! Yeah, a *honeymoon* place!' The song was a real piece of shit, but for a week or two, I thought, 'This is *great.*'

What it comes down to is the volume of mistakes, and giving yourself permission to make them. You must accept that, when you start, you're going to be making a garden in the wilderness. Though digging is easy to learn to do, you're going to be doing an awful lot of it before you can make a nice garden.

When do you think that first started happening for you?
Around about *Go2*, there were a couple of songs built around things that I was observing...

Like 'Battery Brides'?
Yes, 'Battery Brides'. That was a matter of making the connection between the sort of imprisoned, nightmare life of a battery hen and somebody stuck in a little booth at Woolworth's serving people but who's not really there—instead, she's dreaming of a romantic life involving this sort of perfect man. That was one of the first times I started to click in to, 'Oh, here's something I observed. I've made a connection, and I specifically want to write about it.'

'Meccanik Dancing' also is an example of that to an extent, although that came from the slightest of suggestions—boozed-up farmers' boys dancing in a mechanised manner at the Mecca dance hall, and parents going to dance at the Mechanics' Institute—I tried to find a thread running through all this entertainment.

Which you then combined with a very dissonant, metallic-sounding guitar pattern.
Yeah. I thought, 'Well, let's see if I can find something slightly robotic for these farmers' lads to dance to!' At that point, I enjoyed playing the guitar in a repetitive, mechanical manner—and still do, to some extent.

Let's use that as an opportunity to segue into what is a very important aspect of songwriting—how do you marry together lyrics and music? How do *you* do it, and how do you think about it and regard the way others do it?
Wow. [*Pauses.*] I can hear great songs that don't have great lyrics, and I've really enjoyed them. I mean, a lot of Beatles songs don't have great lyrics. They have lyrics that must have taken all of one minute to write—especially the early stuff. 'I love you, you love me, I wanna hold your hand, do you want to hold mine?' It's really surface stuff, but I can still enjoy the whole thing immensely.

What about songs about great lyrics but music that you don't enjoy?
Yeah, there are great lyrics in some Dylan stuff. I was very late to him, but there are songs of his where I really like the lyrics, but if you listen to the music, he's playing G and C on a guitar. So, it's interesting lyrically, but musically, it's nothing.

And then there are people like Bacharach and David, where the structure of the music can be beautiful—the shifts in chords, the melodies—and the lyrics can be apparently workaday, but they tell the story fantastically. And that is a great talent, to be able to do that. I don't think Hal David gets enough praise for his lyrics. Everyone says, 'Oh, I love Bacharach,' and I think, 'No, what you love are the songs that Bacharach and *David* wrote.' It's Hal David's apparent, everyday, conversational lyrics that just tell the story perfectly. Jimmy Webb can do that as well. He can take quite mundane things in a lyric, and turn them into something perfect.

I especially love lyrics these days, and I want each of my lyrics to stand on its own, where you can read one and get a lot out of it without hearing the music. I want the same for my music, of course—if you heard the music by itself, I hope you'd think, 'That's a nice tune, and that's an interesting structure,

interesting chord changes, goes into some nice places, great arrangement—
that's unusual, I'm liking that.'

So, I like all the parts to stand alone as the parts—but when you put them
together, it should make something else again. That's very important for me.

**So, you have these separate things and together they make a whole that's
greater than the individual parts. That's the ideal.**
Yes. Absolutely.

So, we know that you're a synaesthete …*
A little bit, yes!

**I would say *more* than a little bit. You and I have talked about a lot of
your songs, and it's a theme that seems to run throughout the creation
stories for so many of them. You will see something, smell something,
hear something, and it will evoke something else for you. For example, a
sound will bring a colour to your mind. That's a big source of inspiration
for you, and how you pair words and music together. If you were talking
to someone who didn't have that quality—that engine for ideas—what
would you say to them?**
I'd say, 'Make a fool of yourself.' I'm bringing up classic old songwriting ideas
here, but if I ever work with anybody else on a song, one of the first things I
say to them is, 'You've got to be prepared to make a fool of yourself. You've got
to be prepared to say stupid stuff, and to speak in tongues and let gibberish
out, or else you're never going to start pulling out the really valuable stuff.'

And that can be scary.
Yes. And—more importantly—embarrassing.

Right—because you're exposing yourself.
Exactly. You've got to be prepared to make an idiot of yourself—even to yourself!
And that takes some getting used to. Once you can be an idiot to *yourself*, and
feel okay about it, the next step is being able to make an idiot of yourself
in front of other people you're working with. But first, being comfortable

---

* Synaesthesia is a range of neurological phenomena in which stimulation of one sense
produces involuntary responses in another. In one version, chromaesthesia, colours are
triggered when musical notes are played.

enough with yourself to act like an idiot is important—*very* important. You have to *know* yourself. I made a very conscious decision around about the age of eighteen or nineteen that I wanted to know myself, in every facet.

What prompted that?

I'm not sure if it was one event. Probably just the accretion of a desire to get better. I thought, 'I'm never going to be a useful instrument in life unless I know what instrument I am. Am I a garden spade? Am I a butter knife? Am I a telescope? What instrument am I? I must *know* myself.' This process helps in the ability to dig up stuff when you get into an artistic or creative space, whether you're writing a book or writing a song or painting a picture—whatever it is.

You need to be friendly with yourself, as well—don't judge or get irritated with yourself too much. Accept and understand your weaknesses—don't get angry, don't beat yourself up. '*Why* can't I find this?' Don't worry—it's OK.

So, the benefit of acting like an idiot, as you put it, is that you can bring up, or out, a whole lot of ideas, mistakes, whatever, and then, by knowing yourself and having a forgiving attitude, you can put your conscious mind to work on them—start paring away, separating the wheat from the chaff.

That's right. It enables you to bring up *lots* of ideas. And instead of thinking, 'Well, *that's* stupid!' you think, 'Wait a minute! That's *really* useful, and I know that that means! That was about when I was a kid,' and so on.

If you know yourself, you can recognise the value in what otherwise would seem to be gibberish, and you can use it—you can use it like a colour. 'I need some of the colour in that unmarked tube that I just coughed up.' [*Laughs.*]

That ties in to something you've talked to me about before—the value of mining existing songs for bits and pieces.

Oh, yes. Never throw anything away—that's been a constant in my songwriting life. I'm a hoarder, musically.

If you look inside a typical songwriter's brain, maybe there's going to be a fellow with a grand piano, sheaves of music paper, and perhaps a quill for effect. *My* songwriting brain does not look like that. Instead, it looks like one of those sad old fellas who's lived in the same house for fifty years, and can't get in the room because of all the boxes and piles of shit everywhere—that's what it's like. [*Laughs.*] In my songwriting head, I never throw stuff away. I've got little bits of song in there from since I first started!

You have to have some kind of organisation, I would imagine. Otherwise, how would you know what bits to grab?
Perhaps, but it's not a conscious organisation. It seems to work in a kind of blundering way. And I don't want to examine how it works. It's like the fact that I can't notate music. I have a weird fear that if I *learned* to write music down, it would stop me from writing music. Likewise, if I try to figure out how this bits-and-pieces retrieval system of mine works, I might lose the ability to retrieve those bits. It's an irrational fear—but there it is.

You would rather rely on your intuition.
Yeah, absolutely. I've come to rely on it more and more as I get older. In the past, when I've not relied on intuition, too many things have come unstuck.

Give me an example.
You know—when you meet somebody, and they say, 'Oh, just sign this document,' and part of you is thinking, 'No. You're really creepy.' Or, 'I can see evil intent radiating out of you.' If I'd only listened to my 'second brain' first—my gut—in so many instances, I would have been better off. That part is so much more powerful than your rational brain sometimes.

The conscious vs. the unconscious. Many people say that the unconscious is the font of creativity anyway.
I think creativity comes from making mistakes. And the *love* of making mistakes—or of *allowing* yourself to make mistakes. I believe that creativity is simply a matter of, 'What would happen if I just stuck *this* with *that*?'
    If you never made any mistakes, you'd go along on one road all the way to the horizon, then die. It's much better to say, 'Oh, I think I'll just turn the wheel *this* way and see what happens.' You go off-road, then it's a matter of, 'WOW, look what's over *here*!'

You touched on some people whom you admire—Bacharach/David, Lennon/McCartney, Ray Davies …
It's a real toss-up, actually, between some of Ray Davies's writing and some of the best of Lennon/McCartney for who's the top of the pile for me.

In terms of *all* music, or in terms of the modern pop song?
The modern pop song—from the 60s onward. Before then, I think the best writing was probably from musicals. That was quite influential for me. At home we had a box high up on the wall that had two stations piped into it— the BBC Light Programme, and the BBC Home Service, I think it was called. One was music-y, and one was talk-y.

We used to have it set to the music-y one, and all they would play when I was growing up—the best stuff—was show tunes. So I got to hear a lot of those. I had favourites—I would wait for 'Whip-Crack-Away!' from *Calamity Jane* to come on, or 'Bloody Mary' from *South Pacific*. Or stuff from *West Side Story*.

Novelty records also were big for me, because I was a kid, and novelty records are built to appeal to kids. You know, the sped-up voices and all that.

What would you say that you took away from the novelty-record influence?
Psychedelia! [*Laughs.*] Novelty records were just psychedelia in square clothing. They use exactly the same techniques—sped-up bits, slowed-down bits, too much echo, too much reverb, that bit goes backwards. When the generation that grew up on kids' novelty records began making records for themselves, it came out as psychedelia. That genre is just grown-up novelty songs!

That's so funny—I'd never thought of it that way, but of course you're right.
There was no transition to be made. You go from things like 'Flying Purple People Eater' to 'I Am the Walrus'. They go hand-in-hand.

There was no rock'n'roll radio in England when I was a kid. It just didn't exist. And I don't think I would have liked it, because I was too young. I did like the Chipmunks records, or comedy records like those Charlie Drake singles.*

So, you weren't hearing old R&B, or anything like that?
Not at all, no. You might hear a track on a TV show. And you thought, 'Well, that's what older brothers or sisters like. That's *their* type of music. But there's no *fun* in it! Where are all the sped-up voices? Where's the backward bit? Where's the bit where they stop and have a little argument and tell a joke?'

It wasn't until Radio 1, which began in 1967, that suddenly the masses got to hear pop records on the radio.

---

* Charlie Drake (1925–2006) was a comedian, especially popular with children. His early records were produced by George Martin, before The Beatles.

What was happening between 1963 and 1967, then?
There were pirate radio stations, which were illegal stations, either based abroad, or based on a boat in international waters, or something like that. If you knew the frequency, you could get a little transistor radio you'd hide under your bedclothes or something. 'What number was it? Those kids at school said that if I dialled two-oh-eight I could get Radio Luxembourg.'

So, there was a lot of that illicit kind of listening going on. The BBC closed down a lot of the pirates, and then moved in on that territory themselves, because they knew that young people wanted their own music to listen to.

In any case, I couldn't afford records, really, until '67, when I started asking for them as presents—I'd ask for record tokens, or things like that. But otherwise, I was raised on novelty records and show tunes. Occasionally, I'd check out my father's jazz records when he went to work. But I could never admit to him that I liked his records, because that was your parents.

Of course. So, let's work our way through this chronologically. That's what you were listening to growing up. As you became a teenager and a young adult, what songwriters impressed you to the point where you tried to emulate them?
In the mid 60s, loads of great songwriting was going in, but I don't think I was registering how deep it was going in. Then, once I got to about thirteen or fourteen, my brain suddenly opened up. It's that hormonal thing. Suddenly you're not a little kid anymore—your body and your brain are like, 'Whoa— open up there. Let's go seeking!'

I started to hear a lot of stuff where I'd think, 'This is *fantastic*. How do you *do* this?' But I think the songwriting side of it evaded me. I was more interested in the technical side of it—for example, how do you actually *play* a guitar? For several years I concentrated on the technical thing of listening to records and trying to copy what they were doing with a guitar.

I got better and better, and could find more chords. Someone would show me a chord, or I'd figure one out by blundering into it or seeing a diagram in a book. Or, I'd hear a lead line on a record and think, 'What's he doing? What are the notes?' Then you start to see the patterns, and all that.

To be truthful, I never realised the enormous impact of the songwriters of my youth on me until we were already making records. I mean, we'd be in Abbey Road working on the *3D-EP*, and a load of people would be nudging me and saying, 'Hey—Abbey Road! Fantastic! What great songs were made there!' I didn't get it. I was too busy making our own music to think about the fact that, 'Wow, those songs were played on *that* piano or sung down *this* microphone.'

But while we were doing the *Mummer* album, when we got to the middle section of 'Ladybird', I said to the producer, Steve Nye, 'Ooh, I'm a bit funny about how this came out, Steve, because it sounds a bit Beatle-esque to me, and I don't want people to think I'm copying the Beatles.' He said, 'Who *gives* a fuck? That's how you've written it—just *do* it!'

I thought, 'Yeah! I guess they *did* influence the middle of that song, and why shouldn't I just do it?' That's *me* being influenced. I'm not trying to be in a tribute band, that's my genuine influence starting to come out! 'Of course—I'm not going to scrap this middle section—I'm going to do it as it's writ!' That was a little epiphany of, 'Hell yeah—those songs really did influence me.'

And the next thing you know, you're The Dukes Of Stratosphear!
[*Chuckles.*] Yes, and before you can shake a shitty paisley shirt out, we're the Dukes. I think from that moment onward, I started to recognise that those songwriters—the Ray Davieses, the Lennons and McCartneys, the Brian Wilsons—had gone into my head really deeply. They'd set a lot of templates for me.

I realised that I should not be ashamed about digging them up, and getting them wrong, and using them as my template. Because that's another aspect of creativity—taking your influences, mangling them all up, getting them all wrong, sticking a bit of that one to a bit of that other one, doing it your way and it not quite being how they would do it. Then the finished product is some of them, and some of you, and it's all come out wrong—but you've made a new thing!

Absolutely. Every great creative person acknowledges that they stand on the shoulders of giants.
Or on the 'shoulder of giants', as Oasis put it. [*Laughs.*] A one-shouldered giant!

What do you think of music today?
This is really tough to answer, because I actually don't listen to too many people from the last twenty or thirty years. I've been too selfishly making my own music. I have a bit of over-selective laser vision when it comes to today's

music. I certainly don't consume music in the same way I used to as a teen, when I was thinking [*dramatic voice*], '*Everything about this is going to save the world.*' So many mistakes I've made with that.

Are you saying that being a songwriter and recording artist has ruined music for you?
It totally has, yeah. For example, the first few times I heard *Magical Mystery Tour*, I loved it. I could not begin to imagine how you would make any of those songs, write any of those words, or construct any of those chords or melodies. Now, it's just boringly obvious. I know how they did everything! And the fact that they did it first—well, that's the power of it for me now. Hearing it back then completely bowled me over, but I can't hear songs as whole things anymore. I just can't do it.

So, tell the people reading this book how they can save music for you.
They can save music by going out and making something genuinely *new*—which will be very difficult, because most combinations of sounds have been done. But I would like to be delighted to be appalled by hearing things I've never heard before, or combinations of sounds I've never heard before. One thousand cardboard boxes, say, and a trumpet. And the song is an hour long.

Isn't that already a Steve Reich piece?
'Piece For 1,000 Cardboard Boxes And A Trumpet'! Wait, scrap the trumpet. He didn't turn up for the session! [*Laughs.*]
    Nowadays, I want to hear something I've never heard. I don't want to hear any more programmed music. I don't want to hear any more electric guitars. I don't want to hear any more 'Baby, baby.' I find myself turning backwards in music, farther and farther—to the 40s, 30s, 20s, and even the 10s. I found, on a cassette the other day, two songs I wrote last year—it was 100 years since the start of the First World War, and I had thought, 'What songs would my grandad have liked, sat on the Somme? What songs would he have had going 'round in his head?' So I wrote two songs in the style of the sort of music that would have been big in 1914.
    I find myself going backwards farther and farther because I don't know how they do that stuff. *That* is still magic to me—how you arrange a big band swing number, or how you make a syncopated jazz sound. To some extent, I'm even more au fait with classical music than I am with stuff like that.

What do you think the role of technology is in songwriting? Over the course of your songwriting career, you've seen great changes.
I think sequenced music is the only really new thing in the last thirty years—and technology made that possible. Everything else has just involved rejigging guitars, bass, drums, keyboards. But with electronic sequencers, we can now sit and program every instrument that you're hearing. In fact, ninety-nine percent of the top 40 is probably programmed.

A lot of people don't realise that—they think, 'Wow, isn't that good? Don't they really sing in tune, and play in time?' They don't realise that nobody from that band is on that record—it's just somebody sat there and programming it, putting in guitar and drum samples and whatever.

Or maybe they did play on it, but their parts were all corrected and enhanced digitally.
Exactly.

But as a songwriter, don't you find technology to be tremendously useful?
I do, actually. I like repetition, and a lot of my songs have been based on it—everything from 'Battery Brides' to 'River Of Orchids' to 'Travels In Nihilon' to—my goodness, the list is endless. There are lots of 'repetition songs' in my history. And I suppose that's related to the drone—I find the drone to be very powerful and informative.

Why? Because you like that 'foundation'? The reference point it provides?
I do. I like the 'wide path' that you can create and walk along with. And, you know, it's everywhere—if the dishwasher's humming along, I'll sit there and start putting notes over that hum. Or I'll sing along with the blender. Or, if somebody's got a chainsaw or a lawnmower going out back here, I'll harmonise with them.

I know just what you mean. I also love the rhythm you can get from everyday things, like a washing machine.
Yeah! You think, 'I've got to use that in something.' The drone, I think, is core to a lot of folk music and a lot of ethnic music—as is repetition. Perhaps there's more ethnic and primitive music in me than I've been prepared to admit, because I find both of those things enormously influential. 'River Of Orchids' wouldn't have existed without being able to make a little loop out of

a cascade of some orchestral samples. Just as I jam along with a chainsaw, I'm jamming along with the mechanical nature of that loop. Knowing that the pattern is unfailing—that it's going to go round and catch you—enables you to do some crazy acrobatics.

And technology has been tremendously democratising. I can now record, in my garden shed, *almost* to the quality of later-70s studio music without too much effort.

On a wide variety of instruments that you otherwise wouldn't be able to play.
Yes, that's true. I mean, at one time, I could never imagine making a finished-quality recording in my garden shed. Now, with a decent microphone, a converter, a sequencer, and a keyboard to put the information into the computer, I can make music that's sonically as good as a lot of records I bought when I was younger! That's quite staggering.

But the real magic doesn't lay in samples and mechanical means of making music. I think the real magic of making music is in *people* and rough edges and mistakes and doing things in a different way.

I personally have perhaps gotten too hung up on quality over the years. Now, I find myself moving farther and farther back to rougher and more human forms of music. I've been listening to quite a bit of Howlin' Wolf lately—I don't think I've ever heard anything by him that doesn't delight me—and it's about as primitive and rough as you can imagine. It's so far from programmed, mechanical perfection.

You are someone who wrote music to be played live and presented in front of audiences for a good chunk of your career, and then you decided to make the switchover to presenting it in recorded fashion only. What are your thoughts on the two approaches and how your songwriting changed as a result?
At one time, the songs were written and arranged with blinkers on. 'When we play live, we've got two guitars, bass, and drums.'

'This is my palette.'
Yes. 'This is my palette, this is all I can work with. And if I can sing this song, those two can sing backing vocals if they're not doing anything too complex. The drummer refuses to sing.' [*Laughs.*]

Wait—*could* Terry sing? Would you have asked him to sing if he could?
Not really, no. I don't think I've ever really heard him sing, even in jest! He just liked hitting things. [*Chuckles.*]

But that was my palette. It was like having two colours. Then when—thankfully—I got off the live treadmill, those blinkers got removed. It freed me. I could think in other colours. I was mentally released, in lots of ways. It was quite a revelation. And I think our music got a lot better.

Do you think there was an advantage to initially having that limited palette, where you had to work within certain parameters?
Sure. You have to learn to do a lot of things with those limited colours, which forces you to be creative—plus, it lends a more *graphic* design to what you're doing. 'OK, you've got these two shades, and maybe you can water down a little bit of one, or apply the other one a bit thicker, but basically you're stuck with them.'

That said, coming off the road was *really* freeing for me. I know it was freeing for Colin, too, but it was probably limiting for Dave, because with more time to think about songs and their construction and what instrumentation to use, the demos started to get much more ornate.

And you had the advancements happening then in home-recording technology.
That's right. We had multi-track home recording machines being introduced at the same time. So, unfortunately, Dave found that rather than *thinking* of something to play, he was *given* something—'Here, can you play this? I want this piano here, or this guitar part there.'

One of the great things about being in a band is the camaraderie and the creation of a whole that is bigger than the individual parts. But when you're a composer, you create and conduct everything.
Yes.

From a songwriting perspective, how do you view the advantages and drawbacks of each of those models?
The camaraderie thing is very, very important. Pulling toward the same goal is *immensely* important, and it's something I grew to respect and acknowledge as the years went on, whereas maybe I didn't earlier on. They were just blokes

I knew, from the same town as me, who drank similar beer to me, and had similar points of reference. But I started to realise and acknowledge the importance of that camaraderie, which did make the whole so much greater than the individual parts. So I take one of my nine hats off to that.

There are drawbacks, of course. When you moved to the other model, you must have liked being able to more fully realise what you were hearing in your head. As you'd said before, coming off the road was also, coincidentally, the time when you could buy a four-track cassette Portastudio.
It was pretty rotten quality, but it enabled you to 'game things out'—for example, 'I wonder what *this* guitar part would sound like against *that* guitar part.' Rather than having to wait to try something in a rehearsal room in a few weeks' time, you could just go and find out *right now*.

That allowed me to figure out what worked, and tell the others what part to play. It was good for me as an artist—to realise more fully what I was hearing. And as the years went on, I got more skilful at getting out what I was hearing more precisely. Then I went from a four-track to an eight-track machine, and then to a digital machine, and now I'm on a computer and could almost lay down a limitless amount of tracks. I realise that was frustrating for other people in the band.

Because you can lose the camaraderie, the opportunity for the 'happy accident' you've been talking about.
Yeah, sure. Working out initial arrangements together was a great time to discover something you hadn't envisioned—'Ooh, that's great! I hadn't thought of that.'

But even after I got more sophisticated in my approach to creating demos, we would still rehearse the albums, and you can still get that 'Wow! I hadn't envisioned that' moment during those rehearsals, or when you get in the studio with people. They can still say, 'Well, try *this*.' If it's better than what I envisioned, I always would go with what they invented.

I have always been committed to being open to other ideas. If any part that any player came up with was better than what I was hearing for it, their part went in. And, you know, we didn't have too many arguments. The song was king—the song was even above my decision, if you see what I mean. If someone else's idea makes the song better, then it's going in. If it's not, then my default position's going in.

You're the songwriter, so you're the gatekeeper.
I am … who was the gatekeeper in *Ghostbusters?*—I am *Zuul.* [*Laughs.*]

So, what do want the reader to take away from this book? What do they need to do to go out into the world and be songwriters?
If the songwriters today are going to save music, they're going to have to upset people. And they have to realise that great art is made from both misery and joy. People say, 'Oh, you've got to *suffer* to make great art.' Well, that's only half the story—I think you can make great art by suffering, or you can make it if you're really happy about something.

So, great art comes from extremes in emotion.
Exactly. It also comes from knowing yourself, and from recognising the value of, and enjoying, mistakes—because there's so much creativity in 'wrong' thinking. The font of all creativity is thinking 'out of the box'—which is just a polite way of saying, 'You're thinking about it wrong.' Go ahead and think about it wrong! You'll create.

Interview conducted May 28 2015.

ALSO AVAILABLE FROM JAWBONE PRESS

Adventures Of A Waterboy Mike Scott

Becoming Elektra: The Incredible True Story Of Jac Holzman's Visionary Record Label Mick Houghton

I Scare Myself: A Memoir Dan Hicks

Fearless: The Making Of Post-Rock Jeanette Leech

Tragedy: The Ballad Of The Bee Gees Jeff Apter

Shadows Across The Moon: Outlaws, Freaks, Shamans And The Making Of Ibiza Clubland Helen Donlon

Staying Alive: The Disco Inferno Of The Bee Gees Simon Spence

The Yacht Rock Book: The Oral History Of The Soft, Smooth Sounds Of The 70s And 80s Greg Prato

Earthbound: David Bowie and The Man Who Fell To Earth Susan Compo

What's Big And Purple And Lives In The Ocean? The Moby Grape Story Cam Cobb

Swans: Sacrifice And Transcendence: The Oral History Nick Soulsby

Small Victories: The True Story Of Faith No More Adrian Harte

AC/DC 1973–1980: The Bon Scott Years Jeff Apter

King's X: The Oral History Greg Prato

Keep Music Evil: The Brian Jonestown Massacre Story Jesse Valencia

Lunch With The Wild Frontiers: A History Of Britpop And Excess In 13½ Chapters Phill Savidge

More Life With Deth David Ellefson with Thom Hazaert

Wilcopedia: A Comprehensive Guide To The Music Of America's Best Band Daniel Cook Johnson

Take It Off: KISS Truly Unmasked Greg Prato

Lydia Lunch: The War Is Never Over: A Companion To The Film By Beth B. Nick Soulsby

I Am Morbid: Ten Lessons Learned From Extreme Metal, Outlaw Country, And The Power Of Self-Determination David Vincent with Joel McIver

Zeppelin Over Dayton: Guided By Voices Album By Album Jeff Gomez

What Makes The Monkey Dance: The Life And Music Of Chuck Prophet And Green On Red Stevie Simkin

So Much For The 30 Year Plan: Therapy? The Authorised Biography Simon Young

She Bop: The Definitive History Of Women In Popular Music Lucy O'Brien

Relax Baby Be Cool: The Artistry And Audacity Of Serge Gainsbourg Jeremy Allen

Seeing Sideways: A Memoir Of Music And Motherhood Kristin Hersh

Two Steps Forward, One Step Back: My Life In The Music Business Miles A. Copeland III

It Ain't Retro: Daptone Records & The 21st-Century Soul Revolution Jessica Lipsky

Renegade Snares: The Resistance & Resilience Of Drum & Bass Ben Murphy and Carl Loben

Southern Man: Music And Mayhem In The American South Alan Walden with S.E. Feinberg

Frank & Co: Conversations With Frank Zappa 1977–1993 Co de Kloet

All I Ever Wanted: A Rock 'n' Roll Memoir Kathy Valentine

Here They Come With Their Make-Up On: Suede, Coming Up ... And More Adventures Beyond The Wild Frontiers Jane Savidge

My Bloody Roots: From Sepultua To Soulfly And Beyond: The Autobiography Max Cavalera with Joel McIver

This Band Has No Past: How Cheap Trick Became Cheap Trick Brian J. Kramp

Gary Moore: The Official Biography Harry Shapiro

Holy Ghost: The Life & Death Of Free Jazz Pioneer Albert Ayler Richard Koloda